SO-AYZ-829

Journal

of the
Society of Christian Ethics

Spring/Summer 2003

Volume 23, No. 1

See Just -
Peacemky

Editors
Christine Gudorf, Florida International University
Paul Lauritzen, John Carroll University

Editorial Board
Elizabeth Bounds, Emory University
John Bowlin, University of Tulsa
Travis Kroeker, McMaster University
Aaron Mackler, Duquesne University
Margaret Mohrmann, University of Virginia
James Nash
William O'Neill, S.J., Jesuit School of Theology, GTU
Brian Stiltner, Sacred Heart University
Darryl Trimiew, Colgate Rochester Divinity School

Editorial Offices

Department of Religious Studies   Department of Religious Studies
Florida International University   John Carroll University
Miami, FL 33199   Cleveland, OH 44118

Publisher
The Society of Christian Ethics
c/o Regina Wolfe
St. John's University School of Theology-Seminary
P.O. Box 5633
Collegeville, MN 56321-5633

Distributor
Georgetown University Press
c/o Hopkins Fulfillment Service
P.O. Box 50370
Baltimore, MD 21211-4370

Copyright © 2003 by the Society of Christian Ethics. All rights reserved.
The *Journal of the Society of Christian Ethics* (ISBN: 0-87840-340-X; ISSN: 150-7942) is published twice yearly in November and March and is the official publication of the Society of Christian Ethics. Although the *JSCE* is not a proceedings of the annual meeting of the Society of Christian Ethics, material published in the journal is typically generated in relation to activities of the Society of Christian Ethics and its annual meeting. Members of the Society should direct address changes and claims for missing issues to the executive director of the Society of Christian Ethics. Institutions and individuals who are not members of the SCE should direct inquiries about standing orders, claims for missing issues, and notifications of address changes to Georgetown University Press, P.O. Box 50370, Baltimore, MD 21211; remittances should be made payable to Georgetown University Press. Orders for back issues may be placed with Georgetown University Press. Inquiries about reproducing or reprinting material originally published in the *JSCE* should be directed to the editors.

Contents

PREFACE

In the fall 2002 issue of the journal we noted that the *JSCE* was undergoing a number of changes. Two were immediately obvious with that issue. The name of the journal had changed and there was a new cover design. With this issue we inaugurate a less immediately obvious change, for this is the first issue of our new twice yearly publication schedule. You will note one marker of this change in the adoption of an issue number as well as a volume number. Hence, this is volume 23, no. 1. As well as representing a beginning, this issue marks a conclusion. This is the last issue that will be produced through camera-ready copy. We are very grateful to Georgetown University Press for their willingness to assume a greater role in the production process and we are confident that the move to typesetting will enhance both the look and professionalism of the journal.

Christine Gudorf
Paul Lauritzen
Co-Editors

SELECTED PAPERS

Receiving and Responding to God's Grace: A Re-examination in Light of Trauma Theory

Jennifer Beste

Abstract

Christians have traditionally claimed a kind of invulnerability to harm that would render them incapable of responding to God's grace. This claim to invulnerability will be examined in light of trauma theory's insistence that, in situations of overwhelming violence, a person's capacity for responsive agency can be severely disabled. Drawing from incest survivors' experiences of recovery, I argue that a critical re-examination of the human capacity to receive God's grace must include greater appreciation for how God's love is mediated, at least in part, through loving interpersonal relations. Ethical implications resulting from this insight should challenge our communities in profound ways.

The Christian tradition has long affirmed that a person's capacity to receive and respond to God's grace by loving both God and neighbor is not entirely vulnerable to earthly contingencies. How tenable is this, however, in light of recent social scientific research on interpersonal harm? Is it not possible to harm one another to such an extent that our capacity to respond to God's grace is severely diminished, if not altogether destroyed? In this paper, I explore these questions by placing Karl Rahner's theology of the fundamental option in conversation with the insights of contemporary trauma theory as they relate to the experiences of incest victims. Research on incest victims consistently finds that persons' capacities for healthy forms of relationality and agency can be both severely disabled by abusive interpersonal relations and fostered by supportive ones; interpersonal

Journal of the Society of Christian Ethics, 23/1 (2003): 3-20

relationships, I argue, also have the power both to foster and to debilitate one's capacity to respond to God's grace as one strives to love oneself, others, and God. Taking trauma victims' experience into consideration, I suggest that there must be a critical re-examination of the human capacity to receive and respond to God's grace in Rahner's theology and Christian theology as a whole. Drawing from other aspects of Rahner's theology, I contend that a more adequate, contemporary Rahnerian account of human receptivity and responsiveness to God's grace needs (1) to acknowledge and attend to the power of sin against one's neighbor to disable that person's capacity to respond to God's grace, and (2) to articulate how God's love not only directly transforms and heals persons, but is also mediated through loving, interpersonal relations. Lastly, I address the ethical implications of explicitly acknowledging that God's grace is mediated interpersonally.

Rahner's Understanding of the Relation between Grace and Freedom

In his well-known articles on grace and freedom in *Theological Investigations* and *Foundations of Christian Faith*, Rahner strongly affirms that, despite the constraints of sin and earthly contingencies, persons endowed with reason have the capacity to accept or reject God's offer of Godself. Central to Rahner's theology lies his deep conviction that God's offer of self-communication produces a supernatural existential that orients each person toward God and gives him or her the condition to accept God's grace and participate in the life of God.[1] Rahner claims that this God-given "capacity for God's offer of self-bestowing personal love is the central and abiding existential of man as he really is."[2] Rahner views God's grace, then, as liberating human freedom from the enslaved bondages of original sin and concupiscence, enabling persons to accept freely God's self-communication: "It is therefore grace itself which sets free our formal freedom in capacity and in act for saving action, and heals it in itself."[3] Rahner emphasizes that God does not coerce persons to accept divine love; rather, the Divine self-communication is presented to each person's freedom as an offer, and it awaits a free human response. He frequently describes this freedom as the capacity to effect a fundamental option either to accept God's offer of salvation and become the persons God created them to be, or reject the divine offer and turn away from their graced, transcendental orientation to God.

For Rahner, such a fundamental option is formed and actualized through persons' concrete, historical choices and actions: "The entire life of the free subject is inevitably an answer to the question in which God offers himself to us as the source of transcendence."[4] Rahner claims that, being the temporal and historical beings that they are, persons require time in order to achieve final self-disposal to say yes or no to God. Aquinas' insight that individuals' acts leave traces in their being resonates throughout Rahner's reflections about how persons' present acts shape and circumscribe the range of their future options and decisions. Each free action, then, simultaneously affects who one is becoming and one's fundamental option towards God.

What kind of categorical behavior reflects a transcendental yes to God? While Rahner is careful to note that the mystery of human freedom prevents us from identifying certain actions as definitively corresponding to a "yes" to God, he is certain that only love for God ultimately constitutes accepting God's self-offer: "Love of God is the only total integration of human existence."[5] Such love for God, however, cannot exist and be further realized in an interior, private disposition; it can only be mediated and actualized through loving our neighbor: "Love for God only comes to its own identity through its fulfillment in love for neighbor."[6]

Rahner emphasizes that a person can never transfer such responsibility for one's fundamental option onto others: "This self-realization is a task he cannot avoid, and, in spite of all the differences within the concrete material of his self-achievement, it is always either a self-realization in the direction of God or a self-refusal towards God."[7] Rahner thus depicts the human self as "lonely and unsheltered, responsible to himself, who can in no way be 'absolved' of the solitary self, who can never throw himself on to others."[8] Even when considering difficult cases of individuals who appear to have had few options to say yes to God's offer of self-communication, Rahner remains confident that there was sufficient opportunity. In an article titled "The Comfort of Time," he concludes:

> Apparently very little material is required for such total self-achievement. What we may sorrowfully be tempted to complain about as the poverty of opportunities for certain people (in the case of those who died young, etc.), will have to be regarded as the normal opportunity. . . . One must not overrate the significance of the difference in external situation for the proper achievement of man's existence. For otherwise it would be a strange arrangement of life by God, if in most cases of this free spiritual creature—which after all is called to realize its being freely—this realization did not come to its proper fulfillment.[9]

Two theological beliefs undergird Rahner's faith that rational persons have sufficient freedom to effect a fundamental option. First, God creates persons for the purpose of being able fully to realize their true being by loving God and neighbor, thereby responding to God's offer of self-communication. Second, salvation necessarily includes both God's grace and a person's free act of accepting God's self-offer: "A salvation not achieved in freedom cannot be salvation."[10]

Since effecting a positive fundamental option by loving God and neighbor constitutes our human fulfillment, it must be asked why anyone would freely refuse God's self-offer. Rahner soberly acknowledges that, due to the possibility of sin as a permanent existential of humanity, it is possible for us to resist and turn away from the source of our being and fulfillment. Rahner argues that sin and guilt are manifest in external and internal threats that can powerfully hinder our freedom to effect a positive fundamental option for God. He acknowledges how our freedom to create who we finally want to be in our entirety is shaped and constrained by other persons' attitudes and actions in our culture and in history: "Persons' experience says that there are objectifications of personal guilt in the world, which as the material for the free decisions of other persons, threaten these decisions, have a seductive effect upon them, and make free decisions painful."[11] In the end, collective guilt impinges upon, but does not destroy our capacity to respond positively to God's self-communication.[12]

Trauma Theory's Conception of the Self and Freedom

As an instructive way to analyze the adequacy of Rahner's account of the relation between God's grace and human freedom, I now turn to the insights of contemporary trauma theory as it relates to the experiences of incest victims. Trauma is generally defined as a state of being overwhelmed both physically and psychologically: it is the experience of terror, loss of control, and utter helplessness during a stressful event that threatens one's physical or psychological integrity or both. Trauma shatters persons' key assumptions regarding self and one's relations to others in the world, including a sense of self-protection, personal invulnerability, and safety and predictability in the world.[13] In this paper, I narrow my focus on trauma by considering the effects of one particular type—chronic incestuous abuse perpetrated by one's parent. Since social scientific research has found that chronic interpersonal traumas such as father-daughter incest create the most severe distortions in one's identity, capability for effective agency, and capacity for healthy forms of relationality, focusing on this type of abuse serves as an excellent test case for evaluating Rahner's claim that persons, with the aid of God's grace, have sufficient freedom to effect a fundamental option.[14]

Due to the confines of this paper, I will focus on how girls' reactions to chronic incestuous abuse and their subsequent development of post-traumatic stress symptoms severely damage their capacity for free actions and ability to relate positively to themselves, others, and God.[15] Social scientific literature on child maltreatment overwhelmingly demonstrates that children require a great degree of consistent external protection by care providers to develop a healthy sense of self, agency, and the ability to relate constructively to others. When a parent instead sexually abuses a child and violates her bodily and psychic integrity, the child's attachment to her parent is severely threatened. Since such attachment is needed for the child's basic survival, not to mention for crucial developmental tasks, children generally react to sexual abuse by denying its reality. One of the most effective defense mechanisms involves dissociating violent, traumatic events from one's consciousness. Dissociation refers to separating and splitting off elements of the traumatic experience—emotions, thoughts, sensation, location, time, and meaning—into shattered fragments that defy conscious integration. For most children who are sexually abused for a prolonged period, dissociation as a sole coping mechanism will not be effective in consistently denying the reality of the abuse.[16] When dissociation fails, children tend to take full responsibility for the abuse and conclude that there is something intrinsically bad about them that causes the abuse. Interestingly, this process of self-denigration and self-hatred occurs even in children who experience complete dissociation and retain no conscious memories of the abuse.

Since dissociation and self-blame enable the sexually abused child to remain attached to her care providers, one of the obvious consequences is that the abuse is not exposed and stopped. Most children respond by experiencing a host of post-traumatic stress symptoms that frequently persist through adulthood. First, children re-experience the traumatic event in the form of flashbacks, nightmares, intense bodily or emotional sensations, terrifying sensory perceptions, obsessional preoccupations, and behavioral reenactments. Second, re-experiencing the traumatic events causes them to alternate between persistent forms of emotional numbing and hyperarousal, which involves reacting to the slightest environmental stimuli as if everything in one's environment represented potential danger. Irritability, angry outbursts, restlessness, difficulty concentrating, and difficulty sleeping are also common signs. In their attempts to ward off hyperarousal, sexually abused children and other trauma victims experience withdrawal and detachment from emotions and physical sensations. When emotional numbing does not occur naturally, children often resort to forms of autonomic arousal, which include self-mutilation, fasting, vomiting, compulsive sexual behavior, and compulsive risk-taking. Such autonomic arousal offers temporary relief from unbearably negative emotions. Third, trauma victims inadvertently tend to reenact the trauma compulsively by either acting self-destructively, harming others, or becoming revictimized.[17]

Such post-traumatic stress disorder (PTSD) symptoms result in a severely fragmented self. Psychiatrist Judith Herman describes this fragmentation as follows:

All the structures of the self—the image of the body, the internalized image of others, and the values and ideals that lend a sense of coherence and purpose—are invaded and systematically broken down. . . . While the victim of the single acute trauma may say she is "not herself" since the event, the victim of chronic trauma may lose the sense that she has a self.[18]

Incestuous abuse thus distorts and can even destroy central aspects of the self necessary for a healthy self-concept: these include self-awareness, self-continuity, self-coherency, and a minimal sense of self-worth.

Such fragmentation of the self in turn impedes developing an effective sense of agency, which I shall define here as a sense that one has control over one's actions and emotions, and has the ability to deliberate and choose actions that cohere with a life plan consisting of values, beliefs, goals, and ideals that make life meaningful.[19] Many incest victims, due to their post-traumatic stress symptoms and extreme negative self-concept, lack basic skills needed for effectively constructing a life plan.[20] Such abilities include achieving a sufficient degree of self-reflectiveness and self-awareness, possessing a minimal sense of self-worth, and being able to imagine a future for oneself.

Even if an incest victim is able to master the tasks needed to construct a life plan, many of the physical, psychological, and behavioral effects of incest hinder her from being able to reflect on her present options and choose actions that actualize that plan. Cognitive and affective skills of incest victims are often stunted and deformed by the abuse and subsequent PTSD symptoms. Consequently, incest victims commonly have difficulty accurately assessing their situations and often doubt the accuracy of their perceptions. They often react impulsively, making it difficult to protect themselves in threatening situations and to choose the best option to promote their flourishing.

Chronic sexual abuse, in addition to problems it causes with victims' sense of self, can deeply distort incest victims' capacity to relate constructively to other persons. Due to the betrayal of trust in their family of origin and their negative self-esteem, adult incest victims are desperate to find care, protection, and external validation of themselves. Simultaneously, they are deeply afraid of trusting anyone or being abandoned or abused or all three. These conflicting desires make it very difficult to establish and enjoy authentic, intimate relationships. Most often, their abusive families have isolated them from others, thwarting their process of developing social skills needed for authentic connection.

In response to their past abusive experiences, incest victims' attitudes towards relationships vary. Some adult survivors feel threatened by the prospect of intimacy and, as a way to avoid being revictimized, do not form any close relationships. Similar to many Holocaust victims, many incest victims struggle with alexithymia—feeling "dead" and lacking affection or empathy for anyone. They deeply fear that the incestuous abuse has destroyed their capacity to love other persons.[21] Others, by contrast, respond to their abusive past by desperately seeking attachment to others at all costs;

in their desire for social approval, they tend to be "people-pleasers" and risk repeated revictimization.

Just as sexual abuse distorts the way in which one relates to oneself and others, it also can negatively affect incest victims' ability to relate positively to God. Compared to women with no history of child abuse, incest victims tend to perceive God as harsher or more silent, distant, or judgmental towards them.[22] One study found that although many sexual abuse survivors desire intimacy with God, "their perceived unworthiness prevents this from ever being experienced."[23] While some incest victims feel guilty about their abuse and pray to God to absolve them of their inherent badness, others experience a profound loss of trust and betrayal of a God who did nothing to stop the abuse.[24] In her work *Healing the Incest Wound*, Courtney Courtois observes: "Many survivors balk at the idea of God or a higher power, feeling as though they were long ago abandoned by a cruel or uncaring God."[25]

Evaluating Rahner's Theology in Light of Incest Victims' Experience

Rahner's theological anthropology and trauma theory appear to present vastly different accounts of the self and human freedom. Indeed, significant tensions call into question whether Rahner's theology is able to attend adequately to the reality of incest victims. Rahner's conception of the self is an important starting point for consideration. He depicts persons as endowed with a self-consciousness that makes possible the capacity to transcend who they presently are as they actualize their potentialities and grow into greater degrees of being. For Rahner, the exercise of self-awareness, self-reflection, and self-transcendence are dependent on possession of reason.[26] Of course, as spirits-in-the-world, persons are also dependent upon others and the world in the sense that they need to interact with other finite beings and their world to become aware of themselves as knowing subjects and to distinguish between finitude and the horizon of infinite being. The human self relies on other persons, then, in the sense that interaction with others is necessary to experience the continual process of self-transcendence and self-realization.

The experiences of incest victims, by contrast, strongly suggest that self-awareness, self-reflection, and self-transcendence are dependent upon more than reason and interaction with one's environment. Developing sufficient degrees of these attributes appears to be contingent to a significant extent on the absence of overwhelming stress and the presence of supportive relationships. Of course, one's capacity for self-consciousness and transcendence is not utterly destroyed by most bodily violations and abusive relationships; however, as discussed above, the desires to know more, learn, grow, explore, place everything into question, and be open to further possibilities are deeply influenced by one's material and social conditions.

If sufficient degrees of subjectivity and self-transcendence are not immediate "givens" that follow from being rational persons who interact with their environment, but are capacities developed within the context of some form of supportive relationships, Rahner's view of human freedom is challenged as much as his view of the self. As we have seen, severe interpersonal harm and its resulting post-traumatic symptoms can severely disable and even destroy at times the capacity for adequate self-awareness and forms of self-transcendence necessary for one to act freely. This calls into question the warrant for Rahner's confidence that all rational persons have sufficient freedom to effect a fundamental option. Can we know for sure that a severely abused incest victim has realized sufficient freedom to commit enough free actions throughout her life to actualize a fundamental orientation for God?

Lastly, the experiences of incest victims also cast doubt upon the adequacy of Rahner's understanding of how persons receive and respond to God's grace. As noted above, Rahner argues that, besides offering God's very self, God gives each person sufficient grace to receive and accept God's grace. Rahner confidently claims that such grace enables a person to open himself or herself to God's love and experience God as a "hidden closeness, a forgiving intimacy, a real home . . . as a love which shares itself, something familiar which he can approach and turn to from the estrangement of his own perilous and empty life."[27] In many of his writings, Rahner implies that a person's capacity to receive and accept God's grace is invulnerable to earthly contingencies. This understanding of human receptivity to God's grace, though, contrasts sharply with many incest victims' perceived relationships with God. As we have seen, many incest victims despair at experiencing only silence, distance, betrayal, and judgment from God. Such experiences testify to the damage that interpersonal harm can have on one's capacity to receive God's grace in any active sense at all.

Furthermore, incest victims' difficulty relating constructively to themselves, others, and God casts doubt upon Rahner's claim that God's grace sufficiently liberates human freedom from its bondage to sin, enabling one to respond freely to God's grace by loving God and neighbor. How are we to interpret incest victims' compulsive patterns of reenacting trauma by harming themselves and others or being revictimized in subsequent relationships? How do we understand their experiences of feeling "dead" inside and their inability to feel empathy for another person? How much *less* capable might they be of loving and risking themselves radically for another person or God? As we see in Rahner, these kinds of categorical actions actualize one's transcendental "yes" to God's self-offer.

If we accept Rahner's above account of God's grace as fully adequate, we appear committed to the belief that God's grace must somehow enable incest victims' freedom to love God, neighbor, and self; presumably, any failure an incest victim has relating lovingly to others throughout her life is a sufficiently free response that acquiesces to the existential of sin pervading each person's life. As demonstrated by previously quoted passages, Rahner has explicitly denied that external threats have the power to incapacitate entirely a person's ability to respond to God's grace and effect a positive fundamental option. If we follow the logical implications of this position, we are likely to view incest victims as ultimately culpable for their own plight of compulsive, traumatic reenactments and their absence of loving actions for God and neighbor. Besides the fact that this theological response would likely increase many incest victims' alienation and shame, and would figure among the worst pastoral responses imaginable, is such a response theologically credible?

Due to Rahner's own commitment to take human experience seriously when formulating theological doctrines, I am convinced that Rahner himself, if confronted with the realities of incest victims, would have taken steps to qualify his theology to avoid the potential danger of blaming incest victims for their compulsive traumatic reenactments. There are even a number of clear theological insights within Rahner's writings that are in tension with his frequent claims that human receptivity to grace is not wholly vulnerable to interpersonal harm. These insights can be used to construct a more sufficient Rahnerian account of human receptivity and responsiveness to God's grace.

A Revised Understanding of Human Receptivity and Responsiveness to God's Grace

A more adequate understanding of human receptivity and responsiveness to God's grace will include two central claims supported by the findings of trauma research. First, a revised understanding of the workings of God's grace will acknowledge the sober *possibility* that interpersonal harm can severely, and perhaps entirely, impair one's freedom to effect a fundamental option. Note that I am not defending the stronger thesis that chronic incestuous abuse definitively destroys a person's capacity to effect a fundamental option. The mystery of human freedom does not warrant any certainty on this matter. Nevertheless, soberly reflecting on the innumerable cases of incest victims who literally do not even manage to survive, much less realize their freedom to love their neighbors and themselves, forces Christian ethicists to take seriously the extent to which interpersonal harm can damage our freedom to actualize a "yes" to God's self-offer. Second, this revised account will not view the idea of God's grace being directly infused into persons as sufficient; it will also explore the likelihood that God mediates divine grace through loving interpersonal relations.

Regarding the first claim, the experiences of incest victims press theologians to address more explicitly how various assaults on the body and abusive interpersonal relations negatively impede a person's capacity to receive and respond freely to God's grace. To his credit, Rahner may have anticipated the kinds of concerns raised by trauma theory in two short passages found in his later writings. In his 1976 *Meditations on Freedom and the Spirit* he states:

> The idea that man, as a Christian or as the philosophical subject of freedom, is still free, even when he is born in chains, is extremely dubious and may be fundamentally wrong. This is clear from the fact that one man can deprive another man by murder (of his biological or psychological reality as a human being) of the possibility of freedom, even in the theological sense.[28]

Such a statement suggests that Rahner may be open to the idea that in extreme instances, a person may have the power to deprive another of his or her "psychological reality as a human being" and incapacitate him or her from realizing sufficient freedom to effect a fundamental option. Similarly, in his article "Christian Dying," published in 1978, he asserts that, while all persons must view themselves as responsible for effecting a fundamental option, it is possible that some adults may die before realizing sufficient freedom to say yes or no to God:

> It can be said that in the last resort we do not know how or whether this doctrine of the always unique history of freedom passing through death into finality is to be applied to those who die *before* the moment at which, on the basis of ordinary experience, we would be inclined to ascribe to them an actual decision of freedom in the radical sense; nor do we know whether in fact everyone who is "adult" in the sense generally understood really makes that decision of freedom. . . . From the Christian standpoint, all we can really say must be about the "normal" case of human and Christian life.[29]

In this passage, Rahner even claims that such exceptional cases of those who die before realizing their freedom may be numerous. Raising the prospect of possible exceptions suggests that Rahner became more sympathetic later in his career to the possibility that interpersonal harms can severely disable the human capacity to effect a fundamental option.

Interestingly, however, Rahner does not account for this departure from his earlier affirmation expressed in the *Foundations* and articles in *Theological Investigations* that persons endowed with reason are inevitably faced with the task of effecting a fundamental option. He also does not comment on whether the likelihood of exceptional cases calls into question his earlier claims that God always provides sufficient grace to enable a human response to God's self-communication. Instead, Rahner is content to confine his theology of freedom to "the normal case of Christian and human life" and bracket the "exceptional" cases to a realm of their own. By doing so, however, he leaves a host of pressing questions and problems unanswered. Reflecting on these exceptional cases, for example, one is compelled to ask whether marginal cases of adults who die before effecting a fundamental option share certain features in common. If so, is it possible to identify the conditions that hinder persons' ability to realize their freedom and accept God's grace? Can others intervene and counteract these conditions and help such persons realize their freedom?

The experiences of incest and other trauma victims can equip theologians with valuable insights as they grapple with these questions. To begin, trauma theory suggests that interpersonal harm and severe material deprivation constitute key conditions that impair persons' capacities to act freely and relate constructively to others—abilities necessary to effect a fundamental option. As for the possibility of others counteracting the effects of interpersonal harm, social scientific literature on healing and recovery from incestuous abuse is hopeful. This literature consistently emphasizes that reconnecting with supportive persons and learning how to trust facilitates each stage of recovery.[30] The first stage—establishing a sense of safety within one's body and environment—can only occur with the support of others. The second stage—piecing together traumatic memories to form a more coherent account of one's traumatic past—also requires the presence of empathetic persons who are willing to be witnesses in this process.[31] The third stage—reconnecting with ordinary life and developing effective agency—is also sustained by supportive relationships. In short, the experiences of incest survivors testify to the fact that persons are dependent upon the support and love of others to heal and realize their freedom to relate positively to themselves, others, and God.

Such insight into the role of interpersonal relations leads us to the second claim that ought to be included in a revised understanding of God's grace. If interpersonal relations are crucial for healing and enabling one's freedom, then it appears insufficient to conceive of grace as being imparted by God directly to the individual, thereby enabling his or her freedom to effect a fundamental option. These experiences of healing, acquiring a new life-giving identity, and feeling liberated to love freely and be loved are phenomena associated in a theological framework with the effects of grace. Since such experiences occur in the context of interpersonal relations, it appears fruitful to inquire whether it is not actually God's grace that is at work in these liberating experiences. Consideration of the role of interpersonal relations in recovery thus suggests that God also mediates grace through loving, interpersonal relations. Rather than acting unilaterally, God may depend upon on the cooperation of other persons' free choice to love their neighbor in order to mediate grace to each person.

Does the suggestion that God mediates grace through interpersonal relations signify a clear departure from Rahner's theology? The fact that Rahner never explicitly developed such an idea in the *Foundations* or in his central articles on grace and freedom in the *Theological Investigations* gives the impression that Rahner viewed grace as mediated directly from God to the individual or through the Church's institution of the Sacraments or both. However, much of Rahner's material on ecclesiology and the Holy Spirit suggests a more social view of how God's grace is mediated. Since it is beyond the scope of this paper to develop this point fully, I will only highlight several passages which indicate that some of Rahner's writings resonate with the theological conviction that God mediates grace interpersonally.

When discussing why the Church is necessary for the mediation of God's grace, Rahner argues that each person's transcendental relation to God's self-offer must necessarily be mediated historically and socially.[32] Due to humanity's social nature, persons are created to respond to God's self-communication not individually but through fellowship with others:

> There is no experience of God for pilgrim man on this earth which has not been mediated through an experience of the world. Even the immediacy of man to God as constituted by God's self-bestowal in grace . . . is always mediated through the experience of the world which man finds already about him. . . . This relationship to the world . . . is primarily a relationship to a society, the human Thou.[33]

If God's love is mediated through the world and primarily through social interactions, it follows that interpersonal relationships have the potential either to mediate God's abiding love or block such manifestation of God's grace. Although Rahner does not explicitly discuss how abusive relationships can thwart the mediation of God's love, he does positively affirm in his reflections on pastoral theology that all church members have the responsibility to be occasions of God's mediating grace: "Each member of the Church actively shares in building up the Church—conveying grace to individual human beings."[34] He argues that such responsibility to be vehicles of God's mediating grace is grounded in each Christian's unity with Christ: "The bringing to accomplishment of this presence [of God's grace] is the act of all those living in God's grace in the Church. In some form they make this love present and perceptible in the Church's historical and social embodiment."[35] All church members, then, take part in the church's purpose of being a sign of salvation for all: "Every member in the body of Christ can and must serve as a channel of salvation for all others."[36]

If these two claims—(1) that interpersonal harm can severely debilitate one's freedom and (2) that God mediates grace through interpersonal love—

are explicitly integrated within Rahner's overall theology, his understanding of God's grace and freedom is revised as follows: fully embracing Rahner's central conviction that God creates us with the purpose of being able to realize our freedom and accept God's self-offer, we nevertheless acknowledge the possibility that interpersonal harm can severely disable this capacity and possibly prevent some persons from realizing God's intentions.[37] This revised formulation of the fundamental option, then, underscores that interpersonal relations have the potential either to be occasions of God's mediating grace or actually block God's grace from being effectively communicated to an individual. Accordingly, God entrusts the human community with grave responsibility to foster each other's freedom and be vehicles of God's mediating grace to one another. Of course, supportive relationships by themselves cannot cause or necessitate persons' will to say yes to God; these relationships merely enable our capacity to respond to God's grace so that we may realize the freedom needed to effect a positive fundamental option for God.

Resulting Ethical Implications

Since Rahner did not incorporate into his central writings on grace the idea of God's grace being mediated through interpersonal relations, he never explicitly attended to its resulting ethical implications for Christian communities. It is appropriate to ask, then, what follows specifically from recognizing that interpersonal relations have the power both to mediate God's loving presence and severely damage a person's capacity to receive and respond to God's grace.

The primary ethical implication is that this realization transforms and intensifies what exactly is at stake in Christ's call to love our neighbor. It becomes increasingly clear that we are not called to love our neighbor merely to demonstrate obedience and love for God. Neither are we called to love and risk ourselves for others solely for authentic self-realization, as a means of becoming the persons God ordained us to be. What is at stake in our daily decisions whether or not to love and how to love our neighbor is even more far-reaching and profound: God depends on us to love our neighbor in order to mediate God's love and foster each other's freedom to respond positively to God's grace.

Once we understand that God mediates grace through interpersonal interactions, our sense of responsibility for one another is inevitably heightened. If we view God's grace only as directly enabling persons' freedom to love God and neighbor, our actions have no definitive influence on others' freedom before God. However, if we acknowledge the possibility that human sin against one's neighbor can severely impair that person's capacity to respond freely to God's self-offer, we confront the prospect that sin in its most evil manifestations may have the power to deprive a person of fulfilling God's intention for her life: the capacity to realize freely one's "yes" to God as fully as possible within a unique, personal history of salvation. Responding to the power of sin, God entrusts each person with grave responsibility to do all that is finitely possible to ensure that others have sufficient freedom to receive and respond to God's self-communication.

As we realize our responsibilities as God's collaborators, we see that another major ethical implication is the imperative to discern appropriate forms of neighbor love to counteract the conditions that harm persons' capacity to respond to God's grace. Rahner's observation that love for neighbor changes historically has perhaps never been more pressing:

> Concrete love of neighbor, necessarily and constantly, takes on ever new forms in history, one after another, in accordance with the diversity of human beings and their varying historical situations. . . . This is why the Church is constantly encountering new surprises in this area—colliding with demands and tasks for the love of neighbor alive within it with which it has never had to reckon before . . . tasks whose moment for Christianity has come but slowly to Christian consciousness.[38]

Contemplating how to reach out in love to incest victims, for instance, we clearly must go beyond ensuring that their basic material needs are met and that abusive conditions end; Christian communities also need to identify ways to counteract the harms that have spiritually wounded such victims and help facilitate their process of healing. While it is beyond the scope of this paper to elucidate fully how to love in ways that foster healing from sexual violence, I wish to underscore forms of neighbor-love that should take top priority.

The first task is to create a supportive communal context where incest victim-survivors can re-establish a sense of safety and authentic connections with others. Christian communities need to acknowledge publicly and denounce the pervasive problem of child sexual abuse in our society and its devastating effects on victims. During sermons and other moments in the liturgy, Christian leaders must explicitly side with the victims and judge sexual violations as one of the most insidious evils persons can inflict upon one another. Churches must recognize that their past silence about the reality of sexual abuse within and outside their communal boundaries has rendered the church complicit in the denial and minimization of sexual violence. Such silence has made it easier for perpetrators to continue their crimes against those most vulnerable, in many cases maintaining their Christian identity as they do so.

The second task involves a commitment to strive for justice in solidarity with sexual abuse survivors. When confronted with concrete situations of child sexual abuse, Christian ministers and pastors must first act to intervene and ensure the safety and well-being of the victims. Besides reporting sexual violence to public authorities, they need to offer adequate access to pastoral support and make sure victims are aware of existing religious and secular social services. As for their response to perpetrators in their midst, church leaders must use their moral authority and influence to hold them accountable for their abuse. Calling all perpetrators to be responsible for their actions obviously includes reporting Christian ministers or pastors to public authorities when sexual misconduct is suspected or confirmed.

By continuously naming sexual violence as a primary systemic evil pervading our culture and working to achieve greater justice, churches will have laid the necessary groundwork for offering further forms of loving support. During the liturgy, perhaps during collective prayer and singing, the entire community can demonstrate loving solidarity with sexual abuse survivors by publicly honoring their strength and courage. Many sexual abuse survivors find that special healing rituals like laying on of hands, anointing, blessings, and purification rites to be powerful moments of healing in their process of recovery.[39] Of course, communities must be wary of the prospect of retraumatizing sexual abuse survivors during healing rituals. Perhaps participants in these rituals should be limited to incest survivors and those who support them. When more inclusive healing services are offered to the entire community, it is crucial for sexual abuse (and other trauma) survivors to be able to review the content of the healing liturgy before participating.

Besides supporting sexual abuse survivors in their pursuit of justice on an individual level, Christian communities need to raise consciousness about the structural sexism that fuels such a high incidence of sexual abuse in our society. They must also be self-critical about their own participation in sexist beliefs and practices and seek renewal and transformation. Eventually, these forms of consciousness will motivate individuals to use their particular gifts in preventing and eradicating sexual violence; church members will want, among other things, to volunteer at local crisis centers and shelters, educate adults and children about sexual abuse, and seek to change laws and social practices that protect perpetrators and retraumatize victims.

By continuously naming sexual violence as a primary systemic evil pervading our culture and working to achieve greater justice, churches will have laid the necessary groundwork for offering further forms of loving support. During the liturgy, perhaps during collective prayer and singing, the entire community can demonstrate loving solidarity with sexual abuse survivors by publicly honoring their strength and courage. Many sexual abuse survivors find that special healing rituals like laying on of hands, anointing, blessings, and purification rites to be powerful moments of healing in their process of recovery.[39] Of course, communities must be wary of the prospect of retraumatizing sexual abuse survivors during healing rituals. Perhaps participants in these rituals should be limited to incest survivors and those who support them. When more inclusive healing services are offered to the entire community, it is crucial for sexual abuse (and other trauma) survivors to be able to review the content of the healing liturgy before participating.

In addition, when offering pastoral support, Christian ministers and pastors need to be well-informed about the physical, psychological, and spiritual effects upon survivors of sexual abuse and other types of trauma. While Christian religious leaders can dramatically improve their sensitivity to these issues, they also need to be aware of the limitations in their own pastoral training and refer incest survivors to pastoral counselors who specialize in recovery from trauma. Other members in their church community (including those members who have personally experienced the effects of sexual abuse) can also receive training on the effects of sexual abuse and be able to offer individualized support and fellowship to incest survivors. In this way, survivors can build a sufficient network of social support necessary for recovery. Religious communities can also collaborate to make available support groups for those struggling to recover from varied forms of trauma; these groups offer a unique way for incest survivors to forge trusting and empathetic relationships and find within themselves additional strengths to aid them in their recovery.

These pastoral suggestions are obviously not meant to be an exhaustive account of concrete forms of neighbor love for sexual abuse survivors; they represent just a few initial ways in which church communities can begin fulfilling their call to be supportive witnesses for trauma victims in their process of recovery. Hopefully such moments of support and solidarity will serve as occasions for God to mediate divine grace, fostering incest survivors' freedom and their ability to relate and respond positively to God's grace.

Conclusion

I have argued that an adequate understanding of human receptivity and responsiveness to God's grace will include (1) the practical realization both that persons can severely debilitate and foster each other's capacity to respond to God's grace; and (2) the theological conviction that a primary way in which God mediates grace is through interpersonal loving interactions. Such a revised account of the workings of God's grace heightens our sense of responsibility for one another and helps us discern how to love in ways that foster each other's ability to respond positively to God and others.

NOTES

[1] Karl Rahner, "The Dignity and Freedom of Man," in *Theological Investigations*, vol. II (London: Darton, Longman and Todd, 1963), 240.

[2] Karl Rahner, "Concerning the Relationship between Nature and Grace," in *Theological Investigations*, vol. I (London: Darton, Longman and Todd, 1961), 312.

[3] Karl Rahner, "Grace: Theological," in *Encyclopedia of Theology: The Concise Sacramentum Mundi*, ed. Karl Rahner (Kent: Burns and Oates, 1975), 594.

[4] Karl Rahner, *Foundations of Christian Faith* (New York: Crossword, 1978), 101.

[5] Karl Rahner, "Theology of Freedom," in *Theological Investigations*, vol. VI (London: Darton, Longman and Todd, 1969), 187.

[6] Karl Rahner, *The Love of Jesus and the Love of Neighbor* (New York: Crossroads, 1983), 71.

[7] Rahner, "Theology of Freedom," 185.

[8] Karl Rahner, *Grace in Freedom* (New York: Herder and Herder, 1969), 212.

[9] Karl Rahner, "Comfort of Time," in *Theological Investigations*, vol. III (London: Darton, Longman and Todd, 1967), 151-52.

[10] Rahner, *Foundations*, 147.

[11] Ibid., 109.

[12] Ibid., 112.

[13] Ronnie Janoff-Bulman, *Shattered Assumptions* (New York: Free Press, 1992).

[14] Alexander C. McFarlane and Giovanni de Girolamo, "The Nature of Traumatic Stressors and the Epidemiology of Posttraumatic Reactions," in *Traumatic Stress: The Effects of Overwhelming Experience on Mind, Body, and Society,* ed. Bessel A. van der Kolk, Alexander C. McFarlane, and Lars Weisaeth (New York: Guilford Press, 1996), 129; Judith Lewis Herman, "Complex PTSD: A Syndrome in Survivors of Prolonged and Repeated Trauma," in *Psychotraumatology: Key Papers and Core Concepts in Post-Traumatic Stress,* ed. George S. Everly, Jr., and Jeffrey M. Lating (New York: Plenum Press, 1995), 88-90.

[15] I choose to concentrate on female survivors of incest rather than both female and male survivors because the vast majority of incest survivors who have sought therapy and who have participated in studies have been female. Since there has been even greater resistance in acknowledging that males are victims of incest, it is not yet known how prevalent male incest is. Current data suggests that 1 in every 3 girls and 1 in every 8 boys is sexually abused before the age of 18. Given the different socialization of females and males, it would be imprudent to generalize or assume that male survivors of incest have responded exactly the same way as females. More research needs to be done on male survivors of incest before credible comparisons can be made.

[16] Judith Herman, *Trauma and Recovery* (New York: Basic Books, 1992), 103.

[17] All three behavioral patterns are symptomatic of post-traumatic stress.

[18] Herman, *Psychotraumatology,* 94-95.

[19] Susan Harter, "The Effects of Child Abuse on the Self-System," in *Multiple Victimization of Children: Conceptual, Developmental, Research, and Treatment Issues,* ed. B. B. Robbie Rossman and Mindy S. Rosenberg (New York: Haworth Maltreatment and Trauma Press, 1998), 156; James Childress, *Who Should Decide?* (Oxford: Oxford University Press, 1982), 61.

[20] There is much debate whether the term trauma victim or survivor is more appropriate to use when addressing women who have been incestuously abused. The term victim most adequately conveys the long-term negative affects of child sexual abuse, and calls attention to the fact that a percentage of sexual abuse victims do not survive. The term survivor, on the other hand, honors the ways in which the person has coped and survived the abuse. My choice of either term will vary in a given sentence, according to which emphasis fits most appropriately.

[21] Herman, *Trauma,* 194. See also Rebecca Coffey, *Unspeakable Truths and Happy Endings* (Lutherville, MD: Sidron Press, 1998).

[22] Donna Kane et al., "Perception of God by Survivors of Childhood Sexual Abuse: An Exploratory Study in an Underresearched Area," *Journal of Psychology and Theology* 21 (1993): 228-37; Jennifer Manlowe, *Faith Born of Seduction* (New York: New York University Press, 1995); John Lemoncelli and Andrew Carey, "The Psychospiritual Dynamics of Adult Survivors of Abuse," *Counseling and Values* 40 (1996): 175-85; Stephen Rossetti, "The Impact of Child Sexual Abuse on Attitudes toward God and the Catholic Church," *Child Abuse and Neglect* 19, no. 12 (1995): 1469-81; W. Justice and W. Lambert, "A Comparative Study of the Language People Use to Describe the Personalities of God and Their Earthly Parents," *Journal of Pastoral Care* 40, no. 2 (1986): 166-72.

[23] Lemoncelli and Carey, "Psychospiritual," 175-85.

[24] Hall, "Spiritual Effects of Childhood Sexual Abuse in Adult Christian Women," *Journal of Psychology and Theology* 23 (1995): 129-34.

[25] Christine A. Courtois, *Healing the Incest Wound: Adult Survivors in Therapy* (New York: W. W. Norton, 1988), 202.

[26] When analyzing freedom in cases where persons lack reason, Rahner states, "We cannot go into the question whether and how this freedom can be accounted for in those peripheral cases where a person exists on a merely biological level, cases in which we do not recognize any concrete possibility of accounting for subjectivity, for example, the mentally handicapped who, at least by our normal standards, never seem to come to the use of reason. But we cannot understand something fundamental which is experienced at the center of existence in terms of such peripheral cases," (Rahner, *Foundations,* 106).

[27] Rahner, *Foundations,* 131.

[28] Karl Rahner, *Meditations of Freedom and the Spirit* (New York: Seabury Press, 1978).
[29] Karl Rahner, "Christian Dying," in *Theological Investigations*, vol. XVIII (New York: Crossroad, 1983), 237.
[30] See, for example, Judith Herman, *Trauma and Recovery* (New York: Basic Books, 1992).
[31] Herman, *Trauma*, 175-95. See also Dori Laub, "Truth and Testimony: The Process and the Struggle," in *Testimony: Crises of Witnessing in Literature, Psychoanalysis, and History*, ed. Shoshana Felman and Dori Laub (New York: Routledge, 1992), 61-75.
[32] Karl Rahner, *Theology of Pastoral Action* (New York: Herder and Herder, 1968), 47.
[33] Karl Rahner, "The Church's Commission to Bring Salvation and the Humanization of the World," in *Theological Investigations*, vol. XIV (New York: Seabury Press, 1976), 295-313. See also Rahner, *Theology of Pastoral Action*.
[34] Rahner, *Theology of Pastoral Action*, 68.
[35] Ibid., 41.
[36] Ibid., 67.
[37] I am obviously not arguing that interpersonal harm can damn a person *qua passive victim*; I affirm that God's grace can ultimately save persons if their freedom has been impaired by interpersonal harm to such an extent that they die before effecting a fundamental option. For further explication of this issue of a person being damned *qua passive victim*, see Gene Outka, "On Harming Others," *Interpretation* (October, 1980): 381-93.
[38] Karl Rahner, *The Love of Jesus and the Love of Neighbor* (New York: Crossroad, 1983).
[39] Mary Pellauer et al., "Resources for Ritual and Recuperation" in *Sexual Assault and Abuse*, ed. Mary Peallauer et al. (San Francisco: Harper & Row, 1987), 223-47. See also Marjorie Procter-Smith, "Reorganizing Victimization" in *Violence against Women and Children*, ed. Carol Adams and Marie Fortune (New York: Continuum, 1995), 429.

Corporate Selfhood and *Meditatio Vitae Futurae*: How Necessary Is Eschatology for Christian Ethics?

Raymond Kemp Anderson

Abstract

With John Calvin, the Reformed tradition found inseparable linkage between eschatology and ethics. Christians' decision making must include reflection about God's future re-creation of our corporate, corporeal selves, or else individualism or dualism will set in. *Meditatio vitae futurae* is to figure right alongside of the Creator's past word for us and His present intercourse as Spirit among us. Calvin's three foci here, trinitarian in intent, are Christologically informed. Comprising teleological, deontological, and contextual vectors for ethical consideration, they are to work together as orientational constants—a kind of global positioning system—functioning as faith's response to the triune God. This eschatology becomes a key to puzzles in Calvin's ethics: such as why he is reluctant to prescribe patterns of conduct; why he gives such prominence to Christians' freedom; or again, how his world-weary expressions cohere with his astounding activism. Calvin's letters show how anticipation of our future generates normative challenge, proleptic promise, and much more.

Not so long ago, eschatology had almost fallen from the radar screen of ethical discourse. Yet earlier generations of thinkers took it as axiomatic that afterlife concerns are essential for Christians' life formation. Calvin would say, "If the hope of the resurrection were removed, the whole edifice of piety would collapse, just as if the foundation were withdrawn from it."[1] But does

Journal of the Society of Christian Ethics, 23/1 (2003): 21-46

that mean that the personal future had to be individualistic and selfish or that future hopes were to be an escape hatch from the difficult world God loves?

I want to join those who have been asking whether a great deal more attention should not be given to how the eschatology of future promise might properly affect Christians' grasp of their ethical situation—their values, agency, life-style and motivation. My studies have brought me to the realization that Reformation thinkers had some insights here that should be important for us today. They knew why faith's hopes for the future should not open onto a parochial exclusivism or give way to an otherworldly and socially indifferent, "sister-are-you-saved" mentality.

Of course I am far from alone in this contention. I know many of my readers share the view that present behavior depends in part on future expectations. "People live out of the future, even as they understand out of the past," says Walter Harrelson.[2] "It is within the framework of Christian eschatology that social and political concern can be understood most profoundly," says Robert MacAfee Brown. "The future is an intrinsically moral concern" and "eschatology goes hand in hand with ethics," says Ted Peters.[3] "Christian ethics are eschatological ethics," declares Jürgen Moltmann.[4]

So today, we could not say, as Braaten did in 1974, that although "eschatology holds the key to ethics, most of the leading names completely ignore it, especially in America." Thomas W. Ogletree showed us how the prophetic eschatological developments had "enormous ramifications for moral understanding."[5] We have the significant Pauline studies that Nancy Duff undertook with Paul Lehmann.[6] And of course, Jürgen Moltmann's entire "theology of hope" has opened out in this direction.[7]

Carl Braaten's unusual essays in *Eschatology and Ethics* gave us useful insights from the vantage of the Lutheran tradition.[8] In the present study, I have been examining the roots of the Reformed Church tradition in the teachings of John Calvin. My analysis suggests a line of interpretation for the crucial role he found future-life belief to play in the formation of Christians' present action, and for how such belief correlates with the other dimensions of faith. At the outset one faces some interrelated questions: Is the traditional afterlife belief individualistic? Does it distract from our concern for environment, social justice, world health and sustainable economic systems here-and-now? Or could it be, as some claim, that well-understood, it would liberate and motivate action in just these areas?

Prima facie, this latter claim seems to have been the contention of the Reformers—especially John Calvin. For Calvin, the reassurance such belief gives the personal self cannot be an individualistic egotism. The promise it holds for churches should not become a parochial exclusivism. Its vision of a perfected future does not engender indifference to the present world in its social and ecological distress; instead it sparks commitment. An analysis of his attempts to return to an early Christian perspective should show us why.

Orientation for Christians' Freedom:
A Three-Vector Guidance System

As Calvin attempted to lay out an appropriate way-of-life teaching, he hit upon a trinitarian schema that recurs throughout his writing, namely that Christian ethical reflection is always to be spanned between three different theological foci.[9] Each of these, to his mind, provides one essential dimension of a general frame of reference to which we should "refer all our actions." Considered together, these will engender Christologically formed values, norms, and motivation. I will focus on the third of these, which Calvin called "meditation of future life."

The Gospels contain little in the form of ethical directives. But lodged in the back of Calvin's mind was Jesus' broadly stated invitation: "If anyone would come after me, let him deny himself and take up his cross, and follow me."[10]

Accordingly, Calvin termed his first focal reference for life-formation, *abnegatio sui:* badly translated, "self-renunciation" (III.vii). Here we are to reflect upon God's past on our behalf, where we discover that everything we have or are or can hope to be is a vast gift of grace. We contemplate God's action to locate our actions "in Christ." So we can divest the self of any slavish drive for self-enhancement and live free. Our previous struggles for self-worth through legal performance are rendered obsolete by our inclusion in Christ's community. Christians are to take their bearings in part, then, from a consideration of God's law and election pre-formed and pre-possessing us in the past. But it is crucial to keep in mind our memory of the Son, the *imago Christi.* For the living "Law of Christ" is to be understood as the normative embodiment of God's past-perfect will, the *imago dei* for a true humanity. As we reflect on these things, a "renewal of our understanding" and new affections will begin to displace our "*sentiment naturel*," and new motivations will follow (III.vii.4).

Responding to a second focal reference, *tolerantia crucis* (III.viii), we are to reflect on the present companionship we enjoy with the living Christ and empathize with his existential passion for the whole world He is bearing with—tolerating—in love; as he lives beside us through it all, both motivating and comforting. Our response within each new situation is colored by the paracletic accompaniment of Christ, the Holy Spirit.

The third focal reference, our main concern here, was often muted in Christian ethics during the past century: *meditatio vitae futurae* (III.ix). For Calvin, attention to this pole correlates intrinsically with the first two: As we act we are to envision our promised future life together, the community of saints restored in Christ's kind of community with the Father. Calvin, with other Reformers, saw this as indispensable to the formation and motivation of any Christian ethic worthy of the name.

As believers reflect upon these three foci, an ever-new phenomenal field opens up to them, within which "the freedom of a Christian" finds vectored trajectory and motivation. The entire schema is Christocentric, and its normative dimensions Christomorphic—in the sense that they take a liberated, fluidly spirit-responsive shape like Christ's. Indeed the conflicting ways of "doing ethics," prominent within the larger Christian community, may be significantly classified, along these lines, in terms of how different groups have narrowed their focus on one of the three to the exclusion of the others. "Pro-lifers," for example, tend to emphasize God's pre-set orders of nature and fixed laws; while those who accommodate abortion tend to be more contextual in their value formation.[11]

It is significant, however, that when Calvin made his Reformed return to the Emerging Church's life-formation, he found himself having to stress all three of these foci simultaneously. He saw all three references re-defined by Christ. And as such, they are not to be separated into either-or alternatives. Instead, all three are to function together, orientationally.[12] The trinitarian dimensions of God's time-spanning unity taken together become the phenomenal field for any Christ-responsive action. The three Christological foci are not spelled out and labeled so neatly in Calvin—as "deontological, existential and teleological"—but they are there, prominent in his thinking. And once we are sensitive to his frame of thought, we recognize them, expressed in a great variety of language, underlying all his discussions of Christian life.

The third of the Christological foci (III.ix) is so prominent in Calvin's writings that it has appeared to some to dominate his ethics. This once evoked suspicions that the Neo-Platonic revival, fashionable among 16th century dilettantes, had bent Calvin back towards that philosophy's asceticism—where it rejects the material world in favor of a contemplative ideal.[13] In some contexts he can speak of this *meditatio vitae futurae* almost as if it were the cause of the other two foci.[14] In others he speaks as if it were their goal. Observing this, Martin Schulze in the early 1900's made a game of equating Calvin's view of the future with Plato's, and there were those who dismissed the Reformer as a "pure Platonist."[15]

Later writers, such as Quistorp, Bohatec and Boisset, have been more circumspect.[16] We can recognize how Calvin, in the spirit of humanism, could freely borrow Platonic imagery, without our jumping to the conclusion that Calvin's own vision had become Platonic. To be sure, Calvin often enthusiastically contrasted our future life with the present; and if we took such expressions in isolation, we could easily suppose him to be a world-fleeing prophet of denatured spirit.

For example, when he introduces his description of *meditatio vitae futurae* as a focal vector for Christians' life, he says, "We must always look towards this goal: to accustom ourselves to disregard (*mépriser*) the present life," and do that in order "to aspire . . . to the immortality of heaven and strive to reach it."[17] Certainly, Calvin's fusion of Platonic expressions with biblical perspectives on future life remains one of the apparent inconsistencies his critics cannot ignore.[18] It is clear he knowingly borrowed from the imagery of the classics, sometimes sympathetically, often in sharp disagreement.[19] Did he borrow Platonic and Neo-Platonic future imagery simply as illustrative material, familiar to his Humanist readers; or did he share Neo-Platonic premises about a second world of pure spirit to be achieved by suppressing physical attachments in favor of a life of "spiritual" contemplation?

It seems more likely that Calvin, who did his doctoral dissertation on Cicero, continued to look at life's problems through another philosophical optic. Even while he was deeply Christocentric in his quest for answers, the Reformer always retained a Stoic coloration in his assessment of the social problems that exercised him. To his dying day he remained suspicious of unbridled passion and perhaps overly sensitive to the dangers of social chaos.

But it would be a mistake to suppose that he looked to an ethic of Stoic self-detachment or *apathia* for his answers. Again and again he chided those Neo-Stoics among his peers who would counsel us to be impassive "like a stump of wood." In the face of his frequent calls for a healthy disregard for the traumas of our present life, it may be easy to miss his grasp on God's boundless love for the present world, as it evokes humble service between people ("the office of charity"). As said, Calvin sees a dynamic coherence between these things. But he can fall into one-sided expressions: "Our heart . . . is so attached here" he laments, "that it cannot look up on high" (III.ix.3). "There's no mean between these two extremities: either that the earth must be despised, or that it is keeping us attached in an intemperate love of self . . . we should diligently endeavor to disentangle ourselves from these adverse ties . . ." (III.ix.2).

In such passages disregard (*mépris*) for "terrestrial life" begins to sound like a kind of virtue to be achieved in preparation for an escape to a future ideal state—which would seem to be quite out of sync with Calvin's denial of human virtues, in favor of God's active restoration of life. Where attention has come to rest on such expressions, it is no wonder that a sour grapes attitude towards present life has frequently been ascribed to Calvin. His strongest warnings against idolizing things of this world can begin to sound like the Stoic extreme: a rational desire for death.[20] But a wistful nostalgia for God's future was also present in St. Paul. And like Paul, Calvin takes seriously the prospects of a future life in continuity with present existence. Any desire to escape is held in practical check by sharing God's love for the alienated world, and our present calling within it: to bear our crosses in companionship with Christ. Though certainly, nostalgia for the coming life should free people from morbid fears of death.

Although Calvin stressed an ennobled calling in the present, he felt we should remain mindful that we are only pilgrims in transit to another world (see, e.g., III.xxv.2; III.x.1), strangers, exiled from home (III.ix.4). We should transmit our wealth "to heaven, which is our land and our dwelling place." He even spoke of this as a motive for deeds of charity here and now. Our present environment is so alien to the promised heritage that we must suffer earthly life "as lambs destined for slaughter" (III.xviii.6).

Calvin's nod in the direction of "the use of earthly goods and their pleasures" has been much cited as a corrective here. Yet when this nod finally comes in the *Institutes*, it may strike us as all too restrained—as if he dreaded giving any impression of laxity or unbridled spontaneity. When we recall the political situation in which the new Protestant churches faced bloody repression should their emphasis on Christian freedom begin to look anarchic, we may see one reason why.[21] Still Calvin's reluctance here suggests he is fairly comfortable with a freely embraced Stoic self-discipline, even though he is concerned to mark outer limits against an "intemperate" asceticism and crass Stoicism; i.e., one that is not moderated by a person's Christ-response (III.x.1 ff.; see below on moderation).

The Action Impact of *Meditatio*:
An Open-Ended Prolepsis

Follow Calvin's other-worldly expressions and it finally becomes impossible to discount them as simply a pessimistic world-rejection. Lobstein long ago observed that Calvin's concern for the future life could not be understood as world-avoidance (*Weltflucht*) so much as a call to embrace the world in an evangelistic spirit—a challenge to action for Christians.[22]

Calvin himself showed remarkable social and political involvement.[23] He was surely as active as anyone of his century. The scope of his practical concern is astounding. His constant stream of letters engaged heads of state. He urged lower nobility to political resistance, gave legal counsel to magistrates, and founded a public school for education in the classics. Furthermore, he did not embrace Augustine's two-kingdom doctrine in the either-or, heaven vs. earth way that would become so fateful for Lutheran Germany. How many other Humanists could match Calvin's regard for the sweaty workaday world? He declared, "There could be no labor so despised or lowly that it won't sparkle and be extremely precious before God, provided we're serving our vocation in it."[24] Later Calvinism, notorious for its shrewd political and commercial involvement, has its heritage here. For one who has been stereotyped as a champion of "inner worldly asceticism," and who, in fact suffered from painful hemorrhoids and dyspepsia, Calvin had a surprising amount to say about the enjoyment of things of this world.[25]

His Catechism's declaration that we honor God "by depending on Him for all goods" is not only a reference to the future.[26]

It is telling that the *Institutes* discusses the "usage of *terrestrial* goods" as "gifts" of God right after its chapter on meditation of the future life. More than mere juxtaposition, this linkage suggests a relationship that wider analysis will bear out: The future meditation is understood to have one effect and goal here and now—precisely in the joyful use of this world and its goods, not in its dismissal and negation. So it appears that what happens in and for this world correlates with future expectations for Calvin; and it seems unlikely that his future vision would split off from the totality of life as a dynamic whole.

If the world is to be disregarded or "scorned" (*méprisé*), it is only in favor of a fuller vision of this world—healed, elevated and restored—as befits Christ's community. Calvin's *meditatio* calls for a new, realistic perspective, not over against life itself, but against a truncated view of the present life, when it is experienced only empirically under its present burden of mortality and evil ("*estimé en soi*").[27] But the Reformer explicitly distinguishes this from a Stoic's apathy towards life. Such disdain would be a form of ingratitude toward God and is not only unrealistic, but sacrilegious.[28] With God's calling and promise illuminating present life, it is to be esteemed as God's benefit. As such, it is to be seen as already inextricably one with future life (III.ix.4).

God's reign is not only other-worldly and certainly not anti-worldly. Following New Testament usage, Calvin can speak of it as being simultaneously present (or near) and future. So a dynamic continuity is to be seen here: The Kingdom coming seems to stand as norm and judge, as well as final goal for the rule of Christ, which has been founded, long past, but is commanding allegiance and action here and now.

Upon occasion Calvin reflected on the superior desirability of afterlife. But this is not the voice of world-rejection. Such remarks express, instead, a positive longing for life to be freed from the broken relationships that pile new crosses on us every day. Experience demonstrates that "the faithful do have sin living with them always, until they are divested of this mortal body" (III.iii.10); but in his view, if we ever look wistfully towards death, it should be for one reason—that we may "serve God with such freedom as is to be desired" here and now. "It's not the earth that afflicts people, not the air, not the sky, but the evil that man drags around in himself."[29] Future promise actually both enlightens and lightens our bearing-with the present world. So, longing for the future represents not so much a devaluation of this life, as an "awakened" esteem for its promised restoration.

At the same time, Calvin does seem concerned that too much involvement in the vanities of this world can cloud our enlightened grasp of its true and permanent values (III.ix.4). But his "scorn for this life" is only in favor of its future immortality, a constant light from beyond whatever suffering and death we find ourselves presently forced to tunnel through (III.ix.5 See also Com. II Cor. 5:1).[30] Future light clears our way even in the face of severe persecution, such as the Protestants were experiencing in France (III.ix.6). Paradoxically, it is because Christ "will come as redeemer to bring us into the inheritance of his Glory" that we are to find real unity of purpose with this world even in what we today would call its ecological balance.[31]

Towards a Balanced View

An appreciation of the positive side of Calvin's future life orientation comes from Wilhelm Niesel, who counters Schulze's negative view with an overstatement, as if Calvin showed no ambivalence on this point: "The ethics of Calvin are not negativist; they are rather determined by the fact that we have a living Lord who was crucified and rose again and who will come again as our Savior. In the strictest sense they stem from the principle of the imitation of Christ."[32]

Although this statement is largely true, does it not diminish Calvin's witness to a present corporate life of free personal response, to reduce it to bare imitation? What of here-and-now interplay with Christ's Spirit present in entirely new situations? What of unprecedented co-creativity in his company? Calvin's stress was on how we are "in-grafted," "planted," or "inserted," into future-oriented community with Christ (*enté en Christ*). Should we turn Jesus' own person-responses into a deontological law to shape our actions? Even if we could apply such a rule directly in entirely new occasions, such a law (as Paul says of all law) would defeat us. For if it is divorced from Christ's paracletic presence and future promise, even this strict form of the law (Get busy and imitate Christ!) cannot make alive, but frustrates. Calvin says as much explicitly in his Commentary on Romans 6.

We still have to ask ourselves, however, how meditation on the future life keys into a quickened "judgment" over life's present worth. What, if anything, saves this "dual perception" from being what Hermann Bauke used to call Calvin's "compilation of contradictions" (*complexio oppositorum*)?[33] Some have suggested that Calvin may have been pushed into his strong eschatological emphasis by apologetic concerns. Calvin's first sally into theology was an eschatological essay.[34] He wrote it to show that the main Reform was not to be tarred with the same brush as the notorious Libertines. They courted state proscription by brandishing the notion that final perfection was already manifest in whatever they might do. So intent to show his distance from them, the young Calvin over-emphasized the eschatological side, whereas he would later stress a Christologically informed balance between the past, present and future foci for ethical reflection. But the early, one-sided material was later simply taken over into his *Institutes*.[35] To credit such apologetic concerns, however, does not yet explain the functional interrelationship that the Reformer saw between both past and future-directed reflections and present decision-making, as these themes recur throughout his entire life work.

It is striking how often Calvin gives his *meditatio vitae futurae* its significance, not only as a resigned hope for the better future, but as a motivation for forceful action here and now. *Meditatio* is regularly spanned back to the other foci for Christians' action reflection—correlated both with cross-bearing and with *abnegatio* (i.e., the dis-possession, or as we might say, the Christic pre-possession of self). Future orientation helps one embrace suffering and strife in patience (III.ix.2). A moral agent's triply vectored reflections, then, are functionally "moderated" (as Calvin would put it) by each other. Only together do they adequately connect us with the phenomenological field within which faith makes its freely responsive decisions. When we begin to look for it, we find this complementary relationship is a characteristic of Calvin's discussion of each of the three motifs.

As a typical example, when Calvin writes the Duchess of Ferrara encouraging her to put her house in order, his paraenesis takes this characteristic form:

> Call upon [God] then confident in yourself that He is sufficient to provide for our frailties, [in present, living relationship] and meditate upon these lovely promises, which are to raise us in hope of the glory of the heavens [i.e., *vitae futurae*]. For the mere taste should make us forget the world and put it under our feet. And in order to show that the desire to glorify God is enhanced, and is not at all deadened, be advised, Madame, in God's name, not only to bear witness to it in your own personal life, but also to order your house in such a way that the mouths of slanderers be stopped [i.e., consider the Christians' past, as imbedded in tradition and law].[36]

Such passages stressing the practical, this-worldly impact of the *meditatio vitae futurae* are abundant. They suggest its impact within present life is positive, and not just negative; and they lead us towards a unifying hypothesis for Calvin's ethic. Underlying the three centers for ethical reflection, Calvin perceived a necessary, dynamic inter-relationship—an organic harmony between these foci which, when regarded together, structure a Christian's free response.

Vita Futura: **Ideal Trajectory and Living Actuality**

Calvin develops the concept of future life meditation as a main part of what he calls a "general rule to which the Christian could refer all . . . actions" (III.vi.1); but he summarizes this rule in his special section on

Christians' life in terms of a change of heart (III.vi.2). The rule is not simply external. Its dynamism includes our being shown what he calls our own freest, most personal selves.

It is significant that "Christian philosophy," in contrast to Plato, calls us to contemplate our very life and not our death.[37] It is not life in the abstract as a spiritual ideal that we are to contemplate but our own particular life in its promised wholeness. That, of course, is not limited to our present, imperfect state, but is believed to be already perfect in the corporate unity in which God grasps us for good, as one in Christ. This looking forward cannot be an otherworldly narcissism; for the perfected image in Christ is our own image only through grace—a grace that equally embraces others. So rather than carrying us away from the present, it snaps our attention back to the contrast between our present state and what we are to be. The comparison and contrast with our future community in Christ acts as a clear prophetic judgment on much in our present lifestyle and action.[38] Yet such judgment remains from first to last a re-creation promise. Completely personal, it is basically restorative, rather than punitive or threatening. As promise, it evokes joy in place of guilt.

Two characteristic thought patterns enliven Calvin's view of the relationship between future life and the present. One is his image of Christ's own personhood (and of our life "in Christ") as corporate in nature.[39] The other is faith's classical dual perspective on time, whereby our sequential experience of our lifetimes is over-written by belief in what is for God a bridging divine simultaneousness. As Creator and Lord of time, he is not bound within it. So from his side he has a synchronous grasp of all times, which we can experience only sequentially. What remains future for us is present to him.

The life of Jesus of Nazareth stands as the kind of life we are promised in the future: a visible preview of community bonded and bounded by his Spirit. The structural content of our future life, which may also inform the present, then, is none other than our future response to the historical Christ.

As on occasion Jesus' response in the living moment found him re-directing even the weightiest of laws, such as the Sabbath commandment, there may be re-direction in our present. So a wooden imitation of Christ's particular pre-set deeds is not the message here. The *imago Christi* is to become the *imago homini* for us; but Christ was, and remains, the liberated and liberating one. Spirit-responsive, we will make liberal use of his law; but Spirit-responsive, we are also being led beyond its past forms and formulae into absolutely new constellations. All the while our self-view remains constant: we know ourselves as children of God, permanently "*constitué*" in Christ.[40] The old concern for fixed law is re-dimensioned into a person-response and the ethic of personal life is, as Udo Smidt says, "freed from the impossible proliferation of countless detailed demands which tend to annul it."[41]

If it is our own perfected, future life in Christ that we are permitted and called to meditate, our meditation cannot remain only on the other-worldly plane. Its content will become the pattern for our whole life, and so become normative for present action as well. For Calvin the ideal itself has become concrete and actual. It is known in the historical past as the freely responsive character of Christ (I.xv.4). So we look forward to the image of our heritage by looking back at the kind of life he lived for us. One can well say with Ronald Wallace that for Calvin "the focal point of *meditatio* is the ascended Christ."[42]

It must be stressed here that the humanity of God future for us remains thoroughly Christomorphic. This future reference has as its only available analogy and norm the Church's memory of Christ, in the past. This reference back to the Christ-styled life as the permanent image of our future re-creation has always been all-important to the Church. (Every strand of apostolic tradition stresses one way or another how the Psalm 110 image of final judgment has been transmuted by the claim that the all-forgiving healer is the one portrayed "at the right hand of God," as our only judge and gauge of future life). This has its theological parallel in the medieval church's gauge for present life-styles. Where there were any present claims for mystical inspiration, the Great Church insisted on referring back to the memory of Christ—in the past—as normative. God's Spirit present is recognized as he "proceeds also from the Son [*filioque*]." In the same vein, our future restored humanity, has its only visible norm in Jesus' own humanity. As the one insistence guards against aberrant speculation based on claims to present Spirit possession, the other guards against life-distorting speculations based on purely humanistic process and future progress. To be humanly fulfilling both our present and future will need to cohere as life in Christ.

Recalling Paul's word, "Just as we have borne the image of the man of dust, we shall also bear the image of the man of heaven," Calvin makes the *imago Christi* explicit as the subject of our *meditatio;* while at the same time it is the type or mirror or our own future completion.[43] The *imago Christi* also has past reference in the memory of Christ's freely responsive way, and it includes the image of our permanent selves in his community, as present norm. One can well say that for Calvin, "the person who stands in the *meditatio vitae futurae,* is already living the future life, here in this world."[44] But we have not yet grasped Calvin's view here if we have not reflected too on Christ's life as a gauge of our own already permanent, bonded communion. Beyond this Christological image of future life Calvin is reluctant to speculate. He is capable of some poetic imaginings, but these, along with all the Biblical "figures," he sees as only poor hints at the inconceivable human blessedness of which God's boundless creativity must be capable.[45]

The three foci for life, then, work together in harmony. They share the one everlasting Christ-shaped subject—alpha and omega.

> Since He has associated us in and grafted us into His body, we should guard ourselves meticulously that we not contaminate ourselves at all—in view of the fact that we are His members (I Cor. 6:15; John 15:3; Eph. 5:23). Since this one who is our head has gone up into heaven, it is appropriate for us to resign ourselves from all earthly affection, in order to *aspire with our whole heart to the heavenly life* (Col. 3:1-2). . . . Since our soul *and our body are destined to the immortality* of God's kingdom and the imperishable crown of his glory, we should strive to keep both the one and the other pure and unspotted until the day of the Lord (I Thess. 5:23).

> There you see some good and proper bases for constituting our life. One won't find their like in all the philosophers. For they never rise beyond exposing the natural dignity of man, when it a question of showing him what is his obligation (III.vi.3; italics mine).

In all of this there is a kind of two-level reality envisioned which may be reminiscent of Plato; but for Calvin the future ideal is our own completed life, both spiritual *and corporeal* which shares Christ's resurrection of the body. When we are called to live proleptically into that life now, it means to consider it both as our promised hope and as our present goal or law. Our own future life, so understood, with all its promise, joy and freedom actually becomes our present norm—a norm that calls us to be ourselves, in these enduring future terms and not to waste our energy trying to secure what is already ours.

Life-Steering *Meditatio*?

It is important that all three foci for reflection in Calvin's "general rule" for our lives' "address" carry this same noetic quality. In line with the New Testament, Calvin tends to leave the details regarding practical action for people to work out for themselves, as each new situation calls for a new, appropriately reflective response. He was concerned to show political authorities that the Reformed teaching was trustworthy in social ethical terms, but he gives us vastly more on prayer, for example, than he does on other forms of behavior. In fact, as I have on occasion shown, he tended to regard Christians' moral agency as itself a dimension of grace-responsive prayer. Their gracious deeds are but one medium for heart-felt expression toward God. The practice of prayer is the "principal praxis of faith" that precedes all ethical reflection.

Boisset hit the nail on the head when he described the benefit Calvin saw flowing from his *meditatio*: "This 'profit' takes birth and develops in prayer, which actualizes the normal climate for the relations of the man of faith with God, and in which this man tastes the fullness of life."[46] In the final analysis, we have to seek from God, through prayer, the life upon which we meditate, wrought in the warmth of actual companionship with a God who remains faithful for us, past, present and future—never essentially different from Christ.

The three-fold address should be characterized as a call to act freely, with sober realism in view of faith's special grasp of our objective situation. There is an interesting antecedent here to the method we have come to call scientific, namely that one receives stability and direction if one's thought is conducted entirely by the objective structure of its subject. But the subject of life here is the living one in whom we are implanted. No matter how far astray we may have gone, we can at any moment take thought and get our bearings again. We need only reflect upon our actual situation in faith: our past election and adoption in Christ, our present companionship with his accompanying Spirit—challenging, accepting, forgiving—and the all-healing promise of our future together. Our reflections about ourselves are to conform to our future selfhood, as it is to be restored in the Father's community, the Reign of God, pre-imaged by Christ.[47]

As we think upon these things, our motivation will begin to align with them. Thus our moral agency is sustained between the times. This world (where our very bodies are temples of meeting with God's beloved community), is not only a foreign land where we have no home, not only a prison, but also "God's workshop for the active preparation of our lives . . . where the method of hesitation never is valid."[48] Our three-dimensioned consideration acts with organizational force, giving life structure. This is all a "question of ordering our lives well . . ." (III.x.1; III.vi.1). For Calvin, that seems to correspond to the modern concept of becoming well-integrated. But he sees it conjoined with the experience of our vectored "address" to a living goal, which includes all the people we have ever loved in Community, and being ourselves drawn into it. This implies that a future afterlife, while not the whole picture for ethics, is all-important.

Vita Futura: A Prolepsis of Corporate Selfhood

Whatever is said about living proleptically into a future life will distort Christian existence if it is seen only through the optic of our typically American individualism. For Calvin our "in-Christ" status is to be grasped not only as personal and corporeal, but also as a corporate reality. To be ourselves, human, in Christ, we must include as essential to our own being, all those other persons whom God unreservedly loves. They are to be regarded as integral to the completion of our very personhood. Differing interpretations of an expected afterlife radically impinge upon ethical agency; and the Reformers' recovery of the Biblical sense of corporate selfhood is crucial here.

The concretely envisioned future community, in terms of which we are freed to live proleptically, gives a counter-intuitive perspective through which we are to see human beings in a new light, as in essence embodied in a corporate whole (which embraces and enhances their innermost diversity). Salvation itself can only be corporately apprehended.

No one is clearer on the fact that biblical future promise becomes cosmic in scope than Krister Stendahl. Yet he seems to belittle or diminish what this could mean to an individual in her wistful, first-person afterlife hopes. Stendahl is technically quite correct when he reminds us that "the whole concern for individual identity, which is the technical meaning of immortality of the soul is not to be found in the Good Book because its concern and focus is elsewhere."[49]

But he fails to consider what the New Testament's salvation concept means as re-creation of a whole that includes the personal self, corporately grasped. For the Pauline corporate ontology of selfhood "in Christ," re-emerging in the Reformers' thought, should guard future-life orientation against any such individualism. They were sensitive to how this metaphor (that St. Paul used on the order of 200 times to describe our permanently restored status) was clearly a corporate concept. The Body of Christ is none other than the community embraced and bonded by God's love. This is so foreign to the American competitive habit of mind that it is difficult for our students to grasp. Where New Testament eschatology is concerned, no either/or dichotomy may be driven between social concern or systemic, institutional justice on the one hand, and future individual promise on the other. In the wholeness of our restored being, personal selfhood and inter-personal communion are no more to be thought apart, than are body and soul—and about the latter Stendahl is beautifully clear.

Is anything more human than the need for personal assurance in the face of death? Unamuno may not have been far off in seeing that as a human dimension behind all religion. But Stendahl asks us to leave that dimension of our basic humanity behind for an ostensibly higher concern. Should not a clear appreciation of the corporate nature of our essential personhood free us from the guilt he would lay upon us for celebrating our own self-fulfillment alongside, or better, within the social re-creation in which it is imbedded? My selfhood, re-created in its fullness by God, includes relationship to all the others in its very essence. As such, it is immeasurably ennobled and enhanced. But there is no way this burgeoning status can be individualized. So it may be sadly ungracious to tar the joy of personal afterlife as "narrow and selfish," however understandable Stendahl's sentiment might be, as a reaction against individualistic sect Pietism.

Pious, ego-denying programs forget a practical fact of life that Calvin understood: the one sure way to liberate a person from her compulsive struggle for identity and status is to reassure her that she has been given a full permanent worth that is absolutely essential, not only to her own, but also to other people's very selfhood. This is an elevation and liberation for her own self. Such is the paradox of New Testament love. External grace is the source of inalienable status. Permanently self-assured, one never need struggle along in self-centered egotism again. But if such basic assurance is lacking, self-preoccupation becomes compulsive and enslaving.

Meditation upon future re-creation makes a great deal of difference to our view of human selfhood and how it is to be affirmed and expressed. If we can believe that our continuing lives are truly to be freed from the momentum of their own past habits and character (i.e., the life-encrustation that Eastern philosophy describes as the law of karma), then the strangle-hold that our own virtuous or vicious past has on us melts before the promise. Love is free to cling to the permanence of individual selfhood (which the experience-based wisdom of the ages, from the Upanishads through Theravada to Zen, regard as illusory or transient). There is no need for a mystic absorption of ego into the infinite, no pressure for cool self-lessness. Instead, one is invited into a permanent self-fullness upheld in a self-bestowing community of grace. For faith God's total access to our times outflanks the mortal experience of impermanence. His Grace will never become impatient to dissolve our complex stories into the timeless "unity" of an impersonal infinite.

So it needs to be clear that Calvin's corporate conception of self is not impatient of personal distinctness, but embraces and enhances the eccentric personalities we know, in a love which finds no virtue in mushing out individuality into some kind of mystical union. By the same token, neither can this corporate inclusiveness be abstracted into a theoretical universalism. For each of us, our corporate place remains a direct expression of God's own personal freedom to embrace us. Yet since it expresses the limitless whelm of his love, none of us may grasp inclusion as something we may hoard to the exclusion of others. "We are not our own," we do not own even our own selves or bodies, Calvin was fond of saying. We belong to each other in the mutuality Christ both gives and receives. Although Grace-gifted humanity is essentially corporate, any person meditating upon it will discover her individual worth multiplied beyond all imagining. More self-secure, she will find herself opening to others with greater readiness to squander self in generosity.

When Calvin stressed the personal freedom of God, as his active "election" to be for others, in this connection, it was intended to underline his initiative to accept people graciously and quite apart from any prerequisites. This freedom of God to decide to be for and adopt his people out of sheer grace was intended as a Reformation line of defense against the intrusion of institutional powers by the Medieval Church. Although many Roman theologians were in agreement with the Reformers here, the Council of Trent, after a violent struggle, finally declared against them, insisting that God's "preparatory" expressions of grace must finally be earned. We must "merit" acceptance, finally, by "forming" our "unformed faith" in terms of pious canons. (*Fides informata* and *formata* were the crucial terms.) Calvin continually decried the mercenary spirit of a Church that had insinuated a tit for tat stinginess into the heart of God's justice. Was it not blasphemous to snub his grace, on the assumption that it had to be purchased, either in this world or in a temporal Purgatory?[50] God's very glory is revealed in the restorative form of justice exercised by Christ, sovereign in his own good pleasure to heal and forgive.[51]

The Times of our Lives: A Regard for Synchronicity?

Theologically, of course, God's own transcending grasp of time was classically believed to be incomprehensibly synchronistic. As Creator of time itself, He maintains immediate access to our past, present and future as a seamless drama from which nothing worth-while is ever to be lost. God's perfections include something like Random Access Memory. This is another key to why present action and future promise are never to be divorced. And this too, as a counter-empirical faith claim, is difficult for modern minds to entertain.

My study of these themes has been stimulated in part by a problematic gap in the work of Karl Barth, the Reformed Church's most prolific twentieth century interpreter. Although he insisted ethics should be dealt with at every juncture in theology, he remained rather anomalous in his own beliefs about afterlife and seemed in no hurry to complete the planned eschatological section of his Church Dogmatics. He once asked me if I really thought we would go on in an afterlife experiencing new events in parallel to our present experience. I was startled. In my naïveté as a student, I had not considered other alternatives. I suspect he felt common afterlife notions fall far short of Paul's conception. You can believe that the totality of our eventful lives is preserved in the all-comprehending consciousness of God, with nothing worthwhile ever to be lost to us; but does that necessarily postulate an endlessly protracted interpersonal drama?

It became quite clear that Barth was not comfortable with his colleague, Oscar Cullmann's narrowly linear description of the time of our lives marching forward into a future-time-after-time.[52] Barth was too attentive to the totally "other" divine grasp of time. Paul and the apostles tend to speak in the past perfect when coming to terms with God's own perspective upon our final justification. And Barth found the Reformers to be responsive here to what he would describe as a divine synchronism—a kind of divine simultaneity: God treasures and comprehends all of our times in his own immediacy, as a living and detailed whole.[53] "The ribbon of time, which to our eyes is unwound endlessly, is in God's view rolled up into a ball, a thousand years as a day. . . ."[54]

Forensic Justification—and Sanctification?

It is rather broadly recognized that Paul usually used the past-perfect tense when referring to the final justification we apprehend through faith. We can grasp what he meant only when we see it as referring to God's simultaneous time grasp. Another less appreciated dimension of this belief, often implied in Calvin, is the concept that every deed along the way is already comprehended in God's permanent re-creation and preservation of our entire lives. His divine synchronicity includes the hours of decision in our lives. Because of this, we are to recognize his future re-creation of all we are presently doing in our life as something substantial and permanent, to which we may already orient ourselves.[55]

I have sometimes dubbed this dimension "forensic sanctification," using a paradoxical term to describe the synchronicity Calvin found in Augustine and Paul. If God's sovereignty as Creator includes lordship over time itself, his grace puts the seal of permanence, not only on our final, emergent character, but also upon each of our actions along the way. They are all essential to our life as a drama that He grasps and loves as a whole. The future worth-whileness of our lives, their permanent "justification," is actual, not only at a point of arrival, but in process, as well. Our gratitude at the thought should add zest to live in line with such restoration, so as not to waste our times or abuse his kindness.

Meditations that Steer and Moderate Life

If we were to follow further into how Calvin saw his three-vectored ethical orientation working out in actual practice, we would have to explain his ubiquitous appeals for "moderation." Although he occasionally may have in view a prudent Aristotelian mean between extremes, many of his calls for moderated behavior intend anything but a poised, golden mean: They can call for the most extreme passions or self-offering. The solution may well be that Calvin had in mind a meaning for the word "moderation" that has passed out of common usage. To this day, Presbyterian assemblies call their democratic coordinator a "moderator," before whom all enjoy equality or "parity." Active moderation refers to that by which we are willingly led or steered in our own Christ-vectored reflections.[56]

We remind ourselves that where our incorporation in Christ is in view, there can be no such notion as separate, private, good or evil. In Calvin's view, claims to shining virtues are usually vicious things, expressions of anti-christic pride. He did not revert to preaching a middle-way, or middle class virtue.[57] For him to act in appropriate moderation meant to be steered by one's own free response to Christ. The form of his life, past—our prophet, priest and king, a humble healer—the accompaniment of his Spirit present—challenging comforter—and the promise of our permanently bonded corporate future, when taken together, will modulate all our minor initiatives into to the major key of his love. So it is our Christocentric reflections—the past, present and future meditations we have been discussing—that are to be the cybernetic force shaping new, appropriate free action from moment to moment. The "moderation" Calvin always called for was not a cool philosophical stance that reduces every passion by the half. It was a dynamic navigational concept, describing how our own Christ-vectored reflections let us freely steer the course.

If there is any trait in Calvin's writings apt to try a modern reader's patience, it is his constant counsel to be patient. Whenever the leaders and church people he addresses were faced with insurmountable problems (ranging from the growing persecution in France to the chronic illnesses even nobles must suffer), his most prominent pastoral word was patience. Analyze such material, however, and one discovers that this was anything but the passive, stoic virtue we might suppose.

Future Meditation in Action

Calvin's letters—scores of them—are chock-full of social and political nitty-gritty. He was as shrewd about power and intrigue as any career diplomat. On occasion he could even urge magistrates and lower nobility to take responsible action that verged on rebellion. So when he writes such people, "possess your soul in patience," he is not making a virtue of passivity. Instead, he is naming that stance, in which, though victimized by our past or under present duress, we can turn part of our attention to our promised "true rest." As he knew from personal experience, our most desperate times of frustration and mourning can be imbued with a tenacious joy that enables practical realignment and realistic action. Even in such situations ethical paralysis can be relaxed, active energies refreshed, depressions banished.

Calvin's letters are rich with examples of how he saw meditation of the future crucially effecting decision-making—how, as he says in the *Institutes,* "it exercises its pre-eminence in that it guides man's life" (I.xv.6). In a typical letter Calvin urges a woman close to the centers of power to remember how "Paul . . . redoubles his exhortations to rejoice in the Lord . . . supporting with patience the vexations which may annoy us, inasmuch as these cannot prevent us from continually savoring the goodness of our God and Father and the love He bears towards us until we be fully satisfied with them in the place of our everlasting rest. "[58] To another, he counsels a vision of the future as the source of poise: "to find a true rest and abide therein," despite all the confusing vanities of the world that otherwise would "dazzle our eyes and cause us to float in continual anxiety."[59]

To those scattered by persecution, he urges that their ordeal might call to mind how "God will assemble in the heavens His children, who can hardly find a place of refuge upon earth. . . ." "Let the fugitive brethren, after all their wanderings both in body and mind, accustom their thoughts to their final migration" [*meditatio vitae futurae*]. Again, to a group in prison anticipating possible execution, he urges: "Our state is not made worse by death, but if [Our Heavenly King] is pleased to conduct us even to that extremity, He converts it into a blessing and a gain for us; [so] having raised your eyes to heaven, aspire to the palm which is prepared for you."[60]

Such meditation on the future should in no way diminish our gratitude for and joy in the present world:

[Although, on the one hand,] the time of our pilgrimage is short, so that if we reflect on that immortal glory to which God invites us, we shall have no occasion to faint by the way. On the other hand, if we meditate on the inestimable goodness which our indulgent heavenly Father has shown us, and the precious treasures of grace which in every form He has shed on us so abundantly, we shall be base indeed if we are not touched by His love so to forget or despise whatever belongs to the world, in order to break all the ties which hold us back from Him and disentangle ourselves from every obstacle that clogs our march.[61]

In overview then, what is the present ethical impact of believers' afterlife reflections? First we need to keep clear that if Christians' future life is to have orientational force, the only norm remains the memory of Christ's own past life and teaching. It is essentially historical.[62] As we have seen, there is an exact analogy between this and the Western Church's insistence that any claims to the Spirit's present leading must be consistent with Christ's own life and teaching. (Just as medieval spiritualists' claims to eccentric inspiration were challenged by the crucial *filioque* clause, revisionist dreams about our emergent future are also to be restrained.)[63] Any future process for Calvin will be subject to God's judgment and re-creation finally, so must remain essentially Christocentric and Christomorphic.

But the implications of this future orientation are as broad as life itself. Examples could be massed relating to any of the issues that most exercise us in ethics today. Future reference begins to affect our action regarding women's full status and role freedom if we view each other as permanent partners of inalienable worth. Robin Scroggs' important work on "Paul and the Eschatological Woman" backs up Calvin's insights here.[64] Again, it will strengthen our ability to channel or postpone sexual drives, if we really believe the kind of trenchant observations Carl Braaten made about an unending future life together.[65] My testosterone-driven erotic feelings will not have the same disruptive force if my actions are tempered by regard for everlasting, mutually respectful friendships. Even if my culture has been immured in power-mongering chauvinism, such reflections will evoke greater gentility, civility and patience with others' differences.

It will be heartening for a couple who have failed in their attempt to live together in peace, if their divorce is experienced against a background where their original covenant with each other retains a deferred permanence that transcends their present break-up. Where children are concerned, reflection on our future together must stamp our pedagogical style. Thus Calvin exhorts a noble father to reflect on future life with his children: "It is highly necessary that you should train them up for the possession of heavenly inheritance, rather than that of perishable wealth and honors here below."[66]

It effects our treatment of co-workers, if they are not simply "human resources" to be manipulated, but ends-in-selves bonded together for good. America's miserable patterns of incarceration are challenged if we no longer see offenders as nuisances to be locked away in cages and forgotten, but regard them as permanent friends, whose prison experience should contribute more to their lives than education in crime. Our concept of justice will be re-shaped to require concerned contribution to these other lives, rather than angry retribution. It may liberate me to help a friend with his dying if I can believe that even my "limiting case" action in pulling the plug or giving a *coup de grace* is only penultimate and that forced farewells do open onto an unending future together.

Our phenomenal field of action is entirely different if we see continuity between present alienated situations and their re-created future—new heaven and new earth. The political liberation implicit in such future visioning in Calvin's thought can be startling: When a government is destructive of the community promised there, its educated citizenry are empowered to resist godless tyranny and act courageously to establish a more humane government.[67]

Although the leadership Calvin exercised was by medieval custom authoritarian and directive, it was people's free response that he usually was after. Like other Reformers, Calvin had to struggle to grasp the full force of ethical freedom in Grace. Where he succeeded, he began to outline such an open-ended dynamic of Christ-moderated life that it may not even be recognizable as "ethics." Not if we are thinking in terms of rule-bound and sanction-laden patterns of behavior or habitual virtues. Returning to Paul, the Reformers began to grasp an alternative form of ethics, relatively free of institutionalized casuistry. And they began to see how prescribed rules or virtue patterns, although they diagnose and exhibit the life problem, offer no healing solution. The love imperative, the golden rule—even Jesus' "Love as I have loved" encapsulate the law which according to Paul, kills (see e.g., Rom. 5:20; 7:5-8:12 *et passim*).

Christ-mediated grace, however, "makes alive;" it promises not just justification of past actions, and current acceptance, as we are accompanied by the Paraclete he sends, but also future re-creation and restoration of our community-imbedded self. "There can be no doubt but that Christ will bind [us all] together . . . in the same inseparable society, in the incomparable participation of his own glory."[68]

Sharing the Reformation's return to such beliefs, Calvin found powerful backing and direction for Christians' behavior. As we reflect upon the comprehensive wholeness, whereby all of our moments are given permanent value and treasured in the transcending power of God, Christ's own character becomes normative for our perceptions of each of the times of our life—past, present, and future. He is normative not only for the selves we experience as agents in our halting activity from day to day, but also for our abiding life, as God weaves everything we have been into his corporate whole. The underlying unity of our lives is comprised for the Reformers in the Pauline-Augustinian view that God himself, as creator of Time, maintains synchronous random access to all of our moments, past and future. Yet he never collapses them into a moment of final achievement, or a timeless mystic "union."[69]

With life so conceived, the Reformer envisioned a balance between the past, present and future dimensions of life—all to be informed Christologically. This interaction removes misleading dichotomies between this-worldly commitment and future promise, between individual fulfillment and social action, between set law and responsive freedom, between the actions of our maturity and those of our youth. So no one dimension of life's fullness is given precedence over the others, and life guidance remains essentially a dynamic of free personal response. This, for Calvin, makes Christians' action virtually a dimension of prayer.

No matter how far astray we may have wandered, as Christians we can at any moment take our bearings within this faith-formed phenomenal field. A tripolar, or trinitarian, frame of reference is always in view: first vectoring to the past, where the paradigmatic λογος or logic of God's human creation, its freedom in Christ, is to be apprehended as our deontological law; and last, vectoring towards the future. There our inalienable, corporate personhood, "the Body of Christ," is to be envisioned as our teleological promise and challenge. So poised between the times, we act in the existential present, where God's accompanying Spirit embraces us in Christ's quality of companionship—*"Spiritus Sanctus patre filioque processus est!"* Tenaciously bearing with us, he evokes our ever-new and free response.

NOTES

[1] Karl Barth, *The Resurection of the Dead* (London: Hodder and Stoughton, 1933), 222.

[2] "Eschatology and Ethics in the Hebrew Bible," *USSQR*, 42:1 & 2, 1988: 43. This would be true, Harrelson feels, even if the future were envisioned in idealized Platonic terms.

[3] Robert MacAfee Brown, "Eschatological Hope and Social Responsibility," *Christianity and Crisis* 13, no.19, (1953): 147. Ted Peters, *Futures: Human and Divine* (Atlanta: John Knox, 1978), preface.

[4] Jürgen Moltmann, "Liberating and Anticipating the Future," in *Liberating Eschatology, Essays in Honor of Letty M. Russell,* ed. Margaret A. Farley and Serene Jones (Louisville: Westminster-John Knox Press, 1999), 205.

[5] Carl E. Braaten, *Eschatology and Ethics: Essays on the Theology and Ethics of the Kingdom of God* (Minneapolis: Augsburg, 1974), 105. Thomas W. Ogletree, *The Bible in Christian Ethics* (Philadelphia: Fortress Press, 1983), 70, 91 *et passim.*

[6] See Joel Marcus and Marion L. Soards, ed., "The Significance of Pauline Apocalyptic for Theological Ethics," *in Apocalyptic and the New Testament, Essays in Honor of J. Louis Martyn* (Sheffield: Sheffield Academic Press, 1989), 279-96.

[7] See e.g., his "Attempt at a Historical Ethic of Hope" in *Hope and Planning,* (New York: Harper & Row, 1971), 122ff. and his note: "Good works do not build the kingdom of God, but hope in the coming kingdom assumes ethical forms within history. Between optimistic chiliasm and apocalyptic lethargy Christian life stands in the dawn of hope (Rom. 13:11-14)."

[8] Braaten, *Eschatology and Ethics,* 105. See also, *Christ and Counter-Christ: Apocalyptic Themes in Theology and Culture* (Philadelphia: Fortress, 1972).

[9] Calvin, *Institutes,* III.vi-x. Hereafter references to the Calvin's *Institutes* will be given in short form: book and chapter in Roman numerals followed by paragraph locations in Arabic. Unless otherwise indicated, such references are to his final French version: *Institution de la Religion Chrétienne, livres* I-IV, in the edition, *Labor et Fides* (Genève, 1955-58). English translations from the *Institutes* and other foreign sources are my own. This tri-polar Reformation view coalesces strikingly with those alternative philosophical approaches to ethics described by Frankena and others some years ago. Different people espouse different centers of gravity for their value-formation; some focus in the past (stressing deontological, legalistic values), others in the present (making contextual, existential decisions) while others focus in the future (opening to teleological, evolutionary or emergent values). Not only may opposing Christian approaches to ethics be so comprehended, but those of other religions and philosophies, as well. See e.g., summaries in William K. Frankena, *Ethics* (Englewood Cliffs, New Jersey: Prentice Hall, 1963), 14ff.

[10] Mark 8:34f.=Matthew 15:24f.and Luke 9:23f. (which adds the word, "daily"). Compare Calvin, *Commentary Matt.* 16:24, Harm. Ev. (*Corpus Reformatorum: Calvini Opera . . .,* 45.481f).

[11] Despite superficial appearances these three foci or vectors, with their Christic reference, function rather differently from the three ethical positions Tom Ogletree describes as informing ethical reflection in general (deontological, consequentialist, and perfectionist). See Robin Scroggs, "New Testament Ethics: How do We Get from Here to There?" in *Perspectives on the New Testament,* ed. Charles H. Talbert (Mercer University Press, 1985), 76-93. Compare Allen Verhey on "The Bible in Cristian Ethics," *Westminster Dictionary of Christian Ethics* (Philadelphia: Westminster Press, 1967), 58f.

[12] Where some sects of the historical Christian Church have been mired in legalism, or caught up in a libertine individualism, or given over to spiritualized world-abandonment, such excesses may be significantly grasped as having arisen where one of these foci has been regarded in isolation, to the neglect of the others. For the Reformed tradition, such neglect would mean a major dimension of theology is being disregarded: key beliefs about creation, about life in the Spirit or the unity of creation and of salvation have not been grasped as an integrated unity. Christian morality here is always expressive of belief. Ethics are not to be separated from theology—ever.

[13] See P. Lobstein, *Die Ethik Calvins in Ihren Grundzügen entworfen* (Strassbourg: C.F. Schmidt, 1877), 79ff. for collected Calvin loci here.

[14] As said, Calvin's most common designations for these first two foci are cast in the terms taken from Matthew 16:24: self-denial (*abnegatio sui*) and cross-bearing (*crucis tolerantia).* But contrary to a common (and quite understandable) misunderstanding, our research shows that in

Calvin's intent these do not so much press us into an "inner-worldly asceticism" as remind us to rely on God's overflowing grace (and not our own compulsive striving) "for all good things." (Compare *Catechism de Genève*, 1542, Q.7). It is in favor of faith's infinitely higher grasp of the self, whom God loves, that we are free to resign our title to self and our compulsive struggle to achieve status. For we discover the fullest worth has been ascribed to us all the while. Following Calvin's further usage, then, we have found that this "self-denial"—perhaps better translated the dispossession or resignation of self—is not the dualistic, self-repressive act we might suppose. Instead, it refers to the upsurging sense of personal worth we enjoy, when we discover ourselves to be gifted with God's permanent and inalienable love. The old fragile sense of self is rendered *"caduque,"* obsolete, and may be jettisoned like a dead cocoon.

Again, the second focus, cross-bearing means to bear with a present society, in which old status competition and self-bound alienation persist. For Calvin it is not the stoic self-denigration that one might suppose. Quite the opposite, we are called to keep company with Christ's Spirit, as He bears with a world, which does not yet respect people's inestimable status as a gift of grace. This of course is only for the time-being, as our eyes are drawn to the future.

The third focus, *meditatio vitae futurae* (or *coelestis vitae),* as we will see, has us tracking the divine constancy of this grace into the future, so our present free responses will also take into consideration the quality of life together that is permanently ours with the Father.

[15] Martin Schulze, "Meditatio Futurae Vitae, Ihr Begriff und ihre herrshende Stellung im System Calvins," in *Studien der Theologie und der Kirche* (Leipzig: Dieterich, 1901). See e.g., 81 *et passim*. L. D. Streiker, "The Legitimacy of Rational Inquiry," *Christian Century* (April 13, 1966): 460.

[16] See e.g., Heinrich Quistorp, *Calvin's Doctrine of the Last Things* (Richmond, VA: John Knox Press, 1955), 52f.

[17] III.ix.1; III.x.4.

[18] Josef Bohatec traces this characteristic further to include Budé (*Budé und Calvin: Studien zur Gedankenwelt des französichen Frühumanismus* [Graz: Verlag Hermann Böhlaus, 1950], 417, 421); but its significance has been minimized by most, since Schulze first drew a line between Calvin and other humanists, such as Erasmus, here. See also in Jean Boisset, *Sagesse et sainteté dans la pensée de Calvin, Essai sur l'Humanisme du Réformateur français* (Paris: Presses Universitaires France, 1959).

[19] And Platonic imagery does frequently color his picture: The present existence is entombed "in our flesh as in a cave" (IV.i.1) imprisoned in the flesh—at least by contrast with the promised resurrection, where the body will be restored, free from its mortality and its disruptive load of concupiscence (III.vi.3; III.vii.6), divested of this mortal flesh, we will be like angels (IV.i.4; III.xxv.1). As said, however, it would be all too easy to read an other-worldly dualism of Hellenistic stamp into Calvin's program here. We may misread him, I think, where such expressions about future life are taken in isolation. Does all this imply that Kolfhaus was right when he long ago declared Calvin's teachings to be a *complexio oppositorum*? I think not.

[20] III.ix. 4 f.; Com. II Cor. 5:4-6; Rom. 8:9. Compare to II Cor. 5: 2. Calvin's letters and words of counsel keep returning to another rather strange fixed idea that he seemed to think would be helpful in dealing with trying times: They help us develop a patience or resignation that he seems to assume—rather incongruously, I think—will be useful for future life together with God! (See below.)

[21] The open letter to François I, which prefaced the *Institutes,* is very suggestive here. The same apologetic concern probably explains why Calvin put his chapters on the dangerously revolutionary fundamentals, justification of faith and Christian freedom, after his chapters on Christians' practical life control in Book III.

[22] Lobstein, *Die Ethik Calvins*, 110-12.

[23] See, e.g., André Biéler's works: *La pensée économique et sociale de Calvin* (Genève: Georg, 1959; *L'humanisme social de Calvin* (Genève: Editions Labor et Fides, 1961); *L'homme et la femme dans la morale calvinienne* (Genève: Editions Labor et Fides, 1963); and Markus Barth, "The State of the Free . . ." in *Reformatio Perennis, Essays on Calvin and the Reformation in Honor of Ford Lewis Battles*, ed. B. A. Gerrish & Robert Benedetto (Pittsburgh:

The Pickwick Press, 1981). For a short summary see David Steinmetz, *Calvin in Context* (New York & Oxford: Oxford University Press, 1995), 17-20.

[24] III.x.6.

[25] This popular label, pasted on Calvin since the day of E. Troeltsch and Max Weber could about as well describe Lutheran views or even the Roman Catholic economic ethics, as Josef Bohatec, rightly points out (Bohatec, *Budé und Calvin*, 436f.). See also Herbert Luthy, *From Calvin to Rousseau* (New York: Basic Books, 1959) for a reassessment of Weber's views.

[26] *Catechism de Genève*, 1542, Q.7. Wilhelm Niesel, ed., *Bekenntnisschriften und Kirchenordungen der nach Gottes Wort reformierten Kirche* (Zürich: Evangelischer Verlag A. G. Zollikon, 1938), 4.

[27] III.ix.1.

[28] See III.ix.3 and more especially III.x. See further on Neo-Platonic and Stoic traces: Raymond Kemp Anderson, *Love and Order: The Life-Structuring Dynamics of Grace and Virtue in Calvin's Ethical Thought* (Chambersburg: Wilson College, 1973), 57-76 *et passim*. For the most recent digest of this material see Kyle Fedler's "Calvin's Burning Heart: Calvin and the Stoics on Emotions," in the previous issue of this journal (*JSCE*, vol. 22 [Fall 2002]: esp. 137ff.) *"Toute notre vie présente est envisagé sub specie aeternitatis"* [cited by Louis Goumaz, *La Doctrine du salut d'après les Commentaires de Jean Calvin sur le Nouveau Testament* (Paris: Lausane, 1917), 291.] See further *in loc.* on Calvin's commentary to the underlying Matt. 16:24-26 text.

[29] Cited in Bohatec, *Budé und Calvin*, 418. Further, *"toute notre vie présente est envisage* sub specie aeternitatis" (cited by Louis Goumaz, *La Doctrine du salut [doctrina salutis] d'après les Commentaires de Jean Calvin sur le Nouveau Testament . . .* [Noyon, Suisse: E. Cherix, 1917], 291. See further *in loc.* on Calvin's commentary to the underlying Matt. 16:24-26 text).

[30] *"méprise de cette vie mortelle . . . aux prix de l'immortalité future."*

[31] "For St. Paul well teaches the faithful to go briskly to death, not as if they wished to be unclothed, but because they want to be still better clothed (II Cor. 5:2-4). Is it sensible that dumb animals, and even the unconscious creatures down to wood and stones, having some inkling, as it were, of their vainness and pollution, should long for the day of judgment in order to be relieved of it (Rom. 8:19-20), that we by contrast, having first some light by nature, and then, better still, being illuminated by the Spirit of God, should never raise our eyes beyond this terrestrial decay when it puts in question of our very being?" (III.ix.5).

[32] Wilhelm Niesel, *The Theology of Calvin* (Philadelphia: Westminster, 1956), 151. Bohatec (also arguing against Schulze here), shows with abundant examples that Calvin's concern is not basically an other-worldly pessimism. He describes, instead, a kind of dialectic synthesis between pessimism and optimism for the world. There is a clear picture of this world's deep value; but it is framed in an equally clear realism about the ugliness of its pervasive pollution (Bohatec, *Budé und Calvin*, 430).

[33] Herman Bauke, *Die Probleme der Theologie Calvins* (Leipzig: Hinrichs, 1922), 16, 18, 44.

[34] Calvin's Treatise, "Psychopannychia."

[35] See for example Willem F. Dankbaar, *Calvin, sein Weg und Werk* (Neukirchen: Neukirchener Verlag, 1959), 31. Compare Bohatec, who makes a somewhat similar judgment regarding Calvin's apologetic motives (Bohatec, *Budé und Calvin*, 430 and 425).

[36] Lettre à la Duchesse de Ferrare, 2 février, 1555, *Lettres de Jean Calvin, Lettres françaises*, vol. II. ed. Jules Bonnet (Paris: Librairie de Ch. Meyrueis, 1854).

[37] Contrast Schulze, *"Meditatio futurae vitae, Ihr Begriff und ihre herrshende Stellung im System Calvins," Studien der Theologie und der Kirche* (Leipzig, Dieterich, 1901): 81f. (to *Institutes* III.iii.20).

[38] See Calvin, *Harm. Ev. Calvini Opera . . .* 45, 482f.

[39] See Raymond Kemp Anderson, "Corporate Personhood: Societal Definition of the Self in the Western Faith Tradition," in *Becoming Persons*, vol. II, ed. Robert N. Fisher (Oxford: Applied Theology Press, 1995), 599ff.

[40] Calvin used a whole array of terms to indicate this relationship: inserted in Christ, planted, incorporated, associated, etc.

[41] Udo Smidt, "Calvins Bezeugung der Ehre Gottes," in *Vom Dienst an Theologie und Kirche* (Festgabe f. A. Schlatter, Berline: Furche, 1927), 129.

[42] Ronald Wallace, *Calvin's Doctrine of the Christian Life* (Edinburgh & London: Oliver & Boyd, 1959), 87ff. "Now every time one comes to talk about the resurrection, let's set before our eyes the image of Jesus Christ, who ran the course of His mortal life in the nature. He had taken from us in such a way that being made immortal, He is a good gauge of our coming immortality" (III.xxv.3).

[43] Wallace, *Calvin's Doctrine,* 104ff.

[44] A. Göhler, *Calvins Lehre von der Heiligung,* (München: Kaiser Verlag, 1934), 40.

[45] See e.g., III.ix.5 & 6; III.xxv.2 & 10.

[46] Jean Boisset, *Sagesse et sainteté,* 100. Compare Goumaz, "what is the means of penetrating as far as the riches of the new and eternal life that God offers in Christ to our faith? Prayer: that's the medium" (298).

[47] Robert Jensen comes very close to Calvin's application of trinitarian reference in a context where he is speaking of soteriology, rather than ethics. Jensen, *God According to the Gospel: The Triune Identity* (Philadelphia: Fortress, 1982), 22-25. The relation to God-past is not directly to the Father in Calvin, but to the historical Christ, as a redefinition and norm for God's law, as well as an earnest of his present accompaniment and future community with us.

[48] Calvin, "Lettre à Antoine de Bourbon, Roi de Navarre," in *Johannes Calvins Lebenswerk in seinem Briefen,* ed. Rudolf Schwarz (Tülinger: Mohr, Siebeck, 1909), Bd. II: 393.

[49] Krister Stendahl, "Immortality is Too Much and Too Little," in *Immortality and Human Destiny,* ed. Geddes McGregor (New York: Paragon, 1985), 213f. Grace Jantzen, another typical example, has urged that everlasting life should *not* be "so central to Christian thought and practice as is often believed." Jantzen, "Do We Need Immortality," Modern Theology I (1948): 33-44.

[50] Very important here is Calvin's "*Antidotum*" against the Sixth Session of Trent. Latin text in the *Corpus Reformatorum: Joannis Calvini, opera quae supersunt omnia,* ed. G. Baum et al. (Brunswick and Berlin, 1863-1900).

[51] God, free to be Himself, is infinitely more gracious than any church. For Calvin that freedom included the kindness to motivate and gradually restore those He has promised His future Community. ("Those whom God justifies, He also sanctifies," was one of his favorite slogans). It is one of history's great ironies that Calvin did not foresee how some of the arguments he used to get that across would someday be turned to the very opposite purpose. Protestants, bannering his name, would come to indulge in unwarranted speculation: If you think of God's freedom to be saving towards some as an abstract first principle, they would rationalize, wouldn't that lay on Him a necessity to change and become a different Self, as it were, towards others! (Calvin himself was capable of such dark thoughts occasionally, when he was angry enough to call someone "reprobate!" But he knew and frequently stated that people are never in a position to assume such a thing.) Later Calvinist Scholastics, however, armed with this hard-hearted "double-predestination" speculation, presumed to sniff out how God's saving grace was simply not in sight for those who persisted in behavior they judged "unsanctified" (the fateful *syllogismus practicus* doctrine). Carter Lindberg gives, perhaps, the best recent summary of the underlying Calvin connection. *See The European Reformations,* (Oxford *et al.*: Blackwells, 1996), 266f. Jürgen Moltmann comments on the illogic of thus abstracting God's freedom from his grace in *The Trinity and the Kingdom* (Philadelphia: Fortress Press, 1993), 151f; see also 52ff.

[52] See among other titles, *Christ and Time: The Primitive Christian Conception of Time and History* (Philadelphia: Westminster, 1960).

[53] Barth, *Resurrection,* 218. (It is significant that a doctoral candidate of Cullmann's, Jacques Dupont, O.S.B., was drawn by the Pauline texts to recognize how they reflect "*deux points de vue: celui de la vie et celui de la fin des temps. Cette observation est capital . . . .*" Our linear time, as Dupont sees it, persists for us only during "*une periode qui suit immédiatement la morte.*" *ΣΥΝ ΧΡΙΣΤΩΙ—L'Union Avec le Christ Suivant Saint Paul,* "Avec le Christ Dans la Vie Future" [Louvain : Nauwelaerts, 1952], 152f).

[54] Barth, *Resurrection*, 218.

[55] It is in part why Calvin can grasp positively the philosophical maxim that to know oneself is the beginning of wisdom (see e. g., II.i.1-3).

[56] The suggestion seems inevitable, that we may have before us here a source for whatever it was in Calvinist habit of mind that contributed to the emergence, finally, of modern liberal democracy.

[57] Thus Georgia Harkness in *John Calvin: The Man and His Ethics* (New York, Nashville: Abingdon Press, 1958), 219 and chap. VIII.

[58] Jules Bonnet, *Letters of John Calvin...*vol. IV (Philadelphia: Presbyterian Board of Publication, 1858), 43. To one of many notable women embraced by his correspondence, Calvin speaks of her illness and his own as drawing them into an empowering meditation of the future: "in our languishing we are supported by the strength of God's Spirit, and moreover, ... if this corruptible tabernacle is falling to decay, we know that we shall be very soon restored, once and for ever. But there is no repose or satisfaction for us in this world" (to the Comtesse de Sininghen, *Ibid.* vol. IV, 333).

[59] To the Comtesse de Roye, the mother-in-law of the reforming Prince de Condé and sister of Admiral de Coligny, Geneva, (24 September 1561): Bonnet, *Letters . . .*, vol. IV, 228.
In the same vein Calvin will address all the new Reformed churches in France: "we shall possess our souls in patience, because [our divine Master] will be their faithful guardian. And, moreover, if . . . we lose this frail and perishable condition, we shall recover it far better in the heavenly glory. . . . This is the principal lesson which the holy Scripture requires you now to meditate upon when it calls us pilgrims in this world." ". . . since your names are written in the Book of Life, and God approves of you, not only as his servants, but also as his children and heirs of his glory, members of his only Son Jesus Christ and companions of angels" (Bonnet, *ed. cit.*, 51 & 53).

[60] Ibid., vol. IV, 20.

[61] Letter to the house churches in Poitou (3 September 1554), Bonnet, *ed. cit.*, vol. III, 70f.

[62] "Historical" does not carry the secular sense of empirical verifiability here, but refers to faith's common ground in the apostolic canon.

[63] "When the Lord bids us to walk on earth, those who inquisitively argue about how the dead live in heaven are in fact delaying their own arrival in heaven" (Calvin, *Commentary Matt.* 18:1, Harm. Ev. (*Corpus Reformatorum: Calvini Opera*, 45).

[64] Robin Scroggs, *Journal of the American Academy of Religion*, vol. XL, no. 3, (September 1972): 283-303; "Paul: Chauvinist or Liberationist?" *Christian Century* (March 15, 1972): 307-309.

[65] What Jesus meant by a future in which we are together "like angels" with "no marriage in heaven," Braaten says, "can only be imagined in terms of something like a total erotization of all persons endlessly without genital restrictiveness. But that prospect blows my mind; so on with marriage for the time being!" Braaten, *Eschatology and Ethics*, 171.

[66] To a *Seigneur* of Piedmont, Bonnet, *Lettres de Jean Calvin*, vol. 3, 24.

[67] In Calvin's day this meant a freedom for those who had an education and understanding of governance (in France, "the second estate" comprising educated nobility, magistrates and clergy) to undertake responsible resistance—an established revolution—to remedy life-destructive government. The last chapter of the *Institutes* is remarkable here. See especially IV.xx.30-32. It should be noted that Calvin through his new Academy and other efforts to educate the common folk was intent on broadening this educated base and thus, unwittingly, preparing the ground for later liberal democracy.

[68] Bonnet, *Lettres de Jean Calvin*, vol. I, 251.

[69] This line is probably discernable already in Jeremiah and certain of the Psalms. See especially Ps.139.

Three-in-One Flesh: A Christian Reappraisal of Divorce in Light of Recent Studies

Julie Hanlon Rubio

Abstract

The author argues that Christian theologians must consider the suffering of children in their moral evaluation of divorce. A review of recent social science literature shows the negative consequences of divorce, especially in low-conflict cases, and suggests the need to return to the tradition for retrieval of theologies of marriage that include children. In St. John Chrysostom, the author finds a three-in-one flesh metaphor that she claims is a more adequate description of marriage with children as lived reality. With the addition of parallel material from Vatican II and John Paul II, the author argues, it is possible to construct a new theology of marriage that moves beyond relationship to include commitments to spouses, children, and society.

A Lapse in the Discussion

The divorce rate in the United States has been on the rise since the latter part of the nineteenth century, but it declined slightly in the 1990s. Still, about forty-five percent of first marriages and sixty percent of second marriages end in divorce.[1] More children than ever spend at least some of their childhood in single parent homes, while others live in blended families or split their time between two families.[2] While most Americans mourn the frequency of divorce, and some offer proposals for stiffening state or church requirements for marriage or divorce, few would want to go back to an age when divorce was all but unthinkable.[3] Divorce is a large part of contemporary American life, and the great majority of Americans accept it as a necessary, if regrettable, reality.

Over the last three decades, Christian theologians have come to be more accepting of divorce. The major Catholic theological voices on divorce have all argued for more liberal church teachings and practices. The situation among Protestants is similar, but there is less writing on the subject since most theologians agree with the positions of their churches.[4] If the lack of conservative views on divorce is significant, the relative silence of the last twenty years is even more so. In the 1970s, there was a great deal of theological interest in divorce, as theologians argued in the face of a changing society that more tolerance was needed. In the 1980s and 1990s, however, few theologians have addressed the issue. Margaret Farley's 1990 article (which calls attention to the lack of interest in the 1980s) is the last major article by a Christian theologian on the subject.[5] Farley identifies four key developments in Catholic theology that shaped the contemporary theological consensus on divorce: Vatican II's definition of marriage as a community of love, ecumenism, new openness to sharing Eucharist with other Christians, and new biblical and theological studies that raised questions about the traditional ban on divorce.[6] Farley argues that Catholics were mostly silent on divorce in the 1980s because by then most theologians had come to embrace a more tolerant view on pastoral issues, and many had come to believe that divorce in some cases was morally acceptable.[7] Still, they had little hope that the official Catholic position would change.[8] In the 1990s, the silence among Catholic theologians grew and the silence among Protestant scholars continued. As a consequence, there has been little theological development on the issue of divorce over the last twenty years.[9]

In the meantime, social scientists have paid a great deal of attention to divorce. There are whole journals devoted to analysis of divorce, major longitudinal studies have been launched, and hundreds of articles have addressed the topic from various perspectives. Scholars have written about the effects of divorce on the psychological, economic, and social well-being of parents and children. Intact families have been compared to families of divorce. Coping mechanisms that work have been identified and promoted. Custody laws have been analyzed. In short, because of the last twenty years of research, there is now a wealth of information on divorce as a social phenomenon.[10]

However, most theologians have not responded to this new information. The reader used in many Catholic marriage courses throughout the country is an illuminating example. In Kieran Scott and Michael Warren's newly revised *Perspectives on Marriage*, the section on divorce includes five articles by theologians arguing for greater acceptance of divorce, annulment, or remarriage, and one article by a psychologist discussing the negative effects of divorce on children.[11] No more cautious theological voices are included, and no theologian reflects upon the new social science data. The reader is symptomatic of the larger theological conversation in which theology and social science stand side by side but do not enter into dialogue. In this essay I will weave together social science and theology. I want to show how the new studies on divorce might lead to a re-thinking of Christian theological treatment of marriage and divorce. Specifically, I will argue in response to the data, following St. John Chrysostom, that a Christian marriage with children is a three-in-one flesh unity, so divorce in a marriage with children is not the breaking of a two-in-one flesh, but the even more serious rupturing of three-in-one flesh.[12] I will begin by reviewing important currents in contemporary theology, move to an analysis of recent sociological studies, and end with theological reflection, in order to show why a view of marriage as three-in-one flesh union makes sense both sociologically and theologically. I will not attempt to argue here that divorce is impossible or absolutely illegitimate, but I will call into question the mainstream theological consensus that divorce is morally acceptable when spousal relationships fail. Before moving to a study of recent theology, however, it is necessary to understand the earlier analyses of marriage and divorce to which theologians are responding.

Pre-Vatican II Developments in the Theology of Marriage

Until the second half of the twentieth century, the Catholic understanding of sacramental marriage was tied to the language of contract and ends. The marriage sacrament was rooted in the contract between the spouses and was judged legitimate and binding if the contract was valid. The Church taught that the primary (and natural) end of marriage is children, though mutual help and the channeling of sexual desire were viewed as legitimate secondary ends.[13] The official theology was largely legalistic, casuistic, and seemingly unrelated to actual human experience.[14]

This account of marriage was judged inadequate by many Christians, and in 1931 Pope Pius XI, too, realized the "need to build up the human matrix of the sacrament."[15] He did so in *Casti Connubii* by pointing to the "mutual inward molding" of Christian spouses as the chief reason and purpose of marriage.[16] This small movement toward affirming the centrality of the marriage relationship was welcomed by theologians and lay people who found the older language cold and inattentive to the reality of spousal love. Still, the Magisterium continued to use the language of primary and secondary ends, and to give a privileged place to procreation in sexual ethics.

However, liberal theologians of this time picked up on Pius XI's move and took it further by putting the spousal relationship at the center of the marriage sacrament. Hans von Hildebrand distinguished the end of marriage (children) from the "meaning" of marriage (the "union of two persons in love").[17] For von Hildebrand, the complete self-giving of the spouses is the best available example of mutual love and this is why it serves as the best metaphor for God's relationship with God's people.[18] The spousal sexual act is the perfect realization of this relationship, for in it the spousal union becomes "objectively real in its fullest sense—both partners now belong wholly to each other, an objective bond unites them, they are no longer two but one."[19] Marriage exists for its own sake (e.g., for love) not for the sake of its result; it is valuable in itself.[20] It follows that indissolubility flows out of the love of the couple, although it is also indirectly related to the "utilitarian considerations" of children and society.[21] For Von Hildebrand, relationship is the core or essence of marriage.[22]

Like Von Hildebrand, Herbert Doms saw children as the less important end of marriage. He compares them to apples, which are not the only purpose of a tree's existence.[23] The main purpose or intrinsic meaning of marriage is unity. Marriage, real enough in itself, does not need an outside purpose (children) to justify its existence. A child may help a man and woman become closer, but it is the "constant, vital ordination of husband and wife to each other until they become one" that constitutes the essence of marriage.[24]

Both Von Hildebrand and Doms were challenged by conservative theologians like John C. Ford who argued that it was possible to develop theological reflection on the importance of marital relationships without overturning the traditional distinction between the primary and secondary ends of marriage.[25] Ford went so far as to argue that spousal love was not essential to marriage:

> The actual virtue of conjugal love is not essential to marriage. In thousands of marriages we find no trace of it; yet they are real marriages. The actual virtue of conjugal love is no more essential to marriage than the acts of conjugal life themselves. Just as there can be true marriage where the acts of conjugal life are absent, so also there can be true marriage when the love of which these acts should be the expression is absent.[26]

According to Ford, marriage is essentially a juridical bond. While a lifelong partnership of life and love is the goal of marriage, only consent and "the rights and obligations of conjugal life" are necessary to make a true marriage.[27]

Likewise, until Vatican II, when the hierarchy of ends was largely abandoned, official Catholic theology continued to assert that children, not relationship, are the primary end of marriage, and to issue annulments only when the marriage contract was proven illegitimate. For many theologians, the abstractness of a theology of marriage that did adequately value married love and of a theology of divorce which did not admit the possibility of marital death was problematic. After the Council, these theologians attended to the "human matrix" of marriage and the human dimensions of divorce. Most often, they sought greater leniency in Catholic divorce law.

Recent Theological Analysis of Divorce

Contemporary theologians who argue in favor of divorce tend to rely on one or more of the following arguments to support their views: (1) Commitments can be broken for proportionate reasons. (2) Divorce is not ideal, but must be accepted as a tragic reality in the face of human sinfulness. (3) Marriage is in its essence love or friendship, and it can die. I will review these positions below and offer a brief critique.

Commitments Can Be Broken

Although many authors treat divorce as the breaking of a promise or commitment, Margaret Farley's work is the most influential in this category. In her book *Personal Commitments*, Farley develops the idea that human commitments are of their very nature provisional, because their existence implies the possibility of failure. We would not have to make them if we knew we would never break them.[28] Farley argues that a commitment is not binding if it is impossible to keep, or if other obligations override it.[29] She claims that these requirements are difficult, but not impossible to fulfill in the case of marriage.[30]

In her most recent article on divorce, she argues specifically that marriage cannot be binding if it is impossible to sustain, if it no longer serves its intended purpose, or if it conflicts with another obligation.[31] It follows that if one marriage commitment can end, a second one (remarriage) can be entered into.[32] For Farley, marriage is a promise, which, like other promises, can be broken in certain circumstances.

Divorce Is Not Ideal

While Farley focuses on the nature of the marriage vow as it relates to all other vows, Charles Curran argues that in marriage, as with all other ideals, there must be some allowance for compromise. Curran insists that the Church can hold on to the ideal while allowing for inevitable failure. Because human beings are sinful, and because they live in the between times when the kingdom has already been brought into existence by Jesus Christ, but is not yet perfectly realized, lifelong marriage can only be a goal.[33] For Curran, compromise on divorce flows naturally out of a sense of realism and compassion.

Similarly, the late Richard McCormick argued that indissolubility is an "ought" not an "is."[34] It is a moral ideal Christians ought to strive for, not a description of reality. Both theologians see little sense in speaking about marriage in essentialist terms as something that is by its very nature indissoluble, since it is obvious that people fail at marriage or are failed by their spouses (or both) all the time. It makes more sense to speak of lifelong marriage as a difficult but attainable goal, while recognizing that many on this side of heaven will fall short.

Orthodox theologian Vigen Guroian speaks even more eloquently to this point. While the Orthodox Church's theology of marriage places marriage at the center of human existence and speaks of it in the highest of terms, it also accepts the fact that some of its people will not be able to live up to the demands of the sacrament. Because of sin, human frailty, and free will, Guroian argues, it is not possible for all Christian marriages to last forever.[35] He holds up the Orthodox second marriage ritual as a symbol of the penance and joy that should accompany the ending of one Christian marriage and the beginning of another.[36] Divorce is not celebrated but it is accepted with regret and grace.

Marriage Is Love and Love Can Die

Underlying arguments about commitments and ideals is a common understanding of marriage. This understanding is also at the heart of arguments that divorce is acceptable when a marriage relationship dies. At least since the 1960s, marriage has been defined in theological circles as a relationship, or a "personal community of love."[37] Charles Curran notes that marriage defined this way is infinitely more fragile than marriage defined as a contract, because relationships break down.[38] This recognition naturally leads to the crucial question on divorce raised by Theodore Mackin in his groundbreaking work, *Divorce and Remarriage*. Mackin takes the case of a woman abandoned by her husband of twenty-nine years who asks, "With my husband's love going now to another woman after having abandoned me, with our love destroyed, and with us now deciding to be strangers to one another, how does our marriage still image the love of Christ and his Church?"[39] That is, if the relationship is gone, is it still a marriage?

Bernard Cooke offers the strongest negative answer to this question. Cooke claims that marriage is not intrinsically indissoluble simply because it is a sacrament, for the sacrament is in the relationship. If the relationship is over, the sacrament is no longer there.[40] Christian marriage, according to Cooke, is supposed to symbolize God's fidelity, and it cannot do this if the relationship is broken. He claims that the husband and wife together, "are the sacrament, not simply because they are recognizable in the community as two who publicly bound themselves by marital contract, but because and to the extent that they can be recognized as translating Christian faith into their married and family life."[41] If husband and wife are not truly one in faith and in friendship, they cannot be described as one in any meaningful way. Furthermore, because marriage is a process and not an act, it makes sense to talk about degrees of marriage.[42] Marriage, in this view, is not something that happens when vows are made. Rather, it is something that grows between two people over time or dies.

Critique

All three arguments for divorce are convincing at a gut level because they are rooted in a deep sense of what goes wrong in human marriage. Farley is right to point out that commitments can conflict or lose their meaning. Cooke is right to argue that some relationships fail to progress and some die. Curran is right to ask for some acknowledgment of human limitation in a world both fallen and redeemed.

However, all three arguments are limited by a lack of regard for the good of children. Farley discusses marriage as a commitment between two adults.[43] However, if marriage for Christians involves a commitment to a broader community of persons, beginning with children, arguments that take marriage to be only a personal commitment between spouses can only go so far. More importantly, it is limiting to discuss marriage solely as a commitment, as Farley acknowledges when she says that in marriage, spouses "are somehow changed in their beings."[44] This change is symbolized by children, who are a union of their parents. Marriage entails an ontological change in the nature of the being of two persons. When they marry, they grow together. When children are conceived and born, they become one in flesh and blood. A theology of marriage that ignores children and the ways in which spouses change when they become parents cannot be a full treatment of marriage as lived reality.

The arguments of Curran and McCormick are similarly limited. Guroian does give significant attention to children in his theology of marriage, rightly claiming that the "Christian family is a promise, enfleshed in the form of children, of a future filled with joy."[45] Still, his broader understanding of marriage is not reflected in his discussion of divorce. Like Curran and McCormick, Guroian argues that the tragedy of ended love between husband and wife is enough to end a marriage. It is not ideal, but it is real enough. What is missing in the contemporary discussion of the ideal and the real is attention to the reality of children's lives. If they are a part of the marriage (and not simply its result), at the very least, their reality ought to be seriously considered.

Cooke's argument, too, is problematic because it depends on an understanding of friendship as the core of the marriage sacrament. While his personalist assertion that "a Christian man and woman are truly 'grace' to one another" is undoubtedly true, it is not the whole truth.[46] As Cooke himself acknowledges, the couple "are sacrament for each other, sacrament to their children, and sacrament to all those who come to know them."[47] Here he begins to get at the broader meaning of marriage. However, his stress is on the friendship of the couple. If one begins instead with the assumption that marriage is a communion of persons committed to love, children, and community, the marriage relationship as such is not the only important issue.[48] The couple whose romantic love has begun to fade may still have sacramental sign value in the Christian community, if they continue to show compassion for each other and their children, and a zeal for the good of the community. The ongoing commitment to stay together despite continuing troubles can be a witness in itself.

In short, even though some marriages may appear to be commitments that have outlived their usefulness, or relationships that are less than ideal, or friendships that are dying, when viewed from a broader perspective, they may have enduring value. The efforts of couples who struggle to hold their imperfect marriages together for their children, sacrificing the joys of intimate relationship for an unwavering commitment to family and community, may be witnesses to the truth that even if relationships fail, marriages may endure.[49]

Some may argue that asking human beings for such sacrifice is unrealistic, if not cruel. Mackin, for instance, argues that the Church cannot force its people to stay in terrible marriages or live alone. Claiming that a person's joy in sexual intimacy is a fundamental human need that is a key part of her common good, he asks, "where is the compelling reason for denying her common good to a Christian woman trapped . . . in an unforeseen and coerced celibacy?"[50] Leaving aside for the moment the arguable assertion that sexual intimacy is crucial to human happiness, one might certainly claim that the woman in this case could have responsibilities to children that would be complicated by remarriage. It may be cruel to tell the woman to live a life of celibacy, but it may also be cruel to force children to go through remarriage. It is important at least to ask how the needs of children can be balanced with the needs of adults. There is potential suffering in both possible scenarios and it is not obvious that either solution is more or less cruel. What is striking is that in this argument, as in those discussed above, the suffering of adults is taken seriously (as well it should be), but the suffering of children is not considered.

Each of the arguments presented relies primarily on a personalist understanding of marriage as a two in one flesh union that can, in some tragic cases, come undone. Because children are not viewed as a part of marriage, they are marginal in the discussion of divorce. In viewing marriage narrowly as a relationship of two persons, contemporary theologians neglect the needs of an important group of persons whose lives are directly and intimately affected by marriage and divorce. Social scientists, however, are not similarly neglectful.

Recent Studies on the Effects of Divorce on Children

Recent studies on divorce and children are numerous, to say the least. Certainly, it is difficult for a non-specialist to identify major trajectories. However, with the help of meta-analyses that review studies over time, and a focus on top scholars in the field, it is possible to draw some conclusions. First, there is a general agreement among scholars that for the majority of children, divorce has negative effects. Second, most scholars acknowledge that difficulties for children from divorced families begin before divorce and cannot be totally blamed on divorce. Third, it is becoming clear that most children eventually rebound from divorce. Fourth, nevertheless, most adult children of divorce experience continuing pain and difficulties, especially in their family relationships. I will briefly explain each of these conclusions below.

Divorce Has Negative Effects on Children

While in the 1970s and 1980s many researchers believed that if divorce made parents happier, it would also help children, it has become increasingly clear that in most cases, divorce is harmful to children. In one major study, Sara McClanahan and Gary Sandefur studied children growing up in single-parent families and found that, "[c]hildren who grow up in a household with only one biological parent are worse off, on average, than children who grow up in a household with both of their biological parents, regardless of the parents' race or educational background, regardless of whether the resident parent remarries."[51] Their research shows that children from single-parent families are twice as likely to drop out of school, twice as likely to have a child before age twenty, and one and a half times as likely to be out of work and school in their late teens and early twenties.[52] These three factors are important because they are keys to economic success, which is closely linked to personal and social well-being.[53]

Why is the contrast so stark? Children in single-parent homes simply have less support than do those in two-parent families. First, economically, it is more difficult to support two households than one, especially when fathers tend to keep more than half of their income. The average decline in income after divorce for middle-class families is fifty percent.[54] Second, fathers who live apart from their children are usually less committed to them, and this weakened relationship undermines the children's trust in both parents, increases uncertainty about the future, and makes the children more difficult to manage.[55] Third, single mothers experience high levels of stress and depression and are more likely to be inconsistent parents.[56] Less invested non-custodial parents and highly stressed single custodial parents do not make a strong combination, so children are disadvantaged.

Sandefur and McClanahan's negative findings are not atypical. In 1991, sociologists Paul Amato and Bruce Keith, published an article titled "Parental Divorce and the Well-Being of Children: A Meta-Analysis" in which they reviewed ninety-two studies from the 1980s that compared children in intact families to children in single-parent families. The authors conclude that "children of divorce experience a lower level of well-being than do children living in continuously intact families. The view that children of divorce adapt readily and reveal no lasting negative consequences is simply not supported by the cumulative data in this area."[57]

How does this finding square with the recent, well-publicized study that concluded that the overwhelming majority of children of divorce do not suffer from mental illness later in life?[58] While mental disorder is not overwhelmingly common among children of divorce (although it is more common than among children from intact families and more extreme when it does occur) continuing mental distress or anxiety is very common. This anxiety may not be evident in some quantitative studies, but it is clearly revealed in qualitative studies that include in-depth interviewing.[59] When the short-term and long-term are taken into account, it is clear that by the early 1990s, social scientists had enough information to conclude that while divorce may result in more happiness for parents, most often, divorce affects children negatively.

Family Conflict Has Negative Effects on Children

On the other hand, many recent studies are showing that the differences between children of divorce and children from intact families are not overly large.[60] As Robert Emery notes in reference to McClanahan and Sandefur's much-publicized study, even though children of divorce are twice as likely to get into serious trouble in adolescence, most children of divorce do not get pregnant or drop out of school.[61] In addition, Amato and Keith point out that "children in divorced families appear to have a higher level of well-being than do children in high-conflict intact families."[62] Some scholars argue that family conflict, which is associated with divorce, is more closely related to decreases in children's well-being than divorce itself. For instance, one recent analyst of two major longitudinal studies claims that problems evident after divorce actually begin during the pre-divorce conflict period. Parent-child relationships are disturbed, parental commitment to children lessens, and there are fewer economic and human resources to go around. This analyst argues that post-divorce problems can be largely predicted based on negative pre-divorce outcomes.[63]

It is not surprising that negative effects on children begin before divorce and are related to conflict. However, it is important to remember that these families are a minority of cases (about thirty percent) and new research shows that though most children from high-conflict families do better after divorce, most from low-conflict families (the remaining seventy percent) have lower well-being than they would have if their parents had stayed together.[64] Conflict is a part of the negative effects problem, but it is not the whole of it. Family disruption matters, too, as the majority of studies show.[65]

Children of Divorce Cope and Rebound

Despite the fact that most studies on divorce find negative effects on children, there are newer studies that emphasize children's resiliency and their ability to cope. In a comprehensive review of the literature on the effects of divorce on children, David Gately and Andrew I. Schwebel, for instance, found that children of divorce are more mature, have higher self-esteem, are more empathetic, and more androgynous than their peers.[66] These children were able to deal with the challenge divorce presented for them and grow as people. Because their parents had less time and energy to invest in them, they matured faster and became independent earlier. As they coped with the challenges of divorce, they gained in self-esteem. Because they saw human failure and suffering up close, their capacity for empathy increased. In single-parent families, they saw parents taking on dual roles, so they became more androgynous. Stronger children turn the crisis of divorce into an opportunity for growth.

Many newer studies focus on these gains and attempt to extend them by offering strategies whereby parents and others can teach children how to cope more effectively with divorce. One such study ends hopefully with the idea that "factors that lead to positive outcomes of divorce need to be accentuated in order to prevent negative stigmas and self-fulfilling prophecies, including the intergenerational transmission of marital dissolution, as well as dysfunctional families."[67] It illustrates the growing interest among social scientists in fostering "good divorces" in which children bounce back and become stronger, more compassionate people.

However, it is important to acknowledge the sad reality that the positive qualities celebrated in children of divorce are the hard-earned fruits of their suffering the emotional and/or physical loss of one or both of their parents.[68] Children are more mature because they have known crisis. They are more independent because they have been left more alone. They are more compassionate because they have endured suffering. These character strengths may serve them well in later life, but the process that engendered them is not one that anyone would wish on a child.

Furthermore, the research that seeks to enhance children's ability to cope, while necessary and promising in some ways, is disturbing in others. Children are being praised for their ability to be more like adults. They are being asked to transcend childish dependencies. A top scholar in the field recently suggested that future research on coping should ask why some children do not rebound, and assess whether or not these children are "inordinately dependent on both parents," or hindered by a lack of resources other than parents, a low sense of autonomy, or a low tolerance for stress.[69] While it is important to know that children can cope with divorce, it seems clear that in focusing on children's skills or deficiencies, adults are asking children to carry the burden of divorce, and minimizing the effects of divorce on children's lives.

Divorce Has Long-Term Negative Effects

This is particularly disturbing in view of the newest longterm studies. Amato and Keith suggested in 1991 that some researchers were not seeing the negative effects of divorce because they were looking at the wrong kinds of problems. The authors assert that "the long-term consequences of parental divorce for adult attainment and quality of life may prove to be more serious than the short-term emotional and social problems in children that are more frequently studied. Further research on adult children of divorce—in particular, longitudinal studies of children as they enter adulthood—would be of great value in understanding this phenomenon."[70] In the 1990s, researchers started completing those studies and the research now shows that, more often than not, divorce has negative long-term consequences for children. In 2001, Amato updated his influential 1991 study with research from the 1990s. He found that children of divorce score lower on measures of academic achievement, conduct, psychological adjustment, self-concept, and social relationships than children from intact families. He contends that the gap between children from intact and broken families increased in the 1990s, after a slight decrease in the 1980s.[71] The negative effects are clearly shown in the most recent long-term studies.[72]

Among the most significant long-term studies is Judith Wallerstein's. Wallerstein's latest book, *The Unexpected Legacy of Divorce*, reports on the sixty families in her study twenty-five years after she first met them. In earlier analyses of her subjects, Wallerstein reported that she had expected to find that most children would rebound from divorce fairly quickly. Instead she found that after five years, only thirty-four percent of children were doing well, and after ten years, only forty-five percent of children were doing well.[73] At the twenty-five year follow-up, Wallerstein found that even though many eventually put their past behind them, all of the adult children of divorce still suffered from the effects of family breakdown.[74] These results lead her to question the popular myth that if parents are happier, children will be too, and reject the idea that divorce is a temporary crisis that will eventually be overcome. "Divorce," claims Wallerstein, "is a life-transforming experience."[75]

Wallerstein is careful to note that she is not opposed to all divorce, and that she does not believe that divorce is universally harmful to children, but her research clearly shows that compared to children in intact families (even conflicted intact families), children of divorce are usually disadvantaged.[76] As children they suffer the upheaval of the divorce and often get little support from parents who are needy themselves.[77] In post-divorce families, they continue to deal with transitions, new relationships to lovers, step-parents, and siblings. Adolescence includes earlier sexual experiences for girls, more social instability for boys, and greater worries about following in their parents' footsteps for both girls and boys.[78] Those with good support systems and those who naturally need little parenting land on their feet, while the less-supported and more vulnerable suffer.[79] Clearly, problems do not end soon after divorce for children.

Wallerstein sees the most devastating effects of divorce in adulthood. While young adults search for love and commitment, they are haunted by bad memories and hampered by the lack of a template for intimacy. Unlike children from intact families, they expect to fail at marriage and they do so more frequently. This is devastating because "children identify not only with their mother and father as separate individuals, but with the relationship between them. They carry the template of this relationship into adulthood and use it to seek the image of their new family. The absence of a good image negatively influences their search for love, intimacy, and commitment."[80] Although Wallerstein certainly saw children of divorce who succeeded against the odds (most often only after a serious struggle), most of her subjects were simply not able to do it.[81] Her twenty-five year study provides solid evidence that the long-term effects of divorce can be quite serious. It is supported by the work of other researchers who assert that though mental health problems are not common among adult children of divorce, pain, fear of abandonment, grief, anger, and worry are.[82]

Conclusions on the Effects of Divorce

A review of recent studies shows that divorce is much more than a tragedy for spouses who fall out of love. It is also often a tragedy for children who are caught in the middle and suffer the short and long-term effects of their parents' decision to part. It is important not to over-state this conclusion, for it is also true that the conflict that precedes divorce affects children, that divorce does have some positive effects on children, that most adult children of divorce rebound, and that, in most high-conflict marriages, divorce does improve the lives of children. Still, the short-term effects on economic and social well-being are hard to ignore and the long-term picture of anxiety, fear of abandonment, and lack of a template for marriage is troubling. The results of social scientific studies must give pause to theologians who argue for divorce. Indeed, divorce cannot be properly considered without this information. Happily, within the tradition itself, there are resources for a rethinking of Christian theology of marriage that are in harmony with the new data.

Children's Centrality to a Christian Theology of
Marriage and Divorce

St. John Chrysostom's Three-in-One Flesh Model

Although many Christian theologians focus almost exclusively on the relationship between the spouses when talking about marriage, John Chrysostom treats parents and their children as one body. This Greek Orthodox father of the fourth century gave several important homilies in which he developed a unique theology of marriage.[83] His thought provides a firm foundation for a Christian theology of marriage and divorce that includes husbands, wives, and children.

Chrysostom builds on the two-in-one flesh metaphor of Genesis 2:24, and links it to Paul's discussion of marriage in Ephesians 5:21 as a one-body unity. As he sees it, the one flesh referred to in Genesis is really the family: mother, father, and child. The husband and wife only fully become one flesh when they conceive a child, "Then the *one flesh* is the father, the mother, and the child that is conceived from their intercourse. For the child is formed when the seeds mingle together; in this way they are three in one flesh."[84] John develops this idea in his homily on Colossians 4:18, arguing that children are the ordinary way in which two spouses become truly one body:

> The child is a bridge connecting mother to father, so the three become one flesh, as when two cities divided by a river are joined by a bridge. And here the bridge is formed from the substance of each! Just as the head and the rest of the body are one, since the neck connects but does not divide them, so it is with the child. That is why Scripture does not say, "They shall be one flesh," but that they shall be joined together "into one flesh," namely the child. But suppose there is no child; do they then remain two and not one? No; their intercourse effects the joining of their bodies, and they are made one, just as when perfume is mixed with ointment.[85]

The three together are compared in both homilies to Christ and the Church, for just as husband, wife, and child become one body, so, too, do Christ and God the Father.[86] John reads Ephesians 5:31 as a comparison between the husband and wife who become one body and Jesus, who "left his Father and came down and took a bride and became one spirit with her."[87] Most of his focus in the rest of the homily is on instructing husbands how to practice Christian headship over their wives, but unlike many other Christian writers on marriage, his concern goes beyond the spouses to the household, which he calls "a little church."[88] For Chrysostom, it is spouses and children who make a holy, unified, body. He refutes criticism of his celebration of one-flesh unity, arguing that marriage is a Christian mystery, for "the Church was made from the side of Christ, and He united himself to her in a spiritual intercourse."[89] He will not compromise on the ideal that marriage is a holy, spiritual, and fleshly unity. He locates that unity first of all in children, who are the fruit of marriage, and secondly in the sexual relationships of husbands and wives.

Chrysostom's theology is crucial because it recognizes in spiritual terms the biological reality of children and the lived experiences of parents who find that in giving birth to children, they are giving flesh to their already strong union. Even more so than sexual union, in which spouses become one flesh for a time, and then part (even as they increase their spiritual oneness), when a child is conceived, she is a one-flesh union of her parents that never breaks in two. Such a theology of marriage helps makes sense of studies reporting that most children are better off when their parents stay married, even if parents are unhappy. It makes understandable the significance of what Wallerstein calls the lack of a template for marriage in adult children of divorce. Children identify with their parents' relationship because their parents are one in them and for them. When that relationship is broken, they suffer, especially when they try to form relationships of their own. What Chrysostom talks about as a theological truth is not unrelated to the psychological and social effects of divorce.

Although John Chrysostom is the only Christian theologian I have found who uses the three-in-one flesh metaphor, his concerns do have parallels in Christian thinking on sex, marriage, and divorce. He is certainly not the only one to speak of marriage and children in one breath, despite the fact that most Christian theology on marriage and divorce does not give serious attention to children. If theologians are to take seriously the results of the new social science data, there must be a retrieval of theologies of marriage in which children are central.

The Bishops of Vatican II and John Paul II

One important source for such a renewal might be the recent writings of the Catholic Magisterium, for even in the most contemporary and personalist Magisterial discourse, concern for children is evident. Although *Gaudium et Spes* is often rightly cited as the modern Catholic document which provides the impetus for moving to a more personalist, relational understanding of marriage, children are central to the Council's definition of marriage. Marriage is called "an intimate partnership of life and love" in which spouses "surrender themselves to each other."[90] However, the partnership is not an end in itself. "By its very nature the institution of marriage and married love is ordered to the procreation and education of children, and it is in them that it finds its crowning glory."[91] The broader purpose of marriage is emphasized, as the Fathers claim that it exists not just for the good of the spouses, but "for the good of the partners, of the children, and of society."[92] Lifelong fidelity is demanded because of the mutual self-gift of the partners and "the good of children."[93] In its discussion of what marriage is, the goods to which it is directed, and the reasons for its indissolubility, the Council both lifts up the spousal relationship and connects spouses to children.

John Paul II takes this connection even further when he writes in *On the Family* that "[f]ecundity is the fruit and the sign of conjugal love, the living testimony of the full reciprocal self-giving of the spouses."[94] Earlier in the same document, he states, "Thus the couple, while giving themselves to one another, give not just themselves but also the reality of children, who are a living reflection of their love, a permanent sign of conjugal unity and a living and inseparable synthesis of their being a father and mother."[95] The Pope has developed his theology of marriage around the central concept of total self-giving. He sees self-giving as the fundamental vocation of all human beings which is most fully realized in marriage.[96] In the passages quoted above, he indicates that children are the permanent sign of that self-giving. If the one-flesh metaphor is applied here, children concretely symbolize the one-flesh unity of the parents. They are proof, so to the speak, of their parents' love for each other, not just because they are the fruit of sexual union, but also because they are signs of their parents' commitment to give themselves—together—to the vocation of parenting. Though parents' willingness to keep on giving may lag, children remain fruits and signs of their parents' unity. With their bodies, they say, "My parents give themselves to one another."

The Pope thus locates the marital sacrament both in the marital relationship and in the children. This makes sense because most married couples love each other in the context of families. Their relationship does not exist in isolation. Rather, as John Paul II sees, they are united in their parenting and their commitments to church and society. Unlike earlier popes and theologians who seem to neglect the human reality of marriage, and unlike personalist theologians who focus almost solely on marriage relationships, the Pope claims that "[t]he marital sacrament in its fullest expression and in its primary meaning is life in the family."[97] By situating marriage in the context of family, he begins to construct a fuller theology of marriage that treats children not as result or end but as part of the marital communion of love.

This contemporary strain of the Christian tradition illumines the reality that children are a permanent one flesh union of their parents. They are a mingling of two people. Even if their parents come apart, they do not. Even if their parents want to be separated, children cannot separate out the two parts of themselves. It is not the case that ideally children are one flesh unions but in reality they are signs of one or the other parent. Regardless of the actual living arrangements which may mean that children do not live with both of their parents, they are still living reminders of their parents' real (not imagined) unity. In them, their parents are one.

Exceptions to the Three-in-One Flesh Norm

Of course, this argument for parent-child union cannot be absolute. There are times when parents may have to separate from children. For instance, the Christian Church has traditionally approved of adoption if prioritizing blood kinship ties would jeopardize the good of a child.[98] In his writing on adoption, Stephen Post points out that adoption proves that "adults can transcend the 'selfish gene' of the evolutionary psychologists, and that children can prosper without the narrative of a biological lineage."[99]

Post argues convincingly that the Christian approval of adoption is a challenge to our culture's near obsession with genetics and the ties of kinship. "Christianity," he claims, "challenges the assumption that the only real kinship is based on birth, biology, and blood."[100] This does not mean that the Christian tradition does not value the biological connections between parents and children. Rather, "Christianity considers adoption to be an important exception to its teachings and practices that have bound together begetting and rearing children, whether grounded in natural law or covenant love."[101] It is not that adoption and rearing one's own child are equal choices in the sense one may chose one or the other option, but when birth parents cannot raise children, the best interest of the child means that adoption is a moral choice which is not inferior, but secondary.[102] Disagreeing with Paul Ramsey who argues that to bring a child into the world and not rear it is "a refusal of the image of God's creation in our own," he claims that a Christian may legitimately ask when "the mysterious connection between procreation and parental love might be reluctantly set aside in the best interests of the child."[103]

The Christian theology and practice of adoption is an important exception to the norm of three-in-one flesh union. Sometimes it is best for children to be reared by someone other than their parents. One might argue that there are times when children in troubled families would be better off being reared by one parent, by both parents separately, or by one parent and a step-parent. Certainly, there are children in high conflict homes for whom this is true. However, the review of recent research on the effects of divorce shows that it is true less often than one might think.[104] Similarly, the theologies of marriage in which children are central suggest that more often than not, children will be better off with their own parents, with whom they form a one-flesh union. These theologies account for the reality of children's suffering in response to divorce in ways in which personalist theologies that focus only on the spouses cannot. They represent sources for a renewed Christian theology of marriage and divorce centered on children, even as the theology of adoption and studies showing that some children do better after divorce reveal that biological connections are not absolute.

It is critical that arguments for divorce are attentive to this complex reality. The history of the Christian tradition of divorce, however, is largely a history of disagreement about when it is legitimate for spouses to leave each other. Christians have argued about whether or not adultery justifies divorce, whether someone who becomes a Christian may leave a non-Christian spouse, when a marriage is valid, when a marriage can be dissolved or annulled.[105] There is very little recognition of the fact that spouses are almost always parents of vulnerable children. There are virtually no attempts to balance the good of children with the rights of the spouses.[106]

Thomas Aquinas and the Way Forward

The problem is that the two goods or ends of marriage (the loving union of the spouses and the procreation and education of children) are thought of separately, when they ought to be considered together. Thomas Aquinas systematizes the split in the tradition between the two ends of marriage. In Aquinas, as in the tradition, the two ends are always present, but they are treated separately, especially in relation to the third good of marriage: sacrament. Still, Aquinas talks more about children than most and points the way toward a more child-centered understanding of marriage and divorce.

Thomas distinguishes between the natural and supernatural goods of marriage. The natural goods of marriage enumerated by Aristotle are procreation and partnership, but the Christian tradition has added a third, supernatural good of sacrament. Among the first two natural goods, children are more important, because the care of children is the end to which "the entire communion of works that exists between man and wife as united in marriage" is directed.[107] Children are in the natural sense the most essential part of marriage, because men and women marry with the intention of having children.[108] However, in the supernatural sense, sacrament is the most essential part of marriage, because it is the most excellent good of marriage. Sacrament is rooted in the consent of the spouses, not the birthing and formation of children.[109] The two-in-one flesh sacramental union is only possible because man and woman originally came from one being. This, according to Thomas, was "to make the man love the woman and stick to her more inseparably. Knowing that she had been brought forth from himself."[110]

Why then is marriage indissoluble? Again, the distinction between the natural and the supernatural is important. Thomas does relate divorce to the good of children, but gives priority in his discussion to the spousal bond. Children are only the natural reason for indissolubility, while the bond between the partners is at the heart of the sacrament.[111] A summation of his views can be found in his comments on the bill of divorce. He writes:

Indissolubility belongs to marriage in so far as the latter is a sign of the perpetual union of Christ with the Church, and in so far as it fulfills an office of nature that is directed to the good of offspring, as stated above. But since divorce is more directly incompatible with the signification of the sacrament than with the good of the offspring, with which it is incompatible consequentially, as stated above (A.65, A.2, ad5), the indissolubility of marriage is implied in the good of the sacrament rather than in the good of the offspring, although it may be connected with both. And in so far as it is connected with the good of the offspring, it is of the natural law, but not as connected with the sacrament.[112]

Like most in the Christian tradition, Aquinas does not ultimately base his argument against divorce on the good of children. Even though he sees procreation as the main purpose of marriage, he believes that marriage for believers has a higher end and distinct essence. Opposing divorce on the grounds of the good of children is a valuable consequentialist, natural argument, but the Christian tradition, he argues, emphasizes the supernatural, sacramental bond of two believers that cannot be dissolved.

Unlike many contemporary theologians, Aquinas acknowledges that children are a crucial part of marriage, and one reason not to divorce, but he does not see them as part of the sacramental meaning of marriage, and therefore he does not base his argument against divorce on their good. Like most traditional Catholic thinkers, he thinks that spouses have an obligation to consider the needs of children. In contemporary terms, one might say he encourages spouses to think of their duty to children as part of their commitment to the common good. Linked to today's studies on the effects of divorce, Aquinas provides a way to limit divorce simply by considering the good of those who stand to lose by it. Still, for Aquinas this is not the essential point, and for most contemporary theologians, a broken relationship has little reason to continue. The common good argument can only go so far.

However, if children are seen as part of the sacrament of marriage, as the symbol and occasion for one-flesh unity, as John Chrysostom would have it, then children must become a crucial part of theological discussion of divorce. Husband and wife are joined in the marriage promise, in their sexual union, and, perhaps most importantly, in their children. Divorce, then, would be problematic for Christians not simply because of a commitment or bond, but because of the one-flesh union of parents and children. Viewing marriage solely as bond or relationship is insufficient. Instead, marriage ought also to be seen in relation to children, and by extension, community. Marriage is not simply about self-giving love. It is also about passion and love that deepen into solidarity and commitment to others.[113] Unlike personalist definitions of marriage that focus too narrowly on relationship, this definition restores to marriage its distinctively Christian emphasis on the unity of parents and children and the family's broader responsibilities as a domestic church. It assumes that marriage connects more than just two people, just as divorce breaks more than two people apart.[114]

Today, divorce is justified on the grounds that commitments can be broken, relationships can end, and ideals are not reality. Theologians claim that Christians ought to recognize human failure and allow people to move on with their lives. However, sociological research shows that often when relationships become unfulfilling for parents, they are nonetheless important to children. These same studies also show that remarriage does not mitigate (and may even increase) the negative effects of divorce on children. While divorce in high-conflict cases generally decreases children's suffering, divorce in low-conflict marriage most often increases their pain. Based on these findings, it can be argued that while some high conflict marriages should end, most low conflict marriages ought to endure.[115] For Christians, the argument to stay is particularly strong, because the Christian commitment in marriage is not just to one's spouse but to children, God, and community. When spousal relationships fail, marriages can have meaning in shared commitment to children and community. In high-level conflict cases in which no resolution is possible, separation for the good of children would be encouraged, but if possible, a shared commitment to parenting should continue. It would be better in most cases then, first, to endure in imperfect marriage, or, second, to separate but continue as parents, grandparents, and fellow Christians. Theologians must reject a theology of marriage and divorce that focuses solely on the spouses, for it is children, who, together with their parents, constitute the one-flesh unity that is marriage for Christians, just as it is children who are so often torn apart by divorce that disrupts that unity.

NOTES

[1] Judith S. Wallerstein, Julia M. Lewis, and Sandra Blakeslee, *The Unexpected Legacy of Divorce: A 25 Year Landmark Study* (New York: Hyperion, 2000), 295.

[2] David Blankenhorn, *Fatherless America: Confronting Our Most Urgent Social Problem* (New York: Basic, 1995), 18. In 1960, 81% of all children lived with both biological parents. In 1990, only 58% did.

[3] See Don Browning et al., *From Culture Wars to Common Ground* (Louisville, KY: Westminster, 1997).

[4] My focus in this paper will be on Catholic writers. The argument, however, should cut across denominational lines.

[5] An ATLA search in 2001 yielded no new major theological articles on divorce since 1990.

[6] Margaret Farley, "Divorce, Remarriage, and Pastoral Practice," in *Moral Theology: Challenges for the Future,* ed. Curran (New York: Paulist, 1990).

[7] Ibid., 223.

[8] Farley notes that Paul VI and John Paul II reaffirmed Catholic teaching on the indissolubility of marriage. Farley, "Divorce, Remarriage, and Pastoral Practice," 225.

[9] There are a few exceptions: Browning et al., *From Culture Wars to Common Ground*, 53-58, 318-20; Stephen J. Post, *More Lasting Unions: Christianity, the Family, and Society* (Grand Rapids, MI: Eerdmans, 2000), 108-110; Michael Lawler, *Family: American and Christian* (Chicago: Loyola University Press, 1998), 47-79. Even these writers, who draw attention to the negative consequences of divorce, do not enter into specifically theological reflection on the subject.

[10] For an overview of the 1990s and a large bibliography, see Paul R. Amato, "Children of Divorce in the 1990s: An update of the Amato and Keith (1991) Meta-analysis," *Journal of Family Psychology* 15:3 (September 2001): 355-70.

[11] Kieran Scott and Michael Warren, eds., *Perspectives on Marriage: A Reader* (New York: Oxford University Press, 2001), vii-viii.

[12] Obviously, some families are four or more in-one-flesh unities, but for simplicity's sake, I will use three throughout the paper. Sixty-nine percent of divorcing couples have children. Gerard Coleman, S.S., *Divorce and Remarriage in the Catholic Church* (New York: Paulist, 1988), 8.

[13] Lawler, *Family*, 17.

[14] See Lisa Cahill, *Sex, Gender, & Christian Ethics* (Cambridge: Cambridge University Press, 1996), 194-99.

[15] Mackin, *Divorce and Remarriage* (New York: Paulist, 1984), 525.

[16] *Casti Connubii* in *Five Great Encyclicals* (New York: Paulist, 1939), no. 24.

[17] Dietrich Von Hildebrand, *Marriage* (New York: Longmans, 1942), 2. The book was originally published in German as *Die Ehe* (Munich: Kosel-Pustet, 1929).

[18] Ibid., 3-4.

[19] Ibid., 19.

[20] Ibid., 24.

[21] Ibid., 48.

[22] Susan Ross sees Von Hildebrand's distinction as non-hierarchical, but it seems to me that naming relationship as the essence of marriage and discussing children as results constitutes a hierarchical move. See her "The Bride of Christ and the Body Politic: Body and Gender in Pre-Vatican II Marriage Theology," *Journal of Religious Ethics* 71:3 (July 1991): 345-61.

[23] Herbert Doms, *The Meaning of Marriage* (New York: Sheed & Ward, 1939). Originally *Vom Sinn und Zweck der Ehe* (Breslau: Ostdeutsche Verlagsanstalt, 1935), 86.

[24] Ibid., 87.

[25] Ford, "Marriage: Its Meaning and Purposes," *Theological Studies* 3 (1942): 373.

[26] Ibid., 360.

[27] Ibid.

[28] Farley, *Personal Commitments* (San Francisco: Harper & Row, 1986).

[29] Ibid., 74-78.

[30] Ibid., 76-78.

[31] Farley, "Divorce, Remarriage, and Pastoral Practice," 227-29.

[32] Ibid., 232.

[33] Farley, *Personal Commitments*, 85-86.

[34] Richard McCormick, *The Critical Calling: Reflections on Moral Dilemmas Since Vatican II* (Washington, D.C.: Georgetown University Press, 1989), 248-50.

[35] Vigen Guroian, "An Ethic of Marriage and Family," in *Incarnate Love: Essays in Orthodox Ethics* (Notre Dame: University of Notre Dame Press, 1987), 99.

[36] Ibid.

[37] Curran, *Moral Theology*, 95.

[38] Ibid.

[39] Mackin, *Divorce and Remarriage*, 507.

[40] Cooke, "What God Has Joined Together. . . ," in *Perspectives on Marriage*, ed. Kieran Scott and Michael Warren (New York: Oxford, 2001), 347-49.

[41] Ibid., 348-49.

[42] Ibid., 352-53.

[43] In another essay, she argues that children's good is not always served when parents avoid divorce, but does not treat cases in which the children's good would be served. Farley, "Divorce and Remarriage: A Moral Perspective," in *Divorce and Remarriage: Religious and Psychological Perspectives*, ed. William P. Roberts (Kansas City, MO: Sheed & Ward, 1990), 124.

[44] Farley, "Divorce, Remarriage, and Pastoral Practice," 234.

[45] Guroian, "An Ethic of Marriage and Family," 93.

[46] Cooke, "Christian Marriage: Basic Sacrament," in *Perspectives on Marriage*, ed. Kieran Scott and Michael Warren, (New York: Oxford, 2001), 56.

[47] Ibid., 57.

[48] For a fuller treatment of this idea, see my forthcoming *A Christian Theology of Marriage and Family* (New York: Paulist Press, 2003).

[49] I do not mean to imply that this is always the case. Certainly, there are times (especially, for instance, in cases of abuse) when no unity of purpose is possible. In these cases, separation and civil divorce are necessary for the good of spouses and children.

[50] Mackin, *Divorce and Remarriage*, 546-47.

[51] Sara McClanahan and Gary Sandefur, *Growing Up with a Single Parent* (Cambridge: Harvard University Press, 1994), 1.

[52] Ibid., 2.

[53] Ibid., 19.

[54] Ibid., 24.

[55] Ibid., 3-4.

[56] Ibid., 3-4, 27.

[57] Paul R. Amato and Bruce Keith, "Parental Divorce and the Well-Being of Children: A Meta-Analysis," *Psychological Bulletin* 110:1 (1991): 30. See also, Paul R. Amato and Alan Booth, *A Generation at Risk: Growing Up in an Era of Family Upheaval* (Cambridge: Harvard University Press, 1997), 219-20.

[58] P. Lindsay, Andrew Cherlin, and Kathleen Kiernan, "The Long-term Effects of Parental Divorce on the Mental Health of Young Adults: A Developmental Perspective," *Child Development* 66 (December 1996): 1614-34.

[59] Lida Baumann-Billings and Robert Emery, "Distress among Young Adults from Divorced Families," *Journal of Family Psychology* 14:4 (December 2000): 671-87.

[60] Amato and Keith, "Parental Divorce," 38-39.

[61] Robert E. Emery, "Postdivorce Family Life for Children: An Overview of Research and Some Implications for Policy," in *The Postdivorce Family: Children, Parenting, and Society*, ed. Ross A. Thompson and Paul R. Amato (Thousand Oaks, CA: Sage, 1999), 14.

[62] Amato and Keith, "Parental Divorce," 40.

[63] Youngmin Sun, "Family Adjustment and Adolescents' Well-Being Before and After Parents' Marital Disruption: A Longitudinal Analysis," *Journal of Marriage and Family* 63:3 (August 2001): 697-713.

[64] Alan Booth, "Causes and Consequences of Divorce: Reflections on Recent Research," in *The Postdivorce Family: Children, Parenting, and Society*, ed. Ross A. Thompson and Paul R. Amato (Thousand Oaks, Ca: Sage, 1999), 40.

[65] See, for instance, Thomas L. Hanson, "Does Parental Conflict Explain Why Divorce is Negatively Associated with Child Welfare?" *Social Forces* 77:4 (June 1999): 1311. Hanson's analysis of data from the National Survey of Families and Households shows that conflict can explain only part of the problem.

[66] Gately and Schwebel, "Favorable Outcomes in Children after Parental Divorce," in *Divorce and the Next Generation*, ed. Craig A. Everett (New York: Haworth Press, 1992). See also, E. Mavis Hetherington, "An Overview of the Virginia Longitudinal Study of Divorce and Remarriage with a Focus on Early Adolescence," *Journal of Family Psychology* 7:1 (1993): 39-56. Hetherington focuses on the diversity of responses to divorce in her subjects and emphasizes that many rebound.

[67] Lee Ann Kot and Holly M. Shoemaker, "Children of Divorce: An Investigation of the Developmental Effects from Infancy through Adulthood," *Journal of Divorce and Remarriage* 31:1/2 (1999): 161-78.

[68] Robert Emery notes that children may be resilient, but this does not mean that they are invulnerable. "Post-divorce Family Life," 15.

[69] Booth, "Causes and Consequences of Divorce," 45.

[70] Amato and Keith, "Parental Divorce," 40.

[71] Paul Amato, "Children of Divorce in the 1990s: An Update of the Amato and Keith (1991) Meta-Analysis," *Journal of Family Psychology* 15:3 (September 2001): 355-70. See also, Booth and Amato, "Parental Predivorce Relations and Offspring Postdivorce Well-Being," *Journal of Marriage and Family* 63:1 (February 2001): 197-212, which shows that dissolution of low conflict marriages has negative effects.

[72] I have limited my analysis to U.S. studies, but it is significant that studies in other countries have produced similar results. See, for instance, Anna Christopoulos, "Relationships between Parents 'Marital Status and University Students' Mental Health, Views of Mothers and Views of Fathers: A Study in Bulgaria," *Journal of Divorce and Remarriage* 34:3-4 (2001): 179-90.

[73] Wallerstein, "Children after Divorce," 368-69.

[74] Ibid., xxvii.

[75] Ibid., xxviii.

[76] Ibid., xxxiii.

[77] Ibid., 298-99.

[78] Ibid., 299.

[79] Ibid., 300-301.

[80] Ibid.

[81] Wallerstein, "Children after Divorce," 298-301.

[82] Emery, "Post-divorce Family Life," 17.

[83] See Chrysostom, *On Marriage and Family Life* (Crestwood, NY: St. Vladimir's Press, 1986).

[84] "Homily on Ephesians," in *Marriage in the Early Church*, ed. and trans. David G. Hunter (Minneapolis: Fortress, 1992), 83.

[85] "Homily 12: On Colossians 4:18," *On Marriage and Family Life*, 76.

[86] "Homily on Ephesians," *On Marriage and Family Life*, 83.

[87] Ibid.

[88] Ibid., 87.

[89] "Homily 12," *On Marriage and Family Life*, 77.

[90] "Gaudium et Spes," Austin Flannery, O.P., ed., in *Vatican Council II: The Conciliar and Post Conciliar Documents*, rev. ed. (Northport, NY: Costello, 1988), no. 48.

[91] Ibid.

[92] Ibid.

[93] Ibid.

[94] John Paul II, *On the Family* (Washington, D.C.: United States Catholic Conference, 1981) no. 28.

[95] Ibid., no. 14.

[96] Ibid., no. 11. See also the Pope's *Original Unity of Man and Woman: Catechesis on the Book of Genesis* (Boston: Daughter of St. Paul, 1981). I do not mean to imply here that I am in full agreement with the Pope's understanding of self-giving love in marriage. Christina L. H. Traina has raised important questions about the implications of this theory for sexual ethics. See Traina, "Papal Ideals, Marital Realities: One View from the Ground," in *Sexual Diversity and Catholicism*, ed. Patricia Beattie Jung with Joseph Andrew Coray (Collegeville, MD: Liturgical, 2001), 269-88. Still, the linking of marital love and children is, I would argue, true to experience and the tradition.

[97] Mackin, *Divorce and Remarriage*, 572.

[98] Post, *More Lasting Unions*, 120.

[99] Ibid., 212.

[100] Ibid., 123-24.

[101] Ibid., 129.

[102] Ibid., 131.

[103] Ibid.

[104] In particular, remarriage is not, on average, a positive thing for children. See Booth, *The Postdivorce Family*, 41; Barbara Dafoe Whitehead, "Dan Quayle Was Right," *Atlantic Monthly* (April 1993): 47-84; William Jeynes, "A Longitudinal Analysis of the Effects of Remarriage," *Journal of Divorce and Remarriage* 33:1/2 (2002): 131-48.

[105] For an excellent summary, see Mackin, *Divorce and Remarriage*.

[106] The Catholic Magisterium is not an exception. Though children are one of the two ends of marriage, official arguments against divorce and for annulment focus on the legitimacy of the marriage contract or covenant, not the good of children. See John Paul II, *On the Family*, no. 20, 83-84.

[107] Aquinas, *Summa Theologia*, trans. Fathers of the English Dominican Province (New York: Benziger Brothers, 1947), suppl. Q. 49, art. 2.

[108] Ibid.

[109] Ibid.

[110] *Summa Theologia*, Ia. Q.92, art. 2.

[111] *Summa Contra Gentiles*, trans. Vernon J. Bourke, (Garden City, NY: Hanover House, 1955), III:II, ch. 123.

[112] *Summa Theologia* (New York: McGraw-Hill, 1964), supp. Q. 67, art. 1.

[113] Francis Schüssler Fiorenza, "Marriage," in *Systematic Theology*, ed. Frorenza & John P. Galvin, vol. 2, (Minneapolis: Fortress, 1991).

[114] Obviously, not all marriages include children. One could still define marriage normatively as a three-in-one flesh unity, but admit exceptions, as current theology does when it defines procreation as an end of marriage but blesses the marriages of infertile couples and calls them spiritually fruitful.

[115] I have adopted the low conflict/high conflict distinction from the social science literature, because it is a crucial distinction in the most recent studies on divorce. Many studies show that this distinction helpfully explains the differences in children's responses to divorce. It may not be useful in all cases (for instance, when overt conflict is low but adult suffering is high), but it seems useful in most.

Ethical Issues and Approaches in Stem Cell Research: From International Insights to a Proposal

Andrea Vicini, S.J.

Abstract

In recent years and months, human stem cell research has dominated many scientists' interests, the media, public debate, and social policy. This paper aims to consider, first, the major scientific data on stem cell research that are available. Second, I reflect on them by examining how they shaped policies in Europe and the United States. I also point to current changes in policy-making concerning the creation of *ad hoc* committees to address this novel issue and how, in a few instances, different ethical positions are part of the documents produced. In other words, diverse approaches are not solved but kept in tension. Finally, I suggest that the current state of research on human stem cell will benefit from an ethics of risk.

Scientific Issues and Their Ethical Relevance

Defining Stem Cells

The first ethical issue in stem cell research depends on what these cells are and what they could offer to human beings.[1] Stem cells are undifferentiated. They have the "capacity for self-renewal" and are also capable "of forming at least one, and sometimes many, specialized cell types."[2] They can divide indefinitely in culture to give rise to other stem cells and then differentiated cells.[3] However, some scientists argue against stem cell plasticity, or emphasize the importance of cell location on the process of differentiation.[4]

Journal of the Society of Christian Ethics, 23/1 (2003): 71-98

It is well known that the fertilized egg is totipotent, that is, in the first hours after the fertilization it divides into identical totipotent cells. At the early stages of differentiation, before the blastocyst stage, each of these cells can develop into an embryo, then a fetus, when they are placed in the appropriate environment, that is, a woman's uterus. This is also the case with identical twins.

After the initial cell divisions, it seems that totipotent cells lose their ability to develop in an embryo.[5] They begin to specialize in pluripotent and multipotent cells that can develop only into a few cell types (muscle cells, etc.).[6] However, the differentiation process could avoid being marked by a point of no return, an irreversible switch. This approach considers stem cells as an entity. On the contrary, some scientists have proposed that these cells are a function. "The evolving view is that cells have a recruitable but decreasing propensity to act as stem cells as they differentiate."[7]

Stem cells are extremely interesting because of their ability to differentiate and potentially become all cell types. Their availability could address the need for histocompatible cells in medicine, that is, cells that would not be recognized as foreign cells by one's body. Therapy of chronic and degenerative diseases as well as human organ transplantation could greatly benefit from them.[8] Damaged tissue could be colonized and repaired by stem cells. Compatible organs or even body parts could be grown, and then transplanted, whenever medically required.[9] From a scientific point of view the problem is, first, to verify this assumption and, second, to understand how to control the process of differentiation. In the case of patients affected by Parkinson's or leukemia, just to mention two pathologies often associated with stem cell research, these cells could replace either defective or cancer cells.[10]

However, scientists are still trying to define what is "a stem cell in molecular terms, what signalling events control stem cell differentiation, and what does it mean to reprogramme a cell."[11] By using animal models, they are testing the possibilities of transplanting stem cells and assessing the expected benefits, e.g., on spinal cord injuries and stroke.[12] If human stem cells prove to have the same capabilities as mice stem cells, they could be used not only for many therapies but also for a better understanding of our species, particularly embryogenesis and cancerogenesis.[13]

The hypotheses, expectations, and sorting of data that characterize stem cell research today qualify a situation of uncertainty and indeterminacy, marked by hopes as well as possible disappointments and failures.[14] Both uncertainty and indeterminacy make clinical and therapeutic applications yet remote. This is despite the relevance given to their beneficial impact in future medical therapies both in the media and in policymaking contexts.

These scientific aspects associated with stem cells raise ethical issues for two reasons. First, both scientific research and the language that is used to describe its potential are not neutral and require ethical assessment. By studying the history of science, or simply by paying attention to scientific progress in our times, we realize that a critical hermeneutic is the ethical companion needed by scientific progress. To give a recent example, only a decade ago genetic therapy was presented by scientists and the media as the medical procedure that could finally help us to cure a large number of diseases. We are still far from seeing this come true. We should have been more critical of the rhetoric that accompanied research on this therapy.[15]

Second, we cannot dissociate any research from what makes it possible, that is, economic and political powers. Scientific research has its independence. However, economic forces making research possible and controlling it curtail this independence. Therefore, from an ethical point of view, we need to unmask the economic rationales behind the recent hype surrounding stem cell research. The importance of what this research could offer to humankind in terms of medical advances cannot be separated from expected great profits. Therefore, it is understandable that major Western countries want to be an active part in this process and have a share in its economic benefits.[16]

Finding Human Stem Cells

The second ethical issue has to do with stem cell sources. Historically, they were located in teratocarcinomas (i.e., testicular tumor).[17] It is not ethically troubling to do research on stem cells present in many tissues of a person's body, e.g., in bone marrow (adult stem cells, AS), where they are important in tissue repair and homeostasis.[18] In the debate concerning the potential of adult stem cells, recent findings raise doubts on the reported versatility of these cells.[19] Umbilical cords and spontaneously aborted fetuses as sources of human stem cells do not raise ethical concerns either, even if the last one uses embryonic stem (hES) cells or even germ (hEG) cells.[20] In the case of stem cells from umbilical cord blood, the scientific problem seems to depend on the limited number of cells that could be found.[21] On the contrary, we should remember that spontaneous abortions are often caused by genetic or development problems or both. Therefore, it has been suggested that these stem cells are not scientifically appropriate for research aimed at clinical therapeutic applications.[22]

Ethical issues surface when we examine the following three possible hES cell sources.[23] Stem cells could be obtained by using fetuses after procured abortions, frozen embryos stored in private fertility clinics banks as the result of in vitro fertilization (IVF), and by producing embryos for research purposes.[24]

Finally, while these are existing stem cell sources, it could also be possible to produce autologous stem cells, that is, cells immunologically compatible with a patient's cells.[25] Two ways are proposed: first, through therapeutic cloning; second, without producing any embryo.[26] Both procedures presuppose knowledge of the cell differentiation process and the ability to reproduce it in labs.[27] While therapeutic cloning raises ethical issues related to the embryo status, the hypothesis of producing stem cells through reprogramming of somatic cells without creating any embryo could be both scientifically and ethically extremely interesting.[28]

An International Overview

How do we deal with these two scientific issues (i.e., what stem cells are and what are their sources) from an ethical point of view? Stem cell research has provoked responses not only from ethicists but also from ethical committees in many Western countries. This confirms the perceived need to be politically alert to the ethical issues that this research raises. On the one hand, it reveals that we live in a social context increasingly attentive to what scientists do. On the other hand, political bodies have been aware that, in today's more global world, popular support is necessary to sustain any new technology sold in the market. From an ethical point of view, it is therefore interesting to consider what has been proposed and which ethical criteria are operative. Therefore, before making my proposal in the last part of this paper, I examine briefly and incompletely the legal situation and what has been proposed in terms of ethical reports in Europe. Four patterns appear to dominate. For each of them I focus on one European state, that is, the United Kingdom, France, Germany, and Italy. Then I will examine recent developments in the United States.

European Legal Approaches and Ethical Reports

The overview of the European legislation concerning human embryo research and hES derivation highlights four approaches: regulation, prohibition, laws in preparation, and complete absence of any law yet.[29] First, laws regulate both matters in seven countries: Denmark, Finland, Hungary, Netherlands, Spain, Sweden, and the United Kingdom.[30] Second, five countries have laws prohibiting human embryo research and hES cells derivation: Austria, France, Germany, Ireland, and Norway. Third, laws are in preparation in three countries: France, Germany, and Portugal.[31] Finally, no legislation is yet present in Belgium, Czech Republic, Greece, Italy, Poland, Slovenia, Switzerland, and Turkey.[32]

United Kingdom: The United Kingdom is an example of the first pattern, i.e., regulation. Stem cell research has been mostly based on hES cells derived from spare embryos created by IVF, as allowed by legislation and an appropriate authority since 1990.[33] On February 27, 2002, the House of Lords' Select Committee on Stem Cell Research published its report where it indicated that research on embryonic stem cells should be allowed under strict regulation and the Medical Research Council "confirmed its plans to establish a public cell bank to characterize and store adult and embryonic stem cells."[34] The House of Lords report even upholds the government's position that research using cell nuclear replacement (or therapeutic cloning) is justified under the existing law.[35] This issue has been highly debated. Since January 2001, it has been possible to use hES cells to grow replacement tissues, through therapeutic cloning.[36] On November 15, 2001, a ruling by the High Court allowed reproductive cloning by denying the jurisdiction of the Human Fertilisation and Embryology Authority (HFEA) as well as current laws over cloned embryos because they are not created through fertilization.[37] On January 18, 2002, the Court of Appeal overturned this decision by ruling that embryos produced by nuclear transfer are covered by current regulations.[38] Despite the current legislation, as of August 2002, the HFEA has granted only two licenses for research on hES cell lines and no request was pending.[39] Moreover, in September 2002, the J. K. Medical Research Council awarded a contract for the new bank in which stem cell lines (from embryos, as well as fetal and adult tissues) will be collected and distributed to researches.[40]

France: France stands as an example of a country with laws prohibiting human embryo research and hES cells derivation but is also in the process of revising them.[41] In 1994, the Bioethics French Laws prohibited human embryo research for five years.[42] In January 2001, the National Consultative Ethics Committee for Health and Life Sciences (Comité Consultatif Nationale d'Ethique pour les sciences de la vie et de la santé, CCNE) released its opinion (Avis) concerning stem cell research.[43] The document proposes to prohibit therapeutic cloning and the production of human embryos for research purposes.[44] At the same time, it points to "regulated possibilities of research on spare embryos [which are no longer included in a parental project] (article L. 2141-12) *with the agreement of the procreating couple.*"[45] However, "medically assisted reproduction cannot be used to voluntarily stock up on spare embryos so as to be able to use them later for research" and the "embryos which have been used for research cannot under any circumstances be subsequently transferred."[46] Then, as in the United Kingdom, CCNE approves the future creation of the Human Reproduction, Embryology, and Genetics Authority (Agence de la procréation, de l'embryologie et de la génétique humaines, APEGH) responsible to address ethical issues together with CCNE.[47] Finally, at the end of 2001, Prime Minister Lionel Jospin proposed a bill allowing for research on embryos aimed at new therapies.[48]

Two remarks can be highlighted. First, the rationale behind the suggestions made by CCNE is that "society has a duty to encourage therapeutic progress and to hasten improvements in the prevention and treatment of diseases which are presently incurable or difficult to treat."[49]

The need for healing, and even its urgency, should prompt researchers, ethicists, politicians, and society at large to promote this research.[50] Second, on therapeutic cloning the CCNE members are divided and their disagreements are not solved but included in the document with the majority in favor of a controlled authorization to engage in therapeutic cloning.[51]

Germany: As in the case of France, Germany has current bans in place, but is also revising its legislation. At the end of November 2001, the debate on hES cells enlisted the support of the National Ethics Council, established by Chancellor Gerhard Schröder in May 2001, to use imported hES cells and to review the matter in three years.[52] The creation and use of human embryos for research purposes is prohibited. However, the Deutsche Forschungsgemeinshaft (DFG), Germany's main university granting agency, intends to fund research on imported hES cells derived legally from surplus embryos from IVF clinics.[53] Currently, Germany's Embryo Protection Act allows researchers to harvest stem cells from aborted fetuses but not from blastocysts.[54] On January 30, 2002, the German Parliament prohibited scientists "from deriving human ES cell lines" and "fundamentally" banned their import, but "[r]esearchers can import ES cells if they demonstrate that there are not feasible alternative ways to conduct the research."[55] Two more restrictions are set by the Parliament's decision: first, scientists need to wait for a new law "establishing a national commission to review all import proposals, and the soonest such a commission could be in place is early summer [2002];" second, "researchers will be allowed to import cell lines established before" January 30, 2002.[56]

Italy: Without any law regulating stem cell research yet, the Italian debate reveals nonetheless some interesting features. On October 27, 2000, the National Committee for Bioethics unanimously expressed its approval for research on stem cells from adult human beings, spontaneously aborted fetuses, and umbilical cord blood.[57] Division within the Committee was caused by the suggested use of stored embryos and nuclear transfer as sources for stem cells. The Italian Health Minister had also established an *ad hoc* Commission to address the stem cell research issue. The Commission, chaired by the Nobel Prize winner Renato Dulbecco, was composed of twenty experts and released its report on December 28, 2000.[58]

The document's novelty is the proposal of producing autologous stem cells by nuclear transfer without developing embryos (ASNT).[59] While this proposal needs further scientific assessment, its interest depends on the fact that it is ethically acceptable by anyone critical of research involving embryos because it bypasses embryo development. The document indicates that, first, the egg cell with a somatic nucleus cannot be strictly considered a zygote because it does not result from two gametes. To confirm it, this manipulated egg cannot spontaneously multiply, but requires artificial boosts to become a blastocyst.[60] However, the manipulated egg could be forced to develop in aggregated embryonic cells, called embryoid spheres, then directed to become specific cell lines.[61] In other words, this process would not result in an embryo, but a cell that can develop as pluripotent and multipotent stem cells immunologically compatible with the somatic cells from which the nucleus was taken. From scientific and ethical points of view, the problem is to clarify whether the proposed procedure is based on a semantic distinction or a substantial difference.

The nuclear transfer procedure, called by the media "the Italian way to produce stem cells," could therefore be alternative to producing embryos for research purposes. The novelty would be both scientific and ethical.

In reacting to this document, the Pontifical Academy for Life, for example, found the procedure ethically acceptable, if it could be confirmed scientifically. Its judgment on the Commission's proposal is suspended until appropriate scientific confirmation, but the procedure is indicated as a direction in which research should go.[62]

United States: In the United States, a dozen states have laws that "regulate embryo research to varying degrees."[63] Congress prohibits any federal funding of human embryo research and hES derivation, but no other regulation limits privately funded research.

On August 9, 2001, President George W. Bush addressed the nation with his remarks and decisions concerning stem cell research. Besides his emphasis on the care given to examine this issue, he has allowed the National Institutes of Health (NIH) to fund research on some sixty genetically diverse stem cell lines already existing throughout the world before that day. These lines are derived from embryos created for fertility treatments but no longer needed. The couples donating the embryos gave their informed consent, without any financial inducements.[64] Furthermore, President Bush proposed to devolve part of $250 million funding of research on umbilical cord placenta, as well as adult and animal stem cells because they do not involve embryos. Finally, he named a President's Council to monitor stem cell research, to recommend appropriate guidelines and regulations, to consider all of the medical and ethical ramifications of biomedical innovation, and to be a forum for discussion and evaluation. This council will consist of scientists, doctors, ethicists, lawyers, theologians, and others. Dr. Leon Kass, a leading biomedical ethicist from the University of Chicago, will chair the council.[65]

After the President's announcement, on August 27, 2001, the first list of some sixty stem cell lines published by NIH provoked a period of surprise and speculation concerning the exact number, accuracy, and effective availability as well as the characteristics of these lines.[66] On November 7, 2001, NIH posted its registry of hES cell lines, opening the possibility for grant applications.[67]

President Bush's announcement was preceded and followed by lively ethical, political, and media debate.[68] Some considered his decisions inadequate for promoting stem cell research, while others saw it paving the way for stricter regulations. However, compared with the NIH guidelines issued in August 2000, the President's decisions allow researchers more flexibility. Others are pointing to the temporally limited value of his decisions because of the scientific changes that will soon occur.[69]

Some scientists critiqued the President's decisions by claiming that there may be fewer usable cell lines than expected because of biological issues (e.g., inability to survive in long-term culture or occurrence of gene mutations or chromosomal damage).[70] At the same time, legal problems might surface (e.g., material transfer agreements and patents), as well as the presence of "intellectual property rights, licensing fees, and royalties," hindering the availability and use to researchers of these cell lines.[71]

As previously indicated, privately funded research is a multibillion-dollar economy in the United States and the world. While American universities are looking for solutions allowing for greater research independence, President Bush's decisions allow federally funded agencies and researchers to participate to a certain extent.[72] Furthermore, they favor collaborations between government agencies and private companies.[73] Nonetheless, other companies, BresaGen (Adelaide, Australia) and ES Cell International (ESI, Singapore) for example, prefer a different approach. In August 2001, they announced that their ten hES cells lines were given freely to publicly funded scientists. However, "the companies will ask for first rights to license any therapeutics and medical procedures that emerge from the research."[74]

Other agencies intervened in the debate on stem cell research, holding different positions from those established by the President, even without intending a critical stance.[75] Drafted before President Bush's decisions were announced, and without addressing them, the report Stem Cells and the Future of Regenerative Medicine was released by the National Research Council and the Institute of Medicine of the National Academies in September, 2001.[76] It aims to promote stem cell research and its clinical applications. Concerning the need for stem cell lines, the report argues that those currently available are not sufficient, first, because it is possible that genetic mutations will occur in the same cells that continue to multiply; second, because the culture of these cells in animal cell feeders or serum could be responsible for infections.[77] For both reasons, researchers should be allowed to access new human stem cell lines while research on mice stem cell lines continue. Further, the report suggests the creation of a NIH advisory board in which scientists, ethicists, and stakeholders are represented.[78] Public funding is indicated as necessary to promote scientific progress, to attain medical breakthroughs, as well as to ensure scientific standards and public oversight. The report indicates somatic cell nuclear transfer (SCNT) as a possible way to ensure genetic compatibility provided reproductive goals are absent.[79]

Toward a Proposal

Mediations

This incomplete overview on legal decisions and ethical documents highlights a willingness to mediate. First, President Bush's overall decisions appear to be the result of mediation. On the one hand, the President did not want to dismiss the promises made during his electoral campaign, and advocated by his pro-life supporters. On the other hand, he is aware of the need for maintaining federally funded research at a pace compatible to that made by private biotech companies in the United States and in other countries. This is not only an issue of prestige. It is also highly strategic and economic. The future of federally funded labs has to be planned ahead of time with decisions that keep them competitive centers for producing advanced research. Any loss of time and opportunities would have future economic repercussions. Furthermore, the Administration needs to show its commitment to advanced research to avoid any potential emigration of scientists to countries that are strongly promoting stem cell research.

How do we consider ethically this willingness to mediate? On August 24, 2001, Joseph A. Fiorenza, Bishop of Galveston-Houston, President of the National Conference of Roman Catholic Bishops, responded negatively to President Bush's decisions.[80] His rationale is that research on the already available stem cell lines is not ethically acceptable because it "does not respect the rights and humanity of the destroyed embryos."[81] This strong reaction is somewhat surprising in that it does not seem to consider as ethically significant the boundaries set about the source of those cell lines.

Second, as in France, Italy, and, at least partly, in the United Kingdom, President Bush chose to establish an *ad hoc* group of experts to reflect on progress associated with stem cell research and to advise on possible policy regulation.[82] This invites us to reflect on the significance of naming special committees to update and make suggestions but with limited mandates and influence. Forming new groups of experts for consultative purposes could betray a desire to choose its members deliberately in order to have a stronger control over future suggestions made.[83] This approach needs to be contrasted with what occurs in the United Kingdom, that is the existence of an Authority with regulatory tasks (Human Fertilization and Embryology Authority, HFEA).[84]

To Keep in Tension

From an ethical point of view we can ask ourselves how to consider these different ways of mediating. In the case of the proposal advanced by the Italian Commission, President Bush, and the French Avis, I highlight, first, the explicit willingness to favor research on adult stem cells. This source could reduce the use of stored embryos and offer researchers an alternative for producing embryos to obtain hES cells. In all three texts the highly philosophically and theologically complex issue concerning the embryo is addressed, at least briefly, without presenting a definitive solution.[85]

Without dismissing the possibility President Bush's decisions might have been a concession to researchers and a betrayal of the need to protect embryos, we can judge these three approaches differently.[86] First, we can affirm that, at this particular moment, the decisions made concerning stem cell research, which assume the still not fully understood potential of these cells, are not clear-cut. Such a benevolent ethical reading does not eliminate all problematic aspects. It considers the President's decisions as a means to promote preferable directions of research while setting limits. It does not eliminate the gray area that concerns the use of available stem cell lines produced with stored embryos from fertility treatments.

A second element is ethically relevant. How do we deal with pluralism within a committee in charge of advising on public policy? In other words, should we permit diverse approaches within an ethical committee's political advice? Such was the case in both the Italian Commission's report and the French Avis. The Italian document, for example, shows unanimous agreement on allowing for research on stem cells derived from umbilical cords, aborted fetuses, adults, and on the ethically unacceptable hypothesis of producing embryos merely for research purposes. Disagreement surfaced on allowing for research on stored embryos and is documented in the final text.

On the one hand, the minority position considers the embryo's potential for development as human person as already a human being.[87] The minority rationale seeks to preserve and protect human dignity from the zygote stage. It does not consider morally licit any experimentation involving stored embryos, any procedure causing their disposal, or even their use for research that produces stem cells for healing purposes. Healing, as a criterion, is common in public ethical discourse as well as in Roman Catholic teaching in moral theology.[88] However, from this perspective, to heal a living person or the society does not legitimate using embryos.

On the other hand, opposite to this, stands the approach of the Commission majority, largely shared within society. The use of stored embryos is perceived as ethically acceptable in view of the benefits for humankind, particularly when couples indicate they do not want any more embryos transferred and express their informed consent allowing for the use of their embryos for research purposes. The reasons given are, first, that, at the early stages of embryo development the ethical emphasis is placed on the indeterminate and open character of this development. Second, the principle of beneficence is invoked.

Both positions are included in the Italian Commission's report. I consider this choice more than a simple concession of the majority to the minority. It could have greater significance and value. It could express an ethical choice, that is, the awareness that social ethos, and the political choices inspired by it, are shaped even by contrasting approaches on important issues. Hence, the value of promoting dialogue within ethical committees can lead us to keep in tension diverse ethical approaches on specific problems, even in major ethical documents.

I acknowledge that "to keep in tension" could be understood as a sign of failure in composing contrasting assessments and positions, particularly when we move from ethical committees to society at large.[89] At the same time, it could mean that, as a society, we live by keeping our ethical stance open-ended on certain issues that require further scientific clarification. This could lead us to explore and research scientific approaches that offer us more ethical guarantees than today's solutions. In particular, this means that scientific research should aim at reducing the number of extra embryos produced in the case of reproductive technology, particularly IVF with embryo transfer. In such a way, the ethical problems associated with the production of spare embryos, their use for research, and their destruction after a fixed period of time (usually five years) could be progressively eliminated.

From a social point of view, an approach that positively considers the attitude "to keep in tension" raises at least three questions. First, consider the political choices that would be inspired by ethical documents like the Italian Commission Report. How could these choices benefit from this open-ended attitude in search for further elements and verifications? Second, more radically, is there a need for legislative tools (e.g., laws and/or an Authority, as in the United Kingdom and as it has been proposed in France and Germany)? What should these tools be?

Public Policy

The debate concerning appropriate public policy on stem cell research includes a variety of contrasting approaches. Among ethicists a growing concern is that reflection on this new field of research should not be separated from a wider attention to issues of justice in health care today in the United States as well as worldwide.[90] How will future healing improvements, made possible by advances in stem cell research, benefit those who are oppressed and marginalized, like women and the poor, the uninsured, and those with insufficient insurance policies?[91] The current situation makes us believe that those who can afford expensive treatments at experimental and therapeutic stages will benefit from the applications of this research.[92]

Fairness of access and just distribution of medical resources stand as goals to strive for in the years to come.[93] At the same time, some authors call for a ban on embryo research, while others suggest that appropriate oversight is due.[94] According to Cohen, a "National Stem Cell and Associated Technology Advisory Board (NSCATAB) should be established in the United States under the aegis of the U.S. Department of Health and Human Services."[95] While others disagree, some authors agree with the substance of the proposal but suggest different ways to implement it.[96] The need for such boards depends not only on safety issues, but also on societal values, and their importance should not be overcome by the need to favor scientific progress and economic competition.[97] The promotion of public dialogue on this issue could emerge as a particularly important task toward producing the most appropriate solution and bioethicists, not only scientists, should play a particularly relevant role in this process.[98]

In democratic countries, political decisions result from compromise and bargaining. "To keep in tension" could mean that any law regarding today's stem cell research should define the minimal common standing point that needs to be legally promoted and defended. It could require, for example, an accurate inquiry concerning the number of embryos stored in banks and their location as well as on the procedures of fertility clinics concerning the production, transfer, and storage of embryos. It could demand to set rules regulating fertility treatments in those countries that still lack them.[99] At the same time, it could leave room for further scientific developments that can go in the direction suggested by the law itself, e.g., ways in which we can favor research concerning non-problematic sources of stem cells. In other words, legal intervention is not intended to hinder or freeze scientific research, progress and development, but to direct it by selecting preferred directions of advancement.[100]

An Ethic of Risk

From a phenomenological point of view, "to keep in tension" different and contrasting positions increases indeterminacy. It brings us into a sort of waiting zone in which the need for patience dominates. It can even highlight aspects of uncertainty that seem to undermine the clarity and certainty of ethical statements and approaches. Both indeterminacy and uncertainty appear to be particularly present in the case of issues related to technological progress. We could say that, in dealing with high-tech advances, researchers and ethicists enter gray areas in which our scientific and ethical stance is shaped by vulnerability. We become vulnerable to what is going to happen. We lose control of what is happening. We have to wait and see to understand. Of course, we have to assess the benefits, implications, risks, and consequences of our research before we decide on it, while we are doing it, and after we have completed it. Nonetheless, the whole process of scientific and ethical assessment is marked by uncertainty, by a search for better ways of determining what is happening, and by vulnerability.

It is evident to everyone, I believe, that indeterminacy, uncertainty, and vulnerability are experiential states and categories of our time. Since September 11, 2001, we deal with these emotional states both on an international basis and on a very personal one. We experience vulnerability where we thought we could trust our technology, defense system, and control of land and air space. We are exposed in unexpected ways to increased risks.

Just as we should work in the more ethically appropriate ways to reduce indeterminacy, uncertainty, and vulnerability that depend on terrorism, I believe we could try to find ways in which we use all these three emotional states in the case of ethical issues associated with technological progress. Stem cell research seems to be an appropriate example.

I suggest that scientific research concerning stem cells needs an ethic of risk.[101] Of course, risk is a word with multiple meanings. First, risk is always present in scientific endeavors. In an interview on the Italian newspaper *La Repubblica*, Professor Glauco Tocchini Valentini, who coordinates the Italian project on functional genomics at the National Center for Research (CNR), affirmed that today's scientific research demands that we reformulate the relationship between research and risk. We should move from "'risk within research' to 'in search of risk', meaning that the risk needs to be analyzed, examined, and faced, instead of dismissed, otherwise the scientific enterprise will die."[102] Today's bioethics should be able to integrate this dimension of risk by reflecting on the ethical elements associated with specific projects by risking to address questions, making proposals, and suggesting limits to hypotheses and procedures. This approach is opposite to one that presupposes the ability to handle everything in exhaustive ways according to rigid predetermined solutions. As I indicated at the beginning of these pages, because of their novelty, the current scientific studies concerning human stem cells seem to require an ethical approach that allows for further research to obtain information and data in order to future therapeutic applications.

Second, in reading literature on stem cell research, the theme of risk surfaces. For example, in describing the potential application of stem cell research, Donovan et al., highlight three issues.[103] Both for therapy and transplantation, histocompatibility is necessary to reduce risks associated with using stem cells. The authors also refer to the risk of cancer due to stem cell self-renewal and plasticity. Finally, possible infections should be considered as risky aspects of stem cell research for therapeutic purposes.[104] While these issues concern the biological safety of this research and its applications to human therapy, and need to be duly addressed, an ethic of risk goes beyond them.[105]

Third, risk could be understood as restricted to assessment and management of costs and benefits. This approach could be prevalent among investors and biotech companies, both concerned by success in terms of revenues and investments. In this case, risk is both what we intend to avoid as well as part of what we have to undergo in assessing the economic costs that are involved and that are part of the benefits we aim to achieve.[106]

These three qualifications of risk are appropriate and necessary but insufficient. In the case of stem cell research, risk concerns individuals and society. Research on stem cells is risky for those who are working to clarify and expand its potential in terms of therapeutic applications (e.g., researchers) because of failure and disappointment. At the same time, danger, hopes, and promises—that characterize risk—are experienced by the sick who are looking for the benefits in terms of cure that could come to them from stem cells. Also, the Roman Catholic teaching concerning the beginning of human life highlights the ethical risk for society when embryos are produced (e.g., in the case of IVF), stored, and then used for research purposes because this is considered the same as destroying human life, with consequences for the respect due to life within society.

Instead of dismissing the complexity of risks involved in stem cell research, both for individuals and society, it could be considered as ethically relevant at the point of articulating an ethic of risk. Such an ethic would become a specific way to address this research. Besides keeping in tension the presence of these risks, an ethic of risk involves a continuous discerning attitude that moves ahead with the research itself by formulating ethical questions, suggesting caution, and examining possible alternatives when choices are needed. In her recently revised *A Feminist Ethic of Risk*, Sharon D. Welch indicates three aspects that should define and shape this ethic: "a redefinition of responsible action, grounding in community, and strategic risk-taking."[107] These three aspects are deeply related. They are in dynamic tension because the definition of each one requires the others. Furthermore, responsible action, with the challenge, critique, resistance, and commitment demanded from us, takes place because of and within the web of relationships that qualify one's life. We are far from an understanding of responsibility that focuses merely on the individual and one's ability to examine, choose, and act.[108] This seems particularly appropriate when we reflect on research potentially beneficial for humankind as in the case of stem cell research.

To value relationships also means that the ethic of risk is shaped by vulnerability and characterized by a deeply rooted attention to communicate. Both imply attention to who we are by recognizing the importance of those events that marked our past, those realities that qualify our present, and those expectations that concern our future. At the same time, vulnerability and care for communication highlight and promote our relationship with others as members of a social web.[109] On the one hand, both elements help us define our starting point. On the other hand, they promote critical discernment and, thus, they help move us forward.[110]

Concerning stem cell research, an ethic of risk helps us recognize that, from scientific and ethical points of view, we are quite vulnerable. We find ourselves in a situation in which our knowledge is still incomplete.

Furthermore, we are caught between our desire to do all that is possible to relieve suffering and the need to limit our sources of human stem cells.[111] We can appreciate, I believe, the readiness of scientists to inform us about the state of their research.[112] At the same time, we should improve our ability to promote communication and public discourse, ethical reflection, and public policymaking.

Communication is also valuable in the context of different ethical approaches, e.g., in the case of an ethic of control, where it can be seen as a means of controlling ends.[113] The ethic of risk, on the contrary, considers communication part of an active struggle for solidarity instead of a mere search for information, approval, or consensus. As I indicated at the beginning of this paper, in dealing with stem cell research, economic forces are interested not only in participating in scientific development, but also in sharing, or controlling, the benefits that can be derived. Without demonizing market-driven logic and strategies that understand risk in other ways, we can set goals we want to be respected and minimal warranties that we require.[114]

Solidarity is made of recognition and transformation.[115] It is also critical of, and resists, economic powers that limit access to benefits from medical applications of scientific advances only to those few who can pay for them.[116] We should also be concerned with situations of injustice that make access to benefits from scientific advances such as stem cell research insufficient, unrealistic, or even unnecessary in the face of major and prior health needs. The promotion of basic healthcare and healthy living conditions should come before any proposal that aims at making available highly technically advanced therapies like those dependent on stem cell research. The ethic of risk allows us to be involved and support research in this field, still in its initial phase, but, at the same time, sets a direction of development and application by pointing to the need of promoting solidarity.

Solidarity as an active and risky dynamic should imply, first, well documented knowledge about procedures and policies of biotech and drug companies. Second, it should help us find ways to influence these policies, and the ethical criteria that characterize them, with a deeper attention to the needs of less well-off populations.[117] Third, it could lead us to question the choices made in terms of research on which disease is a health priority and on which therapies will be made available as soon as we improve our knowledge of stem cells. An ethic of risk is therefore an ethic of "responsible action within the limits of bounded power."[118]

Conclusion

To "keep in tension" diverse, even contrasting, approaches on stem cell research in the context of the ethic of risk could require that we consider as relevant the objections made by a part of the society to research on embryos, particularly those stored or to be produced for research purposes. Hence, we could accept the challenge to implement other strategies for research that are less problematic. A specific nationally competent agency charged with oversight tasks could make this challenge more achievable.[119] To address issues of justice associated with health care today in Western countries, as well as on a world basis, would further characterize the task ahead. Finally, from the Roman Catholic point of view, we could acknowledge that some levels of research done on existing stem cell lines characterize this transitional phase of research marked by uncertainty and indeterminacy. In this phase, President Bush's limits, as well as the German Parliament decisions, could help researchers obtain information and data concerning stem cells, their development, and embryogenesis by using the available embryonic cell lines.[120]

NOTES

[1] Despite the fact that stem cell research began in the 70s, allowing us to deepen our knowledge of hematopoiesis and mouse embryology, it is only since 1998 that it has been possible to culture human embryonic stem cells. See Natalie DeWitt, "Stem Cells," *Nature* 414. 6859 (2001): 87.

[2] "Pluripotent stem cells can give rise theoretically to every cell type in the animal body." Peter J. Donovan and John Gearhart, "The End of the Beginning for Pluripotent Stem Cells, *Nature*, 414. 6859 (2001): 92.

[3] Stem cells seem to break what were previously thought embryological rules, that is, that "cells derived from one of the three primary germ layers that arise at gastrulation—ectoderm, mesoderm, and endoderm—should not be able to form cell types characteristic of another." Robin Lovell-Badge, "The Future for Stem Cell Research," *Nature* 414. 6859 (2001): 91.

[4] See Sally Temple, "The Development of Neural Stem Cells" *Nature* 414. 6859 (2001): 112, 116. See Sally Temple, A. Spradling, D. Drummond-Barbosa, and T. Kai, "Stem Cells Find Their Niche," *Nature* 414. 6859 (2001): 98-104; I. L. Weissman, "Stem Cells: Units of Development, Units of Regeneration, and Units in Evolution," *Cell* 100. 1 (2000): 157-68; and Emi K. Nishimura et al., "Dominant Role of the Niche in Melanocyte Stem-Cell Fate Determination," *Nature* 416. 6883 (2002): 854-60.

[5] However, it is suggested that in the case of hES this degree of totipotency is lost and hES "cannot be directly implanted into a uterus and grown into a conceptus." Paul Root Wolpe and Glenn McGee, "'Expert Bioethics' as Professional Discourse: The Case of Stem Cells," in *The Human Embryonic Stem Cell Debate: Science, Ethics, and Public Policy*, ed. Suzanne Holland, Karen Lebacqz, and Laurie Zoloth, *Basic Bioethics* (Cambridge, MA, and London, England: MIT Press, 2001), 189. The authors refer to D. Solter and J. Gearhart, "Putting Stem Cells to Work," *Science* 283. 5407 (1999): 1468-70.

[6] "When grown in suspension, pluripotent stem cells will form embryoid bodies, structures originally described in teratomas and which resemble the early pre-implantation embryo. In forming embryoid bodies, stem cell differentiation may proceed in a way related to that occurring in the embryo." Donovan, "The End," 94. However, embryonic stem (ES) cells via

nuclear transfer (ntES cell lines) from adult mouse somatic cells of inbred, hybrid, and mutant strains are "fully pluripotent in that they can differentiate into all cell types, including gametes." Teruhiko Wakayama et al., "Differentiation of Embryonic Stem Cell Lines Generated from Adult Somatic Cells by Nuclear Transfer," *Science* 292. 5517 (2001): 740-43.

[7] H. M. Blaw, T. R. Brazelton and J. M. Weimann, "The Evolving Concept of a Stem Cell: Entity or Function?" *Cell* 105.7 (2001): 637.

[8] In the event that stem cells will be used to treat a great variety of human diseases and many people, they "will be needed in large quantities and be able to differentiate in a controlled manner to form homogeneous populations of cells that are histocompatible with an individual." Donovan, "The End," 95. However, according to recent studies, the patient's immune system could reject transplanted tissues derived from non-immunologically compatible ES cells. See Gretchen Vogel, "Embryonic Stem Cells: Stem Cells Not So Stealthy after All," *Science* 297.5579 (2002): 175a-77.

[9] Stem cell from a donor's cornea can be transplanted in a compatible receiver affected by a corneal disease. See Margherita De Bac, "Le Cellule Staminali del Padre per Ridare la Vista alla Figlia," *Corriere della Sera*, (18 Febbraio 2001): 19.

[10] On the injection of fetal cells into brains of persons suffering from Parkinsonism, and the dubious results concerning both techniques and protocols, see Arthur Caplan and Glenn McGee, "Fetal Cell Implants: What We Learned," *Hastings Center Report* 31. 3 (2001): 6; C. R. Freed et al., "Transplantation of Embryonic Dopamine Neurons for Severe Parkinson's Disease," *New England Journal of Medicine* 344. 10 (2001): 710-19; Gretchen Vogel, "Parkinson's Research: Fetal Cell Transplant Trial Draws Fire," *Science* 291. 5511 (2001): 2060b-61. More recent data seem to suggest positive response to fetal cell implants, see Erika Check, "Parkinson's Patients Show Positive Response to Implants," *Nature* 416. 6882 (2002): 666. However, the transplanted stem cells could become tumors, develop in different cell types, lack specific functions or migrate to different sites from those where they are expected to multiply. To improve therapeutic results and avoid complications, it could be preferable to use differentiated cells instead of stem cells. See Donovan, "The End," 96.

[11] Lovell-Badge, "Future," 88-89. It is even possible that stem cells of male heart transplant receivers colonize the female hearts transplanted. The expression of Y markers indicates the migration in the donors' hearts of receivers' undifferentiated cells expressing stem cell antigens. See Federico Quaini et al., "Chimerism of the Transplanted Heart," *New England Journal of Medicine* 346. 1 (2002): 5-15. See also Caroline Seydel, "Stem Cell Research: Stem Cells May Shore up Transplanted Hearts," *Science* 295. 5553 (2002): 253b-54.

[12] "The discovery of neuronal stem cells in the embryo has opened new avenues for the repair and regeneration of neuronal tissues damaged through disease. Neuronal stem cells have been isolated from embryos, the adult brain, and even the skin of adult animals and humans." J. M. Penninger and J. Woodgett, "Stem Cells: PTEN—Coupling Tumor Suppression to Stem Cells?" *Science* 294. 5549 (2001): 2118. The authors refer to B. A. Reynolds and S. Weiss, "Generation of Neurons and Astrocytes from Isolated Cells of the Adult Mammalian Central Nervous System," *Science* 255. 5052 (1992): 1707-10. A tumor suppressor protein called PTEN controls the proliferation and possibly also the self-renewal of neuronal stem cells. See also B. E. Reubinoff et al., "Neural Progenitors from Human Embryonic Stem Cells," *Nature Biotechnology* 19. 12 (2001): 1134-40; S. C. Zhang et al., "In Vitro Differentiation of Transplantable Neural Precursors from Human Embryonic Stem Cells," *Nature Biotechnology* 19. 12 (2001): 1129-33.

[13] Examples of possible cell-based therapy are: neurodegenerative diseases (like Parkinson's and Alzheimer's diseases), muscular dystrophies, heart diseases, leukemias, AIDS and diabetes type I. See Paul Berg, "Progress with Stem Cells: Stuck or Unstuck?" *Science* 293. 5537 (2001): 1953.

[14] "We do not know yet enough about adult stem cells or ESCs [embryonic stem cells] to make dogmatic statements about the limitations of either." Darwin J. Prockop and Patricia A. Zuk, "Stem Cell Research Has Only Just Begun," *Science* 293. 5528 (2001): 211c.

[15] These arguments are those often used while presenting the opportunities offered by stem cell research. In this paper I will not reflect on the rhetoric concerning the potential for healing of stem cells. See Gilbert Meilaender, "The Point of a Ban: Or, How to Think About Stem Cell Research," *Hastings Center Report* 31. 1 (2001): 9-16; and Suzanne Holland, "Contested Commodities at Both Ends of Life: Buying and Selling Gametes, Embryos, and Body Tissues," *Kennedy Institute of Ethics Journal* 11. 3 (2001): 268-73.

[16] See Lisa Sowle Cahill, "Genetics, Commodification, and Social Justice in the Globalization Era," *Kennedy Institute of Ethics Journal* 11. 3 (2001): 221-38.

[17] See L. C. Stevens, "The Biology of Teratomas," *Advances in Morphogenesis* 6 (1967): 1-31, quoted in Donovan, "The End," 92.

[18] Both in animals and humans research on adult stem cells is less advanced than that on embryonic cells. Recently, scientists have identified a new type of stem cell from the dermis of adult rodent skin (Skin-derived Precursors, SKPs cells). In culture these cells can become several cell types with a different origin (neural and mesodermal): neurons, glia, smooth muscle cells, and adipocytes. See J. G. Toma et al., "Isolation of Multipotent Adult Stem Cells from the Dermis of Mammalian Skin," *Nature Cell Biology* 3. 9 (2001): 778-84. Recently, it appeared that adult stem cells (AS) "are more plastic than previously thought, and in some circumstances can contribute to cell types very different from those in their tissue of origin. This has suggested that patient-specific stem cell therapy can be carried out without cloning" (Lovell-Badge, "Future," 88). For example, neural stem cells can form blood cells and muscle tissue, see Donovan, "The End," 94. The author quotes C. R. Bjornson et al., "Turning Brain into Blood: A Hematopoietic Fate Adopted by Adult Neural Stem Cells in Vivo," *Science* 283. 5401 (1999): 534-37. See also D. J. Anderson, F. H. Gage, and I. L. Weissman, "Can Stem Cells Cross Lineage Boundaries?" *Nature Medicine* 7. 4 (2001): 393-95, quoted in Lovell-Badge, "Future," 89. However, it is not clear yet whether the potential of neural stem cells of becoming muscle cells "is a property of specific rare cells in the population or whether each cell has low probability of differentiating in this direction" (Ibid., 90). Further, "adult CNS stem cells can contribute to cell types of all three primary germ layers after being introduced into blastocysts, where they behave something like ES cells" (Ibid., 89). The author refers to D. L. Clarke et al., "Generalized Potential of Adult Neural Stem Cells," *Science* 288. 5471 (2000): 1660-63. Critics point that "although adult and fetal stem cells may be multipotent—that is, capable of generating many different cell types—they are present only in small numbers, so would not provide a realistic approach to cell therapy of common degenerative diseases unless they could be greatly amplified in culture while retaining a stable karyotype." Anne McLaren, "Ethical and Social Considerations of Stem Cell Research," *Nature* 414. 6859 (2001): 129.

[19] Gretchen Vogel, "Stem Cell Research. Studies Cast Doubt on Plasticity of Adult Cells," *Science* 295. 5562 (2002): 1989-91; Natalie DeWitt and Jonathan Knight, "Biologists Question Adult Stem-Cell Versatility," *Nature* 416. 6879 (2002): 354; Naohiro Terada et al., "Bone Marrow Cells Adopt the Phenotype of Other Cells by Spontaneous Cell Fusion," *Nature* 416. 6880 (2002): 542-5; Qi-Long Ying et al., "Changing Potency by Spontaneous Fusion," *Nature* 416. 6880 (2002): 545-8. Instead of transdifferentiation, as it has been suggested, adult stem cells would fuse embryonic stem cells by creating hybrids with abnormal chromosomes. See also Andrew E. Wurmser and Fred H. Gage, "Stem Cells: Cell Fusion Causes Confusion," *Nature* 416. 6880 (2002): 485-87.

[20] See J. A. Thomson et al., "Embryonic Stem Cell Lines Derived from Human Blastocysts," *Science* 282. 5391 (1998): 1145-47.

[21] Of course, the requirements for ethically sound scientific research need to be fulfilled—in particular, informed consent. In the case of blood samples and human tissue specimens collected and stored for other purposes and tested for stem cells, it is necessary to elaborate ways in which consent can be obtained.

[22] However, human embryonic germ (hEG) cell lines were derived from aborted fetuses. They allowed producing large ES-like cell colonies with potential similar to hES cells. This is an alternative to using early embryos to obtain stem cells. See M. J. Shamblott et al., "Derivation of Pluripotent Stem Cells from Cultured Human Primordial Germ Cells,"

Proceedings of the National Academy of Sciences of the United States of America 95. 23 (1998): 13726-31.
[23] While we consider the types together with their sources, other authors separate them, e.g., Donovan, "The End," 93.
[24] Neural progenitor cells were also isolated and propagated from human postmortem tissues and surgical specimens but further research is needed to confirm possible use to treat neurodegenerative diseases. See T. D. Palmer et al., "Cell Culture: Progenitor Cells from Human Brain after Death," *Nature* 411. 6833 (2001): 42-43. Further, multipotential cell lines were found in liposucted fat (PLA cells). See P. A. Zuk et al., "Multilineage Cells from Human Adipose Tissue: Implications for Cell-Based Therapies," *Tissue Engineering* 7 (2001): 211-28. In the adipose tissue it has to be proven conclusively that there are stem cells because of possible fat contamination with hematopoietic or mesenchymal stem cells from bone marrow.
[25] So far, it appears that compatible cells can be obtained in two ways. First, it is required that "the creation of an embryo by isolating a somatic nucleus from the patient and reprogramming it in an oocyte cytoplasm—so-called therapeutic cloning or somatic cell nuclear transfer." Second, "the existing stem cell lines are genetically modified by homologous recombination to create a stem cell that is compatible with the patient." Donovan, "The End," 96.
[26] "Therapeutic cloning" defines the somatic cell nuclear transfer (SCNT) realized without reproductive purposes. The procedure consists of inserting the nucleus of a somatic cell in an enucleated egg cytoplasm. By activating the cell's division totipotent stem cells can be harvested at the early stage (i.e., blastocyst). See Luigi Lorenzetti, "L'ipotesi Italiana," *Il Regno-Attualità* 46. 873 (2) (2001): 1.
[27] "Science itself points to other forms of *therapeutic intervention* which would not involve cloning or the use of embryonic cells, but rather would make use of stem cells taken from adults. This is the direction that research must follow if it wishes to respect the dignity of each and every human being, even at the embryonic stage." John Paul II, *Address of John Paul II to the 18th International Congress of the Transplantation Society*, (29 August 2000). Available from http://www.vatican.va/holy_father/john_paul_ii/speeches/2000/jul-sep/documents/hf_jp-ii_spe_20000829_transplants_en.html.
[28] From a scientific point of view, it would eliminate all histocompatibility issues while ethicists could promote it as a technique that focuses entirely on healing without involving embryo development and disposal.
[29] In its proposal for the next European Union Framework Program for Research, the European Parliament suggested that funding should be available for stem cell research, but that human embryos should not be cloned for research purposes. On November 14, 2000, the document of the European Commission on stem cell research was presented at the European Parliament. This document is favorable to research on stored embryos, but it does not allow for cloning. On November 29, 2001, the Parliament large majority (316 votes to 37) rejected the report that would have called for a ban on human cloning. See "European Group on Ethics" in *Science and New Technologies, Ethical Aspects of Human Stem Cell Research and Use*, (14 November 2000). Available from http://europa.eu.int/comm/european_group_ethics/docs/avis 15_en.pdf; "Parliament Amends Plans for Framework Funding," *Nature* 414, no. 6862 (2001): 386; Quirin Schiermeier, "European Parliament Rejects Move to Restrict Genetics," *Nature* 414. 6858 (2001): 572.
[30] In the Netherlands, since September 2002, research is allowed on human embryos when no alternative is available, but reproductive cloning is forbidden. See Vogel, "Regulations," 924. The dozen Spanish research groups working with imported stem cells are in turmoil because in August 2001 health-ministry officials pointed that one group was in breach of a 1988 law on assisted reproduction. Therefore, the current legislation seems to be inappropriate. See Xavier Bosch, "Confusion over Law Leaves Stem-Cell Research in the Lurch," *Nature* 413. 6858 (2001): 763. In October 2002, 1.3 million signatures were collected to back stem cell research. See "Spain Stem Cell Standoff," *Science* 298.5594 (2002): 723c.
At the beginning of December 2001, "the Swedish Research Council said that the country's laws governing embryo research allow ongoing work on human ES cells to continue." On

therapeutic cloning, the council did not remark "overriding ethical blocks to such research, but it said the parliament would need to enact new laws to regulate it." Gretchen Vogel, "Bioethics: Germany Dithers over Stem Cells, While Sweden Gives Green Light," *Science* 294. 5550 (2001): 2262a.

In March 2002, the Canadian Institutes of Health Research allowed researchers "to derive new lines of stem cells from embryos left over from fertility treatments or tissue from aborted fetuses under guidelines." This confirms what proposed, in April 2001, "by a blue-ribbon committee." This confirms what proposed, in April 2001, by a blue-ribbon committee. (Wayne Kondro and Constance Holden, "Stem Cell Research: Canada Gives OK for New Cell Lines," *Science* 295. 5561 [2002]: 1816a.) The committee opposed the creation of embryos for research purposes as well as "the donation or sale of gametes to create embryos for the sole purpose of generating stem cell lines. It also urged a moratorium on creating human embryos by somatic cell nuclear transfer [. . .] It suggested forming a national advisory body to oversee stem cell research, both public and privately funded, and possible licensing of researchers. Such an oversight body is expected to be part of long-promised federal legislation on reproductive technologies." Wayne Kondro, "Stem Cell Policy: Canadian Panel Aims for Middle Ground," *Science* 292.5514 (2001): 32.

[31] I choose to list twice France and Germany because, while I am writing this paper, both patterns coexist.In Australia, the state of Victoria prohibits human embryo research and hES derivation, but research on imported cell lines is allowed. In October 2001, an Australian government committee endorsed legislation allowing for hES cell research and the derivation of hES from spare embryos created during IVF. It has also suggested to establish a national licensing body to overview privately or publicly funded research in this area. Finally, it is in favor of creating embryos as a source of genetically compatible hES through therapeutic cloning. See Leigh Dayton and Gretchen Vogel, "Stem Cell Research: Reports Give Green Light in Australia, Israel," *Science* 293. 5539 (2001): 2367a-68. In April 2002, it was announced that in June legislation would be introduced to allow scientists to work with ES cell lines already established as well as "to derive new cell lines from surplus in vitro fertilization (IVF) embryos created before April 5 [2002] that would otherwise be destroyed." Reproductive and therapeutic cloning would be prohibited. Finally, "[a]n ethics committee would be established to review protocols, and the National Health and Medicine research Council will report within 12 months on the adequacy of the supply and distribution of embryos." Leigh Dayton, "Embryonic Stem Cells: Australian Agreement Allows New Lines," *Science* 296. 5566 (2002): 238. Finally, national legislation on stem cell research has been approved by Australia's Parliament in December 2002. Researchers can use existing hES cell lines, as well as create new lines, by using spare embryos from fertility treatments prior to April 5, 2002. See "New Stem Cell Law," *Science* 298.5601 (2002): 2109d.

In Japan, too, hES derivation as well as research on hES cells is in the process of being regulated. In July 2001, guidelines proposed by a committee working for the Japan's science advisory board indicated that stem cells could "only be harvested from spare embryos resulting from in vitro fertilization. The embryos must be donated, with donors giving written informed consent for their use." Dennis Normile, "Stem Cells: Japan Readies Rules that Allow Research," *Science* 293. 5531 (2001): 775a. The cells could be used only for research purposes. On November 5, 2001, Kyoto University approved the request of a Japanese group of researchers to work on hES cells. It is now waiting for approval by the national board. See "Delayed Again," *Science* 294. 5546 (2001): 1435.

[32] In Israel it is possible to derive hES cell lines from spare IVF embryos as well as through therapeutic cloning. The Bioethics Advisory Committee of the Israel Academy of Sciences and Humanities approved both procedures on September 4, 2001, but these decisions do not have legal value. See Dayton, "Green Light." Since 1999, a five-year moratorium prohibits reproductive cloning, but allows therapeutic cloning. See also Gretchen Vogel, "Stem Cells: In the Mideast, Pushing Back the Stem Cell Frontier," *Science* 295. 5561 (2002): 1818-20.

[33] In the United Kingdom, "both private and government-funded research fall under a single regulatory framework, with no restrictions limiting researchers to certain cell lines." Laura Bonetta, "Storm in a Culture Dish," *Nature* 413. 6854 (2001): 346.

[34] See House of Lords, Stem Cell Research Select Committee, *Stem Cell Research - Report*, (13 February 2002). Available from http://www.parliament.the-stationary-office.co.uk/pa/ld select/ldstem/83/8301.htm. David Adam, "Britain Banks on Embryonic Stem Cells to Gain Competitive Edge," *Nature* 416. 6876 (2002): 3. The bank should open in 2003.

[35] On December 19, 2000, the British Government accepted the suggestions advanced by the Chief Medical Officer's Expert Group, chaired by Prof. Liam Donaldson. See Chief Medical Officer's Expert Group, *Stem Cell Research: Medical Progress with Responsibility* (Department of Health, [16 August 2000]). Available from http://www.doh.gov.uk/cegc/stemcellreport.htm. "The creation of embryos by cell nuclear replacement will be necessary to understanding the mechanism by which an adult cell nucleus could be reprogrammed by an enucleated egg. This could lead in the long term to techniques being developed to reprogramme adult cells without the need to create an embryo and to overcome the problems of tissue rejection" (Ibid., 5.4). The HFEA is responsible for allowing research protocols. Informed consent is required from "individuals whose eggs or sperm are used in creating the embryos" (Ibid., 5.6; also 5.10.3).

[36] In January 2001, the 1990 Human Fertilisation and Embryology Act was corrected to allow research using hES cells to grow replacement tissues, even cloned embryos, for therapeutic purposes. In such a way these embryos are compatible with the patient's genetic make-up. See David Dickson, "Parliament Gives Green Light to Stem-Cell Research," *Nature* 409. 6816 (2001): 5.

[37] See David Adam, "Loophole Legalizes Human Cloning," *Nature* 414. 6862 (2001): 3-4; and LeRoy Walters, "Human Embryo Research: Lessons from History," *Science* 293. 5534 (2001): 1401.

[38] See ". . . As British Law Stretches to Make Human Cloning Illegal," *Nature* 415. 6870 (2002): 356.

[39] See Vogel, "Regulations," 924.

[40] See Gretchen Vogel, "British Science: Pioneering Stem Cell Bank Will Soon Be Open for Deposits," *Science* 297.5588 (2002): 1784a.

[41] On January 22, 2002, the National Assembly (*Assemblée nationale*) accepted the revision—also allowing the importing of human stem cells—but it will not become a law until the second semester of the year 2003. However, in June 2002, the new government blocked the revision, and the possibility of importing hES cell lines was suspended. See Vogel, "Regulations," 924.

[42] L.88-1138 (December 20, 1988) on the protection of human research subjects; L. 94-548 (July 1, 1994) on data concerning health; L. 94-653 (July 29, 1994) on respect due to the human body; L. 94-654 (July 29, 1994) on body parts, assisted reproduction and prenatal diagnosis. See Adriano Bompiani, "Le Cellule Staminali e la Clonazione Terapeutica nel Recente Dibattito," *Rivista di Teologia Morale* 32. 128 (4) (2000): 555-57.

[43] See Comité Consultatif Nationale d'Ethique pour les sciences de la vie et de la santé, *Avis sur l'avant-Projet de Révision des Lois de Bioéthique (Opinion on the Preliminary Draft Revision of the Laws on Bioethics): N°67*, (18 January 2001). Available from http://www.ccne-ethique.org/francais/start.htm and http://www.ccne-ethique.org/english/start.htm.

[44] The *Avis* recognizes that "the embryo or fœtus has the status of a potential human being who must command universal respect." It also adds that its preferred definition is "ongoing embryonic process" (*processus embryonnaire en cours*). Ibid. See also Comité Consultatif Nationale d'Ethique pour les sciences de la vie et de la santé, *Avis sur la Constitution de Collections de Cellules Embryonnaires Humaines et leur Utilisation à des Fins Thérapeutiques ou Scientifiques (Opinion on the Establishment of Collections of Human Embryo Cells and Their Use for Therapeutic or Scientific Purposes): N°53*, (11 March 1997). Available from http://www.ccne-ethique.org/francais/start.htm and http://www.ccne-ethique.org/english/start. htm.

[45] Comité Consultatif Nationale, *Avis N°67*. For producing stem cell lines, researchers can use embryos resulting from abortions (without specifying whether spontaneous or provoked), from IVF (and no longer required by their parents), and from somatic cell nuclear transfer. Embryos should be at the end of the pre-implantation stage.

[46] Ibid.

[47] Ibid.

[48] This confirms the French intention to favor biotech progress and development as it is showed by November 2001 proposal to Parliament to provide 60 millions Euro (U.S. $54 million) to biotech start-ups plus 90 million Euro in loans to established companies. See Sally Goodman, "France Boosts Funding for Biotechnology Start-Ups," *Nature* 414. 6864 (2001): 573.

[49] Ibid.

[50] On urgency in healing, see Glenn McGee and Arthur Caplan, "The Ethics and Politics of Small Sacrifices in Stem Cell Research," *Kennedy Institute of Ethics Journal* 9. 2 (1999): 153. For a critical stance and the proposal of a more gradual "[p]rogress at relieving human suffering" without destroying embryos, see Meilaender, "Ban," 12.

[51] See Comité Consultatif Nationale, *Avis N°67*.

[52] See Sabine Steghaus-Kovac, "Stem Cells: DFG Gives Embryo Research a Boost," *Science* 292. 5519 (2001): 1037b-8; and "German Ethics Council Backs Stem-Cell Plans," *Nature* 414. 6864 (2001): 574-5.

[53] At the request of the federal research ministry, on December 7, 2001, DFG postponed "a decision on the first German proposal to use ES cells—submitted by Bonn University neuropathologist Oliver Brüstle—until political leaders and the new bioethics council had explored ethical concerns over such research." Robert Koenig and Gretchen Vogel, "Embryonic Stem Cells: German Leaders Spar over Bioethics," *Science* 292. 5523 (2001): 1811b. "That's a big change from the DFG's initial guidance on ES cell research, issued in March 1999, which counseled scientists to avoid doing research on human ES cells." Steghaus-Kovac, "DFG," 1037b. See also Vogel, "Germany."

[54] "If the import of ES cells does not satisfy scientific demand, the DFG recommends that Parliament amend the ten year-old Embryo Protection Act to allow German researchers to derive their own ES cells from surplus IVF embryos for five years. The creation of human embryos solely for use in research, as well as therapeutic cloning—in which a nucleus of a somatic cell is transferred into an enucleated egg cell—would remain off limits." Steghaus-Kovac, "DFG," 1037b.

[55] Gretchen Vogel, "Stem Cells: German Researchers Get Green Light, Just," *Science* 295. 5557 (2002): 943a. See also Quirin Schiermeier, "German Parliament Backs Stem-Cell Research," *Nature* 415. 6872 (2002): 572.

[56] Vogel, "German Researchers," 943a.

[57] See Comitato Nazionale per la Bioetica, *Parere del Comitato Nazionale per la Bioetica sull'impiego delle Cellule Staminali*, (27 Ottobre 2000). Available from http://www.governo.it/bioetica/notizie/cellule_staminali.html. See also Comitato Nazionale per la Bioetica, *Dichiarazione Sulla Possibilità di Brevettare Cellule di Origine Embrionale Umana*, (25 Febbraio 2000). Available from http://www.governo.it/bioetica/Temi_problemi/epo.html; Comitato Nazionale per la Bioetica, *Protezione dell'embrione e del Feto Umani: Parere sul Progetto di Protocollo del Comitato di Bioetica del Consiglio d'Europa*, (31 Marzo 2000). Available from http://www.governo.it/bioetica/Temi_problemi/protezione_marzo00.html.

[58] See Ministero della Sanità, "Le Conclusioni della Commissione Dulbecco," *Il Regno-Documenti* 46. 872 (2001): 63-72.

[59] The technique is the same as in the case of therapeutic cloning. The difference is in the hypothesis that it is possible to avoid embryo development. According to the Report, human embryos are a primary source from a quantitative, but not qualitative point of view. Umbilical cord blood and adult stem cells are high on a qualitative, but not quantitative level. ASNT [TNSA in Italian] is presented as the best solution qualitatively and quantitatively. See Lorenzetti, "L'ipotesi italiana," 1.

[60] Blastocysts are 4- to 7-day-old embryos.

[61] See Juan de Dios Vial Correa and Elio Sgreccia, "Cellule Staminali Umane Autologhe e Trasferimento di Nucleo: Aspetti Scientifici ed Etici," *L'Osservatore Romano*, (5 Gennaio 2001): 6.

[62] "In linea di principio, non si può tuttavia escludere—a motivo della rapidissima evoluzione delle conoscenze in questo campo e della riservatezza con cui talune indagini scientifiche sono svolte in certe strutture di ricerca—che tale via innovativa alle cellule staminali autologhe possa mostrarsi effettivamente percorribile nei termini in cui è stata proposta, e cioè senza passare attraverso la formazione di un embrione in nessuno dei suoi stadi di sviluppo, da quello unicellulare in avanti. Il giudizio morale sulla liceità o meno di tale ricerca in campo umano – ovvero il TNSA [...] rimane sospeso in mancanza di una adeguata identificazione della materia (oggetto fisico o *genus naturae*) dell'azione, la quale, secondo la tradizione della teologia morale (*Summa theologiae*, I-II, q. 1, a. 3, ad 3; q. 18, a. 5, ad 3; cf M. Rhonheimer, *Natur als Grundlage der Moral*, Innsbruck-Wien 1987, 367 ss.) concorre insieme all'oggetto morale *(genus moris)* a definire l'oggetto proprio dell'atto umano." Ibid. See also Elio Sgreccia, "Nei Congelatori, Embrioni o Ovuli?," *L'Osservatore Romano*, (9-10 Aprile 2001): 12.

[63] G. J. Annas, A. Caplan, and S. Elias, "Stem Cell Politics, Ethics and Medical Progress," *Nature Medicine* 5, no. 12 (1999): 1339. The authors refer to C.L. Feiler, "Human Embryo Experimentation: Regulation and Relative Rights," *Fordham Law Review* 66 (1998): 2435-65. Since September 2002, California allowed researchers to produce stem cell lines and to clone embryos by nuclear transfer for research purposes. See Constance Holden, "Stem Cell Research: California Flashes a Green Light," *Science* 297. 5590 (2002): 2185a.

[64] On August 9, 2001, the criteria indicated by the President were: "Federal funds to be used for research on existing human embryonic stem cell lines as long as prior to his announcement (1) the derivation process (which commences with the removal of the inner cell mass from the blastocyst) had already been initiated and (2) the embryo from which the stem cell line was derived no longer had the possibility of development as a human being." The following criteria were added by the President: "The stem cells must have been derived from an embryo that was created for reproductive purposes; the embryo was no longer needed for these purposes; informed consent must have been obtained for the donation of the embryo; no financial inducements were provided for donation of the embryo." Prohibited areas of research are: the derivation of new stem cells from human embryos; research in which human embryonic stem cells are used to create or contribute to a human embryo; research in which human embryonic stem cells are derived using somatic cell nuclear transfer, e.g., the transfer of a human somatic cell nucleus into a human or animal egg; research using human embryonic stem cells that were derived using somatic cell nuclear transfer, e.g., the transfer of a human somatic cell nucleus into a human or animal egg; research in which human embryonic stem cells are combined with an animal embryo; and research in which human embryonic stem cells are used in combination with somatic cell nuclear transfer for the purposes of reproductive cloning of a human." National Institutes of Health, *Notice of Criteria for Federal Funding of Research on Existing Human Embryonic Stem Cells and Establisment of NIH Human Embryonic Stem Cell Registry* (Office of the Director, [7 November 2001]). Available from http://grants.nih.gov/grants/guide/notice-files/NOT-OD-02-005.html.

[65] On January 16, 2002, the President named seventeen members to serve on the President's Council on Bioethics. The list includes scientists, doctors, ethicists, social scientists, lawyers, and theologians. *President Names Members of Bioethics Council*, (16 January 2002). Available from http://www.whitehouse.gov/news/releases/2002/01/print/20020116-9.html.

[66] Earlier, the NIH also produced an extensive report on opportunities and challenges associated with stem cell research. U.S. Department of Health and Human Services and National Institutes of Health, *Stem Cells: Scientific Progress and Future Research Directions*, (June 2001). Available from http://www.nih.gov/news/stemcell/scireport.htm. See also Holden, "Cloning"; Gretchen Vogel, "Stem Cell Research: NIH Review Outlines 'Enormous Promise,'" *Science* 293. 5529 (2001): 413a. Concerning the stem cell lines, for example, the listed Californian company Cythera was not on the point of making its stem cell lines available to

researchers. See Constance Holden, "Stem Cell Lines: NIH's List of 64 Leaves Questions," *Science* 293. 5535 (2001): 1567a. On September 2001, the NIH were also considering a repository for hES cells to distribute cell lines to researchers taken from those indicated by President Bush on August 9, 2001. See Laura Bonetta, "NIH Ponders Repository for Embryonic Stem Cells," *Nature* 413. 6852 (2001): 99.

⁶⁷ The web site (http://escr.nih.gov) lists five companies and six research institutions with a total of fifty-eight cell lines. Technical descriptions are available for seventeen cell lines and five are ready for researchers. Geron, Inc., and the Wisconsin Alumni Research Foundation offer the same lines. Both were involved in a legal dispute, recently resolved, concerning the rights to distribute those cell lines. See "Stem-Cell Registry Opens Its Portal," *Nature* 414. 6861 (2001): 242-3; and "Dispute over Stem-Cell Rights Is Resolved," *Nature* 415. 6869 (2002): 252. However, in August 2002, U.S. scientists could work only on four of these lines, because of practical and legal hurdles. Furthermore, only a few lines have been characterized, raising uncertainty about whether all of them being stem cell lines. See Constance Holden and Gretchen Vogel, "Stem Cell Lines: 'Show Us the Cells,' U.S. Researchers Say," *Science* 297.5583 (2002): 923-25.

⁶⁸ On February 22, 2001, Lanza faxed a letter signed by eighty Nobel Prizes to President Bush urging to allow government-funded researchers to work on human pluripotent stem cells. See Gretchen Vogel, "Cell Biology: Nobel Laureates Lobby for Stem Cells," *Science* 291. 5509 (2001): 1683-84. On March 6, 2001, three officers of the American Academy for the Advancement of Science (AAAS) board wrote to President George W. Bush in support of federal funding for stem cell research, including cells from embryonic, fetal, and adult sources. The AAAS position on stem cell research had been laid out in its report: Audrey R. Chapman, Mark S. Frankel, and Michele S. Garfinkel, *Stem Cell Research and Applications: Monitoring the Frontiers of Biomedical Research* (Washington, D.C.: American Association for the Advancement of Science and Institute for Civil Society, 1999). Based on months of study by scientists, ethicists, and theologians, this report recommends federal funding for stem cell research and concludes that it is possible to conduct embryonic stem cell research in a fully ethical manner. See Gretchen Vogel, "Embryonic Stem Cells: Rumors and Trial Balloons Precede Bush's Funding Decision," *Science* 293. 5528 (2001): 186-67. Polls seem to be in favor of hES cell research, probably because of the media coverage attentive to emphasize the potential benefits of this research. See Bonetta, "Storm," 346.

⁶⁹ "'As soon as we have some evidence of the potential of ES cells, the whole issue can be revisited,' says Ron McKay, who works on stem-cell therapies for Parkinson's disease at the National Institute of Neurological Disorder and Stroke in Bethesda, Maryland." Bonetta, "Storm," 346.

⁷⁰ From a scientist's point of view, "the more cell lines available to work with the more we will learn about their basic biology." Donovan, "The End," 96.

⁷¹ Thomas A. Shannon, "Human Embryonic Stem Cell Therapy," *Theological Studies* 62. 4 (2001): 822.

⁷² For example, "U.S. academics can work on other human ES-cell lines if they obtain private funds. Harvard University and the HHMI (Howard Hughes Medical Institute) recently announced that they will jointly fund a team to isolate further lines of human ES cells. But such arrangements create severe administrative and logistical problems—the Harvard scientists will have to ensure that no federal money is used to pay for any reagents or overheads costs." Bonetta, "Storm," 346.

⁷³ On September 4, 2001, the Public Health Service (PHS) signed with WiCell, that holds patents on hES cells, to make existing cell lines available. For $5000, WiCell sells to researchers two vials of stem cells and technical assistance to grow them. The agreement with PHS prohibits "to create whole embryos for any therapeutic or diagnostic purposes." (Bonetta, "Storm," 346.) Further, WiCell will not claim patent rights to discoveries commercially relevant, but will negotiate new agreements. WiCell patents are owned by the Wisconsin Alumni Research Foundation. WiCell Research Institute, created on February 1, 2000, is a non-profit facility of the University of Wisconsin that allows this university to work on Geron stem

cell sponsored research. See also Constance Holden, "Stem Cells: HHS Inks Cell Deal; NAS Calls for More Lines," *Science* 293. 5537 (2001): 1966a-67; G. Vogel, "Stem Cells: Wisconsin to Distribute Embryonic Cell Lines," *Science* 287. 5455 (2000): 948-49. The agreement is available from http://www.nih.gov/news/stemcell/WicellMOU.pdf. See also http://www.nih.gov/news/pr/sep2001/od-05.htm.

[74] Jonathan Knight, "Stem-Cell Giveaway Proposed as Confusion Reigns over Cell Count," *Nature* 412. 6849 (2001): 753.

[75] In the case of cell-based therapies, the Food and Drug Administration (FDA) will implement existing statutes or update them. See Robert P. Brady, Molly S. Newberry, and Vicki W. Gerard, "FDA Regulatory Control over Human Stem Cells," *Professional Ethics Report* XII. 2 (1999): 5. These statutes are: the Public Health Service Act (PSH Act: section 351, 361); Federal Food, Drug and Cosmetic Act (FD&C Act); and FDA implementing regulations.

[76] Committee on the Biological and Biomedical Applications of Stem Cell Research et al., *Stem Cells and the Future of Regenerative Medicine* (Washington, D.C.: National Academy Press, 2001). It is partly the result of a workshop held by the National Academies.

[77] See Ibid., 2, 37. A further problem is that many of the recent experiments with stem cells were rarely performed with single cells. Then, there is the possibility of contamination of one stem cell type with another. See Tannishtha Reya et al., "Stem Cells, Cancer, and Cancer Stem Cells," *Nature* 414.6859 (2001): 105-11.

[78] See Committee on the Biological and Biomedical Applications of Stem Cell Research, 4, 38.

[79] Ibid., 8, 25-26, 31, 38-39 and Holden, "HHS."

[80] See Joseph A. Fiorenza, *The Stem Cell Decision*, (24 August 2001). Available from http://www.diocese-gal-hou.org/bishop1mess-080101.asp. On July 11, 2001, Bishop Fiorenza urged Congress not to fund embryonic stem cell research. Then, he made two further interventions, on July 26, and on August 24, 2001. See Joseph A. Fiorenza, *The Stem Cell Debate*, (26 July 2001). Available from http://www.diocese-gal-hou.org/bishop1mess-070101.asp; United States Conference of Catholic Bishops, *Bishops' President Urges Congress Not to Fund Embryonic Stem Cell Research*, (11 July 2001). Available from http://www.nccbuscc.org/comm/archives/2001/01-126.htm.

[81] Fiorenza, *The Stem Cell Decision*.

[82] I refer to the Chief Medical Officer's Expert Group chaired by Prof. Liam Donaldson.

[83] Keep in mind that concerning the UK, the mandate assigned to the National Bioethics Advisory Commission (NBAC) and the report on stem cell research that it produced. National Bioethics Advisory Commission, *Ethical Issues in Human Stem Cell Research*, Executive Summary, vol. I; Report and Recommendations of National Bioethics Advisory Commission, vol. II; Commissioned Papers, vol. III; Religious Perspectives (Rockville, MD: National Bioethics Advisory Commission, 1999). Together with critical reading of the NBAC report, some of the testimonies before NBAC on May 1999 appear in: *The Human Embryonic Stem Cell Debate*. See also R. Macklin, "Ethics, Politics, and Human Embryo Stem Cell Research," *Women's Health Issues* 10. 3 (2000): 111-15; and P. A. Roche and M. A. Grodin, "The Ethical Challenge of Stem Cell Research," *Women's Health Issues* 10. 3 (2000): 136-39.

[84] A similar approach will also characterize Germany where a national commission should review all important proposals, beginning summer 2002. See Vogel, "German Researchers."

[85] Within theological debate, it has rightly been suggested that we should not limit the ethical reflection on stem cell research to the embryo status but include issues of social justice. See Thomas A. Shannon, "From the Micro to the Macro," in *The Human Embryonic Stem Cell Debate* and "Human Embryonic Stem Cell Therapy."

[86] See Bishop Fiorenza's remarks presented earlier.

[87] This coincides only in part with what is affirmed by Roman Catholic teaching on embryos. For example, *Donum vitae* takes a tutiorist approach by affirming that: "From the time that the ovum is fertilized, a new life is begun [. . .] it is rather the life of a new human being with his own growth. It would never be made human if it were not human already." See Congregation for the Doctrine of the Faith, *Instruction on Respect for Human Life in Its Origin and on the*

Dignity of Procreation: Replies to Certain Questions of the Day (Donum Vitae), (1987): I.1. Available from http://www.vatican.va/roman_curia/congregations/cfaith/documents/rc_con_faith_doc_19870222_respect_for_human_life_en.html. The text refers to Sacred Congregation for the Doctrine of the Faith, *Declaration on Procured Abortion*, (18 November 1974). Available from http://www.vatican.va/roman_curia/congregations/cfaith/documents/rc_con_cfaith_doc_19741118_declaration-abortion_en.html. Among the possible alternatives, a tutiorist position chooses that which appears to be the surest.

[88] For example, John Paul II as well as many Roman Catholic moral theologians support somatic cells genetic therapy. See John Paul II, "The Human Genome: Human Personhood and the Future of Society," *L'Osservatore Romano: Weekly Edition in English*, (18 March 1998): 5; William E. May, *Catholic Bioethics and the Gift of Human Life* (Huntington, IN: Our Sunday Visitor Publishing Division, 2000); and Dionigi Tettamanzi, *Nuova Bioetica Cristiana* (Casale Monferrato, AL: Piemme, 2000). Together with healing, the Roman Catholic tradition has focused on the human body, see James F. Keenan, "Christian Perspectives on the Human Body," *Theological Studies* 55. 2 (1994): 330-46; Keenan, "Genetic Research and the Elusive Body," in *Embodiment, Morality, and Medicine*, ed. Lisa Sowle Cahill and Margaret A. Farley, *Theology and Medicine, 6* (Dordrecht, Boston, London: Kluwer Academic Publishers, 1995): 59-73.

[89] See Margaret R. McLean, "Stem Cells: Shaping the Future in Public Policy," in *The Human Embryonic Stem Cell Debate*, 201.

[90] See Shannon, "From the Micro to the Macro" and "Human Embryonic Stem Cell Therapy." These concerns are less present, or totally absent, in scientists calling for governmental support for embryo and stem cell research. For example, see Robert P. Lanza et al., "The Ethical Reasons for Stem Cell Research," *Science* 292. 5520 (2001): 1299b; and K. J. Ryan, "The Politics and Ethics of Human Embryo and Stem Cell Research," *Women's Health Issues* 10. 3 (2000): 109.

[91] See Suzanne Holland, "Beyond the Embryo: A Feminist Appraisal of the Embryonic Stem Cell Debate," in *The Human Embryonic Stem Cell Debate*, 73. The author reminds us that states have a responsibility to encourage human flourishing and "access to adequate, affordable health care is one such need" (75). See also Lisa Sowle Cahill, "Social Ethics of Embryo and Stem Cell Research," *Women's Health Issues* 10. 3 (2000): 134.

[92] See Shannon, "From the Micro to the Macro," 181-83.

[93] See McLean, "Policy," 202-04.

[94] See Meilaender, "Ban," 9. For disagreements, see Michael J. Meyer and Lawrence J. Nelson, "Respecting What We Destroy. Reflections on Human Embryo Research," *Hastings Center Report* 31. 1 (2001): 16-23. Others propose to abandon "treating embryos with respect" "in favor of an examination of whether or not the destruction of certain types of embryos can be justified in terms of the benefits to be produced through their use in research" (Annas, "Politics," 1341). For reflections on respecting embryos, see Karen Lebacqz, "On the Elusive Nature of Respect," in *The Human Embryonic Stem Cell Debate*; and B. Steinbock, "What Does 'Respect for Embryos' Mean in the Context of Stem Cell Research?" *Women's Health Issues* 10. 3 (2000): 127-30. Roman Catholic magisterial teaching is unconditionally against any research requiring the production and/or destruction of embryos and fetuses, except in the case of spontaneous abortion or even voluntary abortion, but only when specific ethical conditions are respected. See Tettamanzi, *Nuova Bioetica Cristiana*, 260ff and Carlo Casalone, "Cellule Staminali: La Decisione del Presidente Bush," *Aggiornamenti Sociali* 52. 9-10 (2001): 708. "Even if stem cell research ought not be banned, it could be situated and controlled on a spectrum of other health care needs through limited funding policies; aggressive peer review; regulatory and legal oversight applying to all research, however funded; and stringent patenting criteria." Cahill, "Social Ethics," 134, quoted in McLean, "Policy," 200.

[95] Cynthia B. Cohen, "Leaps and Boundaries: Expanding Oversight of Human Stem Cell Research," in *The Human Embryonic Stem Cell Debate*, 219. The overview should include stem cell research, IVF, SCNT, and germ line interventions.

[96] The AAAS/ICS report "found no reason for the time being to establish a new body to oversee the research, and recommends using established bodies for approval of research protocol" (Chapman, *Frontiers*; Michele Garfinkel, "Stem Cell Controversy," *Professional Ethics Report* XII. 3 [1999]: 8.) This includes local review at the level of Institutional Review Boards, by normal NIH study sections and, as necessary, review by the Recombinant DNA Advisory Committee. Annas et al. propose "[a] federal oversight panel, independent of the NIH and DHHS" (Annas, "Politics," 1341). See also G. J. Annas, A. Caplan, and S. Elias, "The Politics of Human-Embryo Research—Avoiding Ethical Gridlock," *New England Journal of Medicine* 334. 20 (1996): 1329-32. The authors suggest also the need for an international treaty. Both suggestions aim to contain the power of private corporations.

[97] See Cohen, "Leaps," 219.

[98] The NBAC 1999 Report was calling for more that dialogue, that is, public consensus while arguing in favor of progress in research. See National Bioethics Advisory Commission, *Ethical Issues in Human Stem Cell Research* 51, 55. For critical comments, see Meilaender, "Ban," 14. See also Root Wolpe, "Expert," 195. More forcefully, Zoloth affirms: "Moral vision has to precede research." Laurie Zoloth, "Jordan's Banks: A View from the First Years of Human Embryonic Stem Cell Research," in *The Human Embryonic Stem Cell Debate,* 236.

[99] See Cohen, "Leaps," 212-14; "Ethical Issues in Embryonic Stem Cell Research," *Jama* 285. 11 (2001): 1439, discussion 40; and "Use of "Excess" Human Embryos for Stem Cell Research: Protecting Women's Rights and Health," *Women's Health Issues* 10. 3 (2000): 121-26. The author emphasizes issues of consent, pressure, coercion, and possible overproduction of embryos that affect women and couples and should be matters of concern. She also calls for an oversight panel able to address these issues.

[100] A further problem that relates to the need for regulations concerns the regulatory gap between research performed in private labs and federally funded facilities. However, this issue goes beyond the limits of this paper. See Holland, "Beyond the Embryo," 77-79.

[101] See Sharon D. Welch, *A Feminist Ethic of Risk*, rev. ed. (Minneapolis, MN: Fortress Press, 2000).

[102] Giovanni Maria Pace, "Ma la Colpa è anche Nostra. Siamo Trionfalisti e Provinciali," *Repubblica*, (19 Febbraio 2001): 23. The translation is mine.

[103] See Donovan, "The End," 96.

[104] Because stem cells are grown in animal feeders, viruses can infect them. See Ibid. On the possibility of avoiding feeders, see Bonetta, "Storm," 346; and C. Xu et al., "Feeder-Free Growth of Undifferentiated Human Embryonic Stem Cells," *Nature Biotechnology* 19. 10 (2001): 971-74. Attempts are also made "to produce a synthetic medium that could keep the cells dividing but not differentiating." Gretchen Vogel, "Developmental Biology: The Hottest Stem Cells are Also the Toughest," *Science* 292. 5516 (2001): 615b-17.

[105] In a different area of research, that is, xenotransplantation, still ethically controversial and problematic, the recent document published by the Pontifical Academy for Life understands risk exclusively in terms of safety issues. See Pontifical Academy for Life, *Prospects for Xenotransplantation: Scientific Aspects and Ethical Considerations*, (26 September 2001). Available from http://www.academiavita.org/testi+zip/PAV/prospett%20xenotrap%20-%20doc um%20-%20engl.htm.

[106] See C. Petrini, "Aspetti di Etica nell'Analisi Costi/Benefici per Rischi Sanitari ed Ambientali," *Biologi Italiani* 5 (2000): 40-42.

[107] Welch, *Ethic of Risk*, 46. Zoloth prefers to speak of an "exodic" thinking in bioethics. It aims to define "what would be exemplary research, rather than struggling to figure out if the 'is' presented to us is acceptable or not." Zoloth, "Jordan's Banks," 230.

[108] "Responsible action does not mean the certain achievement of desired ends but the creation of a matrix in which further actions are possible, the creation of the conditions of possibility for desired ends." Welch, *Ethic of Risk*, 46.

[109] It might be interesting to relate the importance assigned by Welch to vulnerability and communication with the relevance given by Jürgen Habermas to analyzing Kohlberg's stages of moral growth (with the vulnerability that they can reveal) and participation in communicative

action. See Jürgen Habermas, *Etica del Discorso, Biblioteca Universale Laterza* (Bari: Laterza, 1993). However, Welch is critical of Habermas' community of discourse, as expressed in his *Theory of Communicative Action*, because of his dismissal of oral traditions as well as the lack of attention to the material condition that are necessary to make discourse possible. See Welch, *Ethic of Risk*, 129-36; and Jürgen Habermas, *The Theory of Communicative Action* (Boston: Beacon Press, 1984).

[110] See Margaret A. Farley, "Roman Catholic Views on Research Involving Human Embryonic Stem Cells," in *The Human Embryonic Stem Cell Debate*, 116.

[111] For a critical reading of "relieving the human condition from suffering," see Gerald P. McKenny, *To Relieve the Human Condition: Bioethics, Technology, and the Body* (Albany: State University of New York Press, 1997).

[112] However, we ask scientists to comply with the requirements concerning peer-review and the sharing of research results. This occurs even in the context of an ethic of risk.

[113] "Our moral and political imagination is shaped by an ethic of control, a construction of agency, responsibility, and goodness which assumes that it is possible to guarantee the efficacy of one's actions." On the contrary, Welch argues for "an alternative construction of responsible action, the ethic of risk." Welch, *Ethic of Risk*, 14.

[114] "[U]nless evil is acknowledged, unless the imbalance of power that causes exploitation is addressed, further change is impossible." Ibid., 52. We can think, for example, about the risky business of investing money in research without being sure of the concrete results that are achievable.

[115] See Ibid., 133-34.

[116] On resistance, see Ibid., 46.

[117] The recent issues concerning AIDS drugs in South Africa and India could be indicated.

[118] Ibid., 45.

[119] By briefly tracing the history of embryo research and policy making on this issue in the United States of America and United Kingdom, Walters invites governments and their advisors to be aware of the need of addressing and solving the issues raised by embryo research when they surface. He encourages an approach "humble and flexible, but also decisive and courageous. Additional surprises surely lie ahead." Walters, "Lessons from History," 1401.

[120] Compared with AS cells, it seems that ES have the ability to divide in culture. This allows us to learn how differentiation occurs. See Gretchen Vogel, "Stem Cell Policy: Can Adult Stem Cells Suffice?" *Science* 292. 5523 (2001): 1820-22.

My gratitude to the staff of the National Reference Center for Bioethics Literature at Georgetown University for their competent help during the last period of research for this paper and to Rev. Winthrop Brainerd for his kind hospitality.

REASSESSING
CHRIST AND CULTURE

The View from Somewhere: The Meaning of Method in *Christ and Culture*

D. M. Yeager

Abstract

Accepting James Gustafson's recent argument that right reading and valid criticism of H. R. Niebuhr's *Christ and Culture* must begin with an informed understanding of Niebuhr's utilization of the ideal-typical method, the author reviews characteristics of Weberian typologies and discusses the levels of criticism to which typologies are legitimately subject. Right appreciation of the text's genre exposes many criticisms of *Christ and Culture* to be misguided, but it also throws into relief those features of the text that cannot be accounted for by that method, revealing the complexity of a text that advances both a comparative descriptive analysis and a bold theological argument. Recognition of this tension prompts the question whether the one so compromises or constrains the other that the enterprise does, indeed, fail as a whole, even though it remains intensely interesting in all its parts.

The 2001 publication of an expanded edition of *Christ and Culture*, which includes not only new introductory essays by Martin Marty and James M. Gustafson but also Niebuhr's 1942 essay "Types of Christian Ethics," provides a welcome opportunity for reflecting once again on the value of the social sciences for the study and refinement of Christian ethical reflection.[1] In the new preface, Gustafson considers *Christ and Culture* in relation to the tools of inquiry developed over the past century in the social sciences, focusing on the ideal-typical method of analysis. He argues that a good deal of "radical misreading" of *Christ and Culture* has resulted from the failure of readers to appreciate Niebuhr's use of this distinctive methodology.[2]

It seems to me that Gustafson is entirely correct in his representation of Niebuhr's intention and achievement. Beginning where Gustafson has left off, I want to use the pages that follow to think, in the company of both Gustafson and Niebuhr, about the nature and function of (Weberian) typologies—and about critical engagement with such typologies. I also want to probe an additional layer of complexity that Gustafson's defense of the book brings much more clearly into view. *Christ and Culture* presents us with a very interesting instance of the difficulties, as well as the benefits, that can arise when theological ethics and a social science method are combined. The book remains important half a century after its original publication for all the reasons Gustafson notes; chief among these is the simple fact that the typology remains remarkably useful not only for theological education but also for lay people (including non-Christians) who need a means of "comparing theological differences" that show themselves in public policy debates and other forums of encounter in a pluralist society. But the book and its criticism, taken together, have an additional kind of importance: they highlight issues relating to the classification of religions, to Christian pluralism, and to the tension between normative theology and the academic study of religion(s).

Three Dimensions of Engagement

Criticism is infelicitous if it invokes standards of excellence that are not appropriate to the genre of the work under consideration. Gustafson identifies three such infelicitous forms of criticism when he structures his "appreciation" around the claims that *Christ and Culture* is "not a history of Christian theological ethics," "not a systematic statement of Niebuhr's theological ethics," and "not a taxonomy of the writings used in the book" (CC, xxvi). I have nothing to add to his reasons for ruling out of court complaints about the book on the grounds of its alleged "historical inadequacies," and I will take up the distinction between taxonomies and typologies in the next section. The question of whether *Christ and Culture* can be rightly read and criticized as a constructive work in theological ethics is more complicated. I agree that it was never meant to be "an account of Niebuhr's systematic and comprehensive Christian ethics" (CC, xxix). I do, however, think that we should consider the possibility that the book may be a mixture of genres—at once an incisive ideal-typical modeling of variations in Christian ethics and also a bold theological argument. To examine this possibility, we must begin by differentiating three dimensions of critical engagement with the text.

First, there seems to be a consensus in the secondary literature that Niebuhr "prefers" the "conversionist" model and that the entire book constitutes a theological argument for the superiority of this model. Whether the conversionist model is, in fact, the superior model then becomes the subject of critical scrutiny (with the commentator almost always taking the position that it is not). This sort of criticism can and frequently does take the oblique form of disputing Niebuhr's alleged representation of the Christ-against-culture type as inadequate. That is, if he has a theological preference for one type, it is because he finds theological fault with another.

Second, a significant number of critics read the book backwards from the "Concluding Unscientific Postscript." These commentators engage the book as a "liberal" theological argument for pluralism (or, as they more often put it, relativism). They give comparatively little attention to the book's content, representing *Christ and Culture* as "a prime example of repressive tolerance." This is the phrase used by Stanley Hauerwas and William H. Willimon in *Resident Aliens.* They frame their critique as an objection to Niebuhr's alleged preference for the conversionist model, but it seems to me clear from the development of their brief remarks that their focus is his emphasis on theological pluralism; indeed, they suggest that it is "his own pluralism" that "underwrote the implicit assumption that his ['transformist'] position (pluralism) was superior to other, more narrow ecclesiology." Moreover, it is by reference to his pluralism that they justify their judgment that the book is "a theological rationale for liberal democracy." This, in turn, justifies their placement of Niebuhr, in their own typology, under the model of the Constantinian church.[3]

Finally, the book can be engaged, as Gustafson recommends that we engage it, as a dispassionate study of Christian diversity that has its roots in the tradition of Wilhelm Dilthey, Max Weber, and Ernst Troeltsch, and employs the tool of ideal types developed by Weber. As Gustafson points out, the book is seldom engaged in this manner. This must seem like an odd claim because virtually every commentary that deals with the book at any length introduces it as a typology and walks us through the five types. Yet if we read these accounts closely, we find that more often than not the representation of types becomes merely the platform from which the commentator proceeds to criticize Niebuhr's own theology in one of the two ways just described.

Often it is not obvious exactly which dimension of the book is being engaged in a particular critical assessment. Generally the criticism shifts about among the three dimensions with no clear demarcation of these passages. John Howard Yoder's long circulated and only lately published critical commentary is a fine example of the way in which the various levels of criticism can shift and blend.[4] It is also, by that very fact, an example of the way such diffuse analysis, moving like a spotlight over a darkened field, picking out first this object and then that, leaves the field itself unilluminated, the argument as a whole untouched. For reasons that will become apparent as the discussion develops, Yoder's criticism of *Christ and*

Culture is the only contribution to the secondary literature that I will try to treat in any detail.

Before I follow Gustafson's lead in exploring how *Christ and Culture* might be better understood as a typology, let me register two caveats concerning the first two dimensions of engagement. Both arise out of my correspondence with Richard R. Niebuhr. From him I learned not only that the "Concluding Unscientific Postscript" was not part of the lecture series originally delivered at Austin Presbyterian Theological Seminary but also that his father did not willingly include it in the book: "my father added the final chapter at the behest of a reader that Harper used regularly" and did so, Richard Niebuhr suggests, with some resistance. If the book can rightly be said to constitute a mixture of genres, this would go some distance toward explaining how that happened. The second point is that Richard Niebuhr himself is skeptical that his father did actually "prefer" the conversionist type. That someone so intimately familiar with H. Richard Niebuhr's theological commitments should be doubtful about what so many take for granted would suggest that on this point we would do well to examine the text and the origins of the critical consensus a little more thoroughly.

Weberian Typologies

In urging that "an intelligent and fair-minded critique" would have to begin with an evaluation of Niebuhr's use of the ideal-typical method, which cannot be accomplished without knowledge of the nature and development of this analytic tool (CC, xxx), Gustafson calls our attention to the importance of distinguishing between typologies and taxonomies (CC, xxix–xxx). He also emphasizes that the objective of the ideal-typical method is *Verstenhen,* understanding or comprehension, not assessment; thus, a successful typology is not by intention evaluative. He further points out that a Weberian typology has a heuristic and comparative, not an explanatory, function. Let us look at each of these in turn.

Typologies and Taxonomies

While forcefully underlining the importance of differentiating taxonomies from typologies, Gustafson admits that the two "readily get mixed or confused" (CC, xxx). He frames the distinction thus: "ideal types are ideal constructs of ideas along a clearly stated axis by which particular aspects of issues of literature are illumined. The purpose of taxonomy is to develop headings about generalizations from a variety of literature which shares similarities" (CC, xxx). Daniel Day Williams's *The Spirit and the Forms of Love* is, he suggests, a taxonomy. Anders Nygren's *Eros and Agape* and Niebuhr's *Christ and Culture* are typologies.

The distinction is a useful one, but fairly subtle. Both typologies and taxonomies abstract from the variability of concrete actuality. Both offer broad classifications within which the authors arrange concrete instances. Both serve to organize or pattern large numbers of instances; therefore, both offer conceptual maps that simplify the "booming, buzzing confusion." Both are, in this respect, essential teaching devices. Neither is meant to function normatively or evaluatively. How, then, do they really differ? Primarily in purpose and use. Consider the comparisons in Table 1.

To see how this distinction might illuminate an example, let us consider Yoder's discussion of the use of types in the section of his essay devoted to "How Do 'Types' Work?"

> The ordinary historical meaning of the word "type" presupposes a degree of normativeness and rigidity in determining the possible forms which reality, by its own deep nature, can take. In ancient philosophy and early Christian exegesis, the "archetype" and the "type" stood in very firm determining relationship.
>
> A typology is therefore in normal usage not an arbitrary, impressionistic, or whimsical principle of classification, nor a mere set of suggestive analogies to provoke interesting insights. A typology is offered as a serious aid in establishing a classification of entities or events, which will throw some needed light on the very nature of those things classified, or on the logic of how they "work" in the mind or in cultures (AT, 44–45).

If I understand Weberian ideal types correctly, they are neither "whimsical principles of classification" nor attempts to express "the possible forms which reality, by its own deep nature, can take." If I have been correct in elaborating how the types in the ideal-typical method differ from the classificatory enterprise of taxonomy, it would seem that what Yoder is describing as a typology would be closer to a taxonomy than a Weberian typology. If so, the implications of the distinction become clearer. There is an obvious difference between, on the one hand, the suggestion that a religious group is, by its nature, opposed to its environing culture and that this social self-definition is self-contradictory and, on the other hand, the suggestion that a religious group, when its practices and beliefs are tracked along several different axes, tends more than others to approximate (but by no means perfectly exemplify) the simplified conceptual model of oppositional tension. In making the latter sort of determination, the Weberian typologist is not stating or implying that the religious community practices a form of Christianity that is intrinsically or in principle hostile to civic arrangements or worldly well-being; the typologist is only saying that, comparatively speaking, this group is more likely than others to believe that obedience to the biblical teachings of Jesus both defines discipleship and is

TABLE 1

TAXONOMY	TYPOLOGY
Intrinsic to work in the natural sciences	Intrinsic to work in the social sciences
Exemplar: Carolus Linnaeus	Exemplar: Max Weber
Explanatory function	Heuristic function
General ideas	Concepts, models
A taxonomy normally undertakes to be comprehensive, to account for all instances.	A typology may be, and usually is, selectively focused.
For any body of instances, there would normally be one and only one taxonomy. If a new taxonomy is proposed, the question of which is correct must be settled.	For any body of instances, there can be (and no doubt will be) multiple useful typologies.
A taxonomy is usually understood to represent the identification of the system implicit in the instances.	A typology is generally understood to bring to light issues of disagreement or points of conflict, and/or the way actual social behavior deviates from systematic conceptualization and logical expectations.
Assumes, more often than not, that there are natural kinds.	Facilitates the recognition of ambiguity and the plurality of sustainable social constructions.
Concrete instances can be unambiguously classified into a particular taxon.	Concrete instances are not expected to conform perfectly to any one theoretical type.
Taxonomies are generally stratified into hierarchical differentiations within the principal categories of classification. The subordinate divisions are the same across the categories.	Typologies generally employ a set of theoretical constructs that are not further differentiated. If there is further differentiation within a type, such differentiation is not ordinarily replicated within the companion types.

TABLE 1 - Continued	
TAXONOMY	**TYPOLOGY**
A taxonomy is essentially the product of scrupulous observation and description.	A typology provides theoretically constructed models that facilitate the subsequent task of description.
A taxonomy rests on the discovery of similarities, and the generalization of those similarities into homogeneous classes.	A typology provides a model of the kind of theoretical consistency (along one axis, at least) that we never find in actual social realities; therefore, it is the deviation from the type, not the confirmation of the type, that is of primary interest. Thus, to employ Peter Winch's word, a typology brings into view not what is common but what is "peculiar."[5]

fairly likely to exact a social cost (lower salary, accusations of disloyalty, ridicule, pity, and at the extreme, imprisonment and death)—so likely that preparation for bearing that cross, and communal support in bearing it, should be central to the life of that Christian community. That Yoder understands typologies in terms of claims about the "deep nature" of possible forms of social reality explains why he construes *Christ and Culture* to be so dangerous to Christian mission and discipleship. Yet the fact that his understanding of typologies differs from Niebuhr's understanding of typologies suggests that he may well be rebutting a characterization of his religious community that Niebuhr never offered.

It is not always self-evident which sort of schema a particular work represents: Does *The Social Teaching of the Christian Churches* actually offer a taxonomy or a typology? What about Gilson's *Reason and Revelation in the Middle Ages*? Once the typologies have been developed, they seem, almost inevitably, to begin to function (if not for the authors, then for those who teach them and build upon them) as taxonomies of social phenomena. That this should happen is not surprising because the conceptual models that constitute the ideal types are themselves generated as a result of the antecedent perception of certain recurring patterns and empirical similarities in the historical record or the sociological data; a typology is not a work of untrammeled imagination. Still, once we begin to be clear about the distinction, we can (1) guard against confusing abstract models with empirical generalizations (let alone attempts at ontological description) and (2) see the very real importance of guarding against such confusion. Certainly Gustafson is right to suggest that certain criticisms of *Christ and Culture* (most especially the complaint that concrete historical and social religious phenomena do not usually fit unambiguously into his "categories") can hardly be maintained once we appreciate the book's function as a typology.

Neutralizing Bias

I think that we can probably all agree that there is no human inquiry that is uninflected by the values and interests of the inquirer. To begin with, the social scientist selects certain things for attention and disregards others. The social scientist does this because she or he has interests (of a wide variety of sorts). This is, of course, a necessary condition of (not a deficiency in) all forms and instances of inquiry. In this sense, all inquiry and all typolgies have values and evaluations built in. But granting this, we can still distinguish broadly between descriptive work (which confines itself to giving us a sense of what is going on) and normative work (which undertakes to advise us as to what ought to be going on or to persuade us that some things that are going on are morally, politically, religiously, or intellectually superior to other things that are going on). A proper typology is not meant to do normative work.

Putting this another way, we can probably all agree that no human accounts of anything are perfectly free of bias, if by "bias" we mean perspective, and if by "perspective" we mean social location and personal investment. Even so, I think that we have no great difficulty, in most instances, distinguishing between comparatively fair and unbiased accounts and accounts that are distorted by commitment, blindness, and desire. It is no easy thing, of course, to drag one's own assumptions up into view, to learn where one is likely to be blind, or to discover, discipline, and neutralize our commitments and desires. What Gustafson suggests, and what I want to emphasize, is that the construction of (Weberian) typologies is a powerful tool in this intellectually essential endeavor. A typology is an admission that my way of looking at things is not the only way, that thoughtful people, reasoning consistently and acting in good will, may truly, consistently, and defensibly think and act in ways that differ from the ways that I embrace with utmost conviction. Niebuhr is quite clear about this in his brief acknowledgment note at the beginning: the book reflects a Troetlsch-inspired "respect" for "the multiformity and individuality of men and movements in Christian history"; it reflects an "acceptance of the relativity" of both the "historical objects" being studied and the observer/interpreter who carries out the analysis.[6] Moreover, implicit in the comparative differentiation that is the heart of the typological approach is the expectation that, by admitting this variation and identifying the advantages and the disadvantages of the various possibilities, I may discover something about my own position that I could not otherwise readily discover. The typological schema enables me to describe alternative positions without incorporating the positions of others into my own interpretive framework, in terms of which they would necessarily have to be represented as deficient or problematic. Typologies grant to the other-than-myself an autonomy and an authority vis-à-vis my own beliefs and loyalties. Typologies give the other independent standing. The typological method is, then, ideally suited to furthering contemporary interests in ways of addressing, representing, and respecting authentic diversity.

Nevertheless, there is a sense in which a Weberian typology can and often does function evaluatively. Once a set of "pure" (that is, perfectly rationally consistent) models has been proposed for our use, our consideration of a given historical/social concrete case that seems to approximate a given model will naturally be a consideration of how closely it approximates that perfectly consistent model and how far it deviates from it. In considering multiple instances, one can, therefore, set up a hierarchy arranged according to how closely different groups approximate the model, with some coming very close (so close that they become identified with the model) and others deviating so widely that they begin to appear to have as much or more in common with one (or several) of the other theoretical models we are using. Note, however, that such deviation from the model is not to be considered a deficiency or a fault unless we insert an additional assumption: namely, that the best social organization is that which most nearly approximates the rational consistency of the constructed model. A typologist may embrace this assumption or may not; it is not an assumption that necessarily inheres in the generation and use of typologies. Weber did not embrace it, and I cannot see that Niebuhr did either.

One can draw up typologies that bear on social phenomena in which one has no particular personal stake, but often, as in the case of *Christ and Culture*, the author might be expected to have a preference for one of the types as his or her own type. Indeed, we might wish to insist that an author should, in the spirit of full disclosure, make explicit which type her or his own position best approximates. Despite the typologist's effort to even-handedly discuss the achievements and the problems associated with each type, it would hardly be surprising if the author had more difficulty specifying the disadvantages and weaknesses of the position closest to the author's own. To what extent this happens in *Christ and Culture* is worth attention and has a bearing on the question of whether or to what degree the book is marred by mixing normative theological argument with sociological analysis.[7] The point here is simply this: If the view is always the view from somewhere, and if even in our most valiant efforts to be fair to views we do not share we end up failing to speak with a pure disinterestedness, the project does not shipwreck on these shoals. We are all pretty sophisticated now in the art of "hearing" the human voice of the thinker who argues from a social location and whose work is informed by a set of loyalties and commitments; we are, in fact, quite practiced in compensating for the partiality of authorial perspective.

Organizing Variousness

As Gustafson remarks, "ideal types do not explain anything" (CC, xxxi). From the point of view of the social scientist, the types precede and make possible explanation. The natural world exists in an array of fairly fixed forms. There may be five million sorts of organisms that have to be fitted into the taxonomy of species, and they may be evolving organisms, but they are still fairly stable morphologically or genetically. The human social world, involving incalculable variables, effects the perpetual construction of the very creature who is trying to study it, and it is, in turn, constantly being built, dismantled, and rebuilt. Moreover, things that at first glance seem the same are often not at all the same if viewed along some other axis. Before any questions can meaningfully be asked about social reality in its extraordinary variousness, some simplifying theoretical constructs must be generated that can serve as benchmarks. That is, they serve to establish some hypothetical standard of the normal, predicted, expected, or rational against which the overwhelming diversity of human activity can be named, compared, and interpreted. These constructs explain nothing, though they are powerful aids to seeing, clustering, comparing, and gaining insight. Once they have been generated, it becomes possible to ask questions about social behavior that we could not ask without them. We might ask, for example, why pacifism, which is usually bundled with the beliefs and attitudes characteristic of smaller Christian groups (groups that develop a strong and distinctive subculture that varies in multiple dimensions from the dominant culture), should, at the turn of the twenty-first century, be growing in the Roman Catholic community which, in its tendency toward a broader theological validation of intellectual and political activity and its historical involvement in the governance of states, has legitimized warfare (or at least some sorts of warfare). The conceptual constructs throw into relief aspects of complex reality that require explanation. The types therefore function heuristically rather than explanatorily.

The Use and Limits of Typologies

A (Weberian) typology is, then, a heuristic device utilized by scholars interested in change, variation, and correlation in human social existence. Methodologically, it creates stable constructs in light of which complex variable structures and practices can be isolated, patterned, and interpreted.

By deliberately legitimating diversity (through the methodological recognition of multiple plausible models), typologies assist the inquirers in identifying and sequestering their own commitments so as to offer a reasonably evenhanded treatment of social possibilities in which they do not participate and which they do not personally endorse.

In the "Postscript," Niebuhr himself reflects on the purpose of the typological method and suggests that typologies function to:

1. bring "conceptual patterns and historical realities into closer relations" (CC, 231),
2. "reduce" "the haze of uncertainty that surrounds every effort to analyze form in the manifold richness of historical life" (CC, 231),
3. "draw" "sharper boundaries between the interfusing, interacting thoughts and deeds of separate men" (CC, 231),
4. "state relatively inclusive and intelligible answers to the problem," where there is an "enduring problem" to which various ad hoc solutions have been and continue to be given (CC, 232), and
5. fulfill our duty to understand the way other Christians solve the problem and why they solve it as they do (CC, 233ff.).

The first four of these form a good fit with what I have already said about typologies, but the last one surely goes beyond anything that has been suggested so far. Why should one, as a Christian (not merely as a sociologist of religion), have a duty not just to tolerate the diversity of Christian answers but to attend to them actively, seeking to understand their internal logic? The answer lies in the "theological and theo-centric relativism" by means of which Niebuhr renders historical relativism meaningful, providing "the context in which the relativities of history make sense" (CC [1951], x; CC [2001], xii). In support of this, he cites Isaiah 10, 1 Corinthians 12, and Augustine's *City of God.* Isaiah 10, which establishes the precondition for the emergence of "a shoot/from the stump of Jesse," is a hymn to the absolute power of God. It promises the punishment of the arrogant, the humiliation of the proud, the smashing of all idols, and the destruction of all who worship idols. Chapter 12 in 1 Corinthians concerns "spiritual gifts" and affirms:

Now there are varieties of gifts, but the same Spirit; and there are varieties of service, but the same Lord; and there are varieties of working, but it is the same God who inspires them all in every one. To each is given the manifestation of the Spirit for the common good. . . . All these are inspired by one and the same Spirit, who apportions to each one individually as he wills (1 Cor. 12:4–7, 11, RSV).

It also contains Paul's metaphor of the in corporation of all the diverse parts of the body into a complete, interactive whole: "If the whole body were an eye, where would be the hearing? If the whole body were an ear, where would be the sense of smell?" The reference to the *City of God* is more obscure because the book is vast and various. Niebuhr might well be thinking of Augustine's emphasis on the idolatry of pride (a pivotal theme in his treatment of Augustine in relation to the conversionist type), but he might also be thinking of Augustine's reflections, in book 19.17, upon the sort of peace that is available to "the heavenly city, or rather the part of it which sojourns on earth and lives by faith." Condemning the fragmentation of divinity but celebrating the harmony of variousness ordered to one God, he writes:

> This heavenly city, then, while it sojourns on earth, calls citizens out of all nations, and gathers together a society of pilgrims of all languages, not scrupling about diversities in the manners, laws, and institutions whereby earthly peace is secured and maintained, but recognising that, however various these are, they all tend to one and the same end of earthly peace. It therefore is so far from rescinding and abolishing these diversities, that it even preserves and adapts them, so long only as no hindrance to the worship of the one supreme and true God is thus introduced.[8]

In his 1942 essay "Types of Christian Ethics," Niebuhr is even more explicit about "the typological method":

> Typology is the effort to order these many elements ["a confusing pluralism of principles and an even greater multiplicity of historic individuals"] into families in such a way that some of the characteristic combinations of principles may be understood. On the one hand, then, typology . . . challenges the assumption that there is only one ethics or one ethical principle. . . . It assumes, on the contrary, that there are multiple principles and a large number of creative individual concretions of the Christian life. On the other hand, typology seeks to understand these unique individuals with the aid of ideal figures or types, that is, of relatively concrete models of combinations of interests and convictions.[9]

With respect to Christian ethics, it is possible, he notes, to develop psychological, socio-organizational, cultural/anthropological, socio-economic, and philosophical typologies. While the time may come for trying to correlate and combine existing typologies into "more inclusive mental models" (that is, models that comprehend several axes of consideration), that time lies well in the future. The task in the 1940s is to refine particular limited typologies so as to use them more productively "for the understanding, not for the explanation, of historical actualities" (CC, xli; AT, 18).

In "Types of Christian Ethics," Niebuhr also makes some incisive comments about the "inadequacies" and "limitations" of the typological method: (1) The "principle" governing the typology (or what Gustafson more helpfully calls the "axis" of concern) may not have been particularly important to some of the individuals, groups, developments, or movements that one is trying to understand. Or, for some of the individuals or groups in question, the factor that forms the axis of the typology might have had its significance only in relation to other factors that the typology leaves out of account (CC, xxxvii; AT, 15). (2) A typology is, by the nature of the case, a one-dimensional schematization of empirical realities possessing many dimensions. A typology may be organized around, for example, anthropological, psychological, or socio-economic factors, but "only confusion results if these categories are mixed" (CC, xxxviii; AT, 16). When this one-dimensionality is coupled with the tendency to confuse correlation (what a typology is designed to uncover) with determination or explanation, there arises the distinct danger that a typology of, say, sociological types of Christian ethics will be misread as an argument that social location is the sole or primary cause of certain ethical teachings. (3) "[A] type is a mental construct to which no individual wholly conforms" (CC, xxxviii; AT, 16). Though Niebuhr does not explicitly say so, I presume that the "limitation" recognized by this observation is the power of mental constructions, if they come to be privileged over the concrete cases, to obscure or distort the very empirical phenomena they are designed to illuminate. (4) It requires constant vigilance to keep evaluative elements from infecting what should be a means of "achiev[ing] some measure of disinterestedness" (CC, xxxix; AT 17).

Ways of Criticizing Typologies

Having clarified what a typology is and how it functions, we can see why some criticism of *Christ and Culture* simply misses the mark: To complain, for example, that it fails as a taxonomy when it was never intended to function as a taxonomy or to engage the book as if Niebuhr had written it to establish the untenability of one or more of the types is to misconstrue the genre. It also becomes plain that there are three different levels at which questions might be legitimately raised about any given typology, *Christ and Culture* included. One of the things that makes Yoder's critical essay so interesting is that he does self-consciously differentiate at least two of these levels. He insists, for example, that "I am not objecting to a typology, I am objecting to a deficient typology" (AT, 46), and he endeavors, toward the end of the essay, to develop criteria for assessing the adequacy or deficiency of typologies.

Criticism of the Typological Method as Such

An individual might reject the very purposes for which typologies are generated and the assumptions that underwrite them. Gustafson has captured the two directions of such discontent with exemplary clarity:

> If critics believe that self-critical disinterestedness and "objectivity" are impossible in principle, and thus that no effort to approximate them is viable, of course the pedagogical interpretive, illuminating power and purpose of the book cannot be appreciated. If critics believe that the purpose of theological education, and particularly of teaching Christian ethics is not to train students *how* to think, but *what* to think, it is clearly a dangerous book [CC, xxxii].

On the one hand, a critic who recognizes full well that a Weberian typology is a strategy intended to achieve disinterestedness may nonetheless be so convinced of the indelible and pervasive character of bias that she or he dismisses the typological method as deluded and self-deceptive. Since nobody can ever fairly describe the position of anybody else, all efforts at fairness will necessarily fail. This kind of objection has a second, somewhat more subtle form. A critic may be so convinced of the fundamental and irreducible heterogeneity of human activity, so suspicious of the ideological (in the negative sense) character of all generalized categories, and so committed to concrete specificity that typologies will seem, by their very introduction of generalized models, to be falsifications of social reality, designed to obscure the truth of heterogeneity and dissent. The impulse in this case, too, is opposition to typologies on the grounds that all conceptual patterning is covertly normative and thus deceptive. Typologists play at objectivity, but they do not and cannot achieve it. Or, worse, they use the pretense of objectivity to conceal ideological manipulation, to silence other voices, and to advance their own agendas.

Conversely, a different sort of critic may object to the typological method because it is not normative enough. Not everyone has been prepared, through the course of Christian history, to regard the diversity of Christian beliefs and practices as a cause for gladness. Not everyone is prepared to do so now. For many, Christian teachings fall into only two classes: true and deviant, orthodox and heretical. From this point of view, a typology like Niebuhr's fails because it does not make the necessary value judgments. Criticisms of *Christ and Culture* that have at their heart an objection to Niebuhr's pluralism seem to constitute, in the end, this kind of rejection of the typological method. Their quarrel is not with his way of modeling Christian diversity; their quarrel is with his legitimization of diversity.

Criticism of a Typology as a Faulty Typology

It is possible, of course, that a set of constructed models might be a bad set, but it seems to me that the only thing that we could mean by a bad set is a set that is not useful. Now it is hardly necessary to waste one's energy arguing against a useless typology. If it is a useless typology, no one will use it. Accordingly, at this level, the only really telling criticism of a bad typology is the presentation of an alternate typology that will, in fact, displace it. It appears from Niebuhr's introductory remarks in *Christ and Culture* that he generated his typology at least partly as a consequence of his own discontent with that of Troeltsch.

Correspondingly, it seems reasonable to assume that a typology that people have found useful over time proves its value in the very fact of its continuing use.

It might, of course, be objected that a set of models could be said to be a bad set if it is excessively ideological, but I am not sure what "excessively" would mean here. As I have already said, the view is always a view from somewhere. Typologies neutralize bias by substituting acknowledged valid variation for the binary division of insiders and outsiders; they do not neutralize bias by creating barriers to expressions of interest. It is precisely the situatedness of the person who develops the typology that permits the definition of an axis of concern in relation to which a variety of models can be developed. If other people share the author's interest in that axis of concern, then they will find the typology illuminating. If they do not, they will not. In that case, they are free to develop a typology that reflects their own interest in the phenomena being studied. The more typologies we have, the more we will be able to notice.

I suspect, though, that the complaint that a typology is excessively ideological would actually, in most cases, be a complaint that the models are functioning normatively to differentiate correct views from incorrect ones. In this case, I would think that what we would want to say is not that the text in question offers a bad typology but that the text in question is not a typology at all. That is why I suggested at the beginning that we should be alert to the possibility that *Christ and Culture* represents a mixture of genres, with each qualifying the success of the other and thus undermining the force of the whole.

It is, however, under this heading that some sustained attention should be given to the work that Yoder has done in his critical essay which, as I said above, is one of the few that attempt to assess *Christ and Culture* as a typology. His complaints fall into several clusters. First, the axis or organizing principle of the typology is, in his view, badly flawed; he complains, for example, that Niebuhr's way of defining the terms creates a problem where otherwise there would not be one and causes him to fabricate a range of, "solutions," specious. Second, Niebuhr's typology is so abstractly constructed that "it can hardly be falsified by any kind of test which Niebuhr could suggest" (AT, 51). Yoder then offers a discussion of various kinds of typologies and of the means by which each can be "verified."[10] Third, the conversionist type is a poorly drawn type, being too vague to bear its weight in the typology. Fourth, the typology is deceptive (this is closely linked to the first criticism), and it actually obscures what it seeks to illuminate. This is because Niebuhr's categories are not apt ones, "for the purpose he wants them to serve" (AT, 37). These claims may be right or wrong assessments of Niebuhr's achievement, but they are, unlike much of the critical response, properly aimed and serious criticisms of Niebuhr's typology *as a typology*.

The question I would raise, though, is whether such criticism of the weakness of Niebuhr's typology has any particular value in the absence of a proposed alternative that can be shown to be more apt for the purposes at hand. In the end, although Yoder seems to recognize that the true answer to the book is "an alternative grid" (AT, 44), he does not provide one. What he gives us instead is a range of seven concrete examples of the way a Christian might, in a given set of concrete circumstances, address herself or himself to representatives of the regnant culture. This is, I think, a clue that Yoder's deepest quarrel with *Christ and Culture* lies at the level of Niebuhr's self-conscious Christian pluralism. Niebuhr takes it for granted that Christian theology is itself plural. Yoder, it seems, takes it for granted that Christian theology is a singular gospel that is expressed in the idiom of a plurality of cultural situations.[11]

Criticism of Concrete Correlations

This third level of legitimate criticism is not really criticism of the typology; it is criticism of the way the typology is actually used (by the person who generated it or by others) to give us purchase on the variousness of human organizations and behavior. We might be perfectly content with Niebuhr's range of abstract models while being thoroughly discontented with his sketchy correlations between particular models and particular denominations. It is, in fact, quite difficult to find fault with the typology since it reflects so neatly a set of logical relations that predict most, if not all, possible relations. For any *x* and any *y*, we can imagine at least five relations: The two could be identical. The two could be on all points incompatible with each other. If they are neither identical nor incompatible, they may be related in at least three ways: sequentially, reconfiguratively, or paradoxically. So once we grant an interest in thinking about the different ways in which Christians relate (or could relate) God and history, these present themselves as indisputably plausible abstract models (even if one or another produces a null class in relation to the matter of concern). But whose Christianity, exactly, we are helped to appreciate by relation to, say, the model of identity is something that we might well argue about.

Here it is helpful to remember that this sort of argument is, in some sense, the very point for which the typology was generated in the first place. It is the *deviation* of the concrete phenomena from the types that is the issue of interest. It is the messiness of reality that the purity of the types throws into relief. Yet at this point we also want to recall the reason for starting with the distinction between taxonomies and typologies. To focus too much attention on whether a particular religious community or a particular religious thinker comes closer to the paradoxical model or the conversionist model is, once again, to miss the point. A typology presents conceptual models in order that we may organize the variousness of social phenomena into sufficiently stable patterns to be able to track change within a community, to ask about the meanings of affinities where we would expect differences, to inquire into the causes of the variation, to correlate variations in doctrine or practice with other factors in social life, and so on.

To the extent that *Christ and Culture* is used pedagogically to introduce students in a fairly neutral way to the range of variation in Christian ethical reflection and social thought, it will inevitably be used more taxonomically than typologically. But as we come to view the book less as a definitive classifying description and more as a conceptual device for defining questions, you may be struck, as I am struck, by the realization that we have perhaps not even begun to use this book as it might be used and ought to be used: as a tool facilitating further inquiry rather than an end in itself.

Enduring Questions

Like Gustafson, I commend the book as a typology and urge that we engage it as such. Much may be gained by a self-conscious effort to differentiate concerns about Niebuhr's use of the typological method from evaluations of his fivefold typology as a typology—and both of these from assessments of the persuasiveness of the particular empirical correlations that he proposes. Such critical clarity would enable us to be more penetrating, as well as more honest, in assessing the value of the work and in accurately identifying its strengths and weaknesses. Moreover, I think a right understanding of the nature of the book has the potential to open up a range of questions and projects that are worthy of investigation.

Yet I am not inclined to think that misreadings—if that is what failures to engage this typology as a typology ought properly to be called—are entirely the readers' fault. As we have seen, Niebuhr gives his typology a theological justification, and there is a normative purpose woven into it which differentiates it from, say, Weber's typologies of theodicies and of forms of mysticism and asceticism. In *Christ and Culture,* we have a tool of the social sciences being put to work in a way that it would not be put to work by a social scientist. The book is a complex crossdisciplinary hybrid rather than an uncomplicated typology. It is not easy to raid one discipline for tools that will work in another, nor is it always persuasive to import a set of findings achieved with the tools of one discipline into a framework where they will be interpreted in light of a different set of assumptions. I can see the book as a Weberian typology, as Gustafson would have me see it, and I can thoroughly appreciate the unexploited benefits of reading it that way. But there is also a theological point of view and a theological argument in this book—and it is a view and an argument that are not indisputable, at least not if we take seriously the supposition of authentic irreducible Christian diversity that funds the typology in the first place. Noticing this tension for what it is seems to me to make the book more interesting, not less. To what extent does the theological purpose undermine the value of the typology as a strategy for achieving a "measure of disinterestedness"? To what extent does it actually enhance the value of the typology by offering a self-conscious disclosure of what is normally hidden: the commitments, interests, and presuppositions that constitute the "somewhere" from which this set of models has been developed as a useful tool? Why construct a typology at all if one has a theological intent? Granting that Niebuhr intended to offer a typology, is the typology itself marred by the dialectical presentation that advances each position as countering and overcoming the weaknesses of its predecessors until we are left with the conversionist model which, as so many have pointed out, escapes unfaulted? Ought we to say that it is a flawed typology? Ought we to try to separate the theological argument from the typology and treat them separately?

We arrive, thus, at an asymmetry and an irony. Let me approach both through a familiar epigram: "There are two kinds of people: those who think there are two kinds of people and those who don't." What makes this funny is the incongruous categorization of the one-kind-of-person person in a taxonomy s/he rejects and the sly triumph of the two-kinds-of-people taxonomist. The consideration of *Christ and Cutlure* and its critics brings us inevitably to a similar asymmetry. Or, to put it differently, it brings us to the collision of the negative capability of the pluralist with the singular vision of the truthfully convinced. The pluralist must account for the antipluralist and can do so typologically, constructing a univocal model and describing with sensitivity and respect groups whose beliefs and practices approximate that model. But try as she will, the pluralist can never account for the antipluralist in a way that the antipluralist will accept and endorse—because the placement of her views within a typology of valid variations places that truthfully convinced person within a framework of diversity that she rejects. The truthfully convinced person, in turn, will find it impossible to construct some more adequate typology of theological types and can only object to typologies in principle—which is what I think Yoder did implicitly and really should have done explicitly. Such a critic can never engage the typological work for what it is, but can only reach beneath it to object to the theological assumptions that made the "mistake" of typologizing possible in the first place.

The antipluralist thus uncovers an ironic circularity in the typology itself: perhaps only Christians who understand themselves as conversionists (or who are semidetached academics steeped in the writings of Troeltsch and the social sciences) would be disposed to construct theological typologies and to find them fair and interesting. If that is so, a typology of forms of Christianity constructed by a Christian theologian cannot avoid being a theological argument, and it is inevitable that the responses of readers of a different persuasion will be so preoccupied trying to get at and correct the theology that they will appear to fail to respond appropriately to the genre that the book represents. It is not that Yoder is a poor reader; indeed, his response to the book is one of the most searching. But Niebuhr's book simply does not make sense to Yoder, though it is luminously clear and helpful to someone like Gustafson or like me. It seems to us that we have made a place for Yoder in the typology, though perhaps it will turn out not to be under the model that we at first thought would be the most plausible. In a way, his essay simply confirms for us the value of the typology. But for Yoder there is one Christ and one gospel and one witness, carried into and spoken of and lived out in diverse cultural milieus. There seems to be no way that that view can be gathered, without falsification, into a typology of diverse forms of Christianity without ceasing to be the view that it is. So it seems that the one-witness Christian like Yoder is obliged, on theological grounds, to denounce a typology like Niebuhr's as deceptive and even pernicious. The Christian pluralist, respecting Christian diversity and admitting the depth of authentic Christian disagreement, attempts, on theological grounds, to acknowledge and even celebrate the distance between his own view and that of Yoder, but he can never put the difference in typological language that Yoder would accept.

NOTES

---

[1] H. Richard Niebuhr, *Christ and Culture* (New York: Harper San Franciso, a division of Harper Collins Publishers, 1951). Republished as an expanded fiftieth anniversary edition, with new front matter, in 2001. Citations for quotations from this volume will be given parenthetically in the text, using the abbreviation CC and the page number. Pagination for the text of *Christ and Culture* is the same in both editions.

[2] James M. Gustafson, "Preface: An Appreciative Interpretation," in *Christ and Culture*, expanded fiftieth anniversary edition (New York: Harper San Franciso, a division of Harper Collins Publishers, 2001), xxvi. It will be obvious, as this article unfolds, that I am deeply indebted to Gustafson's insights, upon which I hope to build in constructive ways. I also continue to be grateful to Howard L. Harrod, who set me on this road nearly a decade ago at a

small conference on *Christ and Culture,* organized in 1993 at the Vanderbilt Divinity School by John R. Fitzmier.

³ Stanley Hauerwas and William H. Willimon, *Resident Aliens: A Provocative Christian Assessment of Culture and Ministry for People Who Know that Something is Wrong* (Nashville, TN: Abingdon Press, 1989), 41. Hauerwas and Willimon, like many others, seem to take it for granted that "Christ" and "culture" are identical with "church" and "world," and that the models are therefore models of the ways in which the church is or can be related to the world. Niebuhr, however, holds that the church belongs to the domain of culture (this is underlined in *Radical Monotheism*). Each of the models implies a distinct understanding of what a Christian community is and how an organized Christian community might be related to other sociological structures, but the "enduring problem" only subordinately leads to reflection about the relation of the church to other social organizations.

⁴ John Howard Yoder, "How H. Richard Niebuhr Reasoned: A Critique of *Christ and Culture,*" in *Authentic Transformation,* by Glen H. Stassen, D. M. Yeager, and John Howard Yoder (Nashville, TN: Abingdon Press, 1996), 31–89. Citations for quotations from this essay will be given parenthetically in the text, using the abbreviation AT and the page number.

⁵ Peter Winch, *Encyclopedia of Philosophy,* s.v. "Weber, Max" (New York: Macmillan Publishing Co. and The Free Press, 1967).

⁶ This quotation comes from Niebuhr's original prefatory remarks, under the heading "Acknowledgments," in *Christ and Culture.* The pagination of these remarks differs in the two editions. In the 1951 edition, this material appears on page x; in the 2001 edition, it appears on page xii.

⁷ Noting that "[m]any interpreters of Niebuhr's typology use the fifth type, Christ transforming Culture, as the key, not just a key to his theological ethics," Gustafson goes on to contrast Nygren's use of his typology with Niebuhr's. Nygren "violate[s] the discipline of the ideal-typical method" by making *agape* "the pure motif of Christianity which was always being corrupted by the infusion of Greek *eros.*" Niebuhr, in contrast, does not use the fifth type as "a polemical tool against the others" (CC, xxviii).

⁸ Augustine, *The City of God,* trans. by Marcus Dods, George Wilson, and J. J. Smith. (New York: Random House, The Modern Library, 1950), 696.

⁹ H. Richard Niebuhr, "Types of Christian Ethics," in *Christ and Culture,* ed. for publication by D. M. Yeager, (New York: Harper San Franciso, a division of Harper Collins Publishers, 2001), xxxvii-xxxviii. Written in 1942, the essay was first published in *Authentic Transformation: A New Vision of Christ and Culture,* by Glen H. Stassen, D. M. Yeager, and John Howard Yoder (Nashville: Abingdon Press, 1996). In that volume, this passage appears on page sixteen. Subsequent citations for quotations from this essay will give page numbers for both books.

¹⁰ What I find so curious about this section is that the one sort of typology that he says Niebuhr clearly is not offering is the one sort that it seems to me Niebuhr *is* offering: a typology of diversification which proves its usefulness by its ability to "simplify helpfully at some points" and "complexify wholesomely at other points" (AT, 49).

¹¹ One of the JSCE referees, who offered welcome, lengthy, and penetrating comments, objected that here and in the elaboration of this contrast in the final section of the article, "the relevant distinction cannot really be Christian pluralist vs. Christian anti-pluralist." Believing that to insist that Niebuhr construes Christian theology as plural is "to deny any substantive meaning to 'Christian,'" this referee recommends reframing the issue this way: "Granting that Christian theology is in some respects singular and in some respects plural, in what respects is it the one and in what respects the other?" Since space constraints have not permitted me to expand the article to properly engage these valuable remarks, I include this summary here so that readers may consider the implications for my argument. It does seem to me that Wittgenstein's notion of family resemblances could be invoked to explain how Christian theology could be truly and irreducibly plural.

Christ and Culture: Still Worth Reading after All These Years

Douglas F. Ottati

Abstract

This essay argues that H. Richard Niebuhr's classic book, *Christ and Culture*, is best understood as a typology of moral theologies. Each of Niebuhr's five types may be regarded as a patterned resolution of four theological relations: reason and revelation, God and world, sin and goodness, and law and gospel. Many of his evaluative comments reflect his preference for what he calls a transformationist or conversionist pattern. However, it is not difficult to imagine evaluative comments on the several types, including the transformationist one, made from the perspective of a different preferred resolution of the four theological relations. Moreover, Niebuhr's scheme remains useful for analyzing more recent texts in theological ethics, such as Gustavo Gutierrez's *A Theology of Liberation*. Thus, while the book is not without its flaws and while readers may wish to enter some emendations and revisions, *Christ and Culture* is still worth reading because the categories it presents for analyzing moral theologies remain unsurpassed in their richness, usefulness, and suggestiveness.

The rather lively recent discussion of *Christ and Culture*—motivated in part by the desire of some to criticize and correct what they judge to be telling deficiencies in Niebuhr's Christ-against-culture type—demonstrates that people read the book in strikingly different ways. My own reading is that Niebuhr's types have a somewhat different and more detailed content and so also a somewhat different and more detailed analytic promise than some recent commentators appreciate. Accordingly, I should like to clutter the interpretive horizon further by outlining my own reading.

The Problem

In order to understand the problem of Christ and culture, it is important to remember that, for Niebuhr, human beings are creatures of faith. Niebuhr believed that people are oriented by commitments to various objects of meaning and value, such as economic production, the nation, or the race. He believed, too, that Jesus Christ discloses God—a new center of meaning and value around which to orient our lives.[1]

Niebuhr's definition of Christ focuses on "that unique devotion to God and . . . that single-hearted trust in Him which can be symbolized by no other figure of speech so well as by the one which calls him Son of God" (27). This unique devotion is what, later in his career, Niebuhr will call "radical faith."[2] Here, it means that Jesus Christ points away from all worlds "to the One who creates all worlds, who is the Other of all worlds," and yet, "since God is *agape*" and because God is faithful, it also means that Jesus Christ, or the one who points to God, points back again toward human beings and toward the world which God loves. Things would be different if the God to whom Jesus Christ was devoted were different. Devotion to God involves Jesus Christ in this double movement "since the Father of Jesus Christ is what He is" (28). Thus, those who believe in Jesus Christ, those who are loyal to his cause, must likewise be involved in this same double movement "from the world to God and from God to the world" (29).

When Niebuhr defines culture, the focus is on a social realm of purposive achievements that reflect commitments to a plurality of values. Culture is a realm of valued ends, material and immaterial goods, such as technical processes, education, science, government, and art. Niebuhr says that these goods, although plural, are dominantly concerned with "the good for man" or what we might call human flourishing (35).

We are ready now to grasp the enduring problem. If Christ directs believers toward the transcendent and faithful God and then back again toward the world God loves, then culture directs them toward a variety of socially defined goods, causes, or values that are understood to advance human well-being. What, then, is the relationship between loyalty to God-in-Christ and the many loyalties and causes to which culture invites our allegiance?

The Logic of the Typical Answers

Niebuhr distinguishes five ways that Christians have answered this question. From his vantage point, two of the answers are radical or extreme; three are more closely interrelated and belong to "the Church of the Center"

(116-20). Niebuhr associates all but the Christ-of-culture type with passages from the New Testament, and he outlines each with reference to classical and modern representatives.[3] This procedure supports his claim that the answers are indeed typical—most in meaningful continuity with scripture and none simply the isolated product of unrepeatable circumstances. So, for example, Niebuhr says that those who insist on fundamental opposition between loyalty to God-in-Christ and commitments to the many causes of culture find scriptural support in 1 John 2:15. ("Do not love the world or the things of the world. If anyone loves the world, love for the Father is not in him.") Classically, this stance is represented by Tertullian and some monastic movements. Leo Tolstoy articulates it during the nineteenth century, while Mennonites and some other groups traditionally tend to view the relation of Christ and culture in this way.

Less frequently noted is the fact that Niebuhr examines the inner logic of each type with reference to four theological relations, points, or questions.[4] The relation between reason and revelation points to an epistemological question: What are the appropriate sources of insight for our vision of God, the world, and ourselves, or for Christian theology and ethics? The question of God and world or, if one prefers, the Trinitarian question, may be stated as follows: How does the God who creates and redeems relate to the world as both nature and history? The relation of sin and goodness raises the question of corruption and the human fault: How does sin affect human capacities, communities, and institutions? Finally, the relation of law and grace or law and gospel points to the question of moral guidance; what sorts of moral norms cohere with or come from our knowledge of God and ourselves in Jesus Christ?

If this is correct, then each of Niebuhr's five types may be regarded as a characteristic or patterned resolution of these four theological questions, and chapters two through six present a typology of options or stances in moral theology.[5] Now for a cannon-ball tour.

The Radical or Extreme Positions

For "against culture" Christians who affirm Christ's sole authority and reject culture's claims to loyalty, the moral life must be considered against the background of a primary question. "Will we remain loyal to Christ or will we compromise with culture's many commitments and thus fall away?" Revelation in Jesus Christ is taken to be the sole valid source of insight in theology and ethics. It furnishes the exclusive standard for conduct, as well as for judging the insights proffered by corrupted cultural sources, such as philosophy and literature. With respect to moral guidance, Niebuhr says that radical Christians tend to emphasize Jesus as the teacher of the new and only valid moral law more than as the bringer of free grace and forgiveness. Again, sin is believed to infect all dimensions of culture. It has the epistemological effect of skewing virtually all cultural reasoning and insight as sources of knowledge of God and true norms and values. But its corruption does not prevent those within the holy community from both apprehending and pursuing the genuine righteousness revealed in Jesus Christ. Finally, with respect to God and world, radical Christians maintain that God created the world as nature, but that fallen culture has corrupted nature and entirely obscured it. The world as culture, then, is almost entirely unreflective of God's good purposes. God's redeeming activity in the world is largely hidden, and it is not mediated through institutions and practices upheld by the wider culture. Indeed, proponents of the "against culture" stance often look for a dramatic eschatological reversal of history and its directions that is forecast only in Jesus Christ.

These resolutions of the four theological relations interact in order to support a coherent Christian stance in the world. For example, the contention that sin and its deleterious effects reside mostly in the wider culture rather than in the church coheres with the ideas that cultural reasoning does not furnish valid sources of insight about moral norms, and that the church can be a disciplined holy community that lives according to the new and true law of Christ. Niebuhr criticizes the "against culture" stance for being unable to formulate a rule for Christian living without recourse to cultural reasoning, supporting a less than universal understanding of sin that largely exempts the holy community from its effects, upholding a portrait of Jesus as a lawgiver that inadequately expresses Gospel grace and forgiveness, and finding it difficult to relate the concentration on Christ's Lordship and the authority of his law to the purposes of the power who governs nature and presides over the histories of societies and institutions (76-82).

Representatives of the Christ-of-culture type tend to interpret Christ as the fulfiller of their society's finest ideals, noblest institutions, and best philosophy (83-84, 103). Revelation in Jesus Christ and the best cultural reasoning are taken as harmonious sources of insight for theology and ethics. Indeed, for thinkers such as Immanuel Kant and Thomas Jefferson, the best reasoning is able to distinguish true revelation from the morass of myth and custom with which it has become entangled. Christ is looked upon primarily as the bringer of a new law or ethical standard that accords with the best moral norms, commitments, and values upheld by culture. Sin tends to be located primarily in nonpersonal but reformable aspects of human nature, e.g., lusts and animal drives, and in evil or bad institutions which aid and abet or at least do not reform them, while the best reasoning remains largely exempt from sin's effects, as do the best cultural movements and institutions. Finally, the world as nature is looked upon as ethically neutral and irrational, while God's governing and redeeming purposes are closely associated with the best tendencies and aspects of culture as they attempt to reform and redirect both human nature and the natural environment.

These resolutions of the theological questions also support a coherent Christian stance in the world; for example, the contention that sin resides mostly in brutish but reformable aspects of human nature accords with a confidence that reasonable moral norms and institutions will bring about a good life. For Niebuhr, "culture Christians" fail to recognize the true greatness and strangeness of Jesus in the New Testament (109, 120). They collapse revelation and reason so as not to do justice to the superrational element or surd that enters in Jesus Christ, exempt the highest expressions of human spirit from sin's deleterious effects, de-emphasize grace and rely on human effort to fulfill the law and achieve human destiny. Again, Niebuhr claims that "culture Christians" identify Jesus with the immanent divine Spirit active in persons and societies. In consequence, they envision redemption as little more than the progressive completion of the best tendencies already at work in culture, and find it difficult to relate the redeeming purposes of Jesus and the Spirit to the Creator of (morally brutish) nature (110-15).

The Church of the Center

"The church of the center," which Niebuhr calls "the great majority movement in Christianity" is marked by agreement on the Trinitarian point that Jesus Christ, or the principle of redemption, is the Son of God, the Father Almighty who created heaven and earth.[6] Centrists therefore believe that the world as culture is not godless, and that Christ the redeemer cannot be simply opposed to it. They also believe that divine purposes are at work in the world as nature (both human and otherwise), and so that nature ought not be regarded as merely negative or inert stuff to be re-shaped by human activity under the influence of God's redeeming Spirit. Centrists agree, too, that sin is both radical and universal; sin infects every dimension of the human personality or spirit, and no person, community, or institution (including the church) is exempted from its effects. They also maintain that, in Jesus Christ, grace and forgiveness are primary, but that law and works of obedience also are necessary. Within this field of agreement, however, there are significant nuances.[7]

Representatives of the Christ-above-culture stance, such as Clement of Alexandria and Thomas Aquinas, try to synthesize redemption with the best in culture without implying a simple harmony or equivalence. With respect to God and world, then, synthesists affirm that nature and culture reflect the single purpose of God the creator and redeemer, but that God's redeeming purpose (for eternal life, or the kingdom, or both) goes far beyond culture's best tendencies and achievements. Similarly, God guides human reasoning along a straight path so that it may identify important truths and moral norms. But, while revelation in Jesus Christ overlaps with and confirms the best reasoning, it also discloses truths and norms that the best reasoning cannot make known. Aquinas' "Treatise on Law" in his *Summa Theologiae*, which distinguishes natural law, positive or civil law, and revealed law, illustrates this same pattern with respect to the question of moral guidance. All forms of law, says Aquinas, have their source in God. By reasoning, people may identify principles of natural law, such as equity or justice, which accord with God's ordering of nature, and on this basis, they may devise more specific, positive rules and civil laws. Revealed law does not contradict good civil law and valid interpretations of natural law, but it goes beyond them in order to direct human life toward its true supernatural end. Niebuhr illustrates.

"Thou shalt not steal" is a command found by both reason and in revelation; "Sell all that thou hast and give to the poor" is found in the divine law only. It applies to man as one who has a virtue implanted in him beyond the virtue of honesty, and who has been directed in hope toward a perfection beyond justice in this mortal existence (135-36).

Niebuhr says that efforts to join Christ and culture, God's work and the works of humans, the eternal and the temporal into a single synthesis have the effect of absolutizing what is relative. Thus, with respect to reasoning about moral norms, the charge is sometimes made that synthesists too easily identify a particular cultural interpretation of the order of nature with God's purposes and requirements, e.g., thirteenth century hierarchical under-standings of political order, Aristotelian understandings of human sexuality. Behind this criticism stands another. Does the confidence that we can accurately identify the natural law mean that sin is less than radical because the best reasoning is largely exempted from its effects?

The Christ-and-culture-in-paradox stance tries to hold together in tension loyalty to Christ and responsibility in culture. Conflict and even duality between the righteousness of God and human righteousness becomes a fundamental issue of religious life, as can be seen in the interplay between sin, good, law, and grace. For example, Martin Luther believes that people are involved in overt rebellion against God's rule. He maintains that, in its civil use, the law curbs and restrains the sinful tendencies of people. In its theological or accusatory use, the law convicts us of our sin so that we may throw ourselves on the mercy of gospel forgiveness (grace alone). The gospel (or strange righteousness of God) is thus for Luther the end of the law with respect to our (spiritual) relation to God, but in its civil use, the law continues to order life in the temporal and social realm. With respect to the epistemological question, dualist Christians understand reason and philosophy to have their legitimate uses in the temporal and cultural realm. But reason is blind in matters having to do with our spiritual relation to

God—there the (ethically irrational) revelation of gospel forgiveness holds sway.

Niebuhr claims that, with respect to God and world, paradoxical estimates of the purposes of God as creator and governor seem perilously close to being at odds with the purposes of God as redeemer. That is, there seems to be minimal continuity between God's rule in the temporal realm, focused as it is on restraining evil, and God's redeeming purpose expressed in free grace and forgiveness. This, in turn, relates to paradoxical estimates of sin. There is a tendency, Niebuhr thinks, for dualists to join temporality and finitude with sin, so that human nature and the world cannot be turned toward good; they can only be restrained from further evil. Moreover, an overly conservative social ethic "is a logical consequence of the tendency to think of law, state, and other institutions as restraining forces, dykes against sin, preventers of anarchy, rather than as positive agencies through which men in social union render positive service to neighbors advancing toward true life" (188).

The Christ-the-transformer-of-culture type emphasizes the sovereign reign of the creator who is also the God of grace. Like the writer of John's Gospel, says Niebuhr, conversionists are fond of the conviction that all things are made and ordered through the redemptive principle (192, 197-99). They believe that, in our mundane interactions in both nature and history we respond to the creative, ordering, and redeeming work of God. Conversionists look upon sin as a radical and universal corruption which subjects all persons, groups, and institutions to God's judgment. As such, however, sin is not an expression of finite human nature, but (in Augustinian fashion) a corruption of good, created human nature. Moreover, like humanity, culture is a corrupted good. "The problem of culture is therefore the problem of its conversion, not of its replacement by a new creation; though the conversion is so radical that it amounts to a kind of rebirth" (194). Our capacity for practical reasoning about values and actions is corrupted by wrong loves and devotions, so that it is inordinately partial to narrow interests, but faith's conversion of our loves and interests may reorder many of our lines of reasoning. Finally, although conversionists refer to Jesus Christ more as redeemer than as lawgiver, they also insist that moral law and norms accompany the gospel of forgiveness. They tend to believe, too, that laws, social practices, and institutions not only restrain wickedness but also pursue good. Together with the conviction that, in addition to God's ordering and judging activity, God's redeeming activity is also present in history, this supports a more hopeful attitude toward culture, its institutions, and our participation in them than is present among dualists. Niebuhr believes that this more hopeful attitude comes to expression in John Calvin's dynamic conception of the vocations and callings of Christians in the world, as well as in F. D. Maurice's religious socialism (217, 221-23).

Estimating Niebuhr's Accomplishment

Many have observed, as I myself did some twenty years ago, that Niebuhr's presentation in *Christ and Culture* is not neutral.[8] His bias comes through in the fact that, while he criticizes theologians such as Augustine and Calvin for departing from the transformationist pattern, he offers no criticism of the inherent theo-logic of the type itself (215-18). Moreover, all of the criticisms that Niebuhr offers of the other types can be made from a conversionist viewpoint, e.g., that radical and cultural stances tend toward legalism, that the "above culture" stance holds a less than radical doctrine of sin, and that a too-close association of sin with human nature contributes to a disjunctive view of God's creating and redeeming activities among dualists.[9]

But is complete neutrality what we really want? At least as early as his contributions to *The Church Against the World* in 1935, Niebuhr believed that our theological stances reflect passionate devotions, and that there is no neutral point from which to analyze moral theologies.[10] A more interesting question is whether *Christ and Culture* is so viciously biased that its categories can only be used to recommend a transformationist stance. Although people may come to different conclusions, let me propose an initial test. Can we imagine something like Niebuhr's book, with its theological points concerning reason and revelation, God and world, sin and goodness, and law and gospel, written from the perspective of a stance other than the transformationist one? (If we can, then its primary categories may be used to interpret moral theologies from another vantage point, and this counts against vicious bias.)

Speaking for myself, I do not find this especially difficult. For example, an "against culture" book would criticize the conversionist stance for being too confident in sources of insight other than revelation in Jesus Christ, underestimating sin's grip on culture's principalities and powers, construing grace and atonement in Jesus Christ in a manner that fails to take seriously his moral teaching and example, and failing to appreciate the importance for God's redeeming purpose of a radical eschatological reversal of history's dominant tendencies. Behind these criticisms will be something like John Howard Yoder's rejection of Niebuhr's tolerance for a legitimate plurality of Christian moral theologies.[11] The larger complaint will be that, like the other types, the transformationist stance finally compromises too much with culture's many commitments and so falls away from genuine witness and discipleship. It is also likely that an "against culture" presentation, would rename Niebuhr's "church of the center" something like "the Constantinian settlement" or "the Constantinian church."

Another test of Niebuhr's accomplishment is whether we can make fruitful use of his scheme to illumine more recent texts. Since I have been doing just this on and off in courses for about twenty-five years, my answer is bound to be yes. But humor me by considering Gustavo Gutierrez's classic, *A Theology of Liberation*. Part of Gutierrez's aim in this book is to connect loyalty to Christ with a commitment to the poor and robust participation in movements for liberation in Latin America. Particularly in the original edition, he makes use of cultural reasoning in the form of a preferred (more or less Marxist) social analysis, as well as the experiences of the best socio-political movements. Insights drawn from these sources having to do with the current situation, the work of liberation, and the creation of a new society harmonize with leading themes of revelation, e.g., God as liberator in the Exodus. Gutierrez maintains that sin as alienation and the breach of communion among people and God has deleterious consequences for persons and societies, but these do not include the radical corruption of the best social analyses and culture's best (liberating) movements. The relation of law and gospel is complicated by Gutierrez's claim that the work of Christ in liberating people from sin's breach of communion has a religious depth that cannot be equated with its political implications, as well as by his recognition that, for Jesus, "the Kingdom was, in the first place, a gift."[12] By and large, however, Gutierrez portrays Jesus Christ, not as the bringer of gospel forgiveness to sinners, but as one who embodies and announces a new (and normative) humanity. With respect to God and world, Gutierrez focuses on the relation between salvation or redemption and the process of human liberation in history.[13] "The God of the Exodus is the God of history and of political liberation more than the God of nature."[14]

These resolutions of Niebuhr's four theological questions interact to support revolutionary movements for social reform. From the perspective of a conversionist stance, perhaps the first issue to be raised about Gutierrez's project will be a Trinitarian one concerning the comparatively distant relation between the God of liberation and nature, as well as the very close association of God's redeeming activity with the best (liberating) historical and cultural movements. The classificatory question will be whether Gutierrez's theology more nearly represents an "of culture" or an "above culture" stance and, on balance, I expect that his understanding of God, nature, history, and culture tilt toward the "of culture" position. But mere classification is of little consequence. The critical issue is whether a Niebuhrian analysis helps us to understand Gutierrez's book, to compare it with other moral theologies, and to move toward our own constructive determinations. I think it does.

However, this does not mean that Niebuhr's book lies beyond important criticisms and emendations. Some concern the accuracy of his treatment of certain thinkers and groups. It may be argued, for example, that his associations of Friedrich Schleiermacher and Walter Rauschenbusch with cultural Christianity indicate a less than full engagement with their positions.[15] John Howard Yoder's complaints about Niebuhr's "against culture" type raise a number of questions. Does Niebuhr misclassify certain persons and movements as belonging to this type, e.g., Tertullian, medieval monks, Mennonites, Leo Tolstoy? Does he overstate the tendency toward "withdrawals from and rejections of the institutions of society" among radical Christians and miss the broader significance of their nonconformity? Does he wrongly assume that radical Christians must simply reject all cultural values and institutions?

I think these last two questions indicate that a Niebuhrian analysis of moral theologies will benefit from a more explicit consideration of the relationship between church and world.[16] I would put the question this way. "How does the community and institution of those who self-consciously acknowledge and are loyal to God-in-Christ relate to those communities and institutions that apparently do not and are not?" Cultural Christians appear to blur the lines between church and society. This is largely because they believe that the "true" church is made up of persons and groups who are committed to the new humanity represented by Jesus Christ as well as by the best cultural achievements. Quite naturally, then, cultural Christianity will be most at home when it tries to advance God's redemptive purpose in history (say the kingdom or cooperative commonwealth) by aligning the "true" church with selected broader social movements and commitments. However, the "flip side" of such alignments will be a rejection of and opposition to those elements in culture and society that are judged to impede needed reforms (say, the entrenched commercial-industrial proponents of laissez faire capitalism).[17] By contrast, I believe that "against culture" Christians draw rather sharp distinctions between the community of radical disciples and the world's fallen principalities and powers. They regard the church or holy community as the one true polity or faithful community whose life and practices stand as an alternative to the dominant society. But, again, this need not mean that radicals shun all cooperative associations and coalitions with others as they pursue specific objectives, e.g., reductions of armaments, medical assistance to those in need, a more humane organization of commerce and industry.[18] It means only that, for radicals, such coalitions constitute piece-meal and temporary strategies that remain secondary to the holy community's essentially nonconformist and alternative witness to the Lordship of Jesus Christ.

When we turn to Niebuhr's "church of the center" types, it seems clear that synthesists favor inviting the world into an established church and then clarifying, strengthening, and relativizing society's best ends by disclosing the supernatural end of redemption and sacramentally dispensing the medicine of grace. That is, the Christ-above-culture type will tend to approximate the parish life of medieval Catholicism. Here, as also with the church–world relation among dualists and conversionists, one may profitably look for more explicit help in Ernst Troeltsch's remarks about medieval Catholicism, Lutheranism, and Calvinism in his *Social Teaching of the Christian Churches*, as well as to Niebuhr's own ruminations about denominations. My point here is simply that the extension of Niebuhr's analysis to the relation of church and world is eminently "doable."

How, then, shall we estimate Niebuhr's accomplishment in the classic text that he published some fifty years ago? Well, the book is not without its flaws, and probably even the most thoroughly H. Richard Niebuhrian among us will want to enter some emendations and revisions. But, all in all, *Christ and Culture* is still worth reading because the categories that it presents for analyzing moral theologies remain unsurpassed in their richness, usefulness, and suggestiveness.

NOTES

[1] By the time he wrote, Niebuhr had been occupied for years with faith as a dynamic factor in human life, as well as with the relationship between faith in God and values. See *The Church Against the World* (Chicago: Willett, Clark and Company, 1935), 127-49; *The Kingdom of God in America* (New York: Harper, 1937), 1-15; "Value Theory and Theology," in *The Nature of Religious Experience: Essays in Honor of Douglas Clyde Macintosh,* ed. by Julius Seelye Bixler, Robert Lowry Calhoun, and H. Richard Niebuhr (New York: Harper, 1937), 93-116; *The Meaning of Revelation* (New York: Macmillan Company, 1941), 128-39; "Faith in Gods and in God" in *Radical Monotheism and Western Culture with Supplementary Essays* (New York: Harper, 1960), 114-26 but first published as "The Nature and Existence of God" in *Motive* (December 1943). These same themes continued to draw his attention after he wrote CC, as is apparent from *Radical Monotheism and Western Culture* and the posthumously published *Faith on Earth* (New Haven: Yale University Press, 1989), 1.

[2] Niebuhr, *Radical Monotheism and Western Culture,* 42.

[3] Niebuhr refers to early non-canonical "of-culture" groups, including "the Judaizers" with whom Paul was in conflict (83), and he questions whether it is possible to formulate an "above culture" or synthetic answer in the modern period (*Christ and Culture*, 138-41, 146-47).

[4] See CC, 11, 76-81, 110-14, 117-19, 142-43, 150-59, 190-96, although he nowhere lists them in mechanical fashion.

[5] It follows, too, that the (disappointed) expectation that CC will furnish detailed studies of moral cases or even extended reflections about moral principles is simply misplaced. See, for example, contributions by John Howard Yoder and Glen H. Stassen in *Authentic Transformation: A New Vision of Christ and Culture* (Nashville: Abingdon, 1996), 42, 142-47.

[6] CC, 117. Niebuhr's understanding of this Trinitarian agreement foreshadows his later account of how religious people who affirm a radical monotheism identify "the Creator and the God of grace." See Niebuhr, *Radical Monotheism and Western Culture,* 32-33.

[7] The close relationship between the stances associated with the church of the center is part of the reason why Niebuhr sometimes speaks of dualist and transformationist motifs (159, 190). John Howard Yoder appeared to regard this as a weakness and he pointed out that, unlike a type, a motif is a theme or an accent which, without inconsistency, may stand beside other motifs. Glen Harold Stassen, D. M. Yeager, and John Howard Yoder, *Authentic Transformation: A New Vision of Christ and Culture* (Nashville: Abingdon Press, 1996), 45. I think it may be worth considering whether chapters 4, 5, and 6 of CC actually present motifs within a broad median type of Christianity.

[8] Douglas F. Ottati, *Meaning and Method in H. Richard Niebuhr's Theology* (Washington, DC: University Press of America, 1982), 121. Paul Ramsey noted Niebuhr's preference in his essay on "The Transformation of Ethics" in *Faith and Ethics: The Theology of H. Richard Niebuhr,* ed. by Paul Ramsey (New York: Harper & Row, 1957), 140-72.

---

[9] The conversionist type also best accords with Niebuhr's position in other writings both before and after the publication of CC. We are therefore hardly surprised to find, as John Howard Yoder reported, that readers of CC often associate themselves with the transformationist pattern. See *Authentic Transformation*, 52-53. Still, there are reasons why even someone as sympathetic to Niebuhr's theology as I am, might hesitate before adopting an entirely consistent conversionist stance. For one thing, while Niebuhr clearly appreciated the theology of F. D. Maurice, whom he called "the most consistent of conversionists" (CC, 224), his other works indicate that he generally found Augustine and Jonathan Edwards (inconsistent conversionists at best) even more illuminating. Also, as Niebuhr himself notes, the types are fluid and one could multiply types, subtypes, motifs, and countermotifs (CC, 231). Again, the press of specific issues may lead us to resolutions that reflect theologies other than the one we think we prefer (in the abstract). Along these lines, Niebuhr's claim that Roger Williams' rejection of Anglican and Puritan attempts to unite politics and the gospel is dualist has always given me pause, as has his intimation that his brother's Christian realism expresses a paradoxical pattern (CC, 183-84).

[10] Niebuhr, *The Church Against the World*, 149. See also H. Richard Niebuhr, "Man the Sinner," *The Journal of Religion* 15 (July 1935): 279. I should add that if Niebuhr meant to feign neutrality in CC, he did a particularly bad job of covering his tracks. John Howard Yoder's contention that Niebuhr transforms the field of ethics from a normative to a descriptive science strikes me as entirely fanciful. See *Authentic Transformation*, 41.

[11] See, for example, the paper by D. M. Yeager in this volume. In fact, the criticisms listed in the previous sentence track some of Yoder's arguments as well as his complaints about "mainstream ethics" rather closely. See John Howard Yoder, *The Politics of Jesus: Vicit Agnus Noster*, 2nd ed. (Grand Rapids, MI: Eerdmans Publishing Company, 1994), 8-11, 19-20, 140-158, 193-210, 213-14, 226.

[12] Gutierrez, *A Theology of Liberation*, 15th anniversary ed., trans. Sister Carrdad Inda and John Eagleson (Maryknoll, NY: Orbis Books, 1988), 32. This is why it is unfair to say that Gutierrrez reduces Jesus to a political figure (a characterization that Gutierrez explicitly denies on 130-34), and why it is also untrue to say that, for Gutierrez, God's kingdom comes simply as the result of human striving.

[13] Gutierrez, *A Theology of Liberation*, 83.

[14] Ibid., 89.

[15] Niebuhr's comments about Rauschenbusch in *The Kingdom of God in America* (New York: Harper & Row, 1959), 194 are more satisfactory, although I doubt whether he ever fully appreciated the sophistication of Rauschenbusch's reflections about human nature, grace, and agency. See Harlan Beckley, *Passion for Justice: Retrieving the Legacies of Walter Rauschenbusch, John A. Ryan, and Reinhold Niebuhr* (Louisville: Westminster John Knox Press, 1992), 72-74.

[16] Jon Diefenthaler notes that this relationship occupied Niebuhr throughout his career, and he also assumes that the relation of church and world is what Niebuhr's types in CC are really about. I agree that the church - world relation often occupied Niebuhr's attention, but I think it is a mistake to reduce the Christ and culture problem to this relation or to any of the other four. See *H. Richard Niebuhr: A Lifetime of Reflections on the Church and the World* (Macon, GA: Mercer University Press, 1986), 65-66.

[17] It is also apparent from Niebuhr's inclusion of fundamentalists in this type that not all cultural Christians select "progressive" elements as representative of the best in culture. Thus, an updated account might include figures such as Jerry Falwell and Pat Robertson who tend to align the church with the right wing of the Republican Party and against "secular humanism."

[18] Niebuhr himself recognized that some radical Christians entered into alliances with other Christian socialists during the nineteenth century (CC, 229).

It Is Time to Take Jesus Back:
In Celebration of the Fiftieth Anniversary of
H. Richard Niebuhr's *Christ and Culture*

Glen H. Stassen

Abstract

In *The Kingdom of God in America*, H. Richard Niebuhr argued that three dimensions are crucial for transformative faith: the sovereignty of God over all; the independence of the living God from captivity to human ideologies or institutions; and a revolutionary strategy with particular normative content from God's self-revelation in Jesus Christ. Without the historically particular content of the way of Jesus, Christian faith has a vacuum only too eagerly filled by alien ideologies. Hence Niebuhr begins *Christ and Culture* with a historically particular and concrete understanding of the way of Jesus Christ, and evaluates the five types with this three-dimensional standard. The puzzle is that the farther the book goes, the thinner Jesus becomes, until the concluding chapter backs off from evaluation. Niebuhr moved back to his more Christocentric ethics before he died, and thus recovered his prophetic edge. To learn from Niebuhr's history and teach a transformative faith not accommodated to ideologies of injustice, ethics needs to recover a thicker Jesus. Helpful resources are emerging from which Christian ethicists can draw rich help: the third quest of the historical Jesus, new exegetical and canonical approaches, the new emphasis on normative practices, historically situated narrative ethics, and some models by Christian ethicists, all of which point to a thicker, richer, historically particular way of Jesus in the prophetic tradition of Israel.

Journal of the Society of Christian Ethics, 23/1 (2003): 133-143

A Transformative Christian Ethic
Needs a Historically Prophetic Jesus

H. Richard Niebuhr's mentor was Ernst Troeltsch. He had other mentors also: MacIntosh, Barth, Bergson, Whitehead, Tillich, Edwards, Mead, and some analysts of language and symbol.[1] But Ernst Troeltsch was very clearly influential especially in *Christ and Culture*. Troeltsch wrote a fine little book, *Die Bedeutung der Geschichtlichkeit Jesu für den Glauben*, or *The Significance of the Historicity of Jesus for the Faith*. There Troeltsch announced the rule he gleaned from the study of the history of religions: a strong religion needs to be centered in worship that pivots around a historical figure—Jews have Moses, Muslims have Muhammad, Buddhists have Buddha, and Christians have Jesus.[2] You cannot build a strong religion around merely an idea, a principle, or a philosophy; you need the central figure. Furthermore, in our time of historical relativism and historical consciousness, or we would say, postmodern awareness, that central figure needs to be rooted in history, so study of the historical Jesus is important. A strong Christian faith needs to be centered in Jesus and rooted in particular history.

It is significant that H. Richard Niebuhr's most influential book focuses on Jesus Christ—and culture. *Christ and Culture* far outsells *The Responsible Self*—itself a fine book—or *Radical Monotheism*. Similarly, Dietrich Bonhoeffer's *Cost of Discipleship*, focusing on the way of Jesus Christ, outsells all his other books. Thomas á Kempis' *Imitation of Christ* and Ignatius Loyola's *Spiritual Exercises* have sold millions of copies. John Howard Yoder's *Politics of Jesus* has far outsold his other books. In terms of book sales, at least, Troeltsch is right about Christian faith and Jesus.

For Christian ethics, a focus on Jesus Christ needs to be related to a particular critical perspective or issue or both, just as Troeltsch was arguing that the focus on Jesus needs to pay attention to the critical question of the historicity of Jesus, and just as Troeltsch's overall work wrestled with the critical question of historical relativism. Thus, *The Meaning of Revelation* combines the constructive work of Karl Barth with the critical perspective of Ernst Troeltsch, and *Christ and Culture* focuses on the critical question of how we are to relate loyalty to the way of Jesus to responsibility in our culture.

My argument is that a historically particular Christocentric emphasis was essential to H. Richard Niebuhr's ethics, and that understanding this will enable us—later in the essay—to understand two peculiarities that have puzzled many about his classic, *Christ and Culture*. Although some know Niebuhr mostly for his lean against Christocentrism in *Radical Monotheism* during the 1950s, the logic of his life work points to a theocentric ethic with essential emphasis on the disclosure of God in the historically particular

Jesus Christ. His life work was Trinitarian; disclosure in the historically particular Jesus is crucial if the three-legged stool is to stand. But a temporary weakening of that leg of the stool had begun during the process of writing *Christ and Culture*. In that we see a critically important lesson for Christian ethics in our time. Niebuhr saw history as the laboratory in which faith is tested, and his own history is a parable for Christian ethics now.

Niebuhr's original trajectory was shaped by his own adoption of Troeltsch's struggle with historical relativism. In this, Niebuhr was our precursor, our pioneer, in facing the reality of postmodernity. He argued that we are in history as a fish is in water, and we can know only what we see in and through our history.[3] Therefore, as Niebuhr argued in *The Meaning of Revelation*, we must understand God's self-disclosure as happening not in a thin, allegedly universal truth, but in particular history. Jesus Christ is our Rosetta stone: We could not know how to trace God's working in all the world's happenings if God were not made "known to us through the memory of Jesus Christ; nor do we know how we should be able to interpret all the words we read as words of God save by the aid of this Rosetta stone."[4] Niebuhr's acceptance of the limits of our historicity logically entailed his focus on historically particular revelation.

Furthermore, Niebuhr's search for the kind of faith that would not simply accommodate to social forces and unjust interests, but would be transformationist and prophetic, led him to his study in *The Kingdom of God in America* of those periods in U.S. history when faith was transformationist: the early Puritan period, the Great Awakening, and the Social Gospel (and had he written the book later, he surely would have included the civil rights movement). In these periods he saw that three dimensions of faith were crucial: the sovereignty of God over all; the independence of the living God from captivity to human ideologies or institutions; and a revolutionary strategy or constitution with some particular normative content from God's self-revelation in Jesus Christ.[5] He concluded the book with these words, "there was no way toward the coming kingdom save the way taken by a sovereign God through the reign of Jesus Christ." As Troeltsch argued that a strong Christianity needs the central figure of Jesus, with some historical particularity and actuality, Niebuhr found that a faith that does not simply accommodate to culture but has transformative impact needs the self-disclosure of God's character and way of working in Jesus Christ. A transformative faith has to stand for something particular; that something has to be God, as particularly revealed. His own "tower experience" of the sovereignty of God had the same trinitarian logic: "the answer to our question what must be done in order that we may be saved . . . directs us to Jesus Christ," not as an example of religious ideals, but as the disclosure of the "I am that I am," where we see "the enemy and the judge of our sin as our redeemer."[6] Furthermore, his ethics of response to God in all actions gets its basic content from the character of God's action—for which the revelation of God's action is critical.

Hence in *Christ and Culture*, Niebuhr begins by defining a Christian as one who belongs to that community for which "Jesus Christ—his life, words, deeds, and destiny—is of supreme importance as the key to the understanding of themselves and their world, the main source of the knowledge of God and man, good and evil, the constant companion of the conscience, and the expected deliverer from evil."[7] He admits there is a great variety of perspectives on Jesus Christ. Nevertheless,

> this variety in Christianity cannot obscure the fundamental unity which is supplied by the fact that . . . Jesus Christ . . . is a definite character and person whose teachings, actions, and sufferings are of one piece. The fact remains that the Christ who exercises authority over Christians or whom Christians accept as authority is the Jesus Christ of the New Testament; and that this is a person with definite teachings, a definite character, and a definite fate. . . . There always remain the original portraits with which all later pictures may be compared and by which all caricatures may be corrected. And in these original portraits he is recognizably one and the same.[8]

He sharply criticizes Bultmann's interpretation of Jesus because it lacks concrete content. "Bultmann can find no real content in the gospel idea of obedience. . . . Moreover, although God is mentioned as the one whose will is to be obeyed, the idea of God ascribed to Jesus is as empty and formal as the idea of obedience." By contrast, Jesus "knows that the will of God is the will of the Creator and Governor of all nature and of all history; that there is structure and content in His will; that He is the author of the ten commandments; that He demands mercy and not sacrifice; that He requires not only obedience to Himself but love and faith in Him, and love of the neighbor whom He creates and loves."[9] Similarly, Niebuhr writes in *Faith on Earth* that in spite of his existentialist effort "to disjoin faith from beliefs about history, nature, and the ethical life . . . Bultmann is unable to separate such faith completely from beliefs in the historical actuality of Jesus Christ, as presented in the New Testament."[10]

Solving the Puzzle of *Christ and Culture*

Christ and Culture proceeds by assessing the five types by the standard of the same trinitarian norms that we saw in Niebuhr's historical study of the kind of faith that is transformative rather than accommodationist, and in his tower experience: God is Creator of heaven and all the earth; God is the living God who cannot be possessed by human persons or communities; and

God is known in Jesus Christ as God-in-Christ and Christ-in-God.[11] Measured by these three tests, the churches of the center do better than the radicals and the accommodationists, and the transformationist type passes all three tests. Yet the puzzle is that the concluding chapter of *Christ and Culture* seems to back off from any comparative assessment, and is "unconcluded and inconclusive."[12] Niebuhr leaves it as a free decision of each believer, without guidance, in the concluding chapter.[13] On the one hand, there is an admirable humility in this openness. Nonetheless, the tone and content of the argument in the concluding chapter is strangely different from the careful assessment and trinitarian evaluation in the body of the book. In spite of Niebuhr's clear affirmation of the normativeness of the specific Jesus of the New Testament in the first chapter of *Christ and Culture*, and his clearly judging the adequacy of the first types that he describes on the basis of their accuracy in representing the way of Jesus Christ, the farther he goes in the book, the less the way of Jesus functions as measure of the types. By the time we get to transformationism, Jesus Christ provides no specific norms for the transformation we are committed to, no specific criteria for distinguishing between those aspects of the culture that must be rejected, or can be affirmed, or are ripe candidates for being transformed—and which direction they should be transformed toward. The danger is that many readers will be convinced that they are transformationists without standing for anything in particular. How is this apparent shift from the normativeness of the way of Jesus Christ to seeming equanimity about the types to be explained?

Niebuhr himself has provided a major part of the explanation. In the 1950s, he intentionally leaned against Barth's Christocentrism and adopted the perspective of *Radical Monotheism*, as a corrective.[14] Furthermore, the shape that his correction of Barth took was influenced by a remaining Kantian residue in spite of Niebuhr's rejection of Kant, as well as by a personal struggle with the omnipotence of God in the midst of the historically particular reality of tragic evil.[15] His theological ethics entered the phase of radical monotheism, with an abstractness that does not fit what he found in his historical research on the nature of prophetic, transformative faith. The consequence was that his own prophetic ethics lost much of its specificity, its strength, its sting. One can see this by examining his writings on peace and war. In the previous decades, he had written strongly, pertinently, and prophetically on nationalism, World War II, racism, and obliteration bombing, and the need for a reconciling rather than self-righteous policy toward Germany and Japan after the war. But in the 1950s, the era of anti-communism and Joseph McCarthy, the Cold War, the Korean War, and the struggle for arms control and a nuclear test ban, as well as the shaping of U.S. policies toward previously colonial nations, he was surprisingly silent on all these questions. His theological language became much more abstract, and in one essay God seemed equally distant from all ethical values. Elizabeth Bounds has written, "Especially in his later writings, the particular historical community became more and more abstract until it seemed to disappear behind a 'universal society and a universal generalized other, nature and nature's God.'"[16] My thesis is that while he was writing *Christ and Culture*, Niebuhr was in the process of making this shift. After he turned in the manuscript, the publisher urged him to add a concluding chapter. But by then he had made the shift. The shift in tone and evaluative perspective in *Christ and Culture* that many have observed enables us to date that shift.

Niebuhr himself was dissatisfied with the result. In the early 1960s, just before his death, he had returned to a more specific focus on Christ, in a way that redefined his faith in the sovereignty of God so that God was not the determiner of all that is, but the One whose will must be distinguished from the evil that is seen in much that happens. The story of Joseph in *Genesis*, the prophetic passage of *Isaiah* 10, with its distinction between what the Assyrians intend and God intends, and the confrontation between Jesus and Pilate, with its distinction between Pilate's power and God's, become highly symbolic of a pivotal turning in his thought. Jesus becomes the "symbolic form with the aid of which men tell each other what life and death, God and man, are *like*; but even more he is a form which they employ as an *a priori*, an image, a scheme or pattern in the mind which gives form and meaning to their experience."[17] He writes once again prophetically on the Cold War and the illusions of military power.[18] Niebuhr's turn away from a thick, particular Jesus thinned out his prophetic faith; his turn back to Jesus as the pattern brought back his prophetic edge. This is Niebuhr's lesson for us in the laboratory of history.

Troeltsch was right: It is our task to develop a historically particular, thick, content-full picture of the way of Jesus Christ in our ethics. We cannot build a strong religious ethic on the basis of a thin principle. We need a central figure with content.

A Thin Jesus Gets Co-opted

Another reason we need a thick description of Jesus is, as Troeltsch shows in *Social Teaching of the Christian Churches*, that history is replete with Jesus getting co-opted for the purposes of some secular ideology. Niebuhr made that point forcefully in *The Social Sources of Denominationalism*. Therefore, he began his search for a Christian faith that would not merely accommodate itself to the ideologies in the culture, but that would have a prophetic, transformative impact. In our time we are particularly aware that Jesus is being hijacked for use by authoritarian movements of the right. We need to take Jesus back. To do that, we need a Jesus who is not merely a thin, Giacometti figure, so lacking in flesh and historical particularity that he is easily accommodated to ideologies of greed, nationalism, militarism, authoritarianism, unilateralism, and empire, but is as thick and definite as we can let him be. The more we teach the Jewish-rooted, prophetic-rooted, historically particular, thick and rich way of Jesus Christ, the stronger our base for resisting the forces of accommodation and the more we are able to take Jesus back from his ideological hijackers.

The twenty-century history of the church offers us a powerful lesson: the forces of accommodation to a culture of greed, domination, violence, and exclusion work to reduce Jesus to a thin Jesus without prophetic content who is marginalized to an ever shrinking space. Accommodationists thus have free reign to pursue their interests without opposition from a marginalized and muzzled Jesus. Constance Benson makes this case sharply in her criticism of Ernst Troeltsch's thin and individualistic Jesus in her recent *God and Caesar: Troeltsch's Social Teaching as Legitimation.*[19] Howard Thurman made it in his classic, *Jesus and the Disinherited.*[20] It is the evasion and rejection of the message of Jesus that we see in those who sought to get rid of him by crucifying him, repeated in different ways throughout our history. Jesus becomes an object of veneration who is not allowed to speak in any concrete way—very much like idolatry.

We still live in the hangover from Christendom, when churches assumed the culture was Christian, so that all that was needed was to baptize those who had been nurtured by the culture and they would spontaneously do what is Christian. So evangelicals assume that the task is to convert people, Pentecostals assume the task is to be receptive to the power of the Spirit, spiritualists assume the task is to feel the presence of the divine, and liberals assume the task is to articulate a philosophical principle, and then the desire to be good, combined with the obvious meaning of goodness that we all know in the midst of our reasonable culture, will produce good Christians. Yet the culture is not Christian; it is good in parts, and it does have a sense of morality, but it is also imperialist, laced with unconscious racism, infiltrated by belief in the myth of redemptive violence, and driven by enormous concentration of wealth that works consistently to weaken or co-opt all possible critics. Unless we teach a thick and holistic ethic with articulate antibodies against those ideologies, Christians will be co-opted, hijacked, and flown off in untrue directions by the forces of accommodation.

New Resources for Recovery of a Thicker Jesus

We live after that watershed of witness to the truth in the midst of astounding co-optation, the Barmen Confession. Over against accommodationist Christianity, Barmen declared decisively that we have only one Lord, Jesus Christ, and Christ is Lord over all of life, not merely one realm.[21] Yet Karl Barth, the author of the Barmen Confession, left a hole for us to fill. He did not succeed in articulating the public meaning of the way of Jesus in a convincing way. He sought to deduce a Christocentric political ethic by a method of deductive analogy, deducing law-based political order from the doctrine of justification, social justice from the doctrine of redemption, individual liberties from the doctrine of grace and the Spirit, the equality of all citizens from baptism in one Spirit, freedom of the press from the doctrine of the free word of God. As Will Herberg rightly comments, Barth's conclusions were ethically right, but this method of deductive analogy is arbitrary and not in line with Barth's mature theology.[22] Barmen left the task of filling in the content and making the connections incomplete. The first step is to recover a thick Jesus, from below, inductively, based on Jesus' roots in the prophetic tradition. For this, we have new resources in our time from several different approaches. Christian ethics can become stronger, and more prophetic and transformationist, by focusing on any one of these approaches.

First, there is new richness from exegetical or canonical approaches, for example Richard Hays' work, *The Moral Vision of the New Testament*; Hays is now working on a new project that is likely to be greatly helpful, focusing on Jesus as rooted in Jewish prophetic tradition. Ched Myers, *Binding the Strong Man*, is wonderfully insightful, and influential. John Howard Yoder, *The Politics of Jesus,* is already a classic, and has been enormously influential for many of us.[23] I have been seeking to help us recover the Sermon on the Mount and the Sermon on the Plain for rich guidance.[24] Walter Wink has focused similarly and fruitfully on Matthew 5:38-42.[25]

Second, the enormous interest in the third quest of the historical Jesus is producing insights with strong ethical content. I judge the most helpful studies to be those that root Jesus in Jewish prophetic tradition rather than in a Hellenistic wandering cynic mode.[26]

Third, there is the approach of normative practices in the New Testament, rooted in Jesus and echoed in the rest of the New Testament. Yoder developed this in his *Body Politics*.[27] James Wm. McClendon, Jr., develops it in his *Ethics*.[28] Duane Friesen's development of normative New Testament practices provides Christ-centered, normative structure for his insightful and sensitive approach to questions of Christ and culture, in *Artists, Citizens, Philosophers: Seeking the Peace of the City*.[29] Perhaps this book deals the most directly, incisively, and concretely, with the questions on which Niebuhr focused in *Christ and Culture*. I commend it as especially helpful.

Fourth, there is the narrative approach of Allen Verhey's *Remembering Jesus*, working in a Reformed tradition as Niebuhr did, emphasizing the lordship of Christ for all spheres of life rather than a compartmentalizing inward emigration.[30] As Yoder's emphasis on the *lordship* of Christ over all of life, perhaps influenced by the Reformed Karl Barth, brought a corrective to some Anabaptist tendencies to limit Christ's lordship only to the church, Verhey's attention to the lordship of Jesus Christ, perhaps influenced by the Anabaptist John Yoder, brings corrective to patriarchal tendencies in some versions of Reformed tradition. His narrative approach fits Niebuhr's pioneering narrative emphasis, and his attention to the concrete, historical context of Jesus' narrative, and our particular historical context, produces more concrete guidance than do some narrative ethics.

Finally, four very nicely argued books model sophisticated ways to restore attention to Jesus' way combined with critical theory. Cynthia Moe-Lobeda's *Healing the Broken World: Globalization and God* perceptively diagnoses the disempowering force of the powers and authorities of economic globalization under the domination of transnational corporations, and argues in a Lutheran and Bonhoefferian vein for union with Christ as providing empowerment for moral and prophetic resistance, and guidance in that resistance.[31] Larry Rasmussen's Grawemeyer-award-winning *Earth Community Earth Ethics* works in a similar mode in ecological ethics.[32] In Lisa Sowle Cahill's nicely crafted *Sex, Gender, and Christian Ethics*, the longest and I think most important chapter in providing the guiding norms for her conclusions is chapter five on Jesus' ethics. She argues that Jesus' ethic of "solidarity with the poor and oppressed" should be understood "in very specific and concrete forms . . . and not leave the values of compassion and solidarity at an ineffective level of abstraction." She demonstrates that Jesus challenged Temple domination, with its practices of bodily purity as separation, and social status and exclusion, and instead advocated positive practices of invitation and inclusion, and challenged social hierarchy, in a way that is much more helpful than Aristotle.[33] William Spohn's *Go and Do Likewise: Jesus and Ethics* begins: "What does Jesus have to do with ethics? We discover in the particular story of this historical figure the one who is often obscured by the abstractions of Christology. . . . Recently, moral theologians are taking a similar turn ['from below,' beginning with the specific stories of the Gospels] to answer the question, 'What moral significance does Jesus have for Christians today?'" Spohn combines virtue ethics and spirituality with "a view in which Jesus plays a normative role as the concrete universal of Christian ethics."[34]

All this adds up to rich help for Christian ethicists to strengthen the prophetic Jesus side of their ethics, and to join in the move to take Jesus back from being hijacked by authoritarian and laissez-faire ideologies.

NOTES

[1] H. R. Niebuhr, *Theology, History, and Culture*, ed. William Stacy Johnson (New Haven and London: Yale, 1996), 21.

[2] It is translated as *The Significance of the Historical Existence of Jesus for Faith* in Robert Morgan and Michael Pye, ed., *Ernst Troeltsch: Writings on Theology and Religion* (Atlanta: John Knox, 1977). But Troeltsch is arguing not only for the historical *existence* of Jesus but for the particular *historicity* of Jesus, and not for faith in general, but for the Christian faith.

[3] H. R. Niebuhr, *The Meaning of Revelation* (New York: MacMillan, 1941, 1960), 48.

[4] Ibid., 154.

[5] H .R. Niebuhr, *The Kingdom of God in America* (New York: Harper & Brothers, 1937), 39, 59ff. 102f. 115.

[6] H. R. Niebuhr, "What Then Must We Do?" *Christian Century Pulpit*, V (July, 1934): 145f.

[7] H. R. Niebuhr, *Christ and Culture* (New York: Harper & Brothers, 1951), 11.

[8] Ibid., 13.

[9] Ibid., 24f.

[10] H. R. Niebuhr, *Faith on Earth* (New Haven and London: Yale University Press, 1989), 10f.

[11] Niebuhr, *Christ and Culture*, 117-19 *et passim*.

[12] Ibid., 230.

[13] Ibid., 233ff.

[14] Niebuhr, *Theology, History, and Culture*, 8f. and conversation with the author. I have analyzed and documented this "leaning" more extensively in Glen H. Stassen, D. M. Yeager, and John Howard Yoder, *Authentic Transformation: A New Vision of Christ and Culture* (Nashville: Abingdon, 1996), 174ff.

[15] Stassen, et al., *Authentic Transformation*, 173ff.

[16] Elizabeth Bounds, "Why Have We Gathered in this Place? A Critical Evaluation of Selected Theories of Community" (Ph.D. Dissertation, New York: Union Theological Seminary, 1993), 100ff. See also Bounds, *Coming Together/Coming Apart: Religion, Community, and Modernity* (New York: Routledge, 1977), 57.

[17] H. R. Niebuhr, *The Responsible Self* (New York: Harper & Row, 1963), 154ff.

[18] I have demonstrated this in Stassen, et al., *Authentic Transformation*, 186ff.

[19] Constance Benson, *God and Caesar: Troeltsch's Social Teaching as Legitimation* (New York: Transaction, 1999).

[20] Howard Thurman, *Jesus and the Disinherited* (Boston, MA: Beacon Press, 1996).

[21] Arthur C. Cochrane, *The Church's Confession Under Hitler* (Philadelphia: Westminster, 1957), 238-42.

[22] See Will Herberg, "Introduction," in Karl Barth, *Community, State, and Church* (Garden City: Anchor Doubleday, 1960), 31ff.

[23] Richard Hays, *The Moral Vision of the New Testament* (New York: Harper San Francisco, 1996). John Howard Yoder, *The Politics of Jesus* (Grand Rapids: Eerdmans, 1972 and 1994).

[24] See *Just Peacemaking: Transforming Initiatives for Justice and Peace* (Louisville: Westminster/John Knox, 1992), chapt. 2 and 3; "The Politics of Jesus in the Sermon on the Plain," in *The Wisdom of The Cross: Essays in Honor of John Howard Yoder* (Grand Rapids: Eerdmans, 1999), 150-67; "The Fourteen Triads of the Sermon on the Mount," forthcoming in *The Journal of Biblical Literature*; and *Kingdom Ethics: Following Jesus in Contemporary Context*, forthcoming from InterVarsity Press.

[25] Walter Wink, *Engaging the Powers: Discernment and Resistance in a World of Domination* (Minneapolis: Fortress, 1992).

[26] N. T. Wright, *Jesus and the Victory of God* (Minneapolis: Fortress, 1996); E. P. Sanders, *Jesus and Judaism* (Philadelphia: Fortress, 1985) and *The Historical Figure of Jesus* (London: Penguin, 1993); Marcus Borg, *Conflict, Holiness, and Politics in the Teachings of Jesus* (Harrisburg: Trinity, 1998); John Meier, *A Marginal Jew: Rethinking the Historical Jesus*, vol. 2, *Mentor, Message, and Miracles* (New York: Doubleday, 1994); William Herzog, *Jesus, Justice, and the Reign of God* (Westminster John Knox, 2000); Geza Vermes, *The Changing Faces of Jesus* (New York: Viking, 2001); Marcus Bockmuehl, *This Jesus: Martyr, Lord, Messiah* (London: T & T Clark, 1994); Gerd Theissen and Annette Merz, *The Historical Jesus: A Comprehensive Guide* (Minneapolis: Fortress, 1998); and Richard A. Horsley, *Jesus and Empire: The Kingdom of God and the New World Disorder* (Mineapolis: Fortress Press, 2003).

[27] John Howard Yoder, *Body Politics: Five Practices of the Christian Church Before the Watching World* (Nashville: Discipleship Resources, 1992). See Michael Cartwright's introduction to Yoder, *Royal Priesthood* (Grand Rapids: Eerdmans, 1994).

[28] James Wm. McClendon, Jr., *Ethics* (Nashville: Abingdon, 1986 and 2001).

[29] Duane Friesen, *Artists, Citizens, Philosophers: Seeking the Peace of the City* (Scottdale and Waterloo: Herald, 2000).

[30] Allen Verhey, *Remembering Jesus: Christian Community, Scripture, and the Moral Life* (Grand Rapids: Eerdmans, 2002).

[31] Cynthia Moe-Lobeda, *Healing the Broken World: Globalization and God* (Minneapolis: Augsburg Fortress, 2002).

[32] Larry Rasmussen, *Earth Community Earth Ethics* (Maryknoll: Orbis, 1996), especially 270-316.

[33] Lisa Sowle Cahill, *Sex, Gender, & Christian Ethics* (Cambridge: Cambridge University Press, 1996), 123, 129ff., 134f., 137, 141, 161.

[34] William C. Spohn, *Go and Do Likewise: Jesus and Ethics* (New York: Continuum, 1990), 1f.

A Discriminating Engagement of Culture: "An Anabaptist Perspective"

Duane K. Friesen

Abstract

Niebuhr's definitions of "Christ" and "culture" set up a problematic dualism that leads to a misrepresentation of the Christ-against-culture type. The paper proposes that instead of Niebuhr's "idealized" Christ (defined by a set of virtues), an embodied Christology locates Christ within culture. The tension, then, is not between Christ and culture, but between different cultural visions. A cultural vision with Christ as norm provides a discriminating ethic of normative practices to engage culture. Many scholars have recognized that Niebuhr not only develops a descriptive typology in *Christ and Culture*, he, also argues that the fifth type, Christ-the-transformer-of-culture, is the most adequate position. Almost everyone identifies with this type. Why is that? The problem is that the variety of meanings of "transformation" is not illuminated by Niebuhr's typology. An alternative typology is proposed which addresses these two problems: a richer development of three types that Niebuhr lumps together in his Christ-against-culture type; and the development of a typology to show that there are four different ways to understand what the church has meant by Christ-the-transformer-of-culture.

A critical assessment of H. R. Niebuhr's typology in his classic, *Christ and Culture*, requires us to consider three related issues: the conceptualization of the problem of Christ and culture, the system of classification Niebuhr develops, and Niebuhr's own normative argument implicit in *Christ and Culture*. I will assume that readers are familiar with

Journal of the Society of Christian Ethics, 23/1 (2003): 145-156

Niebuhr's work, and, therefore, move directly to address each of these issues.

Let me begin with the last issue first, Niebuhr's normative argument implicit in *Christ and Culture*. John H. Yoder has shown convincingly, I believe, that though on the surface it appears that Niebuhr provides us with a descriptive and "objective" classification of five different types of understandings of the relationship of Christ and culture, Niebuhr also argues that the fifth type, Christ-the-transformer-of-culture, is the most adequate, and the first two types, Christ-against-culture, and Christ-in-agreement-with-culture are the least adequate. Niebuhr in particular criticizes the Christ-against-culture position.[1] The issue is not the fact that Niebuhr makes a normative argument. We all stand somewhere, and from within our own particular identities and commitments we both seek to understand and evaluate the complex plethora of Christian positions presented to us. The issue is whether Niebuhr's way of conceptualizing the problem and his definition of the types adequately illuminates the options in a way that fairly represents the alternatives Christians face as they engage culture. I think Niebuhr's normative position leaves us with two problems we need to address: the adequacy of his understanding of the Christ-against-culture position, and the need for more discrimination in how we understand his fifth type, Christ-the-transformer-of-culture.

In my reading of both Ernst Troeltsch's *Social Teaching of the Christian Churches* and Niebuhr I have been unable to "find myself" and the tradition I identify with in their descriptions. The type which supposedly defines my tradition (Troeltsch's "sect type" and Niebuhr's Christ-against-culture type) construct boxes that do not illuminate the best insights of these traditions. Furthermore, their descriptions marginalize these traditions and prevent them from being taken seriously by other Christians. This is particularly serious, since I believe that the stream most poorly represented by their typologies is the one that provides some of the most viable options for a post-Constantinian church in the twenty-first century. One of the reasons, therefore, that I continue to engage Niebuhr is my concern to develop an alternative typological model that better illuminates the type I think is most seriously misrepresented. This is the normative position from which I come, though my concern is to develop a model from within that orientation that fairly represents and describes the other options.

It has also been noted by many that almost everyone who studies Niebuhr's types identifies with the fifth type, Christ-the-transformer-of-culture. This suggests that we need to develop a more adequate understanding of different ways in which "transformation" is understood by Christians. A more adequate typology should also find a way to correct this problem.

Let me now turn to the first two issues: Niebuhr's way of conceptualizing the problem, and his system of classification. On each issue I will state a thesis that criticizes Niebuhr, followed by an alternative thesis that I believe is more adequate.

Conceptualizing the Problem of Christ and Culture

(A) Niebuhr's neo-Kantian conceptualization of the problem as between "Christ" and "culture" (which he inherited from Troeltsch) sets up a problematic dichotomy which fails to adequately illuminate the problem with which we are concerned. For Niebuhr, Christ points to the "absolute" beyond the "relativities" of culture. Culture is defined in the broadest possible way as everything humans do that is not determined by strictly biological forces. Christ is defined in terms of virtues or excellences (love, hope, obedience, faith) that are oriented to a God beyond the world of culture. "As Son of God he points away from the many values of man's social life to the One who alone is good."[2] In this orientation to God, Christ is, then, the mediator to humans. "It involves a double movement—with men toward God, with God toward men; from the world to the Other, from the Other to the world; from work to Grace, from Grace to work; from time to the Eternal and from the Eternal to the temporal."[3] Niebuhr thus defines the problem in terms of a series of dualisms: absolute/relative; Eternal/temporal; God/world; Christ/culture. The neo-Kantian dualism of the "noumenal" and the "phenomenal" (which Niebuhr inherited from Troeltsch) provides the philosophical assumption or conceptual framework for defining the issue.[4]

(B) My alternative thesis is: instead of Niebuhr's "idealized" Christ defined by inward virtues oriented toward God, an "embodied" Christology locates Christ within culture. Christ is not a reality over against culture, but was rather for Christians in the first century the normative cultural option among other cultural alternatives. Christ, in this view, is not defined as an ideal in opposition to culture, but is a bodied person whose model of living and dying is deeply embedded in the Jewish culture of first century Palestine. This Jewish Jesus of the Synoptic Gospels goes to the synagogue and temple, prays to God in Aramaic, and teaches in sayings and parables that fit his cultural context. He is a "political" being whose life and teaching embraces the poor and marginal. He engages the powers and principalities as a prophetic healer/teacher. He teaches people to respond to evil with creative nonviolence, and pays the price of his non-conformity with death on a Roman cross. We might not all agree with the description of the Jesus of the Synoptic Gospels I have just given, and, to be sure, there are a plurality of portraits of Jesus in the New Testament. But one thing is clear, New Testament scholarship in the fifty years since Niebuhr's publication of *Christ and Culture* supports a culturally embodied Jesus, a person with flesh and bones who is integrally bound up with his own cultural context.[5]

The problem, then, should be defined, not as between Christ and culture, but between contrasting cultural visions. By definition, to be a Christian, a follower of Christ, who was himself *sarx*, means to live a particular cultural vision. "The perennial issue confronting the church is the relationship between cultural visions, not between Christ and culture."[6]

Critique of Niebuhr's Typology

(A) Every way of being Christian is culturally embodied. It is nonsensical to describe anyone as "against" culture or in "agreement" with culture. Every Christian "bodies" her identity in language and in practices that are cultural and can be observed empirically. An Amish Christian of rural Pennsylvania and a Harvard theologian of urban Cambridge may embody very different cultural visions, but both are through and through cultural in their identities as Christians.

An adequate typology, therefore, must attend to the varied ways "Christ" is defined by different Christian persons and groups, find out to what degree Christ is normative (and how other norms come into play), and observe how these different understandings of Christ provide a discriminating ethic of normative practices that shape different cultural visions. In this view, culture will be seen not as a monolithic entity, but as fluid and complex. Christians engage culture in a discriminating way and totalistic definitions of "against" or in "agreement" with culture are simply nonsensical.[7]

Diane Yeager, in her paper for the Niebuhr panel at the SCE meeting, raised the question whether my criticism of Niebuhr grows out of a failure to distinguish adequately between a taxonomy and a typology. She rightly points out that a typology is a "logical" construct over against which we can test empirical reality, whereas a taxonomy aims to classify actual empirical options. The question we are still left with, however, is what counts as an adequate typology. It seems to me that a typology should illuminate real "logical" possibilities for relating Christ and culture, over against which we can compare actual empirical manifestations. It seems to me that Niebuhr's first type, "against" culture, is "logically" nonsensical by definition, and thus it fails as a typology. If every Christian view is "bodied" in a cultural vision, then, by definition, Niebuhr has constructed a nonsensical position.[8] The "against" culture type fails to illuminate actual empirical realities, since by definition such a position cannot be practiced. As I have already stated, this problem with the typology is grounded in Niebuhr's problematic dualistic conceptualization of the issue of Christ and culture.

(B) My alternative thesis is: if we could agree as scholars that a different conceptual model for thinking about Christ and culture is needed, then an alternative to Niebuhr's fivefold typology could be developed and worked at collaboratively. However, until a more adequate typology is developed, Niebuhr's model will not be abandoned, because we do need systems of classification that enable us to sort through the vast complexity of empirical phenomena. In developing an alternative typology, however, we need to take into account the following issues.

1. Within particular Christian traditions, we can observe a great deal of variety. We must resist monolithic judgments about whole traditions and not rigidly box all persons within traditions into the categories of our ideal types.[9]

2. In an ecumenical age and in the encounter of scholars who are influenced by a variety of sources, it is difficult to categorize persons and groups within rigid traditional categories, as there is a great deal of cross-fertilization across traditional lines of demarcation. One of the recent examples of this is the work on a just peacemaking theory that has linked common themes and interests of pacifists and just war theorists.[10]

3. It is difficult to classify whole traditions about their view of culture, as if there were a monolithic approach to every issue that is predictable. In fact, it is probably better to classify positions on a particular ethical issue. Christians within various traditions may respond in quite different ways to war, abortion, capital punishment, or genetic engineering. Sometimes we find strange bedfellows. On one issue a Christian group might agree with another, but be on opposite sides on another particular moral or theological issue.[11]

4. We will likely need to abandon classifications that encompass all of culture, as Niebuhr's types attempted to do. For example, Ian Barbour has proposed a fourfold classification of contemporary positions on the relationship of theology and science: conflict, independence, dialogue, and integration.[12] This classification is very helpful in identifying Christian positions on the relationship of the Christian faith to science, but it does not necessarily correlate with views of Christian groups on the arts, or on the relationship of church and society.

5. Finally, a new classification will need to take into account the global church. Niebuhr's typology considers primarily classical positions in church history and the church in Europe and North America. How would we construct a typology if we included the church's engagement of culture in Latin America, Asia, and Africa? I suspect it would require us to do a number of adjustments to Niebuhr's typology.

In the light of the above considerations, below I have outlined a brief sketch of an alternative typology of positions within a limited cultural domain, namely, the relationship of church and society. All we can do here is a sketch. My purpose here is to stimulate scholarly work in imagining and developing a typology that can be more helpful in illuminating the logical possibilities of conceiving the relationship of Christ and culture. Niebuhr's work has played a very important role in our disciplined reflection in Christian social ethics. However, it is time we moved beyond him, both to build on his insights, as well as to improve on the work he began.

The proposed typology is, first of all, organized into two broad streams that reflect how Christians have responded to the "great divide" in the history of the church symbolized by the changes in the relationship of the church and society with Constantine. Constantine symbolizes the shift that occurred in the church when it moved from a minority culture within other cultures to the dominant culture, culminating in the culture of the high Middle Ages. Ernst Troeltsch is in continuity with Constantine when he argues for the more "adequate church type" (vs. the sect and mystic types) because of the church's ability to synthesize with the dominant culture and produce a "unity of civilization." Within each of these two broad streams (Constantinian and non-Constantinian), I have identified three types for a total of six types.

The Constantinian and non-Constantinian streams in the history of the church are shaped by four key interrelated variables: Christology, ecclesiology, the view of history and eschatology, and the ethical norms that shape the engagement of the church with other institutions. The ethical norms that regulate the relationship to the larger culture beyond the church are most vividly illuminated by the question of the "sword," the judicial authority of government and its legitimation of coercive violent force to order society.

The three types within the Constantinian stream of church history all believe the church must cooperate with the dominant institutions of the world in order to shape a relatively just social order. Christians live in a sinful world "between the times" of God's revelation in Christ and the eschatological fulfillment of God's complete redemption. Given the limitations of what can be achieved in history because of the sinful human condition, God providentially works through human cultural agents (e.g. civil authorities; government) to order society toward the common good. Christians may, and indeed are required, to cooperate in the use of the "sword" to protect the good and punish the evil. Christ's teaching of the Sermon on the Mount is a moral ideal for these Christians, but they believe the Sermon on the Mount cannot be applied directly to Christian responsibility in the political sphere. Other norms (e.g., natural law, the common good, Old Testament covenant traditions, Christian realism) are needed to supplement the ethic of Jesus. A more general normative framework is also needed as a basis for cooperation with those (of other religions or secular persuasions) who do not confess the Christian faith. Within the context of these inevitable compromises, Christ's grace and forgiveness offers hope in the face of the sinful human predicament.

The three types within the non-Constantinian stream view the church as a disciplined community called to model an alternative cultural vision distinct from the dominant culture. The alternative cultural stream goes by a variety of names such as the Radical Reformation, the "free church" or the "believer's church." James McClendon Jr. calls it the "small b baptist tradition."[13] John H. Yoder describes this type not as a specific denomination, but rather a perennial position taken, sometimes quite without coordination, in fact often without any knowledge of one another, by scores of renewal communities—including a dozen major, independently viable ones—across the centuries, and by renewal movements within established denominations as well.[14]

The church is called by God to be a people among the nations. The center of history is not empire (Babylon, Rome, Germany, the United States), but a people God has chosen from among the nations to be a light to all the peoples of the world. The ethical norms for all of life are derived from the life and teachings of Jesus. Jesus calls the church to be his disciples, to seek God's righteousness (justice) and make peace by loving the enemy and overcoming evil through nonviolence. Hope is grounded in the Living Christ who is Lord. Christ reveals a God who overcomes evil in history through the nonviolent cross, not through human agents who use violent force to make history come out right.

Within this stream we can identify persons and groups like St. Benedict and the monastic movement, St. Francis, the Waldensians, the Czech Brethren, the Anabaptists, Quakers, Church of the Brethren, the Wesleyan renewal within Anglicanism, Negro slaves in America who preserved an alternative cultural identity (as evidenced in the black spirituals) within the slavery system, the Disciples on the frontier in nineteenth-century America, the black church and Martin L. King, Jr., Oscar Romero who died a martyr's death in El Salvador, and Desmond Tutu in South Africa. These groups are distinguished by two features: (1) They are disciplined ethical communities who live by ethical practices that distinguish them from the dominant culture (i.e., the disciplined practices of nonviolence, economic sharing, inclusive membership beyond race or national identity); and (2) these ethical practices provide a normative vision for engaging the dominant culture within which they exist as minority communities.

Within each of these two broad classifications, we can identify three types, for a total of six types. Within the non-Constantinian alternative culture stream, the three types represent a continuum from indifference or disinterest in relating to the dominant institutions of society to a vision for the transformation of these institutions. All of these types within this stream are shaped by a Christology of ethical formation. All are oriented by a Christ who forms an alternative body, visibly evident in ethical practices such as nonviolence and economic sharing which contrasts them with the dominant culture. They differ in how engaged they are with the larger culture.

Within the Constantinian stream of church history, we can observe a continuum from the tendency to legitimize the dominant institutions of society to an interest in transformation of these institutions. In all of these types the major concern of Christians is to develop a positive relationship to the dominant culture. This means both to acknowledge the significant impact of culture on the church, and to provide a realistic framework that can positively shape and influence the dominant culture in which the church lives.

I will conclude by briefly sketching the three types within each of these two streams. I can only be suggestive by listing a few examples under each category.

Typology of Church and Society

Church as Alternative Cultural Model to the Dominant Culture (non-Constantinian stream)

1. Christ as Founder of Ethical Communities

(A) Amish
(B) Benedictine Monastic Communities

2. Christ as Model for Public Witness

(A) Andre Trocme and the community of Le Chambon, France, who saved 5000 Jews during the holocaust.
(B) Clarence Jordan and Koinonia Farms in Georgia in the 1950s and 1960s.
(C) East German Christians in Marxist East Germany who adopted Jeremiah's model to seek the peace of the city where they dwell.
(D) Roman Catholic priests and bishops in Chile during the Pinochet regime who banned from the Eucharist those who torture, because torture of fellow Christians tears apart the body of Christ.[15] This action was a powerful sign of resistance and witness in the context of repressive violence.
(E) Mennonite Central Committee, with its worldwide programs of service, community development and peace building, through the Ottawa and Washington, D.C., offices, often link testimony from workers in the field to government officials.
(F) Dorothy Day and the Catholic Worker Movement.

3. Christ as Healer of the Nations

(A) Martin L. King, whose vision of cultural transformation through nonviolence is organically grounded in his identity as a Baptist preacher within the black church.[16]
(B) American Friends Service Committee. The series of book length documents with proposals for alternative public policies on disputed

issues are a model of how Christians committed to nonviolence address public policy issues.[17]
(C) Naim Ateek speaks for many Palestinian Christians in calling for a just peace in the Middle East, to be achieved nonviolently.[18]
(D) Desmund Tutu of South Africa. Peace and Reconciliation Commission.

The Church in Collaboration with the Dominant Institutions of Society (Constantinian Stream)

1. The Spiritual Christ who Legitimizes Social Structures

(A) Martin Luther's two kingdom theology is a good example of this type. God has ordained two governments, the spiritual and the temporal. The one produces true inward piety; the other brings about external peace. The Christian prince, saved by God's grace, is called through his office to use the sword to protect the good and restrain evil.
(B) Many evangelical Christians in America believe in Christ the Savior who died to save people from sin at the same time that they support American foreign policy (e.g., the Persian Gulf War and the War in Afghanistan). After Sept. 11, First United Methodist Church in Newton, Kans., began each Sunday service with a "new liturgy for the times" featuring red, white, and blue candles, a wreath, an open Bible, and an American flag.
(C) Apocalyptic Christianity (e.g. the LeHaye novels) emphasizes an "end time" eschatology with minimal attention to existing structures of this world which will pass away.

2. The Christ who Humanizes Social Structures

(A) Humanization of war through the moral categories of just war thinking.[19]
(B) Reinhold Niebuhr's vision of agape love and how it shapes a vision of justice within the limits of existing institutions in a fallen social order.
(C) Efforts by Cardinal Silva in Chile to "reign in" the abuses of the Pinochet regime.[20]
(D) Study document of the Commission of the Churches on International Affairs (CCIA) of the World Council of Churches, the "Protection of Endangered Populations in Situations of Armed Violence," which defines the conditions under which armed force might be justified in humanitarian crises such as Haiti, Somalia, the former Yugoslavia, and Rwanda.

3. The Christ who Transforms Social Structures

(A) John Calvin's vision for a holy commonwealth in Geneva.
(B) Puritan visions for sixteenth century England, and the transfer of this vision to America to be "God's New Israel," "a city set on the hill." William Penn's vision for a holy commonwealth in Pennsylvania.
(C) Conflicts in contemporary America between evangelical and fundamentalist Christians, and more liberal Christians, over what kind of a society America should be.[21]
(D) Liberation theology which is linked to Marxist social analysis and the call for the use of armed force to bring about social change.

This proposed typology corrects two problems that I identified at the beginning of this paper. It provides a much richer description of positions that Niebuhr lumps together in the Christ-against-culture category. We can identify three types within one of the major streams within church history: Christ as founder of ethical communities; Christ as model for public witness; and Christ as healer of the nations. This much richer description of positions enables us to discern more carefully creative alternative options for how the church can relate to society in a post-Christendom age.

Second, this proposed typology identifies several different ways in which one might think of the church's engagement in transforming culture. Within the alternative cultural stream we identified "Christ as model for public witness" and "Christ as healer of the nations." Within the other main stream of church history, we identified "the Christ who humanizes social structures" and "the Christ who transforms social structures." The fact that we can identify four different ways of understanding "transformation" explains why so many have identified with Niebuhr's fifth type, Christ-the-transformer-of-culture. The advantage of my proposed alternative typology is that by enabling us to distinguish quite different understandings of transformation, we are much better able to discern what issues are at stake as we address the normative question of how the church should relate to society.

Within each of the two major streams we can identify negative and positive examples. Within the non-Constantinian stream we can observe the dangers of withdrawal and indifference to society. Within the Constantinian stream we can see the dangers of accommodation to institutional forces of the dominant culture like nationalism. Though the six types do have different views of Christ, the church, history and eschatology, and ethics, nevertheless, all of them embody authentic expressions of Christian faith. The rich variety of manifestations of the Christian faith in the history of the church is testimony to the creative power of the Living Spirit of Christ.

NOTES

[1] See the book by Glen H. Stassen, Diane Yeager, and John Howard Yoder, *Authentic Transformation: A New Vision of Christ and Culture* (Nashville: Abingdon Press, 1996). Note especially Yoder's essay, "How H. Richard Niebuhr Reasoned: A Critique of Christ and Culture," 31-90.

[2] H. Richard Niebuhr, *Christ and Culture* (New York: Harper Torchbooks, 1951), 24.

[3] Ibid., 27.

[4] I support this claim in several other places. See my dissertation, "The Relationship between Ernst Troeltsch's Theory of Religion and his Typology of Religious Association," (Th.D. dissertation, Harvard University, 1972). See a shorter analysis in "Normative Factors in Troeltsch's Typology of Religious Association," *Journal of Religious Ethics* 3/2 (1975): 271-83, and a more extensive analysis in the chapter, "A Critical Assessment of Troeltsch's Typology of Religious Association," in *Studies in the Theological Ethics of Ernst Troeltsch*, ed. by Max Meyers and M. LaChat (Toronto Studies in Theology, Edwin Mellon Press, 1991), 73-118.

[5] For a good analysis of the biblical picture of a ⬚⬚bodied Christ within first century culture see Walter Wink, *Engaging the Powers* (Minneapolis: Fortress Press, 1992), and Richard Hays, *The Moral Vision of the New Testament: Community, Cross, New Creation* (Harper San Francisco, 1996). See Wink's chapter, "God's Domination-Free Order: Jesus and God's Reign," 109-43 for how Jesus addressed the dominant culture with an alternative cultural vision on issues like domination, equality, purity and holiness, racism/ethnocentrism, family, law, sacrifice, nonviolence, women and children, and healing and exorcism. Though Hays does not place his emphasis on the historical Jesus, but rather on the narrative logic of each of the evangelists, he argues (agreeing with Ernst Kasemann) that the "Jesus of history must ultimately serve as a criterion against which the New Testament's diverse formulations of the kergyma must be measured; otherwise, we are in danger of falling into docetism," (160).

[6] Duane K. Friesen, *Artists, Citizens, Philosophers: Seeking the Peace of the City* (Scottdale, PA: Herald Press, 2000), 58.

[7] See Kathryn Tanner's postmodern critique of earlier understandings by anthropologists of culture as an internally consistent whole, which do not adequately recognize the fluidity and openness of cultural identity. *Theories of Culture* (Minneapolis: Fortress Press, 1997), 44. See especially chapter three, "Criticism and Reconstruction."

[8] Niebuhr constructs this type to be logically "impossible." This can be seen in his criticism of its inconsistency because people in the type use language (a cultural phenomena). Niebuhr states that a person within this type must use language because he is a "Christian and a man. If he is to confess Jesus before men, he must do so by means of words and ideas derived from culture." The type is thus constructed as a "disembodied type," in such a way as to be logically impossible in practice (H. R. Niebuhr, *Christ and Culture*, 70).

[9] As evidence for this variety within a tradition, I cite the study I did of Mennonite statements on peace and social concerns between 1900 and 1980. I was able to document five types of responses: separation of the church community from the dominant culture; identification with the dominant culture; spiritualization of Christian social teachings; two levels: radical Christian discipleship and God's will for structures outside the perfection of Christ; and, transformation of the world into the Kingdom of God. Duane K. Friesen, *Mennonite Witness on Peace and Social Concerns: 1900-1980* (Mennonite Central Committee, 1982).

[10] Glen Stassen, ed., *Just Peacemaking: Ten Practices for Abolishing War* (Cleveland: The Pilgrim Press, 1998).

[11] For example, John H. Yoder has developed a much more complex typology of Christian attitudes to war than the familiar Roland Bainton distinction between pacifism, just war, and crusade. See his *Nevertheless: The Varieties of Religious Pacifism* (Scottdale, PA: Herald Press, 1992), 151-56.

[12] Ian G. Barbour, *When Science Meets Religion: Enemies, Strangers, or Partners?* (Harper San Francisco, 2000).

[13] James McClendon, *Systematic Theology: Ethics* (Nashville: Abingdon Press, 1986), 19-20, 31-34.
[14] John H. Yoder, *The Priestly Kingdom: Social Ethics as Gospel* (University of Notre Dame Press, 1984), 1-12. George Williams uses the term Radical Reformation to describe the variety of groups in the sixteenth century continental Reformation that sought to implement the Reformation more thoroughly than the magisterial reformers who remained wedded to the medieval concept of the corpus Christianum.
[15] See William Cavanaugh, *Torture and Eucharist* (Blackwell Publishers, 1998).
[16] See Cornel West, "Martin Luther King, Jr.: Prophetic Christian as Organic Intellectual," in *Prophetic Fragments: Illumination of the Crises in American Religion and Culture* (William B. Eerdmans, 1988).
[17] See John H. Yoder's description of this Quaker approach, "Speak Truth to Power" in his book *Nevertheless: The Varities of Religious Pacifism* (Herald Press, 1992), 145-50.
[18] Naim Atteek, *Justice and Only Justice: A Palestinian Theology of Liberation* (Orbis Books, 1989).
[19] One example is the document of the National Conference Catholic Bishops, *The Challenge of Peace: Gods Promise and Our Response* (United States Catholic Conference, 1983).
[20] Cavanaugh, *Torture and Eucharist.*
[21] See the description of this conflict in James Davison Hunters book, *Culture Wars: The Struggle to Define America* (New York: Basic Books, 1991).

Jesus Changes Things: A Critical Evaluation of *Christ and Culture* from an African American Perspective

Darryl M. Trimiew

Abstract

Christ and Culture remains a useful heuristic device for discerning and interpreting the process of struggle and change produced by the attempts of the church to minister to the world. It is also helpful for ecclesial self-evaluations. While its typologies are conceptually imperfect, they can be used, nevertheless, to disclose important changes in society and within denominations. These attributes can and do help to facilitate the African American church's ongoing liberation efforts and therefore, hopefully, the flourishing of African American communities.

H. Richard Niebuhr's monumental work, *Christ and Culture,* like all of his work, is a product of his time and his place. His sudden death in 1962 left us with an ethical legacy that has yet to be fully realized. His work was produced before the realization of several progressions in the fields of theology, ethics, and political or cultural liberations, global and local.

Niebuhr never had the opportunity to read James Cone, Jose Miguez Bonino, Gustavo Gutierrez, Katie Cannon, or other liberationists. He never lived to realize the complete political overthrow of white political imperialism in Africa, the triumphs of the civil rights revolution, gay liberation, feminism, or the loss of the Vietnam War.

Accordingly, he represents a form of ethics from a different era, from a different world. His work was groundbreaking for its era, but its era is clearly past. How then, in the twenty-first century, should his work serve as a resource for African American morality, among other communities? I will

Journal of the Society of Christian Ethics, 23/1 (2003): 157-165

attempt to answer this question and in so doing review and critique his classic work, *Christ and Culture*.[1]

Today we are forced to ask whether his work might simply be a historical artifact, both beautiful and useful, that exemplifies the successes and failures of the European-American twentieth century. Is it not merely a rich resource for understanding liberal western Christianity, circa 1951? Clearly, without this resource and an insightful understanding of it, we cannot fully understand where we have come from, where we might go, and, more importantly, where we might need to go.

Yet as rich as it is, of what use is it in a constructive sense for a post-liberal, post-modern world? I argue that Niebuhr's work, particularized, relativized, and transmogrified by various communities can serve as a new wineskin to store new moral wine, rather than a derelict cask.

Nonetheless, we must recognize its historic limitations and its limited applications. I will do so with an understanding that I am engaging in revisionism and reinterpreting his Christ-transforming-culture typology. By implication, this paper represents a review, criticism, and use of his heuristic device. We will start with a review of his theory of moral agency and the standard criticisms of it.

As I maintained in my first published work, *Voices of the Silenced: The Responsible Self in a Marginalized Community*, the exercise of moral responsibility by empowered selves is the crux of Niebuhr's approach and vision.[2] His Christ-transforming-culture typology features as its moral agents empowered selves. This orientation is unremarkable given his own location as an empowered self. The key question is whether Niebuhr believed that culture was most clearly transformed in a morally superior fashion only by powerful Christians and whether in his opinion the oppressed could also transform culture. Further it must be recognized (as Niebuhr did not) that the oppressed have a different conceptualization of Christ and of Culture and are themselves generally formed and found in subcultures. Lastly, of great interest is the process by which transformation is thought to take place.

We must note that the liberationists of Niebuhr's generation, the disinherited, such as Martin Luther King, Jr., W. E. B. Dubois, or Jomo Kenyatta were not recognized by him as transformationist.[3] Thus it is not unfair to infer from this lapse that Niebuhr did not see the oppressed as significant transformational moral agents. Or, perhaps he understood that the oppressed of previous Christian subjugated groups had been transformation agents, but was not able to see how his oppressed contemporaries could serve in that capacity.

That he was unable to make this connection constitutes a failure on his part and that of a whole generation of white ethicists. However, it does not follow necessarily that his classic work cannot be of use to the oppressed. But why should a modern liberationist bother to employ his typologies and heuristic devices and to what ends? Could it not be said, once again, that his work represents an important step in Christian social ethics but also constitutes a moral Neanderthal line, i.e., a necessary but now prehistoric dead end?

I believe that his work remains useful but that his conception of transformation is itself what most needs to be transformed. We also need a clearer statement as to how transformation comes about and who is competent to engage in the struggle for its realization. James Cone has raised this issue many times, i.e., the question of who can do theology.[4] Sharon Welch has raised it in a different way, suggesting that her Christ is one who inspires and empowers communities of resistance.[5]

It is the genius of Niebuhr's work that he correctly identifies the reality that wherever Christians have lived and moved, helped and oppressed, they have all claimed Jesus Christ as their inspiration and leader, and felt compelled to relate their understanding of him to their respective cultures. They have all tried to bring their existent understandings of Christ into conversation and harmony with their prevailing culture and, for some of them, their existential subcultures. Further, Niebuhr's typologies have made it clear that different contemporary communities have had competing Christologies and hence, different and competing cultures. His work made it clear that none of these communities and Christologies were immediately self-evident to anyone but the practitioners. Yet time and further consideration of historical events suggests that certain Christian practices that were generated or upheld by certain Christian communities were and are morally superior to others, particularly as they are manifested as political cultures. Martin Niemoller and Dietrich Bonhoeffer expressed Christologies and anthropologies that are now conceded by nearly all to have been morally superior to those of the German National Church. The religious intolerance of the Inquisition and the Puritan commonwealth are now seldom championed over radical reformation and Anabaptist Christologies and practices. Jomo Kenyatta is now considered the father of his country, Kenya, rather than merely a Mau Mau terrorist. Martin Luther King's *Letter from a Birmingham Jail* is considered by all but the most rabid modern racists to be a much clearer expression of a transformative Christ and a Beloved Community than the views of his contemporary white clergy opponents.[6]

This review may sound like Monday morning quarterbacking and so it is, but Monday morning quarterbacking is only possible when Sunday has passed and the game has been decided and, lastly, only when there is a football community that is united in its understanding of great football. Contemporary moralists now reject the historical practices of genocide, religious intolerance and persecution, political imperialism, and violent segregation. The Christs of those oppressive visions, like the Christ of the Afrikaner apartheid-supporting church, are now seen as Christs of oppression, as transformative Christs, but also as brutal and unjust ones.[7] In the case of the Christ of the Afrikaners it eventually became a Christ-of-culture, a civil religion, no longer transforming the land but resisting, most oppressively, transformation. It would be easy to try and say that such visions did not constitute any true vision of Christ or any faithful church, but such an assessment would be fatally simplistic. Those historic communities never held out their Christologies and practices as being anything other than holy. In some cases they saw themselves as a Christian vanguard that was transforming culture (their own for the better) or transforming inferior pagan cultures at the command of Christ. For African Americans, the historical reality has been, as black Muslims are fond of reminding us, that we worship a Christ whose presence was embodied into our communities and culture by rape, genocide, slavery, subjugation, chauvinism, and continuing denigration and misrepresentation of who we are and who Christ is.

With such a history of manipulation by a number of believers one may well wonder, what can be the use of Niebuhr's typologies?

First, these typologies are conceptually defective, because Niebuhr's definition of culture is too broad and because no actual Christian communities actually fit into these typologies.[8] Moreover, actual Christian communities in the modern world manifest these typologies in different ways depending on what particular ethical issue is in dispute. Any particular community can move on any given issue such as capital punishment from one typology to another, sometimes opposing the prevailing culture, (sometimes) transforming it, sometimes merely manifesting it, some times merely floating above it. Yet Niebuhr's typologies have persisted precisely because, flawed as they are, they do serve as a devices for measuring and evaluating how Christian communities are interrelating with other institutions and how they are interacting globally.[9]

All Christian communities are deeply set into patterns of behavior dictated by their past histories and their current interests. Accordingly, most understandings of *Christ and Culture* must be viewed on some level as expressions of that self-interest. This assertion may seem cynical but it is not.

It is no surprise, for example, that marginalized people such as African Americans have in many instances worshipped a Christ who they believed was set on a liberative task on their behalf, transforming a culture that denied their humanity into one that embraced them, among others.[10] In Martin Luther King's Christology, transformation takes place because of what Christ has done and begins with the spiritual transformation of the believer.[11] In this understanding of Christ-transforming-culture, the disinherited are responding to the divine initiative of God in the struggle to overthrow oppressive political cultures. Christ is Emmanuel; Christ is with us, particularly in the struggle as we struggle.[12] It must be said, of course, that this characterization of Christ may be as false as the Christologies of Nazi sympathizers, Ku Klux Klan members, and the worst of the Spanish Inquisition. Since our struggle has not been concluded, it is now currently impossible to assign a definitive moral evaluation to this Christ or to this culture. Those of us who serve this liberating Christ do so in faith, with the knowledge that this struggle may not be won in our lifetimes. Because we are fallen though Christ is not, our struggle may not even be as holy as we make it out to be. Yet it is the immutable task of each generation, as Niebuhr first noted, to take up these cudgels, in faith. God is judging us morally, and doubtless we have failed and will fail morally in some, if not many respects. Yet the Monday morning quarterbacking of the past is not without its uses. Even a cursory review of such aforementioned fiascos compels us to note that "Christs" acting with state or economic powers do seem to hurt the cause of Christ as such praxis is subsequently evaluated by Christian and other moral communities.[13] In short, the Christ of the slaves is morally superior to the Christ of the slave masters; even the sons and daughters of the slave masters now say so.

This matter becomes much more complex the closer we get to our own Sundays of contention. What systems and practices constitute current moral fiascos in the making? Monday morning quarterbacking is, finally, of limited value. Indeed, it is the primary function of ethics to try to determine, within an existential time frame, the better practices, morally speaking, of individuals, groups, and communities. Such a determination would facilitate, when necessary, the discontinuation of certain evil practices as well as the establishment of certain ameliorating practices. In this process, the typologies that Niebuhr has proposed can serve as initial evaluators that enable us to get a handle on what conflicts need what resolutions.

The African American Church, for example, has never been monolithic in its Christologies or its practices, aside from what Peter Paris has called its wholesale adoption of the Christian tradition, i.e., a commitment to non-racist expressions of Christianity in the acceptance of the parenthood of God and the siblingship of humanity.[14] How that inclusivity has been played out has varied depending upon the era involved, class, demographics, and the peculiar church history with which African slaves became converted to being African American Christians. In many respects these typologies, like other aspects of imperially imposed Christianity, were simply stamped upon African American Christians as a side effect of the proselyting process. Where Christ-against-culture churches did the converting, Black churches were, at least initially, also Christ-against-culture. Some abandoned this initial imprinting; some did not.

My own denominational location in the Christian church, Disciples of Christ, is illustrative of this point. The Stone-Campbell movement, which was the founding religious impetus, emphasized a return to primitive Christianity as well as a commitment to freedom and ecumenism.[15] The historic split of the movement into the Churches of Christ, Independent Christian Churches and the Disciples of Christ, was made along theological fault lines.[16] Churches of Christ, by and large, continued a strong commitment to primitive Christianity, and a continued resistance to certain claims of modern culture, i.e., a Christ-against-culture typology. Disciples of Christ, on the other hand, embraced higher criticism hermeneutics, and modern cultural claims towards the American mainstream culture. Disciples have at times adopted a Christ-of-culture stance as well as, on occasion, a Christ-transforming-culture approach. Even the original Stone-Campbell movement sought to transform ecclesiastical culture by championing primitive Christianity and ecumenism in an attempt to halt widespread denominational disputes. Be that as it may, what is interesting to note is that with the historic Stone-Campbell split into two or more separate denominations, black churches simply went with whatever side of the conflict they were on. Black churches that were founded or supported primarily by Church of Christ white believers continued that tradition and the ones likewise established by Disciples of Christ followed that road. Only two golden threads continued between the two black groups that subsequently became two different black sub-denominations. Those two threads were first, a continuation of the cultural cultic worship style of praying, singing, and preaching that is distinctly African-influenced and; second, and more important for the purposes of our current discussion, a political theological commitment to producing and reproducing a non-racist expression of Christianity in a racist Christian culture, which regardless of the intent of the churches was by its nature transformative in its intent. In other words, both black Church of Christ members and black Disciples of Christ members sought to transform their macro-society from one committed to racism to one committed to equality. This is why an examination of each denomination can legitimately find each manifesting the overarching theology and practices of their respective denominations, that is to say purity from worldly influences is continued in the Church of Christ, and a celebration of mainstream cultural experiences in Disciples of Christ settings. These positions are miles apart from each other and yet individual black congregations and pastors in each denomination have worked hand in hand in the ongoing struggle for greater recognition of civil rights. Accordingly, black Church of Christ members and black Disciples of Christ members are much more apt to be found marching together for rights than studying the scriptures together. In this sense, Niebuhr's typologies are merely signposts for how various Christian communities might act in the world with regard to certain issues. Most assuredly, no black churches act monolithically within any one typology.

Still the primary questions will not go away. Of what use are these typologies for black churches? And how, in the larger picture, can these typologies aid in living the Christian life and mission in morally justifiable ways?

Returning to our root metaphor is instructive. Even a Sunday morning quarterback can anticipate that the continued struggle to overcome racism will incline all black Christian churches to manifest in some way a transformative Christ. In some manifestations this Christ may be against culture, of culture, in paradox with it, synthesizing it, or radically and directly trying to revolutionize (radical transformation) it. Accordingly, faulty as these typologies are, they help to describe the various ways that black Christians, among other Christians, have tried and will try to serve Christ faithfully in a hostile world. Various arguments will arise, from time to time, about the usefulness of each type for the process of transforming a racist, sexist, homophobic, and class exploitative American society: such arguments cannot detain us at the present. (The black church itself is riddled with some of these vices.). Suffice it to say, however, that certain historical decisions that have already been made continue to deeply influence further developments. More simply put, it is not accidental that Dr. Martin Luther King, Jr., a Baptist minister, was the leader of the civil rights movement. Most black Christians of his era were either Methodist or Baptist, for certain historical reasons. King was a transformative moral agent and served and projected a transformative Christ. It is unlikely that the leadership of ongoing struggles for transformation against racism, sexism, homophobia, or class difference, will come from a Christian leader who is not theologically inclined to see as his or her role, and as a duty for the Church to engage as part and parcel of its mission, the struggle to transform the world. Thus the Christologies and practices that engage in public discourse, public policy formation and public disputes, are the ones most likely to transform our lives together and this fact was observed long ago by Niebuhr. It is for this very practical reason that whoever will be the next Martin Luther King, Jr. or Fanny Lou Hamer, will not likely come from the ranks of a Christian group whose primary orientation is to simply resist the culture, assimilate into it, or triumph on a personal, individual level without directly challenging the culture.[17]

Niebuhr's typologies, as flawed as they are, are therefore useful for interpreting and analyzing the work of prominent Christian leaders and movements. For blacks, it is important to analyze carefully the shift of recognition and influence of African American "religious leaders" from a civil rights orientation, highlighting prophetic criticism a la, King, Jesse Jackson, or Al Sharpton, to a priestly therapeutic dispensation of balm à la T.D. Jakes. Jakes' meteoric rise has transformed black Christian culture. It remains to be seen what effect this change will have on African American culture in general. Still, for a liberationist, *Christ and Culture,* despite its flaws, is still highly instructive because of Niebuhr's great insight that God and the reign of God cannot be equated with the praxis of anyone, not even Christian liberationists who stand in solidarity with the poor and oppressed, who engage in partnership with marginalized folks in the ongoing struggle against systems of oppression. Such praxis evidences the will of God, but cannot be equated with the One beyond the many who calls us all into question even as we strive to serve Him. Indeed, Christian communities that seek to embody a transformative Christ must accept that we will fail to do so perfectly, even as we try. To achieve true liberation we need checks and balances for our endeavors, engagement with our oppressors, and sometimes even opposition from them when we go astray. What really transforms the world in the best sense of that term does have certain attributes and does encourage certain values. These practices and values can be explained and justified with the use of a variety ethical arguments. Thus a Christ-against-culture group that opposes participation in what David Loy has called our new global religion, the insatiable pursuit of material well-being, the religion of the market, can by its very resistance to our current culture transform it.[18] Similarly, a Christ-of-culture stance with regard to participatory democracy can undergird our morality that has been, historically, doubtfully supported by philosophically questionable arguments and half-baked Deism. The insight that somehow God transcends history and that Jesus is the Christ also allows us to struggle with each other and work with each other and do so with humility. These facts, if no others, constitute excellent reasons for adapting these typologies that Niebuhr insightfully, but imperfectly established.

NOTES

[1] H. Richard Niebuhr, *Christ and Culture* (New York: Harper, 1951).

[2] Darryl M. Trimiew, *Voices of the Silenced: The Responsible Self in a Marginalized Community* (Pilgrim Press, 1993).

[3] Victor Anderson notes the importance of Niebuhr's work for American public theology while noting the under utilization of Black moralists, writing. "This underdevelopment cannot be attributed to an insufficient list of possible representatives. For one may easily draw from the religiously motivated public practices of such figures as David Walker, Frederick Douglas, Sojourner Truth, Booker T. Washington, W. E. B. DuBois, Ida B. Wells, Martin Luther King, Jr., Fannie Lou Hamer, Malcolm X, Elijah Muhammad, and Howard Thurman. Ironically some of these figures are Niebuhr's contemporaries and their work was not utilized by him either in his own work." See Victor Anderson, "The Wrestle of Christ and Culture in Pragmatic Public Theology," *American Journal of Theology & Philosophy* 19 (May 1998): 135.

[4] James Cone, *A Black Theology of Liberation* (Seabury Press, 1975).

[5] Sharon D. Welch, *Communities of Resistance and Solidarity: A Feminist Theology of Liberation* (Maryknoll, NY: Orbis, 1985).

[6] S. Jonathan Bass, *Blessed are the Peacemakers: Martin Luther King, Jr., Eight White Religious Leaders, and the "Letter from Birmingham Jail"* (Baton Rouge, LA: Louisiana State University Press, 2001).

[7] James R. Cochrane's work is illustrative of how this change in theology and perspective took place. See "Christ and Culture: Now and Then," *Journal of Theology for Southern African* 71.1 (June 1990): 39-55.

[8] See especially the insightful criticism by John Howard Yoder in his essay entitled, "How H. Richard Niebuhr Reasoned: A Critique of Christ and Culture," *Authentic Transformation: A New Vision of Christ and Culture,* ed. Glen H. Stassen, D. M. Yeager, and John Howard Yoder (Nashville: Abingdon Press, 1996), 47 and, from a distinctly different point of view, Diane Yeager's article in this *JSCE* issue.

[9] Ibid., 48-49.

[10] What is most amazing is the fact that we blacks have, for much of our church history, maintained Christologies that were oppressive.

[11] Martin writes, "Only through an inner spiritual transformation do we gain the strength to fight vigorously the evils of the world in a humble and loving spirit." *Strength to Love* (New York: Harper & Row, 1963), 13.

[12] Martin writes, "Here on all the roads of life, he is striving in our striving. Like an ever-loving Father, he is working through history for the salvation of his children. As we struggle to defeat the forces of evil, the God of the universe struggles with us. Evil dies on the seashore, not merely because of man's endless struggle against it, but because of God's power to defeat it. Ibid., 64.

[13] Robert Benne, "The Church and Politics: Four Possible Connections," in *Moral Issues and Christian Response*, ed. Paul T. Jersild and Dale A. Johnson (New York: Holt, Rinehart & Winston, 1988), 4-12.

[14] Peter Paris, *The Social Teaching of the Black Churches* (Philadelphia: Fortress Press, 1985), 10.

[15] Colbert S. Cartwright, *People of the Chalice: Disciples of Christ in Faith and Practice* (St. Louis: CBP Press, 1987), 15.

[16] Ibid., 19.

[17] Martin Luther King, Jr., is highly observant on this point, writing, "The church must be reminded that it is not the master or the servant of the state, but rather the conscience of the state. It must be the guide and the critic of the state, and never its tool. If the church does not recapture its prophetic zeal, it will become an irrelevant social club without moral or spiritual authority. If the church does not participate actively in the struggle for peace and for economic and racial justice, it will forfeit the loyalty of millions and cause men everywhere to say that it has atrophied its will. But if the church will free itself from the shackles of a deadening status quo, and, recovering its great historic mission, will speak and act fearlessly and insistently in terms of justice and peace, it will enkindle the imagination of mankind and fire the souls of men, imbuing them with a glowing and ardent love for truth, justice, and peace." Martin, *Strength to Love*, 47.

[18] David Loy, "The Religion of the Market," *Journal of the American Academy of Religion* 65.1 (Spring 1997): 275-90.

JUST PEACEMAKING

Resource Section on Just Peacemaking Theory

Glen H. Stassen

In the 1993 annual meeting of the Society of Christian Ethics, (SCE) a panel including Duane Friesen, Alan Geyer, Bryan Hehir, Edward Long, Glen Stassen, Ronald Stone, and Susan Thistlethwaite began to develop a just peacemaking theory to supplement (not supplant) the traditional paradigms of just war theory and pacifism. Since then twenty-three interdisciplinary scholars, mostly SCE members along with some international relations scholars, continued to work to develop a just peacemaking theory. The result was published as *Just Peacemaking: Ten Practices for Abolishing War* (Pilgrim Press, 1998). The new paradigm brings together ten practices of peacemaking that have been developed and tested since World War II, with its explosive demonstration of the increased destructiveness of war, and the powerful need to prevent war. The authors contend that each practice has demonstrated its effectiveness in making wars less likely; and in combination they have a synergistic effect, making war significantly less likely in areas where they spread. Therefore, persons of faith, and persons who care about peace, are morally bound to strengthen support for and awareness of the practices of just peacemaking.

The authors contend that in addition to the focus of pacifism and just war theory on the question where they disagree—whether a war is justified— public debate also needs to focus on the other crucial question—whether to support and demand the specific practices of war-prevention. They reached a consensus on the ingredients of just peacemaking theory, and they intend the ten practices to be a unified theory, and not merely a list. The ten practices are:

Journal of the Society of Christian Ethics, 23/1 (2003): 169-170

Peacemaking Initiatives

1. Support nonviolent direct action.
2. Take independent initiatives to reduce threat.
3. Use cooperative conflict resolution.
4. Acknowledge responsibility for conflict and injustice and seek repentance and forgiveness.

Justice

5. Advance democracy, human rights, and religious liberty.
6. Foster just and sustainable economic development.

Love and Community

7. Work with emerging cooperative forces in the international system.
8. Strengthen the United Nations and international efforts for cooperation and human rights.
9. Reduce offensive weapons and weapons trade.
10. Encourage grassroots peacemaking groups and other voluntary associations.

The articles in this section of the *Journal of the Society of Christian Ethics* are intended to assist in teaching just peacemaking theory, and in interpreting crises and endemic conflicts ethically. For example, can just peacemaking theory lift up peacemaking practices for attention that are already being advocated in some conflicts in Africa but that need greater popular and civil support? In the current response to terrorism, should U. S. policy focus on advancing human rights, democracy, and sustainable economic development in the Middle East, beyond present actions of repressing terrorism? Is policy sufficiently supportive of cooperative forces in the international system, including the United Nations? Are these questions that an adequate ethical assessment should be asking? The authors were chosen not from those who devised just peacemaking theory, but from other scholars who have distinguished themselves for their expertise in just war theory, human rights, the Middle East, etc. The essays discuss the unity of the theory and assess its usefulness in interpreting some representative cases. This resource section also provides a bibliography for further reading.

The Unity, Realism, and Obligatoriness of Just Peacemaking Theory

Glen H. Stassen

Abstract

Just peacemaking theory is a new paradigm for Christian ethics alongside just war theory and pacifism. It answers a different question than just war theory and pacifism seek to answer: not the question of justification, but prevention. The ethical norms of just peacemaking are not ideals or principles, but realistic, historically situated practices that are empirically demonstrating their effectiveness in preventing war. They are interactive, community practices that inherently engage in dialogue with diverse others, as befits a postmodern or pluralistic age. By no means does just peacemaking theory predict that there will be no more wars, or that the state is withering away, but it focuses on realistic, empirical evidence that ten historically effective practices are in fact preventing wars, and therefore, they have similar obligatoriness as do the principles of just war theory and pacifism.

Introduction

Just peacemaking theory is the consensus after five years of interdisciplinary work by twenty-three scholars, mostly Christian ethicists and international relations specialists, and a few "who have struggled in various ways to make and keep the peace in this often violent age," as called for by the U.S. Catholic bishops in *The Challenge of Peace* (#24).[1] It is intended not merely as ten practices that effectively prevent wars, but as a new paradigm, alongside pacifism and just war theory.

A new paradigm needs to be justified by its bringing to attention important dimensions of concern that previous paradigms overlooked, or did not articulate as clearly as needed. Ten effective practices of war prevention have been developed, mostly since the horror of World War II and the threat of nuclear war demonstrated their need. These practices are showing their effectiveness in preventing war, but are not lifted up for attention by present paradigms, which focus attention on whether a war is justified rather than on effective preventive practices.

But a new paradigm usually finds resistance.[2] Previous paradigms have truth in them, and their truth has helped us to order our worlds. It is only natural that we ask whether and how those truths are reflected in the new paradigm. Accordingly, the authors of *Just Peacemaking: Ten Practices for Abolishing War* make clear that "We intend this work to take its place along with, but not to replace, the established paradigms of pacifism and just war theory" (2).[3] Wars will still happen, and therefore pacifism and just war theory are still very much needed. *The Challenge of Peace* also made clear that we need both a positive theology of peace (just peacemaking theory) and an ethics of the restraint of war (pacifism and just war theory).

Similarly with realism. Questions from the perspective of realism show up in essays in this issue of the *Journal of the Society of Christian Ethics*, and accordingly I hope to show that realism influenced crucial turns in the development of just peacemaking theory.

The Specific Realistic Evidence for Each Practice

The working group of twenty-three interdisciplinary scholars took a decisively realist turn when we rejected defining just peacemaking theory in terms of principles or ideals, and instead decided to focus on practices that are in fact demonstrating their effectiveness in the realistic conditions of present history. We write: "As the realist Reinhold Niebuhr observed, institutions of international cooperation are not created out of nothing by fiat or wish, but built bit by bit as nations act day by day in ways that strengthen their usefulness" (142). *Just Peacemaking* is about those bit-by-bit practices.

Our claim is a limited and empirically realistic claim: that the ten specific practices that we identify are preventing many wars, bit by bit. Each chapter presents empirical evidence—specific historical examples or empirical political science data analysis—that the practice in that chapter is preventing wars. For example, nonviolent direct action effected revolutions in Poland, East Germany, the Czech Republic, and the Philippines without requiring a war. By conflict resolution, former president Jimmy Carter was able to achieve peace between Egypt and Israel, turn the immediately impending violent invasion of Haiti into a nonviolent invasion (and win the Nobel Peace Prize). Independent initiatives have achieved peaceful change and nuclear weapons disarmament (46, 48-51). Turning to democracy empirically decreases the frequency of war: no democracy with human rights has fought a direct war against another democracy in the twentieth century. "The more democratic states are, the more peaceful their relations are likely to be. . . . This has been established by statistical analyses of pairs of states. . ." (97). Empirical study shows that the more nations are engaged with international organizations, the less frequently they engage in wars. We do not merely hope sustainable economic justice will decrease causes of war; we cite the award-winning study by Ted Gurr demonstrating that civil wars and terrorism correlate most closely with relative economic deprivation, and cite wars caused by scarcity in natural resources, including oil and water (112, 118f.). We do not merely hope that just peacemaking practices will reduce military spending and arms trade by developing countries; we show that it was in fact cut by three-fourths from $60 billion per year to $15 billion per year in the seven-year period from 1988-1995 (165), and nuclear warheads were reduced from 47,000 to 15,500 (159). We do not merely hope citizens' peacemaking groups will someday make a difference, but cite numerous examples of their doing so (179-83).

These are empirical results. They are real. We ask ethicists to focus assessment on the empirical evidence of what is in fact happening, not on generalizations about possible futures. The test of the truth and realism of just peacemaking theory is not whether war nevertheless sometimes breaks out, especially where these practices are not used; it does, and it will. The test is whether the empirical claim is true that each of the practices is preventing some wars. If in fact this is happening, and if, therefore, we have a more precise understanding of how to prevent wars, then there is in fact a realistic and disciplined hope that *many* potential wars can be "abolished" or at least prevented, and the war-misery otherwise experienced by millions can be avoided. That is no mean hope, even though it is a realistic hope. If that claim is true, the question then is whether we have an obligation to identify, support, and strengthen the practices and whether this paradigm can enable us to see conflict situations from a new and fruitful angle. It is a research paradigm. We ask ethicists to test it by using it to interpret specific conflicts, as Simeon Ilesanmi and Charles Kimball have done below, and I have done in the September, 2002 issue of *The Council of the Societies for the Study of Religion Bulletin* and elsewhere.

Furthermore, each chapter identifies realistic obstacles to the peacemaking practice it is describing, and seeks to identify ways to reduce these obstacles (40f., 45, 51f., 58f., 60- 64, 69-71, 77-79. 100f., 118f., 122, 136, 140, 148, 154f., 163-65, 168-71, 174f., 177f., 182f.). Lisa Cahill makes a perceptive point in asking us to write more extensively of sin. We do write of sin and guilt (10, 70, 80f., 112, 124f.). But we have intentionally fashioned the practices so that they could be adopted by persons of other faiths or no named faith, by analogy with just war theory. Therefore we write more often of violence, injustice, resistance to acknowledging complicity, and forces that block the practices of just peacemaking.

The fact that the practices are increasingly being employed indicates they are perceived by many governments and other actors as serving their interests. The fact that in some cases they are being blocked indicates they are perceived by some as not in their interests. The question is whether we can help people see how to push politically and perceptively so the interest in these specific peacemaking practices increases.

Furthermore, we believe it is realistic to identify multiple causes of war, not simply one, and to identify ten practices whose effectiveness in preventing war is demonstrated with empirical realism, rather than reducing peacemaking to one practice such as conflict resolution.

Historically embedded practices, as opposed to historical ideals, resemble H. Richard Niebuhr's ethics of the fitting: peacemaking efforts must fit the context. We argue: "On the one hand, peacemakers can recognize and understand the major institutions, forces, and trends working internationally toward peace as resources to encourage, support, and use. On the other hand, if would-be just peacemakers do the opposite—treat the system and its institutions not as a resource to be used and reformed but an evil to be fought or overthrown—then however well-intentioned their activities may be, they are likely to do more harm than good. The message could be put in the words, 'Be wise as serpents and harmless as doves'" (134). Ethicists will recognize the irony: these are the words of Jesus, cited by Reinhold Niebuhr, who here rightly recognized Jesus' realism.

In developing our ethics of practices, we pointed to the function of normative practices in writers as diverse as John Howard Yoder, Michael Walzer, Sharon Welch, Theophus Smith, Larry Rasmussen, Stanley Hauerwas, and James William McClendon, Jr. Our intention was to be broadly inclusive. We wrote that "a practice is neither an ideal nor a rule, but a human activity that regularly takes place and that a sociologist could observe." After extensive discussion, we singled out the ten practices that are demonstrably, empirically, being effective in preventing wars and creating peace (listed in the introduction to this professional resources section).

The turn to practices resolved some major tensions in the group, particularly between realists and idealists, and between international relations scholars and ethicists.

It brought together the realists and the advocates of a liberal-democratic peace, the pacifists, and the empiricists and historians among us. Realism says the world is characterized by power struggles and conflicts of interest, and history does not take leaps, so we have to learn to deal with the world as it is. Idealists say we should focus on ideals, and imagine how we can move the world toward those ideals. The ten practices of peacemaking that we advocate are happening in the real world of power struggles and conflicts of interest. They are in fact making the eruption of power struggles into war less likely and their expression by peaceful means more likely. We are expressing not just a wish, but calling those who have eyes to see to notice what new processes of deliverance are happening among us and spreading globally. We are urging not disembodied ideals or ahistorical oughts to impose on an alien history they do not fit, but support for what is serving functional needs in the midst of the power realities (23-24).

Some of the ten practices may appear to be *sets* of practices working together for a broader goal, such as the several kinds of cooperative forces named in Schroeder's chapter, or the tenth practice, "encourage grassroots peacemaking groups and voluntary associations." But if MacIntyre can call architecture, farming, physics, and the work of a historian practices, and McClendon can call medicine a practice, each of which may be seen as a set of complex and differing practices united by a broad goal, then surely a set of practices like supporting the United Nations or reducing offensive weapons can be called practices.[4] By our criteria, they are historically situated, concretely observable, they work together for peace, and they are therefore ethically normative or obligatory. This, then, is the most important level of unity in just peacemaking theory: these are the practices that are in fact preventing war within our historical experience.

Distinguishing the Two Dimensions of Justification and Prevention

Wars will continue to occur. Furthermore, states are not withering away, nor should they: many wars come from anarchy within states, as in Somalia; or from states that are too weak to hold their people together, as in the former Yugoslavia once Tito had died. Therefore, we still need just war theory and pacifism to debate the justification or restraint of participation in wars. But the new empirical awareness that these ten practices do prevent many wars creates more opportunities for preventing wars, and we need a paradigm that can focus debate about preventive practices.

We may visualize the debate about the justification of a war on the x axis of Figure 1. A spectrum runs from pacifism on the left to just war theory on the right, and beyond to more hawkish interpretations of just war theory, and then nationalists and right-of-staters who defer to the state to decide whether a war is justified.

The y axis is a different dimension. It answers the question of peacemaking practices, not justification. It measures commitment to take peacemaking initiatives that are effective in preventing wars. It articulates the intent in pacifism understood as peacemaking, and the intent in just war theory's provisions of last resort and just intention—an intent, however, which they gloss over because they debate what they disagree about: whether a war is justified, and because they lack an articulate paradigm of peacemaking initiatives. (Public debate focuses on the criteria of paradigms that are ready at hand.) And those paradigms fail to lift preventive actions up for public attention. Debate needs a just peacemaking theory so participants can know how to focus their arguments on preventive actions. When a crisis impends, it is too late to create an ethic *de novo* or *ad hoc*. Therefore, we need a paradigm that focuses public attention on the y axis as well. We need a two-dimensional ethic, not a one-dimensional ethic.

Figure 1. Distinguishing the Dimension of Debate over the Justification of War from the Dimension of Obligation to Engage in the Ten Peacemaking Practices

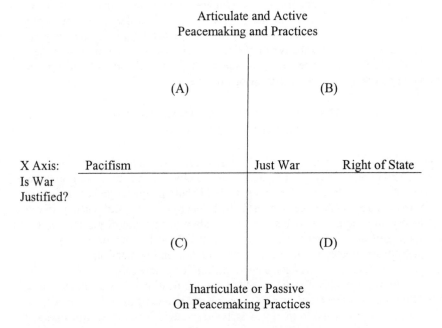

Y Axis:
Are Peacemaking Practices Obligatory?

Articulate and Active
Peacemaking and Practices

(A)   (B)

X Axis: Pacifism   Just War   Right of State
Is War
Justified?

(C)   (D)

Inarticulate or Passive
On Peacemaking Practices

Persons or churches at (A) in the diagram are pacifists who are active peacemakers, such as Martin Luther King, Jr. and many Quakers and other participants in the New Call to Peacemaking. Persons and churches at (B) in the diagram are just war theorists who are active peacemakers, such as Kofi

Annan and many Presbyterians. Persons and churches at (C) in the diagram are pacifists in the sense that they would not participate in war, but they are not articulate about or actively engaged in peacemaking initiatives. Persons and churches at (D) in the diagram support a just war, and are inarticulate or inactive in peacemaking.

Christian realists are used to arguing that the world is sinful and therefore sometimes war is justified to restrain aggressors. Other realists add that governments use the claim to be restraining aggressors to justify their own aggression. When they want yet more realism in just peacemaking theory, what they seem to want is an argument about when war is justified. But *Just Peacemaking* intentionally does not develop a unified position on that x-axis question for four reasons: (1) We want to draw attention to the y-axis question of prevention rather than letting the x-axis question of justification dominate discussion exclusively. (2) We want to establish clearly that one can be a just peacemaker whether one is a just war theorist or a pacifist; there are just peacemakers at both position A and position B. (3) Some of the twenty-three are pacifists and most are just war theorists, and we would not agree on the x-axis question. But we do agree on the y-axis question, and we want to draw attention there. (4) We believe the x-axis question is indeed very important, and we want it to continue to be debated; we recognize that would take another book. Martin Cook suggests insightfully that we need a metatheory uniting the three paradigms. I have been working on that and have taken a first step in *Kingdom Ethics*.[5]

In *Just Peacemaking*, Michael J. Smith argues: "It may be just or necessary for a state to declare its intention to act on its own. . . . And the intervention may still be just even if its motives are mixed. For example, India's intervention in the former East Pakistan and Tanzania's in the Uganda of Idi Amin are often cited as unilateral interventions that nevertheless ended humanitarian disasters" (154). This demands neither that the United Nations have the military force to perform the interventions (it does not), nor that all just interventions be approved by the United Nations (the veto can block them). But normally some international approval provides a realistic check and balance against intervention for unjust reasons.

Just peacemaking theory is unified by its attention to the social context of shared responsibility for preventing wars. Pacifism and just peacemaking theory arose in a social context when speaking of the participation of the people and grassroots groups in shaping policy for peace and war would have been an anachronism. People and churches could decide only whether to fight in a war that rulers had decided on, and bless the war, or to refuse conscientiously. Pacifism as conscientious refusal and just war theory as selective refusal guide those responsibilities. But they are influenced by their history of having a more passive role in the early stages of the powerful drift toward war. They drive the debate toward one question: is it right to make this war? Our debates are much like two persons in a rowboat drifting rapidly toward a waterfall, arguing whether to protest against the fall or to justify taking part in the catastrophe. The force of the drift toward war is powerful, and arguing whether it is right is not enough. We need a third person in the boat who asks early about initiatives to head for the shore while there is still time.

Our social context has changed. We now have responsibility for what governments do in our name, and means to prod them to take peacemaking initiatives. The successful Jubilee 2000 international campaign to cancel billions of dollars of indebtedness by the forty poorest nations, the protests against the WTO, and citizen organizing against the Iraq war, illustrate the change in our social context. They evidence citizen participation in shaping policy and the need for an ethic guiding that participation—different from the Middle Ages. They also concern the most powerful force that is connecting nations together into a global society—economic globalization. Jubilee 2000 was not only a protest against indebtedness, but a constructive solution in line with the theory of just peacemaking practice number six, "foster just and sustainable economic development," with special attention to communities in poor nations. The WTO protest will be effective in the long run only if a constructive change in international policy is developed. The protest against the Iraq war is an advocacy of inspections and working with other nations and the United Nations. Neither is effectively guided only by an ethic of conscientious or selective refusal; each requires a positive theology of constructive peacemaking.

The Transition in the International System

The underlying unity of just peacemaking theory is also seen in the trend toward partial international community, as demonstrated in the chapter by Paul Schroeder. Schroeder was influential in our realist turn to empirical practices, and is considered by many to be the best historian of international relations today.[6] His historical evidence indicates that a transition is occurring in the international system: a web or network of ongoing cooperative relationships and international institutions is transforming the world from an anarchy into an anarchic society.[7] "An anarchic society defines what a just peace means in international relations; the best practical system of rules, norms, practices, and institutions for reducing the anarchic (conflictual, violent, and destructive) elements and promoting the societal (legal, cooperative, and normative aspects) of this anarchic society, while recognizing that for profound reasons it will remain an anarchic society for the foreseeable future (in my view, for any conceivable or desirable one)" (135). Our world is not a pure anarchy of power and national interest, nor is it or will it be the world community advocated by idealism. Reinhold Niebuhr saw the coming transition toward something like an international community: "The world's most urgent problem is the establishment of a tolerable system of mutual security for the avoidance of international anarchy. . . . The historical realists . . . are right in looking to commitments made by the United Nations in [the second world] war as the real source of possibly wider commitments for the future. . . . An economically interdependent world must in some sense become a politically integrated world community or allow potential instruments of community to become instruments of mutual annihilation."[8] Ever since nations formed an alliance to defend against the aggression of Nazi Germany, and subsequently realized that we must not have World War III or nuclear war, the international system has been shifting toward a kind of community in which commitments, norms, and practices become important along with the anarchy. This fits a covenant ethics or common good critique of liberalism's "unsituated, merely interest-driven self."[9] Nations are situated in an anarchic society that gives them incentives and partially coerces them toward means of working together, but also allows war.

Schroeder's masterful work as a historian demonstrates that this shift began to develop in the time of the Concert of Europe, 1813-1854. Cronin, likewise, has argued persuasively that the development of the Concert depended on a change in the popular sense of the legitimacy of government and of transnational identity, which means grass-roots groups and the persuasion of people play a role.[10] The result of the Concert: the ratio of battlefield deaths to the total population of Europe in the nineteenth century was cut to one-seventh of what it had been in the eighteenth century. In our time a much stronger and more global development is happening: four separate but interrelated trends in international history, marked since the early nineteenth century and increasingly powerful and accelerating in the latter twentieth century, have sharply altered the nature of the international system.

A. The decline of the utility of war, that is, a steep rise in the costs and dangers of major war as a tool of statecraft. . . .

B. The priority now placed by most modern states on success in trade and the economy, as opposed to success in war, as the key to domestic order, welfare, and legitimacy. . . .

C. A dramatic increase in the volume, density, and scope of international exchanges, communications, and transactions of all kinds and the increasing integration of these exchanges into organized, complex, international, supranational, and transnational networks, corporations, and other institutions. . . . An equally startling increase in the number, scope, durability, and effectiveness of international organizations of all kinds, both governmental and non-governmental, to which both modern governments and non-governmental groups must pay attention and which they must use for their particular purposes.

D. A gradual, uneven, but unmistakable ascendancy of one form of government, liberal representative democracy, as the dominant legitimate form of governance of modern states and of one kind of economic system, market-oriented capitalism (whether of the welfare-state or a more laissez-faire variety). . . .

Accuracy is crucial in understanding Schroeder's argument and the argument of the book: Nowhere does he or do the book's authors predict that major war will not break out, or that wars will not increase, or that these trends will not be reversed. Again and again, Schroeder rejects idealistic ways out of this anarchic society as "futile and desperate, a Utopian or rather Dystopian dream, promising far worse conflict, tyranny, and war than the present system" (137). Rather, the point is that "These four trends combine . . . greatly to enhance the possibilities of just peacemaking within the existing system. . . . These trends represent potential openings for peacemakers to exploit" (139). Schroeder realistically names six reasons why efforts to form associations of nations have broken down, often disastrously, in the past. He argues that the causes of breakdown are being weakened by the four trends he has identified. "This is not just theory; it is happening. The continued existence and success of organizations like NATO, the European Union, the United Nations, and many others go a long way to make it demonstrable fact. To argue that voluntary associations for peace cannot work better today than in the past seems to me a bit like arguing that manned heavier-than-air flight is not possible for the same reasons it was impossible before 1903" (141). The book is not arguing that the trends are inevitable, but that they are real and they give opportunity for persons to strengthen them and thus reduce the likelihood of specific wars. Thus the countries of Europe that were the source of two world wars are now all democracies with human rights interwoven with international institutions, plus embedded patterns of expectations. War between Germany and France is now almost impossible to imagine.

The book's authors wanted the title, *Just Peacemaking: A New Paradigm.* The publisher, however, being allergic to the word "paradigm" vetoed that, and instead selected the subtitle, *Ten Practices to Abolish War.* The reality is that the publisher has the power to decide the title, has an interest in sales, and the confidence that it knows marketing. Thus the subtitle indicates publisher's interest, not authorial intent. Nowhere does the book suggest just peacemaking will abolish all war. Worldwide nuclear war may break out this year, in India and Pakistan, or in the Middle East. That is not the question. The question is whether we have an obligation to support the ten practices that have been demonstrated to prevent war within the existing system.

The Transition in Realism

Realism, not only as taught by Reinhold Niebuhr, but broadly construed, has greatly influenced "nearly everyone working in the field of Christian ethics" in most of the twentieth century.[11] Niebuhr was my teacher. Accordingly I want to show that the theme in international relations theory of growing interdependence accords with developments within realism itself. No prominent international relations theorist argues from an altruistic or idealist perspective; each assumes states act from self-interest, and each at the same time emphasizes that international structure influences states' perceptions and actions.[12]

The shift in international relations theory is nicely illustrated by the election of Robert Jervis as president of the American Political Science Association in 2001, following the election of Robert Keohane in 2000. Jervis is a realist who has developed a wide reputation as a careful analyst of diverse theoretical approaches, with appreciation for the truth, the logic, and the lacunae in each of them. In two incisive analytical articles assessing the field, he sorts out the similarities and differences between classical realism, neorealism, and the new paradigm of institutionalism, or complex interdependence. He argues they have much in common.[13]

Realism has five basic assumptions:

1. "*States* can be considered the main actors. . . . The state has proven remarkably resilient in the face of multiple social forces and the insistence of scholars that its importance is rapidly waning."[14]

2. *Anarchy*: "The absence of a sovereign authority that can make and enforce binding agreements creates opportunities for states to advance their interests unilaterally and makes it important and difficult for states to cooperate with one another. . . . Agreements must be crafted to minimize the danger of double crosses. . . ."[15]

3. *Self-interest* is what states innately seek. Offensive realists like Hans Morgenthau assume states' interest is to maximize their power, because aggressive states threaten them. Defensive realists like Jervis argue that because war is now so destructive and more is to be gained by alliance, cooperation, and trade, most states' interest is mutual security, and they see effective means of cooperation as in their interest, while still being wary of potential aggressors.[16]

4. *Perception of Intentions* was considered unreliable by Morgenthau, so states should assume others seek power-dominance and act accordingly. Jervis agrees that conciliatory policies may decrease security if others are seeking dominance, but adds that treating states as belligerent when

they prefer cooperation also decreases security. Therefore he has focused significant research on perception of intentions, and has carefully delineated factors that cause misperception.[17]

5. *Military force* is a usable and effective instrument of policy. But war is now so destructive that states usually see it as not worth the cost. "The security dilemma" is that a military buildup threatens other states; so they increase their threatening capability; and security decreases.[18]

6. *Alliances and institutions* are sometimes in the national interest. Classical realism contended that political integration among states is slight and lasts only as long as it serves the national interests of the most powerful states.[19] Neorealism contends that in order to achieve realistic interests in security, order, and economic growth, nations enter into institutions and shared expectations, whose binding force then changes their ongoing interests, perceptions, and actions.

Governments have believed it in their national interest to create an enormous number of international and regional institutions since World War II, which have bound them into various structures, and they are creating more—especially in Europe:

> The great diminution of national sovereignty that we have seen, the delegation of significant power to supranational bodies, and the development of some degree of popular identification with Europe rather than with individual nations were not what most of the European leaders sought at the start, but rather were the product of the institutions they established. The institutions had a "life of their own" in not only binding the states more than the founders foresaw, but in changing beliefs about what is possible and desirable: they shaped, as much as they reflected, interests. . . . I think we have underestimated the importance of these dynamic effects of institutions. . . .[20]
>
> Hence there has been a shift to "the current security community." This involves a change in outlooks and even values among general populations, elites, and national leaders. Rabid and competitive nationalism has greatly declined, war is seen as a brutal necessity if not a crime rather than a glorious activity, and control of historically disputed territories such as Alsace and Lorraine is of greatly decreased concern, in part because the developed countries are democratic and share most values.[21]
>
> The consensus among scholars and, more importantly, elites is that the most powerful states will not fight each other. This situation represents a truly revolutionary change in world politics

and makes particularly relevant the path-breaking analysis of Robert Keohane and Joseph Nye. This does not mean the end of conflict and the struggle for advantage, let alone the end of the state. Thus, I do not believe it means the end of realism; although, since this approach stressed the pervasive influence of the fear of inter-state war, it will have to be reshaped if it is to explain, let alone guide, a world in which security threats are of a very different nature and probably much less important.[22]

Robert Keohane was elected president of the American Political Science Association for 2000.[23] In their influential book, *Power and Independence*, he and Joseph Nye argue that the realist paradigm is still relevant for relationships where war is threatened, especially among smaller regional powers, so an adequate theory must take realism into account.[24] But "we live in an era of interdependence . . . . The very nature of world politics is changing" (3). Therefore they develop a theory of complex interdependence, or institutionalism, to "provide a means of distilling and blending the wisdom in both positions by developing a coherent theoretical framework for the political analysis of interdependence" (4). "We are not suggesting that international conflict disappears when interdependence prevails. On the contrary, conflict will take new forms, and may even increase. But the traditional approaches to understanding conflict in world politics will not explain" conflict with interdependence particularly well (8). Complex interdependence assumes (1) multiple channels—interstate, transgovern-mental, transnational—connect societies, so states do not act as single units but as collections of different levels that relate regularly to similar levels in other societies and other governments; (2) "the national interest" is a melange of different issues operating in different channels, rather than a clear hierarchy dominated by military security interests; and (3) the usefulness and likelihood of use of military force is declining. States rely more on other instruments of power (25-34, 99).

Realism and complex interdependence are ideal types, representing reality with greater or lesser accuracy depending on the issue area and the nature of the changing international system. Accordingly, Keohane and Nye test their explanatory power in four issue areas. They conclude that:

> The realist assumptions fail even to focus on much of the relevant foreign policy agenda—those areas that do not touch the security and autonomy of the state. . . . Yet [those] who believe that social and economic interdependence have totally changed the world fail to take elements of continuity into account. . . . All four of our cases confirmed a significant role, under some conditions, for the overall military power structure (224).

> During the cold war [military security] goals were dominant in oceans politics; but during the [1970s] economic and other goals have frequently overridden military security goals, not only in many small or middle-sized countries but in the world's greatest naval power, the United States. . . . In monetary politics, security goals have periodically been relevant, but they have not been determining (115).

Any judgments must be heavily qualified, but "a strong argument could be made that complex interdependence will *increasingly* characterize world politics, because each of the three conditions of complex interdependence corresponds to a long-term historical change with deep causes of its own" (227). The long-term trend increasingly holds governments responsible for economic security and not only military security. The long-term trend in the technology of communications and transportation strengthens multiple channels of contact. The increasing destructiveness of military weapons, the risks of nuclear escalation, and the opposition of domestic opinion to the costs of the use of force make military force less usable (102, 150, 227f.). Replacing the security threats of the Cold War with Soviet-American detente has caused relationships to approximate complex interdependence more (212, 216). Nevertheless, "lesser states involved in regional rivalries and nonstate terrorist groups may find it easier to use force than before" (228, 246)—a prescient observation.

In the afterward to the 1989 addition, Keohane and Nye observe how their theory has fared in the twelve years since the first edition. "The research program has been fruitful. . . . There is a widespread (although not universal) view among scholars that . . . neorealism narrowly interpreted, is inadequate as an explanatory framework for contemporary world politics" (267). "Much has been learned, especially about conditions under which nations will cooperate with regimes" (267-68; cf. 272). In their new assessment still another decade later, in 2001, they conclude that interdependence has grown not just in degree but in kind: increased density of networks, increased intensity of contact and thus rapidity of institutional change, and increased transnational participation. This is true not only of governmental organizations, but also of international NGOs, "which more than quadrupled from about 6,000 to over 26,000 in the 1990s alone."[25]

> Even today complex interdependence is far from universal. Military force was used by or threatened against states throughout the 1990s, from the Taiwan Strait to Iraq, from Kuwait to the former Yugoslavia; from Kashmir to the Congo. Civil wars are endemic in much of sub-Saharan Africa and sometimes have escalated into international warfare, as when the Democratic Republic of Congo's civil war engulfed five neighboring

countries. . . . Nevertheless, interstate use and threat of military force have virtually disappeared in certain areas of the world—notably among the advanced, information-era democracies bordering the Atlantic and the Pacific, as well as among a number of their less wealthy neighbors in Latin America and increasingly in Eastern-Central Europe.[26]

John Mearsheimer is an offensive realist who disagrees. He admits that institutionalists "accept the assumption that states operate in an anarchic environment and behave in a self-interested manner." Institutionalism "explicitly accepts realism's core assumptions. . . ."[27] But since he assumes states refrain from binding themselves beyond the present, temporary power balance, his either/or thinking criticizes them for incorporating truths of realism in their theories.[28]

Mearsheimer admits that a growing network of international institutions and collective security alliances is forming. "Realists recognize that great powers sometimes find institutions—especially alliances—useful for maintaining or even increasing their share of world power. . . . The debate between the institutionalists and me is about whether institutions can have an independent effect on state behavior, or whether instead institutional outcomes reflect great power interests, and are essentially tools that great powers employ for their own selfish purposes."[29]

Four respondents take issue with Mearsheimer, thus clarifying the debate between his either/or kind of realism and institutionalist theory.[30] His critics agree with him that the question is whether institutions do make a difference in state behavior. Keohane and Martin write that institutions change states' perceptions of their interest, their perceptions of what other states will do, their perceptions of where the focal points for agreement are, and the ability of states to cooperate, so that institutions do have an independent effect on what states do. They point out that Mearsheimer's theory led him to predict the likely disintegration of NATO after the Cold War, and the weakening of the European Union, which turned out to be decisively wrong. Furthermore, since realism rightly says states seek to do what is in their self-interest, it hardly makes sense that states are investing considerable resources in NATO, EU, the UN, GATT, WTO, NAFTA, The European Court of Justice, the Nuclear Nonproliferation Treaty, etc., if international institutions have no power to change outcomes.[31] Mearsheimer's critics offer considerable evidence that institutions do alter national interest and behavior; and they say that he regularly minimizes this evidence. They contend that he regularly distorts their institutionalist theories. My own assessment is that the critics are accurate in these claims, and that they clearly have the best in the debate. The election of Keohane and Jervis as president of the APSA suggests the political scientists also accord their writings the highest of respect.

Mearsheimer writes that his position is unpopular among political scientists because it "treats war as inevitable, and indeed sometimes necessary. . . . Most Americans, however, tend to think it is morally incorrect to fight wars to change or preserve the balance of power."[32] He criticizes his opponents for letting their theories be influenced by moral considerations. His critics, however, say his interpretation of reality is incorrect; the world is becoming more globalized, more mutually interdependent, and this does give play for moral considerations.

We have seen a dramatic demonstration. The Bush administration began by disengaging from the ABM Treaty, the Comprehensive Test Ban Treaty, the International Criminal Court, and the Kyoto Protocol, opposing nation-building, advocating a more unilateralist foreign policy, denigrating and undermining peacemaking efforts between South and North Korea, disengaging from peacemaking between Israel and Palestine, thus leaving Palestinians in a position of bitterly frustrating weakness, and joined Israel in pulling out of the international conference in Durban, South Africa, on racism. This caused unprecedented resentment in many international arenas, especially Arab and Muslim. Then came the attack of September 11, 2001. Responding effectively required intelligence, bases, terrorist account-blocking, and political support from a wide community of nations. The unilateralist policy was shifted somewhat by the realities of the international system into extensive international engagement, as well as pledges of nation-building in Afghanistan after the war. The administration then articulated its determination to make war on Iraq to seek regime change, and denigrated inspections to deal with the problem. World pressure and opposition in the United States, as well as polls saying people wanted the United States to work through the UN and inspections before making war, caused President Bush to go to the UN and the Congress and promise to wait for inspections. At this writing, it appears that the unilateralism may lead to war, but that the United States will pay a large price in international resentment. This may be a factor in the widespread international disinvestment from dollar-denominated stocks, and the consequent decline of the dollar and the stock market. We do not know if the administration will deal with the many complex causes of terrorism, including the underlying injustices, but we do see that the system partly shifted the policy of even the most powerful nation. That nation does have the power to set interdependence back significantly. Just peacemaking theory focuses concern and action on dangers of unilateralism by a nation so powerful it can dominate others, and can be relatively ignorant of the effect on international society.

The Interactive Logic of the Practices

David Tracy suggests that post-modernity is characterized by a turn to interactive reason in the era of globalization, with the presence of diverse other cultures in our midst, and the need to dialogue with mutual respect for the other. Modernity was based on the philosophy of consciousness, the turn to the subject with its purposive rationality; post-modernity is based on communicative reason in which the presence and interaction of the other, dialogically, linguistically, interactively, with mutual participation, is crucial.[33]

Seen from this angle, one might suggest that just war theory represents the purposive rationality of Stoic influence and modernity. It measures the purposive rationality of one side in a conflict: are our cause and our intention just? Are our means and our authority just? Have we tried other resorts? What is our calculation of the reasonable hope of success of our action?

Just peacemaking theory is based on interactive and participative rationality. Each of the practices is a *community* practice in three senses. Each fits the shift in the nature of the international system toward interdependence and community. Each seeks to work with diverse others in the international system, bringing them with their diversity into participative community. Each concerns not only the intention and action of the actor, but dialogical and interactive relation with the other. Several of the practices relate directly to the four changes in the international system toward interdependence or community that Schroeder identified above:

A. The utility of war is declining because of the increased destructiveness of an enemy's retaliatory weapons. This underlies just peacemaking practice number nine: "reduce offensive weapons and weapons trade." When a state has a much larger supply of offensive weapons than a neighbor state has, it may calculate that it can make war without the punishment of great retaliatory destruction. For example, after the split-up of Yugoslavia, Serbia got most of the weapons. Hence Milosevic believed he could make war against Bosnia, Croatia, and Kosovo with a minimum of retaliation. Thus the peacemaking practice of reducing the supply of offensive weapons reduces the temptation to make war. We see this in the reduction of arms imports by developing countries from $60 billion in 1988 to $15 billion, one-fourth as much, just seven years later, in 1995 (165, 156-58). We see it in Gorbachev's withdrawing half the Soviet Union's tanks eastward, behind the Ural Mountains, and removing all river-crossing equipment from the western part of the Soviet Union, so the West could know an attack by the Soviet Union against Western Europe was unlikely (48). This peacemaking practice is interactive: it depends on interaction between offensive capabilities, and on mutual perception. When offensive weapons are reduced, the international system becomes less threatening and more cooperative.

B. Nations now give trade and the economy priority over war. This supports just peacemaking practice number six, "foster just and sustainable economic development." Bitterness about relative economic deprivation recruits terrorists, and causes wars of rebellion (111f.). By contrast, "economic interdependence gives countries a stake in one another's well-being. . . . When countries' trade with each other constitutes a substantial portion of their national incomes, violent conflict and war between them are rare" (102; also 135, 139). Practice number six is thoroughly focused on community development and long-term interaction. "Projects that are not locally supported are likely to decay and not be maintained. . . . Where development consists of projects not rooted in local communities, those undertaking development have little incentive to make sure that social and physical environments are protected in the long-term" (123f.). Aid agencies need to develop long-term relationships with local communities and engage in "holistic work, focusing on the community's many areas of need," and not just a single project like well-drilling (123-26). The word "community" appears seventeen times in the conclusion of chapter six.

C. The dramatic increase in the volume, density, and speed of international exchanges, and in the number, scope, durability and effectiveness of international organizations supports practice number eight, "strengthen the United Nations and international efforts for cooperation and human rights." The United Nations is part of the shift toward international institutions and community, and is the epitome of interaction among diverse nations. The chapter on the United Nations by Michael J. Smith argues realistically that nations may engage in "self-interested interventions thinly cloaked in humanitarianism," and therefore humanitarian intervention normally, though not always, should have the check and balance of multilateral approval. This, too, is interactive.

D. The ascendancy of representative democracy underlies practice number five, "advance democracy, human rights, and religious liberty." The Catholic Church and several other churches have made major contributions to work for human rights. The push for human rights has caused many countries to turn from dictatorship to democracy, from authoritarianism to democratic interaction with diverse others. The result is strikingly effective for spreading peace: no democracies with human rights have fought a war against each other in the twentieth century (96ff.). As democracy spreads throughout Latin America, in several countries in Eastern Europe, and in some countries in Asia, wars are being eliminated from major areas of the world. By contrast, the more dictatorial and less democratic countries in the Middle East are the source of most terrorists, who resent the authoritarian rule of their governments and feel disempowered to bring change by other means. The human rights dimension of practice number five explicitly emphasizes a communal, not individualistic, understanding of human rights, as the introductory chapter, citing John Langan's writings, makes clear (13-15).

The first four practices in just peacemaking theory explicitly embody the themes of participative community and interaction. (1) Nonviolent direct action is designed to respect the adversary, to love the enemy, to disarm the opponent, to pressure the perpetrator of injustice, and to work on his or her conscience. It seeks an outcome in which adversaries can live together without the bitterness and resentment that result from violent confrontation. (2) The practice of independent initiatives is designed to reduce the threat to the other and to initiate a confidence-building or trust-building relation. It has proven especially effective in ending the Cold War peacefully, and in reducing the arsenals of nuclear weapons bilaterally with far greater speed than negotiations had done. It works by its interaction with the adversary, by establishing a common interest in threat reduction, and by eliciting reciprocation. (3) The third practice is named *cooperative* conflict resolution because "it emphasizes the active coworking of parties in conflict; they attempt to develop creative solutions that each can affirm and support. They take on the process of conflict resolution as a shared enterprise, an active partnership in problem solving. . . ." It pays special attention to cross-cultural work, seeking to enter into each others' cultural narratives and to "see cultural differences as resources rather than deficits" (53ff.). (4) The fourth practice is to acknowledge responsibility for conflict and injustice; to seek repentance and forgiveness. This mutually interactive process removes long-festering opposition to community.

The tenth practice is to "encourage grassroots peacemaking groups and voluntary associations." Accordingly, "a just peacemaking theory presupposes not only individual peacemakers but a community of peacemakers. It requires groups of citizens who take peacemaking initiatives themselves and who encourage governments to do so." Analogously with Schroeder, Smith, and Russett's showing that international interdependence is growing, it argues that "a network of interlocking groups of people at a grassroots level" is growing a repertoire of peacemaking processes and skills, and prodding governments to use these skills (176ff.; cf. 141ff.). "In isolation is passivity; in working together is empowerment. The acting unit, for us, is not the isolated individual but the individual in a local group that is connected with a national network of peacemakers" (25).

In sum, community needs these dimensions: economic sustainability, a theory of legitimate authority (democracy, human rights, and religious liberty), a limit to the availability of violent, offensive weapons, interweaving cooperative forces and understandings that govern interactions where there is no government, justice, groups that mediate between individuals and the larger community, and initiatives of peacemaking that can heal the hostilities and conflicts that arise inevitably in any community.[34] These ten practices are not an arbitrary list. They are essential ingredients of community. And they all involve interactive rationality.

The Moral Obligatoriness of Just Peacemaking Theory

As Karen Lebacqz has written, we know what justice is most clearly and vividly when we experience injustice.[35] Similarly, we know the obligatoriness of peacemaking practices when we experience the devastating destruction of war. Many of us were faced with war's destructiveness in World War II, or the Korean or Vietnam War, or the Cuban Missile Crisis and the ongoing threat of nuclear war, or the battle for land between Israel and Palestine in the West Bank. But North Americans have lived a largely separated existence by comparison with the peoples of other nations devastated by war's misery on their own land. Our over-comfortable perception needs the correction that comes from hearing the cries of families of war's victims in nations that have experienced devastating war on their own land. Donald Shriver estimates the number of people killed in war in the twentieth century as above 150 million.[36] Each of those deaths was surrounded by others wounded, families in misery, society-wide impoverishment, and generations of anger, resentment, hatred, and, in many cases, the urge for revenge. The ten practices of just peacemaking theory have emerged into effectiveness in the period since World War II and the nuclear threat, with the widespread realization that we must develop effective practices to prevent war or perish. The world is composed of the cooperative trends identified by Schroeder, but also by drives for dominance, arguably by clashes of civilizations, certainly by nuclear threats, and by seemingly insoluble conflicts like those in the Middle East. Just peacemaking theory does not imply the latter will melt away. As their very presence and force called forth the ten peacemaking practices in response to devastating war, they argue for the need to support these practices that nurture the cooperative forces and decrease the likelihood that the clashes will erupt into escalating war.

The obligatoriness of just war theory is supported in various ways, but perhaps most cogently and directly by the obligation to prevent killing, and to defend justice. Ralph Potter argues that just war theory "is grounded in a strong presumption against the use of violence, a presumption established for the Christian by the non-resistant example of Jesus and for the rational non-Christian by prudent concern for order and mutual security. This presumption against resort to violence may be overcome only by the necessity to vindicate justice and to protect the innocent against unjust aggressors." James Childress argues similarly.[37] The U.S. Catholic bishops write: "The moral theory of the 'just war' . . . begins with the presumption which binds all Christians: we should do no harm to our neighbors; how we treat our enemy is the key test of whether we love our neighbor; and the possibility of taking even one human life is a prospect we should consider in fear and trembling."[38] Lisa Sowle Cahill argues just war theory is best based on justice, and Michael Walzer bases it on justice as right to life, liberty, and community and opposition to domination.[39] This entails a commitment to reduce killing and violence.

The same reasoning makes just peacemaking theory ethically obligatory. The strong presumption against violence, against taking even one human life, and against the injustice that occurs in war, calls all persons, and certainly churches, to do what is possible to prevent wars where they can be prevented. The contribution of just peacemaking theory is to identify which practices empirically do prevent wars. It also outlines ways to seek justice without going to war.

Intrinsic to just war theory is that war must be the last resort, after other effective means have been tried. Just peacemaking theory spells out those other resorts, which are often left mute in explications of just war theory. Also intrinsic to just war theory is the intention to restore a tolerable peace. Just peacemaking theory spells out ways to pursue that intention.

The same kind of reasoning applies to the moral grounding for pacifism. Pacifism rightly understood is not only the obligation to refrain from violence, but also the obligation to make peace. If these practices do make peace, there is obligation for pacifists to support them.

In addition, we argue in the introduction for these practices of peacemaking on the basis of biblical teachings and theological convictions. How to argue this is a complex question. The introduction to *Just Peacemaking* points out differences of approach among our own group between Evangelicals, mainline Protestants, Roman Catholics, peace-church members, and members of no faith tradition. Some methods in Christian ethics prefer to work at the level of basic theological convictions, others with middle axioms or natural law principles. Some favor a thicker, more particularistic or narrativist approach. We were intentional in evaluating the ten practices by their embodying *love* in the sense of community that includes adversaries, *justice* in the sense of deliverance from oppression and bondage into community, and *peacemaking initiatives* in the sense of transforming actions that deliver from vicious cycles of hostility into shared community. These may be seen as general principles. But in each case we also grounded the three themes in specific biblical exegesis, thick narrative of Jesus in continuity with prophetic tradition.[40] Thus, at some key points, our argument comes close to the concreteness of specific, normative New Testament practices expressed as political practices in pluralistic society. We invited other faith traditions to evaluate the ten practices on the basis of guidance from their traditions, not simply thin, universal principles.[41]

The Mandate of the Churches

In the 1980s, several of the major church groups in the United States issued thoughtful and extensive calls to peacemaking. All of those church statements declared that thus far we have been following the ethics of the restraint of war, and now we need a positive theology of peace, a just peacemaking theory. The U.S. Catholic Bishops declared:

> Recognition of the Church's responsibility to join with others in the work of peace is a major force behind the call today to develop a theology of peace. Much of the history of Catholic theology on war and peace has focused on limiting the resort to force in human affairs; this task is still necessary, but it is not a sufficient response. . . .
>
> A fresh reappraisal which includes a developed theology of peace will require contributions from several sectors of the Church's life: biblical studies, systematic and moral theology, ecclesiology, and the experience and insights of members of the Church who have struggled in various ways to make and keep the peace in this often violent age.[42]

We assembled just such an interdisciplinary group to develop the theology of peace that the bishops called for. Similar calls from the Presbyterian Church, the United Methodist Church, the United Church of Christ, and the three peace church traditions, mandated a just peacemaking paradigm. Reading their statements with the now-developed just peacemaking theory in mind, one can see that they were already sensing the emergence of most of these same ten practices.[43] Thus the new ethic of just peacemaking brings to fruition the Catholic and multidenominational Protestant mandate for a just peacemaking theory. We offer it as a gift to those denominations, and to all persons and groups of good will.

NOTES

[1] *The Challenge of Peace* (Washington, D.C.: U.S. Catholic Conference, 1983), # 23 and 24.
[2] Thomas S. Kuhn, *The Structure of Scientific Revolutions*, 2nd ed. (Chicago: University of Chicago, 1962, 1970), 63f., 78, 81, 92f.

[3] *Just Peacemaking: Ten Practices to Abolish War*, ed. Glen Stassen (Cleveland: Pilgrim, 1998), 2.

[4] James William McClendon, Jr., *Systematic Theology: Ethics* (Nashville: Abingdon Press, 1986), 167.

[5] Glen Stassen and David Gushee, *Kingdom Ethics: Following Jesus in Contemporary Context* (Downers Grove: InterVarsity, 2003).

[6] Paul Schroeder, *The Transformation of European Politics 1763-1848* (Oxford: Oxford University Press, 1996) deserves its critical acclaim. See also his "Historical Reality vs. Neo-Realist Theory," *International Security* 19 (Summer 1994): 108-48; and "Did the Vienna Settlement Rest on a Balance of Power?" *American Historical Review* 97 (June 1992): 683-706 and 733-35.

[7] The term comes from Hedley Bull, *The Anarchical Society: A Study of Order in World Politics* (London and New York: Columbia University Press, 1977).

[8] Reinhold Niebuhr, "American Power and World Responsibility," *Christianity and Crisis* (April 5, 1943); and "Plans for World Reorganization," *Christianity and Crisis* (Oct. 19, 1942); reprinted in Niebuhr, *Love and Justice*, ed. D. B. Robertson (Louisville: Westminster/John Knox, 1957), 205, 209.

[9] Eric Mount, "The Currency of Covenant," *The Annual of the Society of Christian Ethics* 22 (1996): 296.

[10] Bruce Cronin, *Community Under Anarchy: Transnational Identity and the Evolution of Cooperation* (New York: Columbia University, 1999), chap. 3 and 6.

[11] John Kelsay and Sumner B. Twiss, "Editors' Preface," *The Annual of the Society of Christian Ethics* 20 (2000), vii.

[12] David A. Baldwin, ed., *Neorealism and Neoliberalism: The Contemporary Debate* (New York: Columbia University, 1993), 9-11. See pp. 4ff. for a helpful analysis of the distinctions among the theories.

[13] Robert Jervis, "Realism in the Study of World Politics," *International Organization* 52 (4) (Autumn 1998): 971-91; and "Realism, Neoliberalism, and Cooperation: Understanding the Debate," *International Security* 24 (1) (Summer 1999): 42-63.

[14] Jervis, "Realism in the Study," 979.

[15] Jervis, "Realism, Neoliberalism," 42. Helen Milner's well respected differentiation of various meanings of "the slippery concept of anarchy" argues "that a more fruitful way to understand the international system is one that combines anarchy and interdependence," in Baldwin, *Neorealism*, 143-69.

[16] Jervis, "Realism, Neoliberalism," 44-45.

[17] Jervis, *Perception and Misperception in International Politics* (Princeton: Princeton University, 1976). I was Jervis's research assistant for this book, and it plus other research at Harvard influenced the development of the perception dimension in my method in ethics. See Stassen, "Individual Preferences and Role Constraints in Policy-Making," *World Politics* (October 1972); reprinted in Chittick, *The Analysis of Foreign Policy Outputs* (Charles Merrill, 1975); and Stassen, "A Social Theory Model for Religious Social Ethics," *Journal of Religious Ethics* (Spring 1977).

[18] Jervis, *The Meaning of the Nuclear Revolution* (Ithaca and London: Cornell University, 1989), 53-58 et passim.

[19] Keohane and Nye, *Power and Independence* (New York: HarperCollins, 1977, 1989), 23-24.

[20] Jervis, "Realism, Neoliberalism," 51f.; cf. 49.

[21] Jervis, "Realism in the Study," 981-82.

[22] "Realism in the Study," 986. For other incisive discussion, see Jervis, "Cooperation under the Security Dilemma," *World Politics* 30 (January 1978): 167-214; and Jervis, "From Balance to Concert: A Study of International Security Cooperation," in *Cooperation Under Anarchy*, ed. Kenneth A. Oye (Princeton: Princeton University Press, 1986), 58-79. Further: Robert Axelrod, *The Evolution of Cooperation* (New York: Basic Books, 1984).

[23] See Robert O. Keohane, "Governance in a Partially Globalized World: Presidential Address, APSA, 2000," *The American Political Science Review* 95 (1) (March 2001): 1-13.

[24] Robert Keohane and Joseph Nye, *Power and Independence* (New York: HarperCollins, 1977, 1989). In the following paragraphs I shall designate references to this book in parentheses, as (3).

[25] Keohane and Nye, "Globalization: What's New?" *Foreign Policy* (Spring 2000): 116f. The conclusion of the article offers a bibliography of literature on interdependence theory, but neglects to mention three important pioneers: Stanley Hoffmann, Karl Deutsch, and Ernst Haas.

[26] Ibid., 116.

[27] John J. Mearsheimer, "The False Promise of International Institutions," *International Security* 19 (3) (Winter 1994/95): 17, 20.

[28] John J. Mearsheimer, "A Realist Reply," *International Security* 20 (1) (Summer 1995): 83-84, 86-88, 90.

[29] Ibid., 82.

[30] In this short space, I can only present the main logic of the debate, and of Jervis, Keohane, and Nye's analyses above. See also Baldwin, op cit.; Stephen Krasner, ed., *International Regimes* (Ithaca and London: Cornell University, 1983, 1991); and Kenneth Oye, ed. *Cooperation Under Anarchy* (Princeton: Princeton University, 1986).

[31] Robert O. Keohane and Lisa L. Martin, "The Promise of Institutionalist Theory," *International Security* 20 (1) (Summer 1995): 40, 42, 47-49; and Ruggie, op cit., 62-67.

[32] Mearsheimer, "False Promise," 48.

[33] David Tracy, "Public Theology, Hope, and the Mass Media: Can the Muses Still Inspire?" in *God and Globalization: Religion and the Powers of the Common Life*, vol. I, ed. Max Stackhouse and Peter Paris (Harrisburg: Trinity Press International, 2000), 232-48. Most of the essays in the first three volumes are characterized by this interactive logic, with an interactive and mutually participative covenant ethic.

[34] See Helen Milner, "The Assumption of Anarchy in International Relations Theory: a Critique," in Baldwin, *Neorealism*, 143-69, for a perceptive analysis of how patterns of expectations, webs of interactions, international governing institutions and a body of international laws serve many of the functions that domestic governments serve.

[35] Karen Lebacqz, *Justice in an Unjust World* (Minneapolis: Augsburg, 1987), 7, 10.

[36] Shriver, "The Taming of Mars: Can Humans of the Twenty-first Century Contain Their Propensity for Violence?" in *God and Globalization*, 143.

[37] Ralph Potter, *War and Moral Discourse* (Richmond: John Knox: 1969), 53, 61 and cf.; also, James Childress, "Review of Walzer," *Just and Unjust Wars*, *The Bulletin of the Atomic Scientists*, 38/8 (October, 1978), 44-48; and Childress, "'Nonviolent Resistance: Trust and Risk-Taking' Twenty-five Years Later," *Journal of Religious Ethics* 25/2 (Fall, 1997): 213-20.

[38] U.S. Catholic Conference, *Challenge of Peace*, #80.

[39] Cahill, *Love Your Enemies: Discipleship, Pacifism, and Just War Theory* (Minneapolis: Augsburg Fortress, 1994), 237ff. And Walzer, *Just and Unjust Wars* (New York: Basic Books, 1977), xv-xvi, 29, esp. 53-54, also 59, 61ff., 70-72, 108, 134-37, 254.

[40] See Stassen, *Just Peacemaking: Transforming Initiatives for Justice and Peace* (Louisville: Westminster/John Knox Press, 1992), chap. 2, 3, and 6.

[41] See the insightful argument for deep engagement of particular religious traditions in Marc Gopin, *Between Eden and Armageddon: The Future of World Religions, Violence, and Peacemaking* (New York: Oxford University Press, 2000).

[42] U.S. Catholic Conference, *Challenge of Peace*, #23 and 24.

[43] Stassen, *Just Peacemaking: Transforming Initiatives for Justice and Peace*, chap. 9.

Just Peacemaking: Theory, Practice, and Prospects

Lisa Sowle Cahill

Abstract

The just peacemaking project is a commendable effort to derive proactive initiatives from the teachings of Jesus and a strong sense of Christian discipleship, and to make these effective in volatile political situations. The project could be strengthened by a more explicit doctrine of sin, and an ethical justification of coercion. Recent debates among political scientists about effective social action in the era of globalization can also offer insights to enhance the political plausibility of the just peacemaking theory.

Glen Stassen's essay, "The Unity, Realism, and Obligatoriness of Just Peacemaking Theory," is an explication and further development of the collaborative project that resulted in the 1998 volume, *Just Peacemaking: Ten Practices for Abolishing War.*[1] Just peacemaking is advanced as a new paradigm that cuts between traditional just war theory and pacifism, combines a biblical faith commitment with political engagement, and aims to unite persons of many faiths and cultures in actually diminishing war and other types of politically motivated violence.

This is an admirable project, a timely project, and on most levels a convincing project. Yet its main strength—to combine pacifism's dedication to nonviolent action with just war theory's commitment to justice—may be a liability to the coherence that Stassen's essay aims to defend. To the extent that any Christian social ethics contends with human evildoing while pursuing a vision of social justice, solidarity, and the common good, exercised consistently with New Testament ideals, it will encounter similar difficulties. The theorists of just peacemaking are not alone. Sin, justice, and love are three irreconcilable realities that must somehow fit together for Christian social action to get off the ground. Whether their integration can happen in theory as well as in practice is an open question.

In my response to Stassen, I will examine how coherently these aspects of social ethics are brought together in the just peacemaking theory, and propose that a more explicit theological reference to sin and stronger ethical endorsement of coercion could strengthen his proposal. The task is to add an Augustinian or Niebuhrian dimension of realism to what seems to have been a meeting of the nonviolence of the historic peace churches and the social optimism of a Walter Rauschenbusch or Pope John XXIII.[2] The trick will be to bring Augustine and Niebuhr under the tent of just peacemaking theory without reverting to Augustine's authoritarian chain of command or Niebuhr's occasionally anomic pragmatism. Both have been known to squelch individual rights for the sake of the common good. What is called for is a Christian social ethics that prioritizes reconciling initiatives but does not exclude coercion, permits coercion as a last resort but maintains limits, and establishes credible procedures of participatory decision-making while still entertaining that some social agents will rightly be coerced by others. This ethic must also embody faithful discipleship while speaking politically in the global sphere. This is a very tall order. Indeed, it requires a synthesis of Christian traditions about faith and politics that are usually rendered as contrasts or opposites.

The double premise of the just peacemaking ethic is that proactive peacemaking initiatives are demanded by the teaching and example of Jesus, and that they are not eschatological ideals but already effective in volatile political situations. The ten practices that constitute the ethic are practices that: support nonviolent direct action; take independent initiatives to reduce threat; use cooperative conflict resolution; acknowledge responsibility for conflict and injustice, and seek repentance and forgiveness; advance democracy, human rights, and religious liberty; foster just and sustainable economic development; work with emerging cooperative forces in the international system; strengthen the United Nations and international efforts for cooperation and human rights; reduce offensive weapons and weapons trade; and encourage grassroots peacemaking groups and voluntary associations.

Stassen's new essay helps to clarify and lift up what I take to be five key emphases of just peacemaking that underlie and unite these practices. The last of these, a realistic appraisal of just how far peacemaking can go in ameliorating the injustices of the present world order, is rendered more strongly in the essay than in the book. In my view, this goes further toward recognizing the tension between love and justice, and strengthens the theory's coherence.

First, then, Stassen's essay stresses that just peacemaking is not only about ideas, theories, or principles, but about normative practices, "historically situated practices." The theory is primarily about community-building, not about forbidding specific kinds of behavior, even killing. This is an important move, because the contraries and incompatibilities of human experience can more readily be woven together in ongoing relations than in academic theories or systems of moral rules. It also reflects the fact that the biblical narratives themselves are full of contradictory and tensive stories and symbols that are best embodied in communal life. The essay complements the book's insight that the practical nature of ethics likewise requires a practical concept of "normativity" by incorporating David Tracy's definition of "interactive reason" to describe the dialogic process through which the normative character of certain practices comes to be theoretically understood.[3]

The second key emphasis is on the long-recognized need for mediating institutions that connect individual action to social change, now given a new reading in light of the impact of globalization on the kinds of institutions that cause or relieve conflict. Social institutions, especially international and transnational institutions, can offer persons of diverse cultures and religions the opportunity to share in common practices. Stassen's essay goes beyond the mutual interest of nation states in maintaining security to include the United Nations, humanitarian intervention (preferably multilateral), transnational trade relationships, and aid agencies that similarly work across borders and beyond national objectives and governments. He emphasizes that nongovernmental organizations (NGOs) seeking to reduce causes of conflict must be rooted in local communities and environments to meet communal needs in an integrated manner (11-12).

The third key emphasis is on establishing in Christian and social ethics a salutary and overdue requirement that claims and mandates be grounded in fact in order to have practical legitimacy. Christian ethics cannot simply deduce obligations from abstract premises or ideals and present them as though they can change behavior, without investigating whether the conditions of possibility of change are in place. From a theoretical standpoint it is easy to exhort that wars should be ended, enemies should be reconciled, nations should serve the common good, the human rights of all should be respected, and wealthy peoples should reduce consumption and commit to the equitable distribution of the planet's material resources. Programs of practical action, however, will disconnect from the very realities they address if they do not incorporate honest and accurate readings of the real facts and conditions that enable or deter the accomplishment of morally admirable goals. Unrealistic ethical systems and norms can even perversely enable violence and other injustices by distracting attention from realities "on the ground" and providing a convenient ideological cover for conduct that in no way actually reduces abuses of power. The history of political uses of just war principles is replete with obvious examples. Just peacemaking theory claims that the practices advocated do in fact enhance global conditions of peaceful coexistence.

The fourth key emphasis is on economics and the connection of both liberal capitalism and the avoidance of war to representative democracy. The essay reiterates a central claim of the book, namely, that modern democratic nations are, in fact, highly unlikely to make war with each other. Democracy promotes cultural norms favoring tolerance and peaceful conflict resolution. A powerful support to the democratic aversion to war is economic interdependence.[4] Economic power has become more important in establishing national eminence than territorial expansion; military conflict interferes with the national and international conditions of free trade and rarely serves the national interest of nations that have access to global trade arrangements.

> The result is strikingly effective for spreading peace: no democracies with human rights have fought a war against each other in the twentieth century (96ff.). As democracy spreads throughout Latin America, in several countries in Eastern Europe, and in some countries in Asia, wars are being eliminated from major areas of the world. By contrast, the more dictatorial and less democratic countries in the Middle East are the source of most terrorists . . . (12).

Here we sense the optimism of some schools of progressive modern Christian social thought, including the social gospel, liberal Protestantism, and the Catholic social encyclicals. Yet, though liberal free-market industrial or postindustrial nations may not fight wars among themselves, recent and proposed ventures in the Middle East have shown that war on a fairly large scale is hardly out of the question when other civilizational players threaten the national security or strategic interests of Western counterparts. Moreover, much of the two-thirds world (former communist states in Eastern Europe and underdeveloped, often heavily indebted nations), far from benefiting from global capitalism, are being further marginalized from the world order arrangements cooperatively negotiated under NATO, the European Union, the World Trade Organization, the International Monetary Fund, and the World Bank. Horrendous wars are still going on in the Middle East, Asia, and Africa, as those who are not in on the global market stake out claims to identity, territory, and goods. Is a globalized market economy simply war by other means? Certainly it leaves many people physically suffering, endangered, or dead in the wake of the "peaceful" regime of the WTO and the IMF. Even if one sees the free market as an essentially neutral or moral institution, one needs to be highly critical of the perversions that unbridled individualism or collective self-interest can wreak on and through it. The fact that solutions must be found beyond the nation-state and its interests confirms the importance of the global "mediating institutions" of the second emphasis.

The fifth and final emphasis, more pronounced in Stassen's essay, is that the global environment still remains an "anarchic society." This term, invented by "realist" political scientist Hedley Bull, appeared in the book's essay by Paul Schroeder.[5] Stassen brings this term up to the front of his present essay to increase the dose of Niebuhrian realism that a contemporary Christian approach to global social transformation must imbibe. He quotes Schroeder:

> "An anarchic society defines what a just peace means in international relations; the best practical system of rules, norms, practices, and institutions for reducing the anarchic (conflictual, violent, destructive) elements and promoting the societal (legal, cooperative, and normative aspects) of this anarchic society, while recognizing that for profound reasons it will remain an anarchic society for the foreseeable future (in my view, for any conceivable or desirable one)" (135). Our world is not a pure anarchy of power and national interest, nor is it or will it be the world community advocated by idealism (1).

Stassen has never maintained that all war will eventually be ended, and now distances the just peacemaking theory from the claim (hinted by the third emphasis on the factual effectiveness of peacemaking) that the historical incidence of war will be on the whole decreased. Instead, global trends toward democracy and economic integration open spaces for peacemaking to "reduce the likelihood of specific wars" (2). Specific peacemaking practices "are preventing many wars" (3).

The critical question here is whether the fifth emphasis on the anarchic society finally undermines the claim that the theory's practical viability is demonstrated by its success in reducing wars. Certainly it makes it more tenuous. At the same time, ethics would not be ethics without any prospect of practical improvement in the way people conduct themselves. What differentiates Reinhold Niebuhr's theological "realism" from the "realism" of today's dominant political theory—and links Niebuhr to the just peacemaking theory—is that Niebuhr offers a social ethics and not merely a description of de facto social behavior presented as a framework for the survival instinct. In other words, Niebuhr's Christian realism presupposes moral forces of love and justice whose incipient presence is real in social relationships and can be fortified and bolstered to serve moral ends, including at least some degree of social transformation. Along with Stassen and colleagues, I would endorse a cautious but strong commitment to social change as essential to the meaning of social ethics. But the three theological convictions and ten practices still need a further Niebuhrian twist.

Although the authors of the just peacemaking theory have tempered pacifist action with a more realistic angle on the necessity and difficulty of changing institutions, the results share certain limits with mid-twentieth century Catholic social teaching, which, while socially engaged, was in hindsight a bit too confident in human reasonableness and the conversion of hatred to cooperation. John XXIII, who convened the Second Vatican Council, also wrote an encyclical on war and peace, *Pacem in Terris* (1963) which he addressed to "all men of good will," and in which he called for a new ethic of international affairs built on "mutual trust" and "sincere cooperation." Decrying the arms race, he called for a truly global commitment to the common good, and for an international governing body such as the United Nations. Pope John was expectant that societies and nations could act reasonably and collaboratively, that the world could progressively be made a more just and peaceful place, and even that violence might be brought to an end.[6]

Reinhold Niebuhr, on the other hand, while never giving up on the transformative effect of Christian love, had a stronger doctrine of sin, and a more pessimistic view of the potential of groups to form and sustain just relationships. He was skeptical about deep structural change. Titling one book *Moral Man and Immoral Society*, he also used the phrase "collective egotism" to describe the inevitable social dynamic by which individuals sublimate their own self-interest to the pretensions and claims of a group, allowing the group to claim virtually unconditioned value, and in the process denying "the determinate and contingent character of [their own] existence."[7] Although Niebuhr would not have been a Christian ethicist if he denied the possibility of social transformation entirely, he did not hold out much hope for extensive reform based on empathy and forgiveness. He believed groups in power rarely, if ever, give up their prerogatives out of altruism rather than coercion. He seemed to think that the dynamics of self-interested power are not going to be overcome or even greatly diminished by any worldwide moral enlightenment.

Niebuhr's theological framework included two concepts related to the process of fortifying and bolstering the human potential for good that I do not find clearly identified in the just peacemaking theory: sin and coercion. Instead, the aims and practices of the theory are formulated in wholly positive terms. For the most part, and especially in Stassen's book introduction and this essay, the practices are types of cooperative, dialogical engagement to which formerly or potentially warring adversaries are benignly invited to respond. Presumably the convergence of these practices with genuine moral existence and social well-being will be adequate to turn aside resort to more destructive alternatives, at least in "many" cases. The practices reflect the tone and commitments of traditional Christian pacifism in adopting nonviolent action: "they confront the other with an invitation to making peace and justice; ... they invite into community in a way that includes, rather than excludes, former enemies and outcasts" (9-10). Historic pacifism did not expect effectiveness though; indeed, it anticipated or even invited hostility and rejection.

The just peacemaking theory, of which Stassen's essay is the most recent embodiment, has incrementally recognized the intransigence of human sin even while it has persistently advocated the way of Christian love. The theory's ten practices also and paradoxically place a good deal of emphasis on the new formations of global economics and politics that make war less appealing precisely because war hurts national self-interest. This seems to suggest that politically realist rather than strictly moral aims are still major, if not sole, determinants of states' behavior, that states are still the major actors on the global scene, and that the best way to deter nations from war is to make it too costly. If collective egotism persists as an important motivator of human social dynamics, then social transformation will depend as much on finding ways to exert coercive pressure to constrain or redirect self-interest, as it will on appealing to humanity's sense of social solidarity or altruistic impulses. It will also require reliance on transnational networks or actors beyond states, both to influence the behavior of states, and to counter or shape the behavior of other international or transnational entities.

The just peacemaking theory's foundation lies in three theological convictions expressed in the book, and these three conform well to the positive aim of social conversion. However, the three may not be sufficient to underwrite the coherence of the theory as a whole, once the continuing fact of individual and group selfishness is fully registered. They are: a concept of discipleship grounded in the life, death, and resurrection of Jesus; a commitment to further God's reign by pursuing justice in a broken world; and a vision of the church as the eschatological sign of God's reign in the world.[8] I suggest that sin has to figure as a key theological doctrine, and force as a peacemaking practice, if Stassen and colleagues are to convince us that their theory is as practical and effective as they say it is. An additional theological conviction, the sinfulness of humanity in this world, should be supplied between the first and second convictions articulated above. The church is the eschatological sign of a community of love, but Christians are called to pursue justice with others in a broken world, and that world continues to be marked with human sinfulness, with which social ethics has directly to contend. This then calls for an additional practice, one that directly refers to the necessary use of countervailing force to raise the profile of justice for those whom a given system has disenfranchised. As Reinhold Niebuhr maintained, the privileged rarely yield their advantage unless forced to do so by an opposite and equal force.

The just peacemaking theory could therefore benefit by the addition of a practice of forceful institutional intervention for social change, in the interests of the vulnerable or those who have already suffered injury. Important parameters of forceful intervention would be: participatory decision making and empowerment of the excluded as participants; resort to intervention by force only subsequent to efforts at moral persuasion; and moderation of force along a scale of directness and severity. Appeals to enlightened self-interest, for example, are an indirect and anticipatory form of coercion, in which an agent rationally considers future or potential negative consequences of a certain course of action.[9] Bad publicity, trade sanctions, and taxes coerce action more directly by making the negative consequences of noncompliance with social norms or laws more proximate. Both national governments and transnational corporations can be pressured into recognizing different constituencies and at least taking a different view of "enlightened self-interest," for example, about responding to genocide or signing onto international conventions.[10] Market pressure and political delegitimization can also be exerted by citizens' movements and NGOs. Physical force, the most direct form of coercion, should theoretically be reserved for cases of extreme threat to the social order (such as terrorism or genocide).

The inclusion of a practice permitting the employment but requiring the restraint of force would draw on some of the positive moral aspects of just war theory. These modifications would lend unity to the just peacemaking theorists' commitment to change and their characterization of the world as an "anarchic society." Although moral example and the appeal of peaceful coexistence may sometimes induce altruistic, pro-social behavior, there are many other occasions on which the carrot of morality will have to be aided by the stick of external pressure, the attractive invitation backed up by an enforceable demand.

There are at least five indications of the use of force in the chapters of *Just Peacemaking* that support forceful institutional intervention as a practice of just peacemaking theory. First, John Cartwright and Susan Thistlethwaite explain the origin of the word "boycott" in a strike of Irish laborers against a nineteenth-century English estate manager named Charles Boycott.[11] Although their essay is on nonviolent practices, this example shows that when relatively powerless individuals take nonviolent direct action, it is usually to exert pressure against perpetrators of injustice against whom the "system" does not protect them, and against whom they also lack the power to use direct force or violence successfully. In such cases, nonviolent collective action is an available form of coercion that aims to compel its object to comply with demands, whether or not compliance is also motivated by conversion to a different vision of social order.

Second, linking domestic and international scenarios, Duane K. Friesen illustrates how voluntary organizations can pressure governments to change policies on a number of issues, including human rights, arms control, disaster relief, environmental protection, poverty, and hunger. In some cases in which voluntary organizations have actually effected change, they do so by collective witness to alternative patterns of social behavior and organization that successfully converts others. Yet in not a few instances, if not the majority, the public visibility given to a cause constrains the actions of leaders by undermining popular or international support, and thus disabling a repressive regime or unfair policy.

Third, an excellent chapter on economic development in *Just Peacemaking* links sustainable development to justice and peace, arguing that the lack of a chance to make a useful livelihood leads to social disorder and even war.[12] The authors (David Bronkema, David Lumsdaine, and Rodger A. Payne) all too rightly allude to "subjugation," and observe that "people who are poor are easy targets for abuse by economically powerful persons and institutions." They note that "powerful domestic or foreign interests may seek to expropriate the property of small cultivators or to capture and abuse government power for their own purposes."[13] The chapter calls for reorganization of the international economic system, urges that the focus of development be on the poor and their long-term self-sufficiency, through grassroots and holistic collaboration. Yet the chapter concludes in a litany of eschatological "shoulds." For example, "peacemakers should support networks of agencies that work toward protecting the legal rights of the poor," "wealthy states should increase their foreign-assistance programs and work to transform bilateral and multilateral development institutions," and "people and companies should harvest primarily renewable products."[14] If the reality of sin and the need for coercive power are taken seriously, the attainment of just economic development will require contrary forces of economic, political, and even revolutionary or military pressure. An important question to ask for the just peacemaking ethic is how voluntary associations, mediating institutions, and regional and international organizations like the United Nations can bring pressure to bear in support of such changes, as is suggested by the invocation of "legal rights."

Fourth, the book's chapter on the arms trade (by Barbara Green and Glen Stassen) refers to pressure that can be exercised by the United Nations in concert with nations, NGOs and citizens' organizations to curtail the international sale of weapons that adds greatly to the profitability of and incentives for war. Surely here we are dealing with countervailing force against recalcitrant leadership. The authors address both nuclear weapons and the trade in conventional weapons, especially the momentum for a worldwide ban on land mines. One reason that purely moral appeals are ineffective in such problem areas is that the manufacture and sale of weapons is highly profitable, and the influence of money corrupts the political processes in which arms reduction decisions are made in the manufacturing nations, including the United States. Six major suppliers account for most sales to the developing world, and manufacturers make substantial contributions to political campaigns in the United States. Nevertheless, a bill was introduced in Congress that would prevent the sale of weapons to countries that do not meet human rights standards and participate in the UN Register of Conventional Weapons. Transparency discourages arms build-up by enabling neighboring nations to make reliable estimates of one another's arms capacity.[15] Pressure can be exerted on purchasing nations as well. First of all, Stassen and Green claim that as nations modernize and become more democratic, the need for weapons decreases. Furthermore, the IMF requires reduced expenditures for weapons as a condition of receiving aid.[16] The authors argue that such efforts have met with success in limiting global nuclear proliferation and weapons sales, but they have hardly closed the "nuclear club" or put traders out of business. It is difficult to muster adequate interventionary force to reverse even those institutions of greed that kill millions and threaten death to the entire planet.

Finally, Michael Joseph Smith, in commenting upon the eighth practice, "strengthen the United Nations," provides the most direct defense of coercive power in the just peacemaking book, up to and including even violence and killing in the service of justice. He proposes that resort to military force outright may sometimes be called for. He wants a better-equipped United Nations with a standing volunteer military force, prepared if necessary to go beyond peace-keeping and peace-enforcing to war-fighting. Though flawed, he says, the United Nations is still the best nexus of international debate, consensus, and multilateral action against egregious human rights violations and threats to the global common good.[17] In a similar vein, J. Milburn Thompson has developed just peacemaking theory for the international theological journal, *Concilium*. Thompson identifies the danger today as disengagement, and includes under the mandate of the UN tasks of nation building such as disarming combatants, equipping a respectable police force, establishing a judicial system, and bringing in the aid, investment, and technical assistance necessary for economic development and grassroots participation.[18] Welcome though these calls for forceful intervention under global, participatory authority may be, they too serve strikingly to highlight the distance of present circumstances from the ideals we desire.

In summary, then, this review of just peacemaking theory brings me to two critical comments and one affirmation, made in great sympathy with the theory's proponents. First, along with Reinhold Niebuhr, the theory needs to find a niche for a theological conviction of human sinfulness and a peacemaking practice of forceful intervention for justice, especially on behalf of and empowering those formerly unable to defend themselves. Second, even with these modifications, the "effectiveness" claim remains weak. Third, and affirmatively, I want to help fortify the effectiveness claim and so advance the positive, engaged approach to justice and the social order that just peacemaking theory shares with Catholic social teaching, as well as augment the appeal of this theory in the public arena. To do that, I would like to introduce for discussion some recent debates in political science about globalization, world order, and the possibility of achieving greater justice.

The focus of my discussion will be Richard Falk of Princeton University's Woodrow Wilson School. Although Falk is regarded as a leftist utopian by supposedly more mainstream and "realist" political theorists, his reading of the human situation is not far from that of Niebuhr.[19] Moreover, Falk keeps insisting, like the just peacemaking paradigm, that our condition is more amenable to improvement in the globalization era. Recent events, he thinks, are "suggestive of the extent to which the actual range of possibilities for the future far exceeds the realist calculus of plausibility."[20]

The primary points of contact between Falk and the just peacekeeping theory are that he is an advocate for "humane global governance" in the face of the predominant political theory, realism; that he terms his reformist agenda "rooted utopianism," in that it is rooted in real possibilities already present in globalization; that he appeals to an emerging "global civil society" as the locus of more participatory global decision making about economics, government, and conflict; that he is "realistic" (if not a political "realist") in the sense of acknowledging barriers to real change; that he is agnostic about the eventual success of some moral tasks, like developing reliable criteria and institutions to guide humanitarian intervention; and that he deals directly and consistently with the need for participants in global civil society to exert both positive and negative pressure on key institutions of the dominant social order. He has a bigger, or at least more overt, place for enlightened self-interest and for more coercive actions and institutions in reducing poverty and exploitation.

Innumerable commentators have noted the mixed effects of globalization, primarily understood as economic integration enabled by rapid information and communications technologies, on the world historical scene. In a concise overview in *Foreign Affairs*, Stanley Hoffman interrelates economic, cultural, and political globalization and then surmises in a discouraging tone that:

> We live in a world where a society of uneven and often virtual states overlaps with a global society burdened by weak public institutions and underdeveloped civil society. A single power dominates, but its economy could become unmanageable or disrupted by future terrorist attacks. Thus to predict the future confidently would be highly incautious or naive.[21]

That may be so, but other political scientists support the just peacemaking theorists' more hopeful reading, even if peace will not result from the progressive modernization of nation states alone. According to Joseph Nye, globalization is simply "networks of interdependence at worldwide distances."[22] These are pervasive. Communications technologies enable participation in public institutions, connect superstructures with grassroots communities, and create networks among those communities themselves.

Although Nye believes a "hierarchical world government" (like a truly authoritative United Nations) is "neither feasible nor desirable," he highlights the "many forms of global governance and methods of managing common affairs" that are springing up in a much more pluriform and polycentric way. "Hundreds of organizations now regulate the global dimensions of trade, telecommunications, civil aviation, health, the environment, meteorology, and many other issues."[23] Although complaints that such organizations, and even more so international institutions, are undemocratic are partly true ("the democratic deficit"), it is also true that democracy and transparency are the watchwords of the day for all who seek political legitimacy.

After the failure of the world trade talks in Seattle in 1999, *The New York Times'* David Sanger commented that the developing nations were, for the first time, able to join forces and resist, "what they view as a relentless American onslaught to reshape the world on Washington's terms."[24] Mobilization and coalition-building among AIDS activists, the governments of second and third world countries, UN leaders, NGOs like Doctors Without Borders and Oxfam, and small, local manufacturers of generic AIDS drugs campaigned over a number of years to sharply reduce prices for sufferers in Africa. They eventually broke the strength of the major pharmaceutical companies, who had been holding out on patent rights. Lacking significant direct influence on the regulatory regime of the WTO, they applied the pressure of public disgrace to undermine shareholder support, as well as threatening blatant violation of patent law, a move that would have opened up third world markets to competition from far less expensive generic drug producers. At the World Trade Organization meeting in Doha, November 2001, poor countries with millions of AIDS victims won important concessions. A new interpretation of international patent law will permit such countries to declare national emergencies without retaliation from rich trading partners, and to manufacture or import cheaper copies of patented AIDS drugs.[25]

This success might seem to pale in comparison with the experience of massive economic and political disenfranchisement that is among the contributing factors to the terrorism manifested apocalyptically on September 11, 2001, and that resonates almost daily in the Israeli-Palestinian conflict. Yet in the longer view Richard Falk believes, like the proponents of just peacemaking, that "transnational democratic forces" may still have a chance to create a "global civil society" strong enough to offset the control of global market forces. He calls this prospect "'rooted utopianism,' a horizon of hope and aspiration that currently appears beyond reach," yet is supported by recent developments. These include: the end of the cold war without nuclear conflict, the nonviolent collapse of Soviet Communism, the reunification of Germany, and the repudiation of apartheid by the white elite in South Africa.[26] Falk's rooted utopianism (or "embedded utopia") amounts to a defense of the very idea of a constructive social ethics for globalization, a defense of the reform agenda as indicating concrete possibilities for change.[27] What he calls "normative democracy" is in fact being created by the local and transnational forces of "globalization from below."[28] The democratic energies now finding expression in grassroots action and new transnational institutions may result in a global reordering toward more democratic and humane governance, less poverty and pollution, and fewer human rights violations.[29] A concrete example of "globalization-from-below" was the mobilization of consumer power, led by Greenpeace, in a boycott of Shell Oil when it proposed the sinking of an oil rig in the North Sea. "The civil sector can make trouble transnationally" by disseminating information about harm that will result unless a targeted activity is halted.[30]

Falk outlines the emergence of "global civil society" constituted by voluntary, nonprofit citizen initiatives, sharing a global orientation to society, responsibility, and agency. Though the manifestations of global civil society can be chauvinistic or extremist (Al Qaeda), they also furnish important positive alternatives to market and statist outlooks.[31] Falk hopes we are in a "Grotian moment," a point of transition between an old and a new order, in which the statist framework of Westphalia is giving way practically and theoretically to a differently constituted world order.[32] In the wake of Seattle, Falk wrote that even the WTO, the World Bank, and the IMF were recognizing the need for "greater citizen participation in the international order."[33] Nonprofit organizations are on the rise in number and have begun to act as an independent international force, meeting cooperatively at or in anticipation of large international conferences of states. Elite business participation is similarly becoming institutionalized, for example, through the World Economic Forum in Davos, Switzerland, and the International Chamber of Commerce. Corporate elites have already been influential in shaping global policies compatible with their neoliberal outlook. Global civil society has not yet attained this kind of leverage. Yet Falk suggests the time may have arrived for a "global parliament," in which business and civic representatives would work together to achieve "stakeholder accommodation" and close the "democratic deficit." A global parliament might even "serve as an attractive alternative to those people who, out of enlightened self-interest or even public-spiritedness, wish to see the international system become more open and democratic."[34]

Nevertheless, the future is hardly secure. Local organizing connected to new transnational constituencies is not always benign. Moreover, hegemonic interests can still obstruct support for "global public goods," as for instance when the United States refuses to sign on to global environmental protection treaties, the International Criminal Court, or attempts to strengthen the United Nations and its peacekeeping role.[35] Falk sees the gap between "geopolitical priorities and humanistic imperatives" to be particularly evident in the areas of peace and security. As one example, he offers the

1997 opinion of the World Court on the legality of nuclear weapons. Prompted by anti-nuclear mobilization "from below," especially in the form of the World Court Project, the opinion was a compromise that encouraged the forces of civil society, which had managed to place their issue on the international legal agenda, but which also avoided alienating the nuclear powers by not declaring nuclear weapons clearly illegal or seriously threatening their current policies.[36]

A particularly acute challenge to principled global governance can be found in the complexities of humanitarian intervention, and the reigning anti-intervention ethos. In addition to the fact that nations or coalitions usually act selectively on a calculation of their own prospective costs and advantages, it is often not clear with whom the responsibility or authority to intervene resides. National governments, domestic constituencies in the intervening state, regional coalitions, the United Nations, and transnational nongovernmental organizations may all be involved. In the case of humanitarian emergencies, domestic protest and transnational pressures may all be necessary to prompt action by states, but the likely danger remains that the response will not be backed with the major resources needed to make it effective.[37] Indeed, even resources that are expended can be employed in such a way that the peoples in whose defense they are supposedly marshaled are ultimately impeded from achieving a stable and participatory society of their own. Even the United Nations and transnational aid organizations can implement social rebuilding projects that undermine the social structures they mean to support because planners act like "globalization from above," following an imperial masterplan devised in a foreign capital, interfacing inadequately or condescendingly with local authorities and customs, and delegating only day-to-day administration to local agents.[38]

Falk finally concedes that although humanitarian intervention is called for in acute circumstances, it is unlikely that it will occur in the absence of strong strategic interests or mobilized domestic constituencies favoring action.[39] Hence, Falk concurs with the peacekeeping theory that the best way to avoid human rights violations, humanitarian disasters and violence, including violent intervention, is to be engaged diplomatically and economically in a preventive mode.[40] We need a "critical geopolitics" that, combining prudential forecasting with moral commitment, will raise recognition that "investment in conflict-prevention, human rights (economic, social, and cultural, as well as civil and political), and conflict resolution is conducive to global stability and prosperity."[41]

In conclusion, Falk's quest for humane global governance and the just peacekeeping theory's practical approach to avoiding war can be brought together as efforts to change the framework of discourse about globalization, justice, world order, and governance. Violent relationships and solutions to problems will become secondary because nonviolent, cooperative, conciliatory, and diplomatic ones seem plausible, realistic, and achievable in the order of serious political possibilities. The framework of discussion determines what is perceived to be desirable and possible. In his 2000 Presidential Address to the American Political Science Association, Robert Keohane points out that even the meaning of self-interest depends on people's values and beliefs. Citizens of liberal democracies, at least, believe that legitimate institutions should be participatory and accountable. They also value persuasion over coercion and purely interest-based bargaining. According to Keohane, we need "to recognize, and seek to expand, the scope for reflection and the normative principles that reflective individuals may espouse."[42]

By promoting a different world vision as politically plausible, Stassen and colleagues, as well as Falk, Keohane, Nye, and others, foster global institutions that operate more frequently by participation, reflection, and persuasion. These values and practices have increasing legitimacy in the "real world" of international and transnational relations. As students of one of the oldest and most effective NGOs, the International Labor Organization, have noted, social models and lines of argument help establish "cognitively available choices and the discourse that frames discussion" about interests and prospective action. Cultural understandings, embodied for instance in international conventions, shape behavior on both the national and international levels.[43]

Religious communities have traditionally been among the most influential and active in promoting public discourse that is critical of resort to violence and that consistently puts forth symbolic legitimation of nonviolence and cooperation. Religious critiques have also raised the profile of harm to civilians and to social infrastructure that war and conflict bring in their train. Such discourse and symbols are all the more persuasive when they can meet the practicability criterion of governments, interest groups, and political theorists by making concrete connections with actual social and political conditions. The just peacemaking theory's evidence for growing effectiveness and Richard Falk's "rooted utopianism" are alike in this regard. They offer theoretical support and a discursive edge for a "normative" and constructive transformation of the world order presented by globalization, especially its effects on violent conflict.

Even Stanley Hoffman, who is pessimistic about the emergence of the kind of "humane governance" and "civil society" for which Falk hopes, thinks normative theories can make a difference. He calls for a renewed "political philosophy," guided by "the fate of the victims of violence, oppression and misery," and having as its goal, "material and moral emancipation." He even grants it is "possible to loosen" the "formidable constraints of the world as it is."[44] Altruism based on compassion for victims, though, won't be sufficient to loosen the constraints in the real world that cause governments and businesses to choose exploits favoring power and profits, or avoid democratic reforms that do not. But practices and theories of compassion, inclusion, and reconciliation can still change domestic and international politics—partly by legitimating these values, and partly by underwriting forceful institutional intervention against backsliders and outliers.

NOTES

[1] Glen Stassen, ed., *Just Peacemaking: Ten Practices for Abolishing War* (Cleveland: The Pilgrim Press, 1998).

[2] Although Stassen mentions Niebuhr's caution that international institutions are only gradually built (3), I do not find major implications of Niebuhr's "Christian realism" to be carefully distinguished from political realism, nor fully integrated into the just peacemaking proposal.

[3] David Tracy, "Public Theology, Hope, and the Mass Media: Can the Muses Still Inspire?" in *God and Globalization: Religion and the Powers of the Common Life*, vol. I, ed. Max Stackhouse and Peter Paris (Harrisburg: Trinity Press International, 2000), 232-48.

[4] See Bruce Russett, "Advance Democracy, Human Rights, and Religious Liberty," in *Just Peacemaking*, 93-98.

[5] Paul W. Schroeder, "Work with Emerging Cooperative Forces in the International System," in *Just Peacemaking*, 134-437. See Hedley Bull, *The Anarchical Society: A Study of Order in World Politics* (London and New York: Columbia University Press, 1977).

[6] The encyclical is available in *Catholic Social Thought: The Documentary Heritage*, ed. David J. O'Brien and Thomas A. Shannon (Maryknoll, NY: Orbis Books, l998), 129-62. See especially nos. 109-119 on disarmament and international relations.

[7] Reinhold Niebuhr, *Moral Man and Immoral Society* (New York: Charles Scribner's Sons, 1932); and Reinhold Niebuhr, *The Nature and Destiny of Man, Volume I, Human Nature* (New York: Charles Scribner's Sons, l964), 213.

[8] Stassen, *Just Peacemaking*, 6.

[9] On "enlightened self-interest" as a necessary line of appeal in overcoming inequality, see Orlando Patterson, "Beyond Compassion: Selfish Reasons for Being Unselfish," *Daedalus* 131/1 (Winter 2002): 26-38.

[10] Samantha Power, *"A Problem from Hell": America and the Age of Genocide* (New York, NY: Basic Books, 2002). According to Power, the United States has a very effective policy in place of nonresponsiveness to genocide, because the risks and costs outweigh the benefits to Americans. Her book is an attempt to expose the problem and create an alternate domestic politics, which would in turn pressure presidential administrations to take a different stance toward genocide, even if a particular intervention did not serve the so-called "geopolitical" goals of the United States.

[11] John Cartwright and Susan Thistlethwaite, "Support Nonviolent Direct Action," in *Just Peacemaking*, 33.

[12] David Bronkema, David Lumsdaine, and Rodger A. Payne, "Foster Just and Sustainable Economic Development," in *Just Peacemaking*, 112.

[13] Ibid., 124.

[14] Ibid., 127-28.

[15] Ibid., 166.

[16] Glen Stassen and Barbara Green, "Reduce Offensive Weapons and Weapons Trade," in *Just Peacemaking*, 165.

[17] Michael Joseph Smith, "Strengthen the United Nations and International Efforts for Cooperation and Human Rights," in *Just Peacemaking*, 152-55.

[18] J. Milburn Thompson, "Humanitarian Intervention, Just Peacemaking and the United Nations," in *The Return of the Just War*, ed. Maria Pilar Aquino and Dietmar Mieth (London: SCM Press; *Concilium* 2001/2), 91.

[19] For example, replying to their work, Falk characterizes the British realists Hedley Bull and John Vincent as "variously suspicious, and even somewhat scornful, of my more skeptical attitude toward statism, regarding my level of criticism as 'utopian' or 'salvationist' because it seemed to them to be advocating a post-statist type of world order as more desirable than the world of states that existed and—what was worse in their eyes—implying that a differently constituted and better world order might even be attainable in the near future under certain conditions" (*Predatory Globalization: A Critique* [Cambridge and Oxford, UK; Malden, MA: Polity Press, 1999], 35). Falk sees Samuel Huntington and Joseph Nye as translating the realist and modernist outlook into the idiom of the post-cold war world (*Predatory Globalization*, 36).

[20] Falk, *Predatory Globalization*, 60.

[21] Stanley Hoffman, "Clash of Globalizations," *Foreign Affairs* 81/4 (July/August 2002): 114.

[22] Joseph S. Nye, Jr., "Globalization's Democratic Deficit: How to Make International Institutions More Accountable," *Foreign Affairs* 80/4 (July/August 2001): 2.

[23] Ibid., 3.

[24] David E. Sanger, "A Grand Trade Bargain," *Foreign Affairs* 80/1 (July/August 2001): 66.

[25] See David Barnard, "In the High Court of South Africa, Case No. 4138/98: The Global Politics of Access to Low-Cost AIDS Drugs in Poor Countries," *Kennedy Institute of Ethics Journal* 12/2 (June 2002): 159-74.

[26] Falk, *Predatory Globalization,* 59-60; and Falk, *On Humane Governance: Toward a New Global Politics, The World Order Models Project Report of the Global Civilization Initiative* (University Park, PA: The Pennsylvania State University Press, 1995), 14.

[27] Richard Falk, *Law in an Emerging Global Village: A Post-Westphalian Perspective* (Ardsley, NY: Transnational Publishers, Inc., 1998), 190.

[28] Ibid., 220. See also 190-91 on the normative character of the emerging global civilization.

[29] Falk, *On Humane Governance*, 14-16, 207-55; Falk, *Law in an Emerging Global Village*, 189-224.

[30] Falk, *Law in an Emerging Global Village*, 219.

[31] Falk, *Predatory Globalization*, 138-39. See also, Paul Wapner, "The Normative Promise of Nonstate Actors: A Theoretical Account of Global Civil Society," in *Principled World Politics: The Challenge of Normative International Relations,* ed. Paul Wapner and Lester Edwin J. Ruiz (Lanham, Boulder, New York, Oxford: Rowman and Littlefield Publishers, Inc., 2000), 261-74.

[32] Falk, *Law in an Emerging Global Village*, 3-31. Grotius was a seventeenth-century Dutch jurist who is regarded as supplying the beginnings of international law to correspond to the transition from the medieval world to the world of sovereign territorial states.

[33] Richard Falk, "Toward Global Parliament," *Foreign Affairs* 80/1 (January/February 2001): 214. For a converging view of the pro-social potential of business, see George C. Lodge, "The Corporate Key; Using Big Business to Fight Global Poverty," *Foreign Affairs* 81/4 (July/August 2002): 13-18.

[34] Ibid., 218.

[35] Falk, *Law in an Emerging Global Village*, 213.

[36] Ibid., 180-85.

[37] Ibid., 100, 103.

[38] See Michael Ignatieff, "How to Keep Afghanistan from Falling Apart: The Case for a Committed American Imperialism," *The New York Times Magazine,* (July 28, 2002): 31, 54. For a discussion and case studies exploring the ways in which aid agencies do or do not encourage or remedy local violence and conflict, see Mary B. Anderson, *Do No Harm: How Aid Can Support Peace—Or War* (Boulder and London: Lynne Rienner Publishers, 1999).

[39] Falk, *Law in an Emerging Global Village*, 104-105.

[40] Ibid., 107.

[41] Ibid., 107.

[42] Ibid., 12.

[43] David Strang and Patricia Mei Yin Chang, "The International Labor Organization and the Welfare State: Institutional Effects on National Welfare Spending, 1960-80," *International Organization* 47/2 (Spring 1993): 236-37.

[44] Hoffman, "Clash of Globalizations," 115.

So that Peace May Reign: A Study of Just Peacemaking Experiments in Africa

Simeon O. Ilesanmi

Abstract

Post-colonial Africa's political stability, economic growth, and human development have been impeded by a vicious circle of ethnic rivalry and civil wars. This article examines the various attempts in Africa to move beyond the traditional lens of pacifism and just war theory in curtailing the deleterious effects of war. These attempts, which are also consistent with the theoretical proposal of just peacemaking, have had mixed results on the continent. The article focuses on Liberia and Rwanda to illustrate the strengths and weaknesses of just peacemaking theory, and concludes with a few suggestions on how its vision might be better pursued in Africa.

Are Things Falling Apart in Africa?

The horrors of war are a painful fact of which Africans do not need to be reminded. For the past two decades nowhere has the scope and intensity of violence been as great as in Africa. While the general trend of armed conflict in Europe, Asia, the Americas, and, until last year, the Middle East fell during the 1989-99 period, the 1990s witnessed an increase in the number of conflicts on the African continent. A total of thirty sub-Saharan states experienced civil wars and interstate violence during this period.[1]

In 1999 alone, the continent was plagued by sixteen armed conflicts, seven of which were wars with more than a thousand battle-related deaths.[2] The situation precipitously deteriorated in subsequent years. The resurgent heavy fighting between Eritrea and Ethiopia claimed tens of thousands of lives in the lead-up to a June ceasefire and ultimately the signing of a peace accord in December 2000. The intermittent violence in Sierra Leone, Burundi, Angola, Sudan, Uganda, and Nigeria, as well as the unexpected outbreak of violence between Guinea and Liberia, in Zimbabwe, and in Côte d'Ivoire, brought both hardship and bloodshed to the continent.[3] Among the plethora of conflicts on the continent, perhaps the worst and most intractable war is in the Democratic Republic of Congo (DRC). Since 1998 this conflict has involved the armed forces of nine different states and at least nine rebel groups.[4] According to the UN Secretary-General Kofi Annan, the complexity of this conflict, along with the vast territory in play, partly explained the initial reluctance of the international community to get involved in the conflict.[5] Even now, the potential exists that more civil wars, like those that gripped Sierra Leone and Liberia during the 1990s, will occur on the continent.

Recognizing the massive human suffering that these conflagrations have caused and the profound long-term effects they are going to have on development, one cannot but conclude that the continent has reached a nadir. According to the World Health Report, released in June of 2000, forty-four of the fifty-two countries with life expectancies less than fifty years are in Africa.[6] Other published reports indicate that 3.8 million people became infected with HIV in sub-Saharan Africa in 1999, bringing the total number of people living with HIV/AIDS in the region to 25.3 million or 8.8 percent of the adult population. In 2000, the pandemic reportedly claimed the lives of 2 million Africans, in addition to 1 million who died from malaria and tuberculosis.[7] It is now widely agreed that there is a correlation between Africa's wars and her underdevelopment.[8] The just released *Human Development Report 2002* shows that of 50 African countries, at least 13 spent more of their GDP on the military than on health, and at least 5 spent more on the military than on health and education combined. In comparison, each of the top 22 ranked countries on the Human Development Index, from Sweden to Israel, spend more than 5% of a much larger GDP on health.[9]

As the devastating confluence of economic, health, and political problems continue to submerge the continent in the vicious circle of poverty and conflict, one has to ask whether there is a way out. Or is the seeming predilection of Africans for violence a symptom of their political and moral immaturity? A brief detour into the scholarship on the ethics of war is in order at this juncture.

Is Pacifism or Just War Theory the Answer?

Moral reflection on war has historically oscillated between two competing options, pacifism and just war theory. The former is categorically opposed to war and all forms of violence while the latter insists on the moral ambiguity or even the nonmoral character of war, and therefore grants its justifiability if certain criteria are met. Neither theory takes a simplistic approach to war, but both have been severely criticized for their inadequate solution to the moral quandary of war.

There are those who denounce the idealism of the pacifists and their apparent indifference to the demands of justice in the face of suffering and oppression that are, within limits, avoidable.[10] Just war theory has also faced a similar credibility crisis, not the least of which is its failure to deter war and its susceptibility to rationalization by the state, which is perceived to be compulsively bellicose.[11] Despite certain fundamental theological and political convictions that both theories share, their intractable disagreement about the permissibility of war has the potential to fuel moral cynicism and create programmatic paralysis.[12] The disagreement could be taken as proof of the irredeemably subjectivist nature of morality and its utter irrelevance to matters of statecraft.[13]

Although both pacifism and just war theory continue to shape our thinking and attitudes toward war, there is a new theoretical venture—a third option of a sort—which seeks to overcome the apparent moral impasse created by these two dominant stances. A growing number of scholars believe that *just peacemaking theory* offers a new possibility for not simply thinking through the labyrinth of war but actually abolishing or preventing many wars.[14] Thus contrary to the armchair debate about whether or not one ought to conscientiously participate in war, the focus of this new approach is on waging peace. Indeed, just peacemaking is more than a theory; it is chiefly a moral discipline with an array of principles and practices that are intended to transform situations of conflict into ones of harmony and reconciliation. It draws its inspiration from historical clues or signs, theologically informed religious visions, and worldwide human aspirations for peace.[15]

Unlike the just war theory which grants the possibility of using lethal force to achieve some political-ethical goods, just peacemaking theory holds that such goods often can be attained in a nonviolent and constructive manner. But also unlike pacifism, which seems to make a fetish of peace as the highest ethical good in a political society, just peacemaking is not content with establishing any kind of *modus vivendi* between enemies. Peace achieved at the price of justice is worthless; in much the same way that justice pursued in a non-peaceable spirit would be regarded as mean or cruel. This is a profound lesson of history, according to the proponents of just peacemaking theory: When peace is pursued without justice, the effort usually "leads to appeasement, while the pursuit of justice without peace leads to a crusade mentality."[16]

The complementarity of justice and peace as proposed by just peacemaking, though attractive, opens this theory to the charge of redundancy. At the surface, it could be argued that since just war theory and pacifism respectively affirm these values, there is nothing new being offered by the ostensible third option. For instance, some scholars of just war theory would contend that both values—justice and peace—and more, including order, are at the heart of just war thinking, in both its justification of resort to violent force and limitations on such force.[17] Pacifists may also argue that if there is any difference at all between their position and that of just peacemaking theorists, it is superficial. Despite the fact that just peacemaking theory does not rule out the use of force as part of a comprehensive peacemaking strategy, and pacifism clearly rejects this, even as a last resort, both theories are united in their ranking of peace over justice, and in that respect, they have greater affinity with each other than either does to just war theory.

But dismissing just peacemaking theory on the basis of this charge of substantive ambiguity only betrays a shallow appreciation of its tenets. The theory is intentionally proactive; its objective is to deaden the political urgency of war and ultimately render it obsolete in our moral lexicon. It is also flexible in its practical prescriptions, as it recognizes the validity of diverse pathways to reconciliation. These pathways are worth repeating here: employing nonviolent direct action; taking independent initiatives to reduce threat; use of cooperative conflict resolution; acknowledging responsibility for conflict and injustice and seeking repentance and forgiveness; advancing democracy, human rights, and religious liberty; fostering just and sustainable economic development; working with emerging cooperative forces in the international system; strengthening the United Nations and international efforts for cooperation and human rights; reducing offensive weapons and weapons trade; and encouraging grassroots peacemaking groups and voluntary associations.[18] But whether a single peacemaking method or a combination of several is needed to accomplish the objective of the theory is not entirely clear. It is reasonable to assume, though, that different situations will call for different strategies of peacemaking.

In fact, what we see in Africa is a pragmatic approach to socio-political reconstruction, illustrated by the involvement of different actors and the deployment of various strategies of conflict resolution and management. As already indicated, Africa has had more than its fair share of wars and violent conflicts, and one wonders whether there is a reasonable basis for generalizing about the causes of these wars. Undoubtedly, each of the war-ridden countries has its sociological peculiarities; it is a fact that all African countries are artificial creations of European colonialism, and are similarly affected by the perceived scourge of cultural pluralism, ethnic rivalry, material pauperization, and the pervasive corruption of the ruling elite.

In addition, all African countries are affected by a hostile international environment dominated by political blocs whose policies toward Africa are remarkable for their inconsistencies, incoherence, and condescension. As one leading student of African politics points out, the decision of Western nations to meddle in African affairs sometimes hinges on whether they have "a strategic interest in supporting a weak or bad government."[19] This strategy is compounded by the conflicting national ambitions among major Western powers active in Africa (France, the United States, and, to a lesser extent, Britain), and among some less powerful countries, notably Libya (in Chad and Liberia), Israel (in Sudan), South Africa (in Lesotho and the Democratic Republic of Congo), Iran (in eastern Africa), and Egypt (in Rwanda and Somalia). Nowhere are the conflicting ambitions of these external powers better demonstrated than in Rwanda where

France was deeply involved in shoring up the autocratic Juvenal Habyarimana government in defense of *La Francophonie* as the government battled English-speaking Tutsi insurgents whose families had been exiled to Uganda in the 1960s. The same Anglophobic consideration governed France's support for the Mobutu regime of former Zaire in its waning days.[20]

Another observer links the West's morally ambiguous dealings with Africa to a more sinister reason. Comparing the difference between the West's response to the Kosovan war and its response to the 1994 genocide in Rwanda, John H. Morrow argues that the West refused to intervene in Africa because the West's "threshold for viewing atrocity remains lower for those perpetrated on Whites than for those perpetrated on black people."[21] This explains why, he continues, the United States and European countries see the most gruesome horrors perpetrated on Africans, and do little or nothing, while they see less done to Europeans, and increasingly urge a military response. Samantha Power corroborated this view in an article published in *Atlantic Monthly*, which debunks the widely held contention that the U.S. failure to respond to the Rwandan genocide was because it did not know what was happening. Power argues that the U.S. government knew enough about the genocide early on to save lives, but passed up countless opportunities to intervene:

> In reality the United States did much more than fail to send troops. It led a successful effort to remove most of the UN peacekeepers who were already in Rwanda. It aggressively worked to block the subsequent authorization of UN reinforcements. It refused to use its technology to jam radio broadcasts that were a crucial instrument in the coordination and perpetuation of the genocide. And even as, on average, 8,000 Rwandans were being butchered each day, U.S. officials shunned the term 'genocide,' for fear of being obliged to act. Indeed, staying out of Rwanda was an explicit U.S. policy objective.[22]

One way to make sense of this grotesque failure of moral and political will on the part of the international community is to understand it against the backdrop of the dramatic global events located around 1989 and which are generally purported to have ended the superpower rivalry and the tense confrontation between the East and West. The end of the Cold War occasioned a shift in the strategic interests of the two major superpowers. Neither side has compelling reasons to continue guaranteeing the security of client peripheral states, whose value to these powers did not go beyond that of pawns in now obsolete ideological and strategic battles. The absence of superpower protection and the increasing threats from within have made African states most vulnerable to explosive conflicts.[23]

Whether understood as tough love or an abdication of moral responsibility, the perceived international inertia forced Africans to seek homegrown solutions to their own problems. In each of the trouble spots on the continent, there are unsung heroes and heroines—individuals and organizations—who took independent initiatives and cooperated at many levels to transform their societies from being zones of genocidal slaughter into havens of peace. Although the remainder of my discussion will focus on Liberia and Rwanda, any African country could have been chosen as a case study. These two countries, however, because of their geographical location, will give us a balanced regional picture of the peacemaking experiments on the continent.

Just Peacemaking Experiments in Liberia and Rwanda

Liberia and Rwanda descended to a state of anarchy and total failure in the early 1990s. As the decision-making centers of their respective societies collapsed, both became paralyzed and inoperative. As symbols of identity, they lost their power of conferring a name on their people. Lacking a central sovereign government, neither was able to maintain law and order within its borders. Their respective authoritative political institutions lost legitimacy, as neither was receiving support from or exercising control over its people.[24] The principal actors in the Liberian civil war were Charles Taylor (a civilian rebel at the time and now the president of Liberia) and the late Sergeant Samuel Doe, then president of the country. More warlords emerged as the war dragged on. Scholars generally agree that the longstanding mutual suspicion and hatred between the minority Tutsis and the majority Hutus, and the colonial and Christian missionaries' historical manipulation of ethnic identity, lay at the root of the Rwanda genocide.[25] There is no need to belabor the point that both societies suffered monumental proportions of carnage and humanitarian catastrophes. What is relevant for our purpose is the steps that were taken to prevent the tragedies of Liberia from occurring and to de-escalate the violence after it had broken out, and the efforts that are underway in post-genocide Rwanda which are designed to prevent a repeat of the 1994 experience.

Historically, one major obstacle to peacemaking, especially through the instrumentality of military intervention, has been the doctrine of sovereignty and the concomitant principle of non-interference in the internal affairs of states. African heads of state have typically understood this doctrine to be about each state's doing entirely as its current government pleases, at least within what it itself defines as its own territory: not only may the state sometimes do wrong, it may decide for itself what wrong it may do, without restriction.[26] The scale of humanitarian nightmare during the Liberian war challenged this mindset, forcing many African leaders to regard continued adherence to sovereignty as scandalous. Salim A. Salim, then Secretary-General of the defunct Organization of African Unity (OAU), first signaled this changed perspective when he argued that the principle of non-interference enshrined in OAU's Charter does not provide for indifference to such magnitudes of disaster. The Economic Community of West African States (ECOWAS) went a step a step further by forming the ECOWAS

Ceasefire Monitoring Group (ECOMOG). The latter's tasks included, *inter alia,* conducting military operations for the purpose of monitoring cease-fires; restoring law and order to create the necessary conditions for free and fair elections; supervising the implementation and ensuring compliance by the warring factions with the provision of the ceasefire; and remaining in Liberia, if necessary, until the successful holding of general elections and the installation of an elected government.[27] These cohere with the advocacy of humanitarian intervention in the just peacemaking chapter on strengthening the United Nations and international efforts for cooperation and human rights.

Much of the rest of the world only knew about ECOMOG's peacekeeping/military intervention in Liberia. In point of fact, this effort was also paralleled and complemented by a vigorous diplomatic peace process aimed at finding a political solution to the conflict. This diplomatic process predated ECOMOG intervention, dating back to the early stages of the conflict when ECOWAS assumed a mediation role, and included not only key ECOWAS countries but also a host of indigenous actors such as inter-faith groups, women's organizations, various associations of Liberians residing abroad, and local non-governmental organizations. Not a few students of Liberian politics believe that had some of the proposals of these groups been implemented, the war in Liberia could have been averted.

Notable among these proposals was the idea of "collective presidency" contained in the Abuja Accord crafted at the end of a series of secret meetings and behind-door discussions at Nigeria's federal capital, Abuja, and involving the leaders of all the warring parties.[28] This was the use of cooperative conflict resolution method par excellence, reflecting the warring parties' acknowledgment of power imbalance among the constituting ethnic groups as a major cause of the conflict, as well as accepting their culpability in manipulating ethnic identity and difference for selfish and narrow political gains. Under the arrangement devised in the Abuja Accord, there would be a Council of State with one chairman and five vice-chairmen of equal status. The Dutch political theorist, Arend Lijphart, described this model of governance as "consociational democracy," which is different from the winners-take-all model associated with some Western democracies.[29] To allay fears of ethnic insecurity and marginalization in a pluralistic society like Liberia, it is necessary to devise a political structure capable of accommodating natural human needs for self-determination, identity, and recognition.

The "governing partners" were to be selected from each of Liberia's ethnic groups. This idea, together with other aspects of the Abuja Accord, gave rise to widespread euphoria about the dawn of peace in Liberia, as all the warring parties and their respective constituencies accepted and affirmed it. The euphoria was heightened by one of the factional leader's (Charles Taylor) announcement on various local and international media that he was returning to tell his fighters that the war was now over and that they should lay down their arms.[30] Although no one underestimated the difficulties that the implementation of this arrangement would entail, it was clear from the "active coworking" of the warring parties that they were prepared to transform their "deadly conflict" into "non-lethal controversy."[31]

The other actors in this peace-searching process endorsed the idea of collective presidency, but they also made other contributions to the process. The Inter-Faith Mediation Committee (IFMC), for example, called for "sit-home" strikes to protest the indiscriminate use of force by all the warring parties against civilians. In addition, it continually warned against the polarization of Liberian society along ethnic lines, the intransigence of warring factions to disarm, and had the singular honor of being the only group to raise the issue of justice in post-war Liberia.[32] The Liberian Women's Initiative (LWI), a national organization of women, was instrumental in drawing local and international attention to the plight of women, especially their sexual exploitation by the fighters, and in channeling women's views to national and international mediation groups. Their involvement and that of other interest and non-governmental groups in the negotiations was to ensure that the peace being sought would not be purchased at the price of justice.

Although the failure of the warring parties to implement the Abuja Accord and embrace other proposals from the various indigenous mediation groups inevitably plunged Liberia into one of the deadliest conflicts in Africa, it must be mentioned that the mode of mediation adopted at the time was inspired by Africa's traditional methods of conflict management, which emphasize the use of elders—men and women—as mediators instead of adjudication as advocated in the *Just Peacemaking* chapter on "Cooperative Conflict Resolution." The method is a further extension and application of the traditional African concept of family, village, or clan elder intervening in a "palaver." Rather than apportioning blame, it is more interested in preventing bitter recriminations, soothing jarred sensitivities, and seeking compromise. The use of the method allows the disputants to benefit from the wise and perceptive experience of the elder-mediator and provides a stable environment for negotiation derived largely from the respect accorded to the person in charge of the mediation.[33]

The 1994 genocide in Rwanda was a tragic and explosive culmination of a long history of Hutu-Tutsi antagonism, characterized by an entrenched tradition of politics of exclusion, and preceded by numerous smaller-scale bloodsheds.[34] By 1994, there were practically no social and political ingredients for communal harmony. The state had been converted into a fiefdom and an instrument of terror by a clique of Hutu extremists, for whose exclusionary politics the religious institutions—principally Roman Catholic and Anglican Churches—provided a sacred canopy.[35] Rene Lemarchand, perhaps the leading authority on Rwanda and Burundi, asserts that "the politics of exclusion," by which he means "exclusion of specific ethnic communities from *effective political participation*," lies at the heart of the Hutu-Tutsi problem.[36] Whenever members of one group hold the power, the other ethnic group does not feel safe, and vice versa. The oppressiveness of the group in power usually lends credence to this feeling of mutual insecurity; hence a vicious circle of political instability and violent overthrow of government:

> Exclusion leads to insurrection, insurrection to repression, and repression to refugee flows to neighboring states, where the refugees become the source of renewed confrontation. This is all the more likely where "kin rallying" is the norm, and where the fears and aspirations of refugee diasporas are shared by their ethnic kin in countries of asylum.[37]

The Tutsi-led government knew it had to overcome this legacy if it was to have any chance of building peace and reconciliation in the country. Among the first steps taken was the creation of a National Reconciliation Commission, headed by Aloysie Inyumba, which was charged with the responsibility of holding consultations throughout the country on issues related to coexistence. Its mandate also included seeking to highlight common problems and solutions and to promote a common history for all Rwandans, remove myths, and confront bigotry in all its forms. Perhaps its most innovative mandate was to monitor all government programs to determine how they affect peace, reconciliation, and national unity.[38]

The government also initiated a number of interim steps designed to promote discussion about the nature of democratic participation and to establish a bottom-up approach to rebuilding governance, which resembles the just peacemaking practice of democracy. The inherited legacy of over-centralization, in which blind obedience to authority was the objective of the leadership, made state-sponsored genocide possible. The bottom-up process aims to decentralize decision-making power and destroy a culture of blind obedience to authority. Discussing democratic values, allowing participation, and focusing on solving problems are seen as methods to lay the groundwork for the transition to some form of multi-party democracy. Elements of this transitional strategy include: (1) a Constitutional Commission, which will elicit wide input and discussion on the nature of the constitution, the form of elections, and issues related to ensuring Hutu participation and Tutsi security; (2) a bottom-up election process, starting with the cell and sector levels, aimed at moving up the chain of political and social organization, culminating eventually in national elections; (3) a decentralization process aimed at transferring decision-making authority for development and other critical responsibilities, to the local level, initially through community development committees; (4) a series of "Saturday discussions," in which the president hosts debates about the central issues facing Rwanda; (5) a series of meetings between Rwanda's political parties on the nature of a future political system and their roles in it; and (6) a more participatory justice process.[39]

The government has also attempted to supplement the efforts of the International Criminal Tribunal for Rwanda (ICTR), which the UN Security

Council established in 1994 to prosecute perpetrators of genocide and other crimes against humanity. Even if one can justifiably describe ICTR as a symbol of atonement for the indifference of the international community toward the genocide, its purpose was to demonstrate that establishing accountability and breaking the cycle of impunity are key to creating conditions for peace and stability in Rwanda. However, the progress of this formal justice system has been handcuffed by a number of problems, such as bureaucratic delays, internal power struggles, under-staffing, and under-funding. In response to this, the Rwandan government took a creative step in early 2000 by instituting a Rwanda justice instrument called *gacaca*, which it hoped would move the process of justice along at a faster pace. *Gacaca* derived from a traditional dispute-resolution mechanism, and is expected to allow communities to establish the facts and decide the fate of the vast majority of those accused of lesser offenses, while at the same time addressing reconciliation objectives and involving the population on a mass scale in the disposition of justice. The court system will continue to try planners and organizers of the genocide, while the cell, sector, and commune levels will handle the rest of the cases.[40]

In a program aired recently by the South African Broadcasting Corporation, it was reported that ordinary Rwandans have greater confidence in this indigenous justice system than the Arusha-based ICTR. Time will tell, however, whether *gacaca* is a blessing or a curse. It certainly has the potential to undermine the rule of law and perpetuate the culture of impunity because the communalistic orientation of African societies tends to discourage people from publicly humiliating friends, family members, and neighbors, which is how people typically perceive a legal ritual, whether traditional or modern trial. The press has also expressed concern about the suggestion that churches should undertake their own process of "*gacaca christu*," a confession and forgiveness ritual that many people believe has the potential to emasculate the actual *gacaca* process and guarantee a sort of religiously sanctioned impunity.[41] This, no doubt, is an attempt to borrow from the Truth and Reconciliation experiment in South Africa. But as scholars have shown, not all South Africans agree with the fairness of that experiment or that it was even the right route for South Africa to take in dealing with its history of contradictions.[42] Thus, unless both Hutus and Tutsis are convinced that ICTR and *gacaca* are impartial in their dispensation of justice, no matter who the perpetrator and the victim are, genuine reconciliation and social development will be difficult to achieve in Rwanda.

CONCLUSION

My purpose in this essay has been to locate the just peacemaking experiments in Liberia and Rwanda within the wider context of African political history and institutions. Like war, waging peace is a complex undertaking, requiring the full commitment and perseverance of the parties involved. More important, it requires hope—hope in the redemptive quality of justice and forgiveness, and in human capability to generate and sustain these virtues. It will not be an exaggeration to say that just peacemaking theory is grounded in this high estimate of human nature, or else in actual interests and system changes that explain why the just peacemaking practices are being implemented in cases identified in the book, and in fact are beginning in Rwanda and Liberia, along with oppositional and destructive forces that are surely present and active. But this optimistic perspective on politics may also be the undoing of the theory, for as we have seen from the two countries studied, human beings seldom behave in ways that reflect the best of their nature or that are conducive to their best interests, rightly understood. The crucial test for just peacemaking theory in the two cases we have examined is whether realistic incentives and interests are identified that move people to support the just peacemaking practices and whether people can be persuaded to support the practices or instead will revert to destructive war again because of the power of forces that block just peacemaking.

Charles Taylor of Liberia is worse today as president than he was when he was in the bush as a rebel and warlord. Similarly, Paul Kagame, President of Rwanda, is showing all the signs of a dictator rather than a statesman. He eased Pasteur Bizimungu out of the country's leadership, a moderate Hutu who was appointed President after the genocide when Kagame was appointed Prime Minister. The offense of Bizimungu, who is still languishing in jail, was suggesting that all recruitments to government and the army be on a 50-50 Hutu-Tutsi basis. Kagame is also opposed to holding elections, press freedom, and the trial of Tutsi soldiers whose atrocities against the Hutus during the genocide and the counter-insurgency war of 1996 were no less significant than those committed against the Tutsis.

Both Taylor and Kagame are invoking security needs to justify their Draconian approach to governance, but it is an open question whether these needs could not be better met through a genuine opening of the political system to all the groups with stakes in their respective societies. To be sure, their autocratic manipulations of the system are providing a semblance of peace, but at the high price of justice. Perhaps, it is for this reason that the just war tradition insists on the criterion of legitimate authority as an integral component of justice, which ought to be the primary aim for which to resort to the use of lethal force. The central concern of this tradition, as a political rather than a merely military tradition, is to build a just, and because it is just, a stable political order, in which ordinary men and women can engage in the kinds of things that make life good—marriage, raising children, cooperating with neighbors on projects of substance, etc.[43] Against this backdrop, political legitimacy is measured not by a leader's ability coercively to transform citizens into a bevy of sycophants but by his or her embodiment of, and service to, the just interests and concerns of fellow citizens. There is much in just peacemaking theory that lends support to this comprehensive view of political society, but at the moment, neither Taylor nor his counterpart in Rwanda seems interested in building, let alone nurturing, such a society.

NOTES

[1] Studies of various dimensions of wars in Africa include Abdel-Fatau Musah and J. Kayode Fayemi, eds., *Mercenaries: An African Security Dilemma* (London: Pluto Press, 2000); Abiodun Alao, *The Burden of Collective Goodwill: The International Involvement in the Liberian Civil War* (Aldershot: Ashgate Publishing Company, 1998); Stephen Ellis, *The Mask of Anarchy: The Destruction of Liberia and the Religious Dimension of an African Civil War* (New York: New York University Press, 1999); Christopher Clapham, ed., *African Guerrillas* (Oxford: James Currey, 1998); Alison Des Forges, *"Leave None To Tell The Story": Genocide in Rwanda* (New York: Human Rights Watch, 1999).

[2] Peter Wallensteen and Margareta Sollenberg, "Armed Conflict, 1989-99," *Journal of Peace Research* 37, 5 (2000): 638.

[3] See reports by Africa Policy Information Center at http://www.africaaction.org.

[4] SIPRI Yearbook (2000).

[5] See http://www.un.org/News, (24 January 2000).

[6] Salih Booker, "Combating HIV/AIDS in Africa: 21st Century Strategies" (A Special Plenary Address delivered at the African Studies Association Annual Meeting, Nashville, TN, November 18, 2000).

[7] See http://allafrica.com/health.

[8] Michael Barratt Brown, *Africa's Choices: After Thirty Years of the World Bank* (Boulder, CO: Westview Press, 1997), 100-13.

[9] See http://www.undp.org/hdr2002.

[10] David R. Mapel, "Realism and the Ethics of War and Peace," in *The Ethics of War And Peace: Religious and Secular Perspectives*, ed. Terry Nardin (Princeton: Princeton University Press, 1996), 55-77; Reinhold Niebuhr, "Why the Christian Church is not Pacifist," in *Christianity and Power Politics* (New York: Scribner's, 1940), 5-18.

[11] See Stanley Hauerwas, *Against The Nations: War and Survival in a Liberal Society* (Notre Dame: University of Notre Dame Press, 1992).

[12] See Richard B. Miller, *Interpretations of Conflict: Ethics, Pacifism, and the Just-War Tradition* (Chicago: The University of Chicago Press, 1991); Joseph L. Allen, *War: A Primer for Christians* (Nashville: Abingdon, 1991), 32-35.

[13] On the supposed autonomy of politics from ethics, see Hans J. Morgenthau, *Politics Among Nations: The Struggle for Power and Peace* (New York: Alfred A. Knopf, 1954), 10-12.

[14] See, inter alia, Glen H. Stassen, *Just Peacemaking: Transforming Initiatives for Justice and Peace* (Louisville, KY: Westminster/John Knox, 1992); Glen Stassen, ed., *Just Peacemaking: Ten Practices for Abolishing War* (Cleveland, OH: The Pilgrim Press, 1998); J. Milburn Thompson, *Justice and Peace: A Christian Primer* (Maryknoll: Orbis Books, 1997).

[15] Stassen, *Just-Peacemaking: Ten Practices For Abolishing War*, 3-28.

[16] David Steele et al., "Use Cooperative Conflict Resolution," in *Just Peacemaking: Ten Practices for Abolishing War*, ed. Glen H. Stassen (Cleveland, Oh: The Pilgrim Press, 1998), 55.

[17] See James Turner Johnson, "Human Rights and Violence in Contemporary Context," *Journal of Religious Ethics* 26.2 (1998): 320.

[18] These are the ten practices for abolishing war discussed in Stassen, *Just Peacemaking*.

[19] Goran Hyden, "Sovereignty, Responsibility, and Accountability: Challenges at the National Level in Africa," in *African Reckoning: A Quest For Good Governance*, ed. Francis M. Deng and Terrence Lyons (Washington, D.C.: Brookings Institution Press, 1998), 37.

[20] David Bourmaud, "France in Africa: African Politics and French Foreign Policy," *Issue: A Journal of Opinion* XXIII, 2 (1995): 58-62; Marina Ottawy, "Post-Imperial Africa at War," *Current History* 98, 628 (1999): 202-207.

[21] John H. Morrow, Jr., "Why Kosovo, Not Rwanda," *Emerge* (1999): 62.

[22] Samantha Power, "Bystanders to Genocide," at http://www.theatlantic.com, (September 2001).

[23] S. P. Riley, "Intervention in Liberia: Too Little, Too Partisan," *The World Today* 49, 3 (March 1993): 42-3.

[24] For a helpful discussion of the concept and characteristics of a failed state, see I. William Zartman, ed., *Collapsed States: The Disintegration and Restoration of Legitimate Authority* (Boulder and London: Lynne Rienner, 1995), 1-11.

[25] On Liberia see Stephen Ellis, *The Mask of Anarchy: The Destruction of Liberia and the Religious Dimension of an African Civil War* (New York, NY: New York University Press, 2001). Also, Abiodun Alao, *The Burden of Collective Goodwill: The International Involvement in the Liberian Civil War* (Brookfield, VT: Ashgate Publishing Company, 1998); and on Rwanda, see Gerard Prunier, *The Rwanda Crisis, History of a Genocide* (New York: Columbia University Press, 1995); Alison Des Forges, *"Leave None to Tell the Story"*; Philip Gourevitch, *We Wish To Inform You that Tomorrow We Will Be Killed With Our Families* (New York: Farrar Straus and Giroux, 1998).

[26] For critical assessments of sovereignty doctrine and the principle of noninterference, see Richard Falk, "Sovereignty and Human Dignity: The Search for Reconciliation," in *African Reckoning: A Quest for Good Governance*, ed. Francis M. Deng and Terrence Lyons (Washington, D.C.: The Brookings Institution, 1998), 12-36; James Turner Johnson, *Morality and Contemporary Warfare* (New Haven and London: Yale University Press, 1999), 71-118; J. Bryan Hehir, "Military Intervention and National Sovereignty: Recasting the Relationship," in *Hard Choices: Moral Dilemmas in Humanitarian Intervention*, ed. Jonathan Moore (Lanham, MD: Rowman & Littlefield Publishers, 1998), 29-54; Abiodun Alao, *Brothers At War: Dissidence and Rebellion in Southern Africa* (London: British Academic Press, 1994).

[27] See M. Wellner, ed., *Regional Peacemaking and International Enforcement: The Liberian Crisis* (Cambridge: Cambridge University Press, 1994); Abiodun Alao, "Thus Far, Still Far: The Prospect for Peace in Liberia," *International Security Digest* 1, 9 (1994).

[28] See M. A. Sesay, "Civil War and Collective Intervention in Liberia: A Strange Case of Peacekeeping in West Africa?" *Review of African Political Economy* 23, 67 (1996).

[29] His many publications on this topic include: *The Politics of Accommodation: Pluralism and Democracy in the Netherlands* (Berkeley: University of California Press, 1968); *Democracies: Patterns of Majoritarian and Consensus Government in Twenty-one Countries* (New Haven: Yale University Press, 1984); "Unequal Participation: Democracy's Unresolved Dilemma," *American Political Science Review* 91 (1997): 1-14. The South African democracy along the line of "proportional representation" is the closest political experiment to consociational democracy.

[30] See M. A. Sesay, "Politics and Society in Post-War Liberia: Challenges for the Twenty-first Century," *Journal of Modern African Studies* 34, 2 (1996).

[31] David Steele et al., "Use of Cooperative Conflict Resolution," in *Just Peacemaking: Ten Practices for Abolishing War*, ed. Glen Stassen (Cleveland: Pilgrim Press, 1998), 53.

[32] Sesay, "Politics and Society in Post-War Liberia."

[33] See Simeon Ilesanmi, "Human Rights Discourse in Modern Africa: A Comparative Religious Ethical Perspective," *Journal of Religious Ethics* 23.2 (1995): 304-307; J. K. Olupona, *Kingship, Religion, and Rituals in a Nigerian Community: A Phenomenological Study of Ondo Yoruba Festivals* (Stockholm: Almqvist & Wiksell International, 1991), 34-57; Jomo Kenyatta, *Facing Mt. Kenya* (New York: Vintage Books, 1965), 177-221; Kwame Gyekye, *Tradition and Modernity: Philosophical Reflections on the African Experience* (New York: Oxford University Press, 1997), 115-43.

[34] Between 1962, when Rwanda became an independent republic under Hutu rule, and the 1994 genocide, there had been fourteen separate instances of massive bloodshed due to Hutu-Tutsi struggle.

[35] Timothy Longman, "Empowering the Weak and Protecting the Powerful: The Contradictory Nature of Churches in Central Africa," *African Studies Review* 41, 1 (1998): 49-72.

[36] Rene Lemarchand, "The Fire in the Great Lakes," *Current History* 98, 628 (1999): 195. Emphasis mine.

[37] Ibid.

[38] Cyprian Fisiy, "Of Journeys and Border Crossings: Return of Refugees, Identity, and Reconstruction in Rwanda," *African Studies Review* 41, 1 (1998): 17-28.

[39] John Prendergast and David Smock, "Postgenocidal Reconciliation: Building Peace in Rwanda and Burundi," at http://www.usip.org.

[40] "Gacaca's Challenge: Going Beyond the Pain And Bitterness," *Internews* (Arusha), (9 August 2002). This may be said to implement just peacemaking practices of conflict resolution, acknowledging complicity, and democracy.

[41] See http://www.sabc.co.za/. This initiative is also similar to the fourth just peacemaking practice of acknowledging complicity and seeking repentance and forgiveness.

[42] Audrey R. Chapman, "Coming to Terms with the Past: Truth, Justice, and/or Reconciliation," *Annual of the Society for Christian Ethics* (1999): 235-58; Wole Soyinka, *The Burden of Memory, The Muse of Forgiveness* (New York: Oxford University Press, 1999), 23-92.

[43] I am grateful to John Kelsay for his helpful comments on this point.

The Just Peacemaking Paradigm and
Middle East Conflicts

Charles Kimball

Abstract

Turmoil in many parts of the predominantly Muslim world is connected both to common themes and specific historical, political, social, and economic circumstances in various countries. While short-term threats may require forceful actions to neutralize violent extremists, the longer-term challenge requires painstaking work in the dense thicket of the particulars present in each situation. The just peacemaking paradigm provides an invaluable framework for addressing constructively the multiple root causes of conflict in the Middle East. This article identifies four specific practices from the just peacemaking theory, practices that provide meaningful ways to build trust, nurture hope, and move intentionally toward a more healthy future.

For more than thirty years, the Middle East has received far more media attention than any other part of the world. Much of that attention has been connected to conflicts and violent upheavals in Israel/Palestine, Lebanon, Iran, Iraq, and to a lesser extent in Syria, Jordan, Egypt, and Saudi Arabia. The flood of images from major events—the Arab-Israeli-Palestinian conflict, the multi-sided civil war in Lebanon, the Iranian revolution and hostage crisis, the Iran-Iraq War, the 1991 Gulf War and, most recently, the events on September 11, 2001, the subsequent U.S. "war on terrorism," and the heightened focus on potential danger—has been highly disproportionate to the coverage of major events in Africa, Asia, Europe, or Latin America.

Unfortunately, for most people in the West, the result of his massive media attention is a kind of "detailed ignorance." While almost everyone has hundreds of disconnected or semi-connected images in his head, surprisingly few people can articulate a wider framework for understanding the ongoing events or developments. This is somewhat understandable since most people rely primarily on television media for news. Television, more obviously than print or radio journalism, gravitates strongly toward the most sensational stories and images. Simplistic views abound about inherent and eternal violence among people in the Middle East. If most people cannot cogently put particular events into a comprehensible context, even fewer can identify clearly the most productive ways to endeavor to resolve the destructive and dangerous conflicts that threaten both those who live in the region and the wider world community. The just peacemaking paradigm is an extremely valuable framework for understanding and addressing the multiple sources of conflict constructively.

The stunning events on and after the September 11, 2001, attacks on the World Trade Center and the Pentagon provide a window through which we can identify multiple sources of frustration leading to violence. The most hopeful ways to deal with these sources of frustration and move forward involve key elements of the just peacemaking paradigm.[1]

Understanding Militant Islamist Groups

In the immediate aftermath of the September 11th attacks, the most frequently asked question related to militant Muslims: Why do they hate us? Various other questions repeatedly cycled through the thousands of articles and interviews over several months: What does the Qur'an teach about *jihad*? What is the face of "true" Islam? Is it a "religion of peace" as many Muslim leaders and President Bush repeatedly claimed? Or, did Osama bin Laden and the Al Qaeda ("the base") offer a more accurate picture of the world's second largest religious tradition?

What is the meaning of *jihad*? The Arabic word means, "striving or struggling in the way of God." Muslims should strive to know and do the will of God. Historically, the "greater" *jihad* refers to the struggle each person has with him or herself to do what is right. Human sinfulness, pride, and selfishness are our major obstacles. The "lesser" *jihad* involves the outward defense of Islam. Muslims should be prepared to defend Islam, including military defense, when the community of faith is under attack. While the vast majority of Muslims reject the violent extremism manifest on September 11, 2001, some Islamist leaders and groups clearly attempt to justify their behavior in the context of a holy war or struggle in defense of Islam. Thus, Osama bin Laden called on the "nation of Islam" to join with him in this holy war.

Why are many Muslims so angry? How can they justify turning airplanes into bombs and killing some 3,000 people as heroic actions? The answers are not simple or straightforward. Labeling the perpetrators terrorists or evildoers rings true, but it does not answer the questions. We can begin to get some clarity, however, through a synthetic analysis, a layered approach that takes seriously religious, historical, political, social, and economic dynamics.

Common Themes and Specific Circumstances

A number of factors are operating simultaneously in predominantly Muslim countries. There are common themes one can discern through study and personal interaction with Muslims over time. These inform many of the politically active individuals and groups, often referred to as Islamists. At the same time, there are very specific historical, political, social, and economic circumstances giving rise to different movements in particular settings.

Many Muslims are convinced that Islam can provide a framework for the future. They point to the past and note how Islam led the world civilization for centuries. A famous saying attributed to Muhammad enjoins Muslims to "seek knowledge wherever you may find it, even unto China." For many centuries, Muslim scholars and thinkers did just that. The popular Western image of Islam as unsophisticated and anti-intellectual quickly disappears in the face of even a cursory survey of Islamic history. The error of this image is particularly ironic in view of the major ways Islamic civilization helped shape Western society as we know it. When Europe was languishing in the "Dark Ages," Islamic civilization was thriving from Spain to India. For several centuries, Muslims led the world in areas such as mathematics, chemistry, medicine, philosophy, navigation, architecture, horticulture, and astronomy.

Muslims are proud of their history and civilization. But something went wrong. From the sixteenth through the twentieth century many of the lands with a Muslim majority were under the control of outside powers. European colonial powers dominated prior to the rise of the two superpowers following World War II. In the last decade, the United States has stood alone as the world's superpower. Resentment against the history of colonial domination can readily translate into resentment against the United States, if it is perceived as supporting structures of economic and political domination.

The formation of many new nations during the past sixty years adds another layer. Muslims who hoped and worked for revitalized, contemporary Islamic states have been thwarted time and again during recent decades. Although many Muslim lands now have indigenous leaders, there are not many examples where those who govern are in power by virtue of popular choice. Instead, one finds dynastic rule by kings or military and political leaders who seized and maintain power through force.

Movements for political reform have frequently been marginalized or crushed. Despicable human rights records in many Muslim countries add to the frustration. The details vary from country to country, but the pattern is all too familiar. The data are available through Amnesty International, Human Rights Watch, and the annual reports published by the U.S. Department of State.

Economic disparity and perceptions of exploitation are additional ingredients contributing toward political instability. Extraordinary wealth enjoyed by the ruling elite coupled with images of opulence in the West provide evidence for those who argue that their countries are still very much controlled by external powers.

There is a widespread belief that Islam can once again provide a viable framework for the state and for society. There is also a strong sense that many existing political, economic, and social systems have failed. When most avenues for political change appear to be blocked, more and more individuals and groups are attracted to revolutionary movements.

Working with the churches in the Middle East during the 1980s brought me in contact with many groups working for political change. I became aware of some of the groups that attracted considerable attention subsequently, namely: Hizbullah, Islamic Jihad, Hamas, and the Islamic Salvation Front. It is vital to understand these and various other groups and movements in their respective contexts. There are general themes and perceptions running through the Muslim world. But individual leaders and groups take shape in specific places with distinctive histories and contemporary circumstances. It is this piece that many analysts seem to miss.

Islam is not monolithic. Sweeping generalizations devoid of careful contextual analysis will lead inevitably to erroneous conclusions. Egypt is not Algeria; Algeria is not Afghanistan; Afghanistan is not Iran; and so on. One must be very careful about generalizations based on one setting or one group. When journalists and pundits engage the question, "Why do they hate us?" they find partial answers in clashing value systems and general grievances related to inconsistent U.S. foreign policies. But the roots of frustration go much deeper. They are lodged in particular settings.

Consider Egypt as a case study. I was studying in Cairo in 1977-78, the year Anwar Sadat stunned the world with his sudden trip to Jerusalem and the subsequent Camp David peace process. I have been there many times since. My experiences in Egypt—as a student and working with the Coptic Orthodox Church and Muslim leaders—have been extremely positive. But there are longstanding frustrations and deep undercurrents in this overpopulated country. Widespread poverty and substantial limitations on democratic participation in policy making are major factors feeding the frustration. For many centuries, Egypt, and al-Azhar University in particular, have been at the intellectual center of the Muslim world. Early in the twentieth century, Egypt gave birth to the Muslim Brotherhood. Various reform movements have come and gone and some have been radicalized over the decades.

Although Sadat was popular in the West, not all Egyptians felt the same way. Muslim extremists assassinated him in 1981. Fringe groups convinced that the regime of Hosni Mubarak is beyond redemption have surfaced in Egypt on a number of occasions over the past twenty years. They have attacked tourist groups from Japan and Germany as a way to dry up an indispensable source of revenue for Egypt: tourism. Their goal was to destabilize the Mubarak government.

A small group of Egyptian nationals, led by the blind cleric, Umar abd al-Rahman, was convicted of the first attempt to blow up the World Trade Center in 1993. They also had plans to kill Mubarak and Butros Butros Ghali, the Egyptian who served as General Secretary of the United Nations. The apparent ringleader for the September 11th hijackings and attacks was Muhammad Atta, an Egyptian. Taped messages from Osama bin Laden also featured the number two leader in the *Al Qaeda* movement, an Egyptian physician named Ayman al-Zawahiri. These extremists have grown in a context of crushing poverty, minimal democratic participation, the breakdown of traditional values, and harsh crackdowns on dissenters.

To understand the religious, political, and social dynamics informing Hizbullah, one must look closely at the convoluted history of Lebanon. Similarly, the Islamic Salvation Front is inseparable from the French colonial and more recent history of Algeria. Hamas—which includes educational, social, political, and military institutional structures primarily in Gaza—cannot be understood apart from the tortured history of the Israeli-Palestinian conflict.

The desire for clarity about the Islamic connections to turbulent forces is understandable. Bringing the picture into focus requires both an awareness of widespread aspirations among Muslims and a lot of hard, painstaking work in the dense thicket of the particulars present in specific situations.[2]

An Islamic State?

While many share the vision that Islam can provide the framework for their respective societies, there is no consensus on precisely what an Islamic state should look like. If we were to give fifty Islamist leaders a blank notepad and ask them to write out their vision for an Islamic state in the twenty-first century, the results would be anything but consistent. Recent attempts to develop Islamic states illustrate the disparate visions. Following the 1979 revolution, Iran developed an Islamic Republic, a governmental structure based largely on the model of a Western parliamentary democracy. Pakistan, the only country created explicitly to be an Islamic state, has had a tumultuous history for more than fifty years. No Muslims I know look to Pakistan as the model they seek to emulate.

In Afghanistan, the Taliban seized power in 1996 after fifteen years of devastating warfare. They imposed an extraordinarily rigid and extreme version of Islamic law to the horror of most of the world. Prior to September 11th, only three countries—Pakistan, Saudi Arabia, and the United Arab Emirates—had diplomatic relations with the Taliban. There is no evidence that Muslims (other than a few people with close ties in neighboring Pakistan) were interested in taking courses from the Taliban on how to organize an Islamic state.

There are many other voices within Islam.[3] Given the nature of our pluralist, interdependent world, some Muslims believe secular democratic states that guarantee religious freedom is the best model for the future. Many Muslims are deeply troubled by the very real problems of religious intolerance, persecution of minorities, and the treatment of women within their societies. This debate will continue.

Why Is There Such Hostility toward the United States?

Anger and frustration inspiring violence directed toward the United States is not new. For 444 days, student militants held 52 U.S. citizens hostage in Iran. The initial reason for taking over the embassy in Tehran and holding hostages was tied to their fear that the United States was preparing to return the Shah to power, as it had done two decades earlier. In 1982, a teenage suicide truck bomber blew up Marine barracks in Beirut killing 239 Americans. Five years ago, Muslim extremists connected with Osama bin Laden destroyed the U.S. embassies in Kenya and Tanzania. In 2000, 17 Navy personnel were killed when a suicide bomber attempted to sink the USS Cole near Yemen. The depth of anger toward the United States is unmistakable. Their numbers may be relatively small, but, as we now know, it does not take many people to wreak havoc.

The search for simple answers continues with some Muslims and many analysts citing United States support of Israel as a primary source of anger toward the United States. Such rhetoric reflects only part of the truth. The deeper issues are tied to the enormous power of the United States and the inconsistency of policies affecting the Muslim countries in question. Far too often, the U.S. government has pursued short sighted, self-serving policies that contradict the ideals most Americans believe we espouse. Most Americans do not pay much attention to the inconsistencies in foreign policy. People in other parts of the world who feel the impact of those policies pay close attention when U.S. policies support the status quo in countries with authoritarian governments and deplorable human rights records.

In the late 1970s, the United States helped train Osama bin Laden and his forces. They were considered "freedom fighters" since the enemy in Afghanistan was the USSR. Muslim revolutionaries operating at the same time in neighboring Iran were labeled "fanatics." During the 1980s, the United States supported Iraq in the ten-year war of attrition against Iran. Many public policy advocates, myself included, were highly vocal in opposition to the support of Saddam Hussein. His human rights record was among the worst in the world and he used chemical weapons repeatedly on both Kurds in his country and Iranians. Much later, President Bush labeled Saddam Hussein "an evil man" in his press conference on October 11, 2001, noting that he "gassed his own people." True. Where was the "official" outrage when these events were taking place during the Reagan administration? The operative policy in these instances was simple: the enemy of my enemy is my friend. The fallacy of such short-term, expedient policies is now all too clear.

Osama bin Laden and most of the terrorists of September 11th were Saudis. Saudi Arabia is governed by a tight family circle. Free discussion, political parties, elections, and citizen input are all suppressed. Opposition groups see U.S. government support for the ruling regime in Saudi Arabia and the presence of U.S. military forces as reinforcing the status quo. Opposition leaders consider the U.S. military a deeply offensive secular presence in the land which safeguards the sacred cities of Mecca and Medina. The ramping up of U.S. military bases in response to Iraq's 1990 invasion of Kuwait was a decisive turning point in the thinking of Osama bin Laden.[4]

Although not many Americans were paying attention, Muslims around the world know that the United States supported the regime in power in Algeria when it halted elections in the early 1990s after the first of two rounds. It was clear that Islamic parties were going to win the elections with eighty percent of the popular vote. Some in Congress were confused as well, thinking that the United States supported democratization and self-determination. Why would we help stop free elections? A top official from the Department of State was summoned for congressional testimony. He explained that our policy is "One person, one vote." "But," he added, "we are not for one person, one vote, one time." Should the Islamic parties win, he suggested, they would abolish democracy. So, the reasoning went, the United States cannot support a process whereby parties will use democracy in order to get power and then abolish democracy. So, the policy actually turned out to be this: One person, no votes, any time.

Many Muslims around the world are unimpressed by presidential speeches calling Americans freedom loving, peaceful people who cherish democracy. They see cancelled elections and the subsequent arrest of Islamist leaders in Algeria. They see United States support for many repressive regimes they consider illegitimate. They see the pervasive influence of hedonistic Western culture on their traditional societies. Combine these ingredients and you have got a volatile mix.

The Just Peacemaking Paradigm

The just peacemaking paradigm is predicated on the idea that there are multiple and identifiable root causes fueling animosity and conflict. The ten practices represent specific steps or actions that can—individually and collectively—reduce the movement toward war. It is important to underscore this foundational premise since there are substantial voices who argue against it. Cable news programs, talk radio, and opinion pages frequently feature "analysts" who argue essentially that the United States must simply crush those forces which appear to threaten its "vital interests." Some prominent figures openly reject any position that takes root causes seriously.[5] Not only is this approach morally indefensible, in my view, it is a recipe for disaster. While there are no easy answers or simple solutions, sustainable peace and stability require concerted efforts on several fronts.

Just peacemaking theory directs our attention to the worldwide push for *human rights and democracy* (practice 5), and thus alerts us to the dammed-up resentment of those who long for change in predominantly Islamic countries, people who are frustrated by repressive policies of authoritarian governments. Violent extremists come mostly from countries ruled by authoritarian and non-democratic governments. They do not view the United States as the paragon of democracy most Americans see in their mirrors. Rather, the United States is perceived as the powerful ally of repressive regimes for the sake of oil, arms sales, and a wider system of economic and political hegemony.[6] Based on extensive empirical analysis, Rudolph Rummel found that democratic forms of government experience far fewer massacres, civil wars, and terrorist violence than do dictatorships.[7] Surely this is confirmed by our contemporary experience with terrorism. If the "war on terrorism" is to be effective, U.S. policy must shift toward encouraging human rights and democratic reforms among Middle Eastern nations. Ray Takeyh rightly makes the connection:

> The collapse of the Soviet Union and the emergence of democratic regimes in Eastern Europe, Latin America, and East Asia electrified the Arab populace. Their demands were simple but profound. As one Egyptian university student explained in 1993, "I want what they have in Poland, Czechoslovakia: freedom of thought and freedom of speech."[8]

Takeyh points to "a new generation of Islamist thinkers, who have sought to legitimize democratic concepts through the reinterpretation of Islamic texts and traditions. . . . Under these progressive readings, the well-delineated Islamic concept of *shura* (consultation) compels a ruler to consider popular opinion and establishes the foundation for an accountable government."[9] In the *hadith* (sayings and actions of the prophet),

Muhammad taught that "difference of opinion within my community is a sign of God's mercy." So there are solid foundations upon which Muslims can explore options for viable political structures. Participatory government systems will surely vary in Muslim lands as they have in other newly emerging democracies. Cultural and historical factors will shape the processes in particular settings. Takeyh underscores this point: "Even though Islamic democracy will resist certain elements of post-Enlightenment liberalism, it will still be a system that features regular elections, accepts dissent and opposition parties, and condones a free press and division of power between branches of the state."[10]

Hopefully, new and viable structures can be fashioned over time. One such potentially positive experiment is the Islamic Republic of Iran. The basic Iranian government system is a Western parliamentary democracy, a republic. Iranians elect their president and representatives in the *majlis* (Parliament). The 1979 revolution did not produce a return to the time of Muhammad or Ali's caliphate. Rather, it resulted in a new form of government that endeavored both to draw on tradition and to adapt to the contemporary circumstances. Iran is not a pure democracy. The government structures include distinctive and powerful roles for Shi'ite clergy leaders. Even so, clear signs of moderation among many elected leaders over two decades suggest that democracy is alive and functioning in the Islamic Republic.[11]

To the degree to which the United States is perceived to be genuinely supporting democratic reforms, anger toward the world's superpower as a defender of the status quo will diminish proportionally. Nowhere is this more needed than in Palestine. The ability of Palestinian leaders to slow and halt the tide of terrorism—most visibly seen in the rapid rise in suicide bombings during 2002—depends on hopeful alternatives. In my experience, many Palestinians look also to the dramatic changes in South Africa as a source of hope for nonviolent change and movement toward genuine self-determination. These hopes have been thwarted time and again both by repressive policies of Israeli military occupation and various types of corruption within the Palestinian authority. Much more transparency, an independent judiciary, a stronger legislature, demonstrable respect for the rule of law, and checks and balances against corruption are essential. Deficiencies in these areas are powerful tools in the hands of militant Islamist leaders.[12]

In the midst of various violent clashes between Israelis and Palestinians, there have been signs of hope from within the U.S. government. For the first time, an American president, George W. Bush, has identified an independent Palestinian state as the desired outcome of the exceedingly difficult peace process. President Bush and Secretary of State Colin Powell have stressed the centrality of fair elections and democratic reforms within the Palestinian Authority. These affirmations, combined with unrelenting commitment to human rights and justice for all peoples, are foundational for the just peacemaking paradigm.

Just peacemaking theory directs us also to the importance of *sustainable economic development* if we are able to reduce violence and diminish the sources fueling violent extremism. Chapter seven of *Just Peacemaking* refers to *Why Men Rebel* by Ted Gurr, a now classic study deemed the "best book of the year" by the American Political Science Association.[13] On the basis of massive longitudinal and cross-national data, Gurr argues that relative economic deprivation is a, or *the*, major cause of international violence. Terrorism is a form of rebellion, bred by bitter resentment over perceived injustices and a sense of victimization. Violent extremists feel powerless to fight back by other means. Terrorism is a weapon of the weak. Examples abound in the Middle East and elsewhere.

Effective assistance in nurturing and developing sustainable economies is not only morally responsible, it is also dramatically less expensive than an ongoing, multi-year violent war against terrorism. Strobe Talbott reports that half the people on earth are struggling to survive on less than two dollars a day. The numbers of the poor are growing faster than the wealthy and the gap between them is widening.

> Disease, overcrowding, undernourishment, political repression, and alienation breed despair, anger and hatred. . . . Programs that are instrumental in getting at the roots of terrorism are more in jeopardy now than they were two months ago. The blank check Congress seems willing to write is for enhancing military defenses (including a national anti-missile system). . . . In the budget crunch ahead, there will be a temptation to squeeze down the very programs that will allow us to move from reactive, defensive warfare against the terrorists to a proactive, prolonged offensive against the ugly, intractable realities that terrorists exploit and from which they derive popular support, foot soldiers, and political cover.[14]

The strong argument advanced by Talbott, a former U.S. Ambassador in the Middle East, rings true with my experience over many years. In dozens of conversations all across the political spectrum in Israel/Palestine and Lebanon—with political and religious leaders, activists, academics, people in refugee camps, and others—better economic opportunities always surfaced as an essential ingredient. In the face of tremendous suffering and strong perceptions of injustice, people on various sides of bitter conflicts repeatedly softened their positions when prospects for the cessation of violence included specific plans for economic development. In a word, even bitter enemies are capable of exploring options for peaceful coexistence when they include the real possibility of a better future for their children and grandchildren.

Rampant poverty and hopelessness are breeding grounds for extremism. Economic opportunities provide reason for hope; they are practical, tangible components that appeal to the self-interest of everyone. Many Palestinians look to the example of South Africa as a model for change. Despite horrendous conditions for black South Africans living under apartheid, pressure from the world community, democratic reforms, and economic incentives helped persuade people on both sides that the only way forward involved negotiations around a table, not at the point of a gun. In the case of the Israeli-Palestinian conflict and the wider Arab-Israeli conflict, economic self-interest will be a critical factor in any sustainable peace process. Long-term issues of limited water resources and the crushing defense expenditures will necessitate cooperation and peaceful coexistence. People on all sides knew this and had begun to make meaningful progress in multi-lateral negotiations during the 1990s before renewed conflict sidetracked discussions and undermined the minimal levels of trust between adversaries.

Another just peacemaking practice is *independent initiatives*. These are desperately needed in the context of Israel/Palestine. The strategy of independent initiatives is designed to decrease distrust. It absolutely requires that initiatives take place by the announced deadlines in order to decrease distrust; postponement or excuses in the face of announced deadlines can easily destroy the minimal level of trust that has been established. In 1993, when the two sides signed the Oslo agreement recognizing Israel and its need for security, and setting dates for the return of land for Palestinian rule, Palestinian support for the agreement was initially at sixty-seven percent; popular support among Palestinians rose to eighty percent as the first portions of land were returned and the Israeli army withdrew after over twenty-five years of military occupation. Violence directed toward Israelis was remarkably low when Benjamin Netanyahu became Prime Minister of Israel in 1996. Netanyahu postponed the return of the land indefinitely, the settlement process expanded substantially. Polls among Palestinians revealed a marked decline in expectations that the "peace process" would lead to a permanent settlement. During Netanyahu's first year in office, the decline in Palestinian expectations dropped from forty-four to thirty percent. When Ariel Sharon became Prime Minister in 2000 and cancelled the negotiations, only eleven percent of the Palestinians held out hope for a permanent, negotiated settlement. Support for violent action directed at Israel increased inversely, both in the polls and in actuality.[15]

Israelis, too, can cite examples of promises and agreements that have been broken. Both sides offer familiar refrains about political leaders on the other side who say one thing to the other side and the press while promulgating a different message among their supporters. All of this undermines bases for trust. Independent initiatives are particularly valuable since they do not have to wait for long-delayed and complicated negotiations; they may be taken when the atmosphere is too hostile or distrustful to support successful negotiations. One side can help break the stalemate and finger-pointing through a series of visible and verifiable initiatives that decrease the threat to the other side. It signals the purpose of decreasing the threat to the other side and inviting reciprocal action. Trust is created when a date is announced and specific initiatives are implemented regardless of efforts by those on either side who oppose any process of negotiation.

The sad reality during much of 2002 revealed how independent initiatives worked in reverse. When Prime Minister Sharon declared repeatedly that there could be no negotiations unless all violence ceased, he effectively empowered suicide bombers and extremists among the Palestinians. One person taking a violent independent initiative could stop any hope for meaningful negotiation. One person could and did provide justification for massive military crackdowns and occupation of cities in the West Bank. The level of distrust on both sides in 2002 was higher than anything I have experienced in twenty-five years of direct involvement.

The Way Forward

Where do we go from here? I suggest a two-track approach. The immediate, short-term threats are very real. The events of September 11, 2001 speak for themselves. Some violent extremists may be beyond negotiation. One has to assume that a small number of extremists will use whatever weapons of mass destruction they can acquire and deliver. The stakes are exceedingly high—not only for the United States, but for the world. Whatever their grievances, terrorist actions eliminate any moral authority. The short-term requires a careful, systematic, global effort to neutralize these misguided, violent extremists. The challenge involves pursuing military, political, and economic policies that will not effectively drive many more frustrated and angry people into the ranks of the Al Qaeda network. Patience and a great deal of collective wisdom are needed.

The longer-term challenge moves at a very different level. As the world's superpower, the United States must find new ways to work with others in the community of nations in pursuit of peace and stability. This is not wishful thinking. I am not talking about lighting a candle, joining hands, and singing "We are the World." Rather, the United States must take a hard look at our own policies and resolve to take principled, consistent positions in support of fundamental human rights, self-determination, democratization, and genuine economic opportunities.

Constructive leadership requires critical self-analysis. The fourth just peacemaking practice is *acknowledge responsibility for conflict and injustice; seek repentance and forgiveness.* As we have seen above, just peacemaking points toward the kind of analysis that can reduce the causes fueling terrorism. Just war theory alone tends to focus on whether it is right to use violence in retaliation against violence and terrorism. As suggested in the first-track response, this may be needed in extreme situations. Nonviolence may be the ideal, but in the face of weapons of mass destruction, serious consideration must be given to issues of proportionality and approaches that would likely result in the least harm. But, it is essential to think and move beyond short-term policies. This is where the Israeli-Palestinian conflict appears to be stuck at the time of this writing. Similarly, the United States must not become stuck in the "war on terrorism." The second track, one which addresses root causes with a longer term perspective, is precisely where the just peacemaking paradigm can and must guide our thinking.

In many parts of the world, especially the Muslim world, we see boiling pots. Working with others in the community of nations as well as non-governmental groups and organizations, the United States must endeavor to help take the lids off those boiling pots. People of goodwill in all communities must strive to provide bases for hope that a better future is possible. Put another way, the community of nations must find ways to replicate the kinds of political, economic, and social pressure for nonviolent change we have witnessed in South Africa. There is no magic wand or quick fix. The road ahead will be circuitous and full of major obstacles. But the way forward is not blocked.[16] A better informed public must encourage courageous leadership in pursuit of peace, justice, and stability. It is the right thing to do; it is the only approach that ultimately makes sense.

NOTES

---

[1] This article is based both on three decades of scholarly inquiry and personal experience working in the midst of the major conflicts in the Middle East. Some personal background information is important. My doctoral work at Harvard was focused on Islamic studies and contemporary Jewish-Christian-Muslim relations in the Middle East. I was one of seven clergy invited to Iran in the early stages of the Iranian hostage crisis in order to meet with the Ayatollah Khomeini, top Iranian officials and the student militants holding the hostages in the U.S. embassy in Tehran. I was twice more invited back to Iran during the 444-day crisis to help facilitate communication and pursue non-violent ways to resolve the crisis.

From 1983 to 1990, I served as Middle East Director for the National Council of Churches based in New York. A major focus on that work included gathering information and facilitating initiatives for relief, development and conflict resolution. This involved working with top government officials (in the United States, Israel, the PLO, Lebanon, Jordan and Egypt) as well as hands on involvement in war zones, refugee camps. Efforts to formulate policies and encourage constructive steps by the various parties—including the U.S. government—required continual meetings with academics, journalists, and various activists in widely diverse communities. This work required numerous trips to and throughout the Middle East as well as twenty to thirty trips to Washington, D.C., each year. Between 1977 and 2001, these endeavors have included more than thirty-five trips to the Middle East.

Over the past two decades, I have written four books, and numerous articles and opinion pieces related to Islam, interfaith relations and the contemporary conflicts in the Middle East. This present article is based, therefore, on both a longstanding study of and direct involvement with several major conflicts in the Middle East. Portions of the analysis presented here were first published in *The Christian Century* (October 24-31, 2001) and in *When Religion Becomes Evil* (Harper San Francisco, 2002).

[2] See John L. Esposito, *The Islamic Threat: Myth or Reality?* 3rd ed. (Oxford: Oxford University Press, 1998) and John L. Esposito, *Unholy War* (Oxford: Oxford University Press, 2002) for detailed and helpful overviews of revivalist movements and widespread political debates within and about predominantly Muslim countries.

[3] See Charles Kurzman, ed., *Liberal Islam: A Sourcebook* (New York: Oxford University Press, 1998) for an instructive array of essays by thoughtful Muslim scholars and activists in various settings.

[4] Esposito, *Unholy War*, 11-12.

[5] See, for instance, Alan M. Dershowitz, *Why Terrorism Works: Understanding the Threat, Responding to the Challenge* (New Haven: Yale University Press, 2002) and Daniel Pipes, *Militant Islam Reaches America* (New York: W. W. Norton & Co., 2002).

[6] See Charles A. Kimball, *Religion, Politics and Oil: The Volatile Mix in the Middle East* (Nashville: Abingdon Press, 1992) for an extended analysis of ways economic considerations about oil and arms sales shape U.S. policy in the Middle East.

[7] Rudolph Rummel, *Power Kills: Democracy as a Method of Nonviolence* (New Brunswick and London: Transaction Publishers, 1997).

[8] Ray Takeyh, "Faith-Based Initiatives: Can Islam Bring Democracy to the Middle East?" *Foreign Policy* (November/December 2001): 68.

[9] Ibid., 69.

[10] Ibid., 70.

[11] Thomas Friedman articulated this view when he wrote about his visit to Iran in *The New York Times*, June 16, 2002. Friedman writes about the "third wave" of Iranians, the new generation that wants the good life, good job, more individual freedom, and more connections with the outside world. Friedman's many articles underscore the centrality of addressing root causes of conflict and careful analysis in particular settings. See Thomas Friedman, *Longitudes and Attitudes* (New York: Farrar, Straus and Giroux, 2002).

[12] Khalil Shikaki, "Palestine Divided," *Foreign Affairs* (January/February 2002): 89ff.

[13] Ted Gurr, *Why Men Rebel* (Princeton: Princeton University Press, 1970). See also Glen H. Stassen, *Just Peacemaking: Transforming Initiatives for Justice and Peace* (Louisville: Westminster John Knox, 1992).

[14] Strobe Talbott, "The Other Evil: The War on Terrorism Won't Succeed Without a War on Poverty," *Foreign Policy* (November/December 2001): 75ff.

[15] Stephen Zunes, *Middle East Policy* 8 (4) (December 2001): 66ff.

[16] There are literally dozens of groups and organizations working for reconciliation across political and religious lines. For those who see the Israeli-Palestinian conflict as hopeless, see Marc Gopin, *Holy War, Holy Peace: How Religion Can Bring Peace to the Middle East* (New York: Oxford University Press, 2002). Gopin offers over 100 pages of "practical applications" for people serious about facilitating peace in the Middle East.

Just Peacemaking: Challenges of Humanitarian Intervention

Martin L. Cook

Abstract

Just peacemaking proposes that it is a creative "third way" between just war and pacifism for Christian engagement with international affairs. It claims that its proposals result from the convergence of a number of important characteristics of the contemporary international scene that cumulatively make this a *"kairos"* for novel and creative modes of reflection and action. Further, it claims to offer workable and realistic counsel for action in the contemporary world of international relations. This paper critically assesses both claims. It reviews various interpretations of the direction of contemporary international affairs and raises some cautions about too enthusiastic an embrace of just peacemaking's vision of cooperative internationalism. It then focuses specifically on situations that invite intervention in the name of humanitarian concerns. There, the author finds some elements of just peacemaking to be an important supplement to the capabilities of military forces to intervene effectively and to transition successfully to nation-building activities that are necessary if intervention is to have a lasting positive effect.

Introduction

Just Peacemaking: Ten Practices for Abolishing War is a collaboration of twenty-three scholars, each of who contributed to chapters spelling out various practices that together comprise the essential elements of just peacemaking. This paper will not attempt a full-fledged assessment of the

Journal of the Society of Christian Ethics, 23/1 (2003): 241-253

coherence, adequacy, and practical value of all elements of the just peacemaking proposal. Rather, it will focus on the specific issue of the use of military force for humanitarian intervention.

This focus is worthy of attention because, as a practical matter, much of the debate in recent years has swirled around the twin concepts of universal human rights, on the one hand, and the difficulties of gathering political and military support to act on their behalf, on the other. It is precisely the persistence of such questions that indicates the importance and need to balance the just peacemaking proposal with an equally robust framework for the justified use of military force in war, in operations other than war (including peacekeeping and peacemaking), and in the current environment in the far-flung "war" against terrorism.

Some misunderstanding of the just peacemaking proposals has been generated by the book's subtitle, "ten practices for abolishing war." Taken at face value, it would suggest that the authors believe that their practices cumulatively will indeed achieve such a grand effect. If so, then just peacemaking stands in sharp contrast to both pacifism and just war. In contrast to pacifism (at least the most profound kinds), just peacemaking advocates quite vigorous engagement with the world of international affairs and foreign policy; in contrast to just war, if just peacemaking is understood in these terms, it displaces entirely just war's claim for an abiding and appropriate place for war (and other uses of military force) in morally legitimate statecraft.

Despite that confusion, many places in the book, and subsequent work by Glen Stassen, the volume's editor, strongly assert that just peacemaking is intended to supplement and not supplant just war. This paper will argue that, understood in this way, both just war's criteria and just peacemaking's practices form a continuum of tools to be employed as practical wisdom and circumstances dictate, in pursuit of common moral aspirations in international affairs. The paper will proceed by means of an overall assessment of just peacemaking's interpretation of the current international scene, turning then to specific questions of the role of just peacemaking's practices in assisting our thinking and our acting in humanitarian intervention in particular.

In the *Just Peacemaking* volume, Michael Smith's chapter advocating such humanitarian intervention is, by the editor's own admission, one on which some of the other authors did not agree.[1] Yet it is the only chapter that deals directly with the issue of political/military power—the defining characteristic of the nation state as it has evolved, and the central issue of the international order. It is in that context that Smith advocates willingness and ability to harness military power to the pursuit of the moral values of human dignity and human rights.

This suggests an important area for clarification in the just peacemaking proposal itself. While the volume says at various points that it recognizes that war and the use of military force for purposes other than war will continue to be an important element in the international scene, it is perhaps less clear than it ought to be in demarcating the boundaries between areas of international life where the just peacemaking practices might usefully be applied and those areas where military force remains an important element of international agency.

This essay, therefore, will attempt to sharpen the discussion by exploring some of the areas of international life in which continued use of military force in pursuit of humanitarian ends serves the same ethical ends as those sought by the just peacemaking practices.

The Current International Scene: Alternatives of the Just Peacemaking Proposal's View

A fundamental assumption of the just peacemaking proposal is that the post-Cold War international scene is a time of unprecedented opportunity for new initiatives for peacemaking. In religious terms, it represents a *kairos*, a moment of unique opportunity.

The interpretation of the international scene that underlies the just peacemaking consensus (including Smith's model of intervention) is resolutely internationalist and cosmopolitan. Drawing on the work of Paul Schroeder, the contributors share a belief that the direction of historical development points to an ever greater interlocking international economy, a spreading network of non-government organizations, strengthening international authorities, and so forth.[2] Cumulatively, these trends will progressively create a world in which military force is rendered increasingly unnecessary and superfluous and in which its cost in proportion to any conceivable benefit will render it manifestly irrational—at least for large-scale inter-state warfare.

Just peacemaking claims the connection between traditional just war principles and just peacemaking is that the various just peacemaking practices "fill in the contents" of just war's "underdeveloped principles of last resort and just intention—to spell out what resorts must be tried before trying the least resort of war, and what intention there is to restore a just and enduring peace."[3] On this account, just peacemaking expands the repertoire of alternatives in advance of armed conflict, and expands the scope of analysis of just settlement of those conflicts (and just international arrangements generally).

As a practical action guide, the requirement that in any and all circumstances these practices must actually precede use of military force seems imprudent and unwarranted. The absolute requirement that they be tried before force is used is asserted without any justification. While it is important, of course, to be sincere and honest about the last resort criterion, the idea that any "check list" of absolute requirements can capture the judgment of practical wisdom for all cases is, on the face of it, almost certainly misguided. It would make ethical reasoning much simpler, of course, if there were such a checklist, but in any real-world conflict, honest people of good will almost always disagree about whether the last resort criterion has been sincerely respected.

Michael Smith's picture of the emerging world, while also quite idealistic, is fundamentally different than the dominant one held by the just peacemaking "consensus." Perhaps because he is grounded in the discipline of political science rather than theology, necessarily his perspective is to some degree closer to the real world of political decision-makers. Rather than a freely cooperative and peaceful world, Smith's vision maintains a prominent place for the coercive role of military power. His ideal world is one of states of diminishing sovereignty. These states increasingly cede authority to a much-strengthened United Nations. The United Nations, so reorganized, possesses a volunteer military force prepared to intervene in the name of human rights globally.

Smith's is a picture of universal values and rights married to a universal political structure possessed of coercive power to enforce the values of the international community on a nation that commits especially egregious massacres and violations of human rights such as Rwanda, Somalia, or Kosovo and individuals and groups that attempt to act at variance with them.

Sharing a vision of the objective with his fellow just peacemaking scholars (increasing respect for human individuals, their rights, democratic government, economic prosperity), Smith still presumes that there are many actors on the world stage ready, willing, and able to aspire to regional hegemony and perhaps "irrational" actors (as at least the emerging global consensus understands "rational") prepared to develop and use weapons of mass destruction or to turn their power against their own people.

For Smith, the fundamental moral question is not "military force or no military force;" rather, it is "force for what ends and under what authority." His concern is that national sovereignty no longer rules the international scene, and that it be replaced with a much-strengthened United Nations. This new UN is capable of coherent political action and is willing, able, and possessed of sufficient military force to impose the will of the international community on errant actors. Not surprisingly, Smith's muscular international community would vary considerably from the model of peaceful cooperation that dominates most of the other authors of the just peacemaking project.

One might argue that the difference in perspective is also a difference in time. On its most optimistic interpretation, just peacemaking might assert that its practices would, if engaged in sufficiently early and with sufficient resources, be capable of obviating virtually all need for the use of military force. But that optimism might be tempered by the recognition that there will frequently be situations where such early and aggressive just peacemaking was not practiced and the situation was allowed to erode to the point where the stark alternatives of standing idly by or using coercive military force for humanitarian ends remain the sole practical alternatives. If one reads the just peacemaking proposal in this way, it offers a comprehensive model of conflict avoidance in theory, while recognizing the real world limitations that will keep its practices from being deployed consistently and in a sufficiently timely manner to be effective in all (or even most) cases.

Alternatively, one might hold that just peacemaking's practices might not work at all in certain intractable conditions and recognize that, for those contexts, coercive military power will remain the sole effective instrument. This interpretation, (which I believe is Smith's) gives greater scope to the perversity of human nature, to irrational and evil actors on the international scene, and to the inherent limitations of knowledge and resources that will keep just peacemaking's practices from being effective with consistency and regularity on the international scene.

It is important to note, however, that from the perspective of many realists in political science and international relations, Smith's humanitarian world order is itself often viewed as unduly optimistic and overly enthusiastic about the prospects and limits of international organizations. Smith's vision expects a degree of "felt cosmopolitanism" among powers that I doubt to be present and, arguably, desirable in the foreseeable future.[4] While UN peacekeepers have performed most valuable service in separating willing parties and defusing potential conflicts when the parties wish them to be defused, a UN force capable of forced entry and peace enforcement against a militarily significant unwilling party would require a level of interoperable equipment, training, and logistics very hard to imagine in the foreseeable future.

In the absence of a militarily powerful UN force, pursuit of the internationalist agenda will be left to the military forces of willing sovereign states and regional "coalitions of the willing." While Smith and Schroeder are certainly correct in noting the diminution of the power of sovereignty in many areas of contemporary international life, control of military forces is one area where it remains robust. Pursuit of humanitarian intervention in this political environment will inevitably be piecemeal, substantially intertwined with national interests of the interveners, and frustrating to all who, like Smith, wish to see universal principles backed up with consistent uses of military force.

Indeed, if one wishes to see relatively consistent and effective use of military power for humanitarian ends, one would be very reluctant to shift the "right authority" aspect of the judgment to the United Nations as it exists now or for the foreseeable future. Such a shift would be a recipe for inaction in many of the most urgent cases Smith and other proponents of intervention would advocate.[5] The veto power of any of the permanent members on the Security Council would block proposals in which a major power had a stake (witness the problem of authorization for Kosovo). If one wanted frequent and effective humanitarian interventions, in the foreseeable future one might think developing the capability of NATO and other regional alliances to undertake them under some kind of effective international agreement on acceptable conditions would be preferable. Such alliances are more likely to be motivated because of proximity or common interest to intervene and to possess the kinds of military forces and logistical support necessary to execute the mission in any but the most benign environment.[6]

In one important respect, however, the just peacemaking project's consensus is significant and broad enough to embrace both Smith's military interventionism and the dominant just peacemaking thrust toward non-military initiatives: they all assume the post-Cold War world is moving forward into a more globalized future. Underneath the disagreement over the continuing role of military force lies a conviction that the vision of the Enlightenment of a democratic world system, linked inextricably by bonds of commerce and shared values, lies, if not in the near future, at least within our sight and grasp.

This is probably the deepest critical question one may raise about the entire project. A number of very astute scholars have written powerfully of a quite different future for the world. Instead of global village, they suggest, the future holds some stark choices: *Jihad vs. McWorld*; the clash of civilizations.[7] As these scholars survey the same set of facts as the just peacemaking scholars, they see not an emerging global society of shared values, but either a knife edge walk between competing and incompatible visions or, even more grimly, a struggle to the death between utterly incompatible values and cultural forces. Some see this as a moment in which "America sleeps" and fails to recognize the need for even more robust military forces and their more frequent use in pursuit of the strategy our sole remaining superpower status makes possible.[8] The terrorist attacks of September 11, 2001, clearly warrant a large-scale and far-flung use of military force to control and eliminate the sources of future attacks. The degree to which the international cooperation that has characterized the early days of that conflict will continue is a complex matter politically, but also (given the absolute disparity in capability between the United States and even its closest NATO allies) militarily as well.

What is the relevance of these quite different pictures of the future for the cogency of the just peacemaking proposal? At a minimum they raise a useful caution against a premature or too-enthusiastic embrace of a single vision of the possible/probable human future. There was much in the international scene that allowed reading that future as the *Just Peacemaking* authors do; there was much to inform the much darker and more conflict ridden vision.

There were many indications that the darker vision was likely in recent years. But certainly in the aftermath of September 11, 2001, if not before, one should expect a serious hearing for these forecasts as well. It is, at the very least, now abundantly clear that forces are at work which would, if they had the capability, destroy the foundations of the emerging international order envisioned by any version of the just peacemaking proposal. Those forces stand willing to do so, even to their own destruction, and almost certainly with weapons of mass destruction if they had them. They are unlikely, to put it mildly, to be dissuaded by just peacemaking's practices.

At its root, just peacemaking may, with much of the academic community, significantly underestimate the depth of the conflict and the hatred that realistic international policy must be prepared to confront. For example, it presupposes that the assumptions about human rights and democratic government are universally shared. In this worldview, there is a kind of manifest destiny that those political values, notions of human rights, globalized economy, and so forth are waves of the future.

What if, instead, the real world practical choice is a struggle to the death between competing visions of human civilization and culture? What if, like the situation of the early Christians at the beginning of the fifth century, the question is not the triumph of moral idealism, but rather the persistence and success of the civilization itself? What if the price of military and cultural defeat is the loss of the cultural gains of millennia and the collapse of high civilization itself?

To raise these questions is to pose a fundamental issue to the just peacemaking project. It rests on a particular interpretation of the historical moment. Of course the reasons offered for that interpretation of the future are plausible. They are not, however, fundamentally different from those offered by Immanuel Kant in the eighteenth century in his vision of "perpetual peace." Naturally, the vision of advancing into a peaceful, democratic, prosperous, and united human future is attractive. As an eschatological vision it is unassailable. Whether it provides useful practical advice here and now is more debatable, in particular if it blinds the individuals and communities that share it to very real threats that need to be dealt with today.

To his credit, Smith's proposal assumes only an emerging international consensus on what the human rights *norms* should be and not on the breadth and depth of resistance to them. His conclusion that "a revitalized United Nations equipped with a standing volunteer military force" (155) is desirable but does not specify that force's size or operational tempo. In my view, if it were to execute his vision of consistent action in defense of human rights globally and effectively, it would be very, very large, and very, very busy.[9]

All these observations point out sharply the need for a meta-theory that incorporates the important contributions of the just peacemaking practices, but also provides clarity in thinking about where just peacemaking might be useless or inappropriate. Ideally, it should also frame use-of-force questions in such a way as to provide guidance to coercive peacemaking endeavors and also continuing legitimate war-making employment of military force. Only with such a comprehensive vision can just peacemaking's proposals fit within a sufficiently realist framework and avoid the hint of utopianism that clearly is not the intent of the *Just Peacemaking* authors.

Given the frequent assurances of the *Just Peacemaking* authors that they recognize international conflict will occur and given their insistence that they intend their recommendations to be practical and politically realistic, perhaps what is needed from a moral perspective is a moral principle that underlies practical engagement in worldly matters. "Use all elements of national and international power and cooperation so as to advance the cause of justice and minimize human suffering and loss of life," may be such a formula.

In some circumstances, that principle will counsel prompt use of overwhelming military force; in others, the cultivation of international cooperation and non-violent means to advance those causes. Those inclined to reach for military means may often overlook alternatives and thereby violate the principle by increasing suffering and death; those inclined to place great hope in internationalism and cooperation may delay effective military action in hopes of finding alternatives, also to the violation of the fundamental moral principle. Knowing which situations call for which approach is the essence of practical wisdom.

The Contribution of Just Peacemaking's Practices to Humanitarian Intervention

We turn now to the much narrower question of the contribution of just peacemaking's practices to humanitarian intervention. This question is premised on the assumption that military forces will be used to maintain peace when warring parties consent and to enforce peace and to prevent atrocity and violation of human rights, even when the perpetrators do not consent. I leave to the side the questions of the frequency, consistency, and authority for those interventions as well as of the agency that executes them. Given that the military has created a relatively stable and relatively peaceful environment where previously there was none, what is the value of just peacemaking's practices in enhancing our view of how to proceed? Alternatively, in circumstance where time and resources permit, what contribution can just peacemaking's practices make to preemption and forestalling deterioration of a situation to the point where coercive means are the only timely interventions possible?

It is here that the practices of the just peacemaking proposal have the greatest immediate practical applicability. Time after time the world has witnessed military interventions that were extremely effective in solving the particular problem that justified the intervention (deposing a dictator, stopping ethnic cleansing, restoring deposed elected leaders to power). But once the military operations were essentially completed, the "exit strategy" and final disposition of the situation have more often than not been badly handled.

Because often it is the only well-disciplined force capable of maintaining order, the military is tasked to fulfill missions (e.g., law enforcement, food distribution, health care, etc.) for which it is not prepared or which do not constitute the best use of its skills. Often the military is left deployed in an environment because no one knows how to restore civil society to the point where the heavy hand of military order is no longer required, lest factions resume killing each other. Still worse, at some point the sustained deployment is no longer possible (politically, economically) or violence is done to the military force and it is abruptly withdrawn (e.g., Somalia, to some degree Haiti), leaving the country at best only marginally better off than it was before the deployment.

The just peacemaking practices of cooperative conflict resolution, independent initiatives for threat reduction, acknowledgment of responsibility, advancing democracy and human rights, fostering just and sustainable economic development, working with cooperative forces (NGO, United Nations, and regional), and reducing weapons trade (especially in small arms) all speak to this very real gap in humanitarian interventions.

What are needed to fill the gap are well-trained and well-disciplined groups prepared to follow the military into these environments and prepared and capable to take the handoff when military forces are no longer the appropriate instruments and where nation building is really the major remaining issue. The very distaste for nation building expressed in the most recent presidential election stems from the valid perception that the United States and the world community lack precisely the "force structure" (to use the military term) to execute that phase of any humanitarian operation effectively. But the experience of Afghanistan also shows that it is impossible to exit when the central military mission is completed without undermining the moral justification of the entire intervention or even its long-term political success.

If the practical effect of just peacemaking's practices is to create such organizations and units, it will have provided an absolutely essential element for truly successful humanitarian interventions. Indeed, governments and international organizations might be much more willing to use their military forces for humanitarian interventions (as Michael Smith wishes they were!) if they knew that there would be competent, well-trained, well-disciplined nation-building forces ready to take the handoff when their military missions are complete.

Needless to say, those forces would have to be willing and able to link up tightly with military forces, to gain the respect and trust of military and civilian leadership and, perhaps, to be prepared to take casualties in execution of their mission. At present, some of the most effective groups in these areas are NGOs—although the appropriate UN agencies are important and their effectiveness and funding could be increased as well.[10]

For citizens of the United States, just peacemaking's practices might have very practical and political consequences. For example, groups and individuals who take seriously the importance of just peacemaking's various practices might advocate a policy that the U.S. government fund and build deployment capability into other Federal departments and agencies. To cite only a few examples, why could not the Department of Justice be tasked, funded, and prepared to deploy for the rebuilding of legal systems? Why could not the Department of Agriculture be given the mission of deploying personnel in the wake of humanitarian intervention to help establish sustainable agriculture? Why could not the FBI have units trained, funded, and equipped to help re-establish effective local law enforcement?

Similarly, non-governmental teams skilled in the practices of cooperative conflict resolution and in facilitating acknowledgment of responsibility, repentance, and forgiveness may be absolutely essential in a conflict such as occurred in Bosnia. In such deep-seated conflicts where memories are long, one suspects no amount of institutional rebuilding will ever bring a stable and just society if those more fundamental issues of inter-communal conflict remain below the surface. This is, of course, precisely the kind of work David Steele (one of the participants in the just peacemaking conferences) is attempting in the Balkans. It is precisely the kind of cultural engagement which is necessary, and which militarily imposed order can, at best, only make possible. Because of the cultural sensitivity it requires, here is a place where just peacemaking NGOs are most likely to be the effective agents rather than U.S. military or government entities; the challenge will be to build the trust in the professionalism and dependability of such NGOs to the point where the military views them as an asset in their overall pacification strategy. This is by no means utopian: witness the close cooperation between military forces and the Red Cross addressing humanitarian concerns in modern conflicts.

Just peacemaking's practices are indeed an essential augmentation to the short term ability of military forces to intervene and provide the stability that is the precondition for, but not the solution of, the underlying cultural, religious, and economic conflict. Here, the practices of just peacemaking are an essential contribution to the overall effectiveness of any policy that would move a given country, region, or the world, in the direction of a more peaceful and stable future.

Much of the judgment about when to deploy some or all of the practices of just peacemaking in a given situation will, of course, depend on where one starts the clock in one's assessment. At any given time, some situations cry out for immediate use of military force to bring a halt to the killing and massive violations of human rights. Others appear to be at the beginning of a path that, if allowed to evolve unchecked, may well develop into situations like the first. In such cases, just peacemaking's practices may well be effective in diverting that descent and preventing deterioration into conflict. What is required here is, of course, practical wisdom and accumulated experience to determine what kinds of interventions inserted at what point can effectively prevent conflict. Lastly, the persistence of causes of international conflict will necessitate the existing categories of just war and the use of military force.

For all these reasons, it is critical to a comprehensively adequate conceptual model to treat both just peacemaking and just war as a range of tools in a large and complex toolbox available to leaders of nations, religious organizations, and NGOs. If the goal is to minimize loss of human life and suffering while increasing the respect for human rights, each of these tools, and various mixes of them, will be required in varying circumstances.

The just peacemaking proposals contribute to the ultimate goal of a full range of strategies that, taken together, provide political leaders and NGOs with a range of options. What is ultimately required is shrewd practical judgment to understand when to employ which approaches in order to create and sustain as peaceful and just a world as we can attain. It is essential that just peacemaking's practices not be artificially polarized from or viewed as inherently morally preferable to just war's criteria for the use of force: both perspectives share a common moral imperative to act in realistic and practical ways to advance common moral goals.

Just peacemaking's practices helpfully remind just war thinkers of a wider range of tools available, depending on circumstances, than they might ordinarily consider. Just war and alternative readings of the current world circumstance urge caution upon just peacemaking's perhaps unduly optimistic *kairos* interpretation of the present situation. For religious ethics and church communities in particular, it is critical that a deep recognition of the complexity and, often, brutality of our world requires a wide range of responses. Perhaps "be wise as serpents and innocent as doves" remains the best advice.[11]

NOTES

[1] "We do not all agree with Michael Smith's affirmation of humanitarian intervention, but we think it should be included." Michael Joseph Smith, "Strengthen the United Nations and International Efforts for Cooperation and Human Rights," in *Just Peacemaking: Ten Practices for Abolishing War*, pt. 1, ed. Glen Stassen (Cleveland, OH: Pilgrim Press, 1998), 26.

[2] Schroeder's contribution to the volume is the most nuanced in its analysis of the international situation. Less than many of the other articles, it does not so much see an inevitable evolution of the international system in a single direction as a tension between competing models, each of which focused on different constellations of values. His claims are quite modest: Just peacemaking "strategies and tactics can work far more widely and durably than they used to, or than many think; that where they do not work, often nothing else will work either; and that plenty of evidence from recent peacekeeping and peacebuilding illustrates their

value." Paul Schroeder, "Work with Emerging Cooperative Forces in the International System," in *Just Peacemaking: Ten Practices for Abolishing War*, pt. 3, ed. Glen Stassen (Cleveland, OH: Pilgrim Press, 1998), 143-44.

[3] This is stated perhaps even more strongly in the Cartright and Thistlethwaite essay: "Citizens and governments must support and work with such campaigns in situations of actual or potential conflict before the condition of 'last resort' can be employed to justify violence. Hence the practice of nonviolent direct action is an obligatory norm where nonviolently it can transform festering injustice into constructive change." John Cartwright and Susan Thistlethwaite, "Support Nonviolent Direct Action," in *Just Peacemaking: Ten Practices for Abolishing War*, pt. 1, ed. Glen Stassen (Cleveland, OH: Pilgrim Press, 1998), 31. This assertion is, of course, ambiguous if not confused on the character of the "oughts" it is asserting. The first sentence asserts as an absolute principle that nonviolent means must always be tried before the last resort principle can legitimately be satisfied. The second sentence makes the requirement conditional: it is a norm "where it can transform" This seems to suggest the more reasonable view that one may make a good faith judgment whether, in a given fact-set, nonviolent means are likely to be effective.

[4] Martin L. Cook, "Immaculate War: Constraints on Humanitarian Intervention," *Ethics and International Affairs* 14 (2000), 55-65. I argue that, although national leaders will feel the impulse toward humanitarian intervention, they are rarely going to be willing to spend blood and treasure on such interventions above a certain (pretty low) threshold of pain. I further argue that this constraint is not merely political, but ethical: political leaders of nations have fiduciary obligations to their own nationals. While legally soldiers are obligated to obey all legal orders, expending their lives and national treasure for purposes not linked to national interests will be unsustainable—perhaps especially in a democratic state. Of course this dilemma is one Smith proposes to remove by the creation of a genuinely international military force.

[5] Smith is well aware of the problem. He writes, "This process [of approving interventions] should, in my view, be multinational. For all the flaws of the United Nations, it does provide a forum for international debate and for the emergence of consensus. And insistence on collective, multilateral intervention—or, as in Haiti, collectively approved unilateral action—can correct for self-interested interventions thinly cloaked in humanitarianism. At the same time, it may be just or necessary for a state to declare its intention to act on its own." Smith, *Just Peacemaking*, 154. This states the problem accurately, but with a bit more confidence in the power of consensus to emerge than I believe experience warrants.

[6] Even that presents far more complications than may be obvious. The NATO intervention in Kosovo was clearly a humanitarian intervention. NATO executed it, the best integrated and prepared military alliance in human history. Yet even NATO found it difficult, nearly to the point of impossible, to maintain unity of command and effort to conduct the mission successfully. Even a cursory reading of Wesley K. Clark's book, *Waging Modern War* (New York: Public Affairs, 2001), ought to give serious pause to anyone advocating that NATO conduct another similar mission—let alone attempt to imagine a UN military capable of effective action in combat. Also, few regional powers have the kinds of well-disciplined forces one may really want to unleash, even if with multinational authority: witness the conduct of the Nigerian forces in Sierra Leone.

[7] Just a small sampling of significant alternative perspectives includes: Benjamin R. Barber, *Jihad vs. McWorld: How Globalism and Tribalism are Reshaping the World* (New York: Ballantine Books, 1995); Samuel P. Huntington, *The Clash of Civilizations and the Remaking of World Order* (New York: Touchstone, 1996); John Lewis Gaddis, "Living in Candlestick Park," *The Atlantic Monthly* 283/4 (April, 1999); and Michael Ignatieff, *Blood and Belonging: Journeys into the New Nationalism* (New York: Farrar, Straus and Giroux, 1994).

[8] Donald Kagan and Frederick W. Kagan, *While America Sleeps: Self-Delusion, Military Weakness, and the Threat to Peace Today* (New York: St. Martin's Press, 2000). I attempted to provide a parallel, but somewhat more internationalist vision in "On Being a Sole Remaining Superpower: Lessons from History," in *The Journal of Military Ethics*, vol.1. no. 2 (2002): 77-90.

[9] As a practical matter, I very much doubt the feasibility of an effective military force under UN control for any but the first of Smith's three categories of international forces. Smith, *Just Peacemaking*, 152-53. Even peace-enforcement, not to mention genuine war fighting, requires a level of training, interoperable equipment, operational security, unity of command and control, etc. which is difficult for a single state to attain; very challenging for any coalition (even, as I mentioned above, NATO, which has worked on those issues for fifty years); and I suspect impossible unless and until the United Nations truly served as a world government rather than a loose coalition of states. For that reason, I find even Smith's contribution to the just peacemaking project utopian—and it is the most realistic.

[10] A very important contribution to this question has been made recently by the "Brahimi Report" to the United Nations (http://www.un.org/peace/reports/peace_operations/). This report, and the various responses to it (also available on the UN's website), very critically assesses the strengths and limitations of historic UN peacekeeping operations and makes important and constructive suggestions about how the UN's ability to conduct such operations might be dramatically improved.

[11] The views expressed in this article are those of the author and do not necessarily reflect the official policy or position of the Army, the Department of Defense, or the U.S. Government.

Realist Criticism of Just Peacemaking Theory

Ronald H. Stone

Abstract

Many of the ten practices to abolish war of just peacemaking theory can be appropriated by classical realist thinkers to illumine possibilities of more peace for the post-cold war situation. The optimism of just peacemaking theory about abolishing war, however, does not need to be appropriated. Realist participation in the just peacemaking project can proceed but only with reservations about what seems to be a mixture of optimism and Kantian idealism about the future peacefulness of a capitalist world, and the illusion that war will disappear from the world. Realism, grounded more in the prophets than the just peacemaking project and more in the prophets' moral critique than in Thucydides' cynicism, provides a stronger foundation for policy advice than the Sermon on the Mount which did not focus on international relations. The striking lack of attention by Jesus to questions of the management of the Roman Empire and the ethics of war and peace permits Christians to consult books of the Bible where international relations and foreign policy are prominent for moral wisdom on the subject.

Realist Criticism of Just Peacemaking Theory

Christian realism associated with Reinhold Niebuhr, John Bennett, Kenneth Thompson, and Roger Shinn, et al. provided guidance for main line Protestant approaches to international politics during the cold war years. The critiques of realism by liberation theologians within the church and liberals or international organizational thinkers in politics weakened realism's hold on the Protestant centers of thought about international relations. Hans J.

Morgenthau, the Jewish philosopher of politics, allied with Reinhold Niebuhr, received a lot of critique posthumously as well. In the last half a dozen years, a reemergence of just peacemaking theory in ecumenical and denominational thinking about foreign policy has also criticized the earlier realism. Was the earlier reform-oriented realism too pessimistic about the future of international politics? In the early post-cold war years an optimism, partially Christian and partially from secular philosophy, began to suggest international politics was in a more cooperative, transformative time and that paradigms of just peacemaking were needed.

Some denominations, an ecumenical group guided by Glen Stassen associated with the Society of Christian Ethics and the National Council of Churches of Christ in the United States of America all articulated theories of just peacemaking in the last six years. All of these participated somewhat in the liberal, internationally oriented optimism of the post-cold war times.

Not only the events of September 11, 2001, but also the lack of a philosophy for the hegemonic, super-power United States raise the need for fundamental thinking about U.S. foreign policy. While the just peacemaking insights and recommendations contain needed emphases, the underlying philosophy of just peacemaking does not seem persuasive enough to guide and limit the policy of the solitary super-power. Just peacemaking remains as a vision and as a set of practical policies, but a more politically oriented Biblical or prophetic realism is needed as the public theology to impact and reform U.S. policy for the new century. This essay attempts to contribute to the dialogue by providing a prophetic realist critique of just peacemaking, reflecting on the just peacemaking critique of realism, reviewing the origins of prophetic realism within the Biblical prophets, and providing a few conclusions. This essay will focus on the ecumenical discussions of just peacemaking associated with Stassen and the Society of Christian Ethics. I also personally believe more of the morally concerned realist perspective was needed in some of the concurrent denominational and National Council of Church projects on peacemaking in which I participated.

In 2003, Christian realism affirms the struggles for peacemaking and justice and recognizes the ontological and theological embraces of peacemaking and justice. However, it expects less peace and justice to be realized than just peacemaker writers in their transformative models affirmed. The struggles for justice will continue sometimes to involve armed force and the threat of violence. The suppression of terrorism will require more justice, peacemaking policies, and the application of armed force. Sometimes peacemaking will be achieved without justice.

To the extent that the practices of peacemaking attempt to parallel the principles of just war, they fail. The principles of just war are articulated to limit the fighting of war while sometimes morally affirming war. The practices of just peacemaking are not to limit peacemaking and peacemaking requires no moral justification in itself. The ten principles of just peacemaking have a better analogy with the Ten Commandments than with the principles of just war.

Realist Criticism of Just Peacemaking Theory

The great significance of the conception of just peacemaking is that it provides a paradigm for religious thinking about peacemaking beyond the concepts of agonized participant, pacifism, just war theory, obey the state positions, or crusade attitudes toward war. It also provides for Christian church policy making a responsible framework into which other problems like an ethic for military intervention for humanitarian rescue can be placed. It has continuity with many of our denominational quests for peace thinking, while in presenting a rather complete paradigm it is an advance. For example, the existence of the material and the process of the just peacemaking-working group assisted the Presbyterian Church to collect together the major teachings of its own peacemaking policies and order them in a single peacemaking conceptual paper.

Just peacemaking is an emerging concept that has received an additional boost by the publication of *Just Peacemaking.* It is referenced in the policy paper resolution of the Presbyterian Church U.S.A. in their document *Just Peacemaking and the Ethics of Humanitarian Intervention* (1998).[1] I appreciate this sense of an emerging concept which was more developed in Glen Stassen's earlier book *Just Peacemaking* than it is in this collection, which has an introduction titled "Just Peacemaking as a New Ethic." Its precedents in official religious language are at least as old as the debates among the theologians during the 1940s in the Federal Council of Churches Commission on a Just and Endurable Peace. The ten "practice norms" or principles of action have been documented as already existing in church social teaching in this century.

A decision was made between the final meeting of the group at the Carter Center and the book's publication to place the major discussions of international relations in the third part of the book. Responding to students who read the earlier draft, issues of conflict resolution and theories of non-violent peacemaking action were brought to the fore. So, the book now moves from a New Testament-based peacemaking theology introduction into non-violent action praxis to independent initiatives toward peacemaking and conflict resolution and the practice of forgiveness in politics in the first four chapters. As one who appreciates these resources, I would still wish for more of an Old Testament introduction where the realities of the sources of conflict in injustice, pride, anarchy, and conflicting religions are clearer. While recognizing that individuals and groups have a role in international peacemaking, I would still place more weight on the structured realities of nation states and economic structures by moving these discussions to roles of greater prominence.

Similarly, I would plead for a little more resistance to editors who attach subtitles. The working group did not discuss abolishing war and the subtitle "Ten Practices for Abolishing War" gives it, to my Christian realist ears, a utopian cast. Some of us read the Bible, particularly *Isaiah* 2, which contains the UN's motto about "swords into plowshares," as making it pretty clear that anarchy, injustice, and pride will need to be overcome before the necessary agreements in ultimate commitments and penultimate laws can be achieved that will abolish war, and the need to study it. One can agree with Stassen's exegesis of the Sermon on the Mount and its powerful message of initiating peace without believing that it and the adoption of these ten practices by several countries would abolish war. I think the New Testament itself anticipated the continuation of war within human history.

The ethic of just peacemaking continues five of the six principles of the Federal Council of Churches' *Six Pillars of Peace*. It is good news that it did not need to continue the fourth pillar: "(4) The peace must proclaim the goal of autonomy for subject peoples, and it must establish international organization to assure and supervise the realization of that end." At least some colonialism is over. This still begs the question for Kurds, Palestinians, Tibetans and others, but the claims of these peoples were not elevated to one of the ten principles. Four of the other principles of a UNO, international regulation of international economy, controlling military establishments, and human rights have continued in the ten with modification. John Foster Dulles's principle of flexibility to adapt the treaty structure of the world to changing conditions is not continued, but can be seen as subsumed under using peacemaking initiatives and cooperative conflict resolution in the new principles. Interestingly, as the just peacemaking project was publishing its work, the National Council of Churches was engaged in rethinking and refurbishing the Six Pillars of Peace for the twenty-first century. This is all to say our work on just peacemaking is not all that new. We must be careful about claiming we have practices to abolish war, and that our work on just peacemaking is still in process. Though eschewing the need for assurance of success, the editors wrote in 1998, "We live at a moment when historical evidence of the promise of just peacemaking surrounds us."[2]

The chapters on non-violent strategies of social change, independent initiatives for peacemaking, and the importance of religious peacemaking support for organizing voluntary peacemaking organizations are all advances beyond the Federal Council of Churches' Six Pillars of Peace. Still, Michael Smith's transformative, optimistic approach into a new, stronger United Nations with its own military force will strike many as utopian. Paul Schroeder's emphasis on cooperating with the trends of the present system requires a lot of optimism about the market system producing sufficiency, justice, and legitimacy to protect this order. His dismissal of finding the causes of war in human nature and the anarchy of the present system seems premature. The realism of Kenneth Waltz's *Man, State and War*, drawn from generations of political theorists, reinforces a realist reading of scripture that both human nature and the lack of sufficient order in a world of conflicting religious and pseudo-religious ideologies incline us toward war. The melioristic reduction of the numbers of wars and the expansion of the realm of peace will call forth our full efforts. Let us follow St. Paul: "If it is possible, so far as it depends on you, live peaceably with all." (*Rom.* 12:18)

Just Peacemaking's Critique of Realism

Glen Stassen's own text *Just Peacemaking* criticizes Reinhold Niebuhr only on his understanding of Jesus' ethic and tries to preserve Niebuhr's realism about the human situation. Actually, in his later life, Niebuhr learned from W. D. Davies, as Stassen did, about the Matthean construction of teachings attributed to Jesus. Niebuhr thought that W. D. Davies' work could have spared him a lot of problems. Davies' work on the gospel clarified the constructed nature of the Sermon on the Mount distancing it from the literal speech of Jesus which Niebuhr earlier had represented as the ideal presented in ethics. Stassen is correct that Niebuhr's idealistic understanding of Jesus' ethic separated it from the world of politics and international ethics while he still insisted that the love ethic was relevant to every situation. Stassen's presentation of the Sermon on the Mount in advocating initiatives in peacemaking and reconciliation is very powerful. He also notes how Paul, particularly in *Romans* 12, develops many of Jesus' themes. Despite the facts that terms like peacemaking, Messiah, and the nations in *Matthew* 25 are present in Matthew, the implications that Jesus had a political message as seen by John Yoder or that Jesus taught an approach to resolving problems of international conflict seem as strained to me as the early Barth's claim that Jesus was a socialist. Of course, the gospels do not ignore political reality nor the Roman Empire, but the arguments that Jesus taught an ethic for international relations is not persuasive to me. Stassen is better than the earlier Niebuhr in finding concrete guidance for life in Matthew, but Niebuhr remains wiser in refusing to locate Jesus directly in international politics. I would also want to emphasize that when we are exegeting the beatitudes of either Matthew or Luke, we are exegeting those books and not any text of Jesus. Matthew is past the fall of Jerusalem and Jesus is pre-fall. Niebuhr is probably correct that it is the love teaching of Jesus that is directly relevant to international relations and not the specific ethical guidelines of Jesus, though they, too, may be helpful.

There is less restrained criticism in the edited volume *Just Peacemaking*. (1) It is suggested that Niebuhr taught students: "to be skeptical of major changes in history (20). (2) "A realist critique often characterizes international relations as similar to the 'prisoner's dilemma' in game theory" (63). (3) Alan Geyer found Niebuhr guilty of having: "Discounted severely the relevance of Jesus' gospel of love and forgiveness to the realities of world politics and even of international conflict" (78). When he quoted Niebuhr on forgiving love in international politics, he found Niebuhr to be "ambiguous and even contradictory" (78). (4) Bruce Russett characterized the realist extremist as treating: "All states as potential enemies" (108), while he argued for recognizing a peaceful side to international relations particularly among democracies. (5) Paul Schroeder recognized himself as a realist in the sense of acknowledging the relative anarchy of the international system. Still, he wanted to distance his position from realist assumptions "that there must always be great wars" or that "war is rooted in human nature" (135). The concluding sentence of his essay identifies his position as that of a problem solver and neither as a "realist" nor an "idealist."

A realist response would be that Niebuhr certainly affirmed a pragmatic or problem solving approach while mixing elements from idealism and realism. (5) He would stubbornly hold though to the values of a philosophy of humanity and history in discussions of international politics. (4) Realism was not the discoverer of the tendency of democracies to be peaceful among themselves and has stressed conflict models, but they were highly cognizant of long-term international cooperation and common interests. Still, it seems true that within its two hundred years of history, the United States has had wars or military conflicts with most of the major nations (India and France are exceptions). (3) Realists recognize forgiveness as important but do not expect it often among nations, and within that framework, the quotations of Geyer from Niebuhr do not seem contradictory but rather nuanced, subtle, and accurate. One does not need to subscribe to Niebuhr's portrait of Jesus from 1935 to recognize that Jesus did not give explicit advice for international politics. Alan Geyer provides three quotes from Niebuhr, two from 1935 and one from 1952, and finds them ambiguous or contradictory. I would not argue that Niebuhr's formulations are always consistent, particularly over a period when he switches from a leader of the socialist party to a New-deal Democrat. The historical period in question was marked by World War II and the advent of the nuclear age. However, the quotations are typical Niebuhr material. The relationship of divine love to sinful politics is paradoxical. Politics is criticized by love and never fulfills it perfectly. Yet love and forgiveness are great solvents to human brutality when they are found. They are not found that often in the prideful behavior of statespeople. However, as much forgiveness as we can get in international politics is good, but we should not expect too much of it. Geyer is probably correct that the roll of forgiveness in international politics is not a pacifist-realist dispute. Niebuhr's Rauschenbusch lectures of 1934 that Geyer quotes were polemically directed at Christian liberal optimism. Perhaps Geyer still retains more of that optimism than realists and therein rests the need for Geyer's critique. Many Christian ethicists will even see signs of very old debates between political ethicists from Union Theological Seminary and Boston University to be a stake. (2) It is rather silly to treat political realism as game theory of the "prisoner's dilemma" type. Realism is too historically oriented and too cognizant of the irrationalism of politics to enter significantly into the rationally-modeled world of various forms of game theory. (1) On history most readers of Niebuhr find him perceptive in seeing the shifting dynamics of America from a continental growing republic to imperial power or the rise and fall of various empires in *The Structure of Nations and Empires*. It would be strange for prophetic realists like Niebuhr, Morgenthau, and Tillich combining Biblical realism and debt to Nietzsche for their dynamic concepts of power not to expect change. If the authors meant that Niebuhr did not expect inevitable progressive improvement in international politics, they were correct. On balance, Niebuhr's Biblical realism still seems closer to our 2000-year post-Christ history than either Schroeder's enthusiasm for peace as a result of worldwide capitalist-democracy or Smith's Kantian optimism about the United Nations Organization (UNO).

An exposition of the Biblical sources of what I would call prophetic realism illustrates the different hermeneutic of the Biblical sources of prophetic realism and just peacemaking.

Prophets and International Relations

The prophets of Israel were crucial for the political thought of four religiously-based political philosophers of the third quarter of the twentieth century. Three were very explicit in their debt: Abraham Heschel, Reinhold Niebuhr, and Paul Tillich. Hans J. Morgenthau's debt is seen in his youthful Jewish studies and in his old age return to practicing Judaism and in the contours of his morality regarding international relations.

Amos represented God's voice to the northern kingdom of Israel during the prosperity of Jeroboam II's reign of 786-746 B.C. It was a time of relative richness and luxury for the establishment which Amos detailed. His eye was also on the suffering of the poor, and one of his most outstanding characteristics of his speech for the Lord was the demand for justice. As the earliest of the prophets whose oracles are extant, he stamped the demand for justice on the very meaning of the role of the prophet. Twenty-eight centuries later, the same words of justice would be used by the prophetic realists and forever connected to the civil rights movement of the 1950-1960s by their friend Martin Luther King, Jr. (5:21-24).[3]

For Paul Tillich, this emergence of the union of justice with universal monotheism was the deciding characteristic of prophetic consciousness correcting the myths of nature. The prophets demanded justice in both of its expressions as the correctness of the legal system including the structures of the society and as the more personal righteousness that makes for correct and fulfilling relationships. They include not only the formal requirements of society but the pursuit of right relationships in actions. Justice, *mishpah,* and *tsedeqah*, righteousness, are used in parallelisms to reinforce the demand of the prophet, speaking for God for right behavior.[4] Justice included obedience to the codes of Israel, but it was more than that as it pointed to God's requirements for correct behaviors in economics, sociopolitical issues, cultic issues, special concerns for the poor and defenseless, and international relations particularly in diplomacy and war.[5] In these four contemporary realists, regarded here as prophetic, the central social moral issues were: economic justice, race relations including protection of Jews, the state of democratic politics and government, and international relations particularly issues of diplomacy, war and nuclear weapons. The continuity between the macro concern issues of the eighth century B.C. and the twentieth century A.D. is remarkable. To some degree, the issues are simply major issues; but at another level, the impact of choices of Amos, Hosea, and Isaiah have been communicated through scripture, the church, Judaism and teachers to morally concerned exponents of those traditions in the twentieth century.

James Muilenburg reminded his readers that the demands of the prophets were concrete and particular.[6] The book of Amos begins its account of "Which he saw concerning Israel in the days of Uzziah King of Judah and in the days of Jeroboam . . . King of Israel." Amos and those who follow in the school of prophetic religion get very particularized; they do not stay at the general, innocuous level. He spells out the historical destruction to be directed to the Syrians, Gaza, Ashkelon, Philistia, Tyre, Ammon, and Moab. In each case, the victims of Assyria's wrath were indicted for war crimes. Judah's crimes were the rejection of the law, the mistreatment of the poor, misuse of the cult, and sexual malpractice. Israel deserted justice, mistreated the poor, cheated in trade and its fate was destruction, even though a gloss in the last chapter of the book promises the redemption of a remnant and an eventual rebuilding of ruined cities.

Amos details war crimes before there was international law. There is a judge who mysteriously weighs the life of the nations and uses war and the destruction of cities to carry out the divine will.[7] Hope here, in the view of a God whose will surrounds all nations, is only in the remnant and a future rebuilding. The lord is like a lion devouring prey. Israel had been saved before like "a brand plucked out of the burning" (4:11), but this time the hope of any salvation follows the destruction. Very little hope is given for international relations. Israel is a minor player in the world of nations and her days as a player are about to be suspended by Assyria, a major player who will also meet judgment. "Prepare to meet your God, O Israel" (4:12). She has always been a pawn in the hands of the nations whose fates are determined by God. God is a mover of international relations and a judge whose love for Israel has been disappointed in this scripture. The breaking of Assyria is a theme of the later prophet Isaiah. "I will break the Assyrian in my land" (*Is.* 14:25). The reader must also wait for the opening of Isaiah's prophecies to see hope for history. By this time Israel is gone and the hope is in Jerusalem as Zion:

It shall come to pass in the latter days that the mountain of the house of the Lord shall be established as the highest of the mountains, and shall be raised above the hills; and all the nations shall flow to it, (2:2)

and many peoples shall come, and say: "Come, let us go up to the mountain of the Lord, to the house of the God of Jacob; that he may teach us his ways and that we may walk in his paths." For out of Zion shall go forth the law, and the word of the Lord from Jerusalem. (2:3)

He shall judge between the nations, and shall decide for many peoples; and they shall beat their swords into plowshares, and their spears into pruning hooks; nation shall not lift up sword against nation, neither shall they learn war any more. (2:4)

Even this hope has an eschatological quality for it requires the nations' obedience to the moral law of God from Jerusalem which rules the nations. Disarmament can then be real as well as conversion to peacetime uses, and with law established, the learning of war can be abandoned.

In Amos we have the emergence of radical monotheism to be expressed even more strongly in *Hosea* 13:2 in the connection of sin and idols and 13:14 in the teaching of knowing of no other God but the Lord and that there is no other savior. The demands of social justice and international justice are clearly explicated, as is the characterization of this God as the universal ruler of all nations. Max Weber probably had Amos in mind when he entitled Yahweh as a specialist in international relations.

The prophet proclaimed that the "Day of the Lord was darkness and not light." Except for the editorially disconnected hope for a remnant rebuilding at the end, the book is one of unrelieved pessimism. Realistic polemics in the second quarter of the twentieth century needed to provide historical hopes to save them from the charges of unrelieved pessimism. Their commentaries on European descent into evil from 1932-45 were pretty pessimistic. But, in that pessimism was accuracy as Berlin, Brussels, Amsterdam, Kiev, Paris, Rome, and Tripoli had their lights extinguished. The fascist terror and punishment was no less than the Assyrian terror which swept down the Mediterranean coast crushing Gaza, Askelon, the remnant of Philistines, and Tyre. As Japan threatened Hawaii, Midway, Burma, Thailand, Hanoi, Jakarta, so Amos prophesied the destruction of Edom, Damascus, Samaria, and Jerusalem. Both periods were times of international terror. The realists found strength in God's strengthening of democratic forces in Britain, the United States, and authoritarian forces in Russia and China. Likewise, in the third quarter of the twentieth century they found hope in deterrence, industrial strength, democratic government, a shared responsibility with Russia for avoidance of nuclear war, and God given human striving over the long travail toward freedom and responsible government. Still, as with the eighth century prophets, there was much to condemn on both sides of the cold war.

Isaiah 52-53 portrays the promise of the Lord's servant to be in the bearing and redeeming of the world's suffering as revealed in the great eschatological council of nations. So, in the gospel of the servant as reinterpreted by Matthew, the secret of salvation in *Matthew* 25 is revealed as the nation's representatives caring for prisoners, feeding the hungry, and watering the thirsty.

But even more hopeful is the vision of a common moral law, nations reasoning together, the conversion of weapons to tools, and finally the unlearning of war. In Isaiah, it is an eschatological vision, and while we cannot rule our nations with eschatological vision, this one provides a sense of direction. Policies may be eschatologically inspired while ethically informed. Law, council, disarmament, and the disestablishment of war are both prophetic and relevant policy goals.

They are goals which place prophetic realists who embrace them in conflict with the U.S. government. One of the most famous of these conflicts was explicitly based upon Amaziah's denunciation of Amos in Amos 7. In the chapter, Amaziah, Jeroboam II's chaplain denounces Amos and expels him from the capital city. Amos denounces the king's chaplain and proclaims the end of Israel. Reinhold Niebuhr used the story to denounce the White House Chapel in which sermons supported President Nixon and shielded him from anti-Vietnam religious criticism. Niebuhr compared J. Edgar Hoover to Amaziah who served to protect the king in the king's court. Niebuhr's adoption of the Martin Luther King, Jr. cause and his critique of the war policy earned him much assault from the religious and political interests supporting Nixon and the Vietnam War. In America, Niebuhr could not be easily silenced. But, the White House could and did intensify the FBI's investigation of the aging prophet as Mr. Ehrlichman was the last Nixon official to examine the over 600-page file from the Federal Bureau of Investigation. Again, domestic justice, international war policy, the King or President's chapel were all integrated in prophetic critique of official religion and policies.

Abraham Heschel regards Isaiah (1-39) as more concerned with domestic injustice and idolatry than with international relations. Yet, his book *The Prophets* was published before the heat of the Vietnam War overshadowed, for a time, attention to the corruption of American domestic politics.[8] Still within the totality of Isaiah 1-66, Israel is a pawn of the superpowers achieving autonomy and some international standing only in the Southern Kingdom under Uzziah. Particularly, Assyria stands astride Palestine destroying the Northern Kingdom and subjecting the Southern Kingdom. Isaiah's polemics against treaties aside, Assyria, Egypt, Babylon, and Persia all play with Israel. She has to learn her survival at the hands of the superpowers regarded by all these prophets of Amos, Hosea, and Isaiah as being used by God to punish the faithless Israel. There is little doubt that God is in control in those prophets. Yet, the Lord's punishment is indistinguishable from the policies of the nations. Israel, the home of these prophets, is chosen to witness to Yahweh whose will is expressed internationally. Nations fall because of internal corruption, unfair business, the cruelty to the poor, the pride of the inhabitants, and because of unethical and idolatrous religions. Pride led to destruction clearly, could moral conduct, recognition of international standards, humility, fairness, and ethical religion have prevented destruction? Perhaps! Yet Isaiah pointed both in chapter 2 and chapter 66 to the need for a religiously based international law, an international council, disarmament, and the learning of ways other than war. The focus of both eschatological passages on Jerusalem reveals the limits of the prophets, but they provided, even with their limits, much wisdom so long ago.

Conclusion

For the just peacemaking paradigm to succeed, it needs to engage the classical realism of North American theology and international relations more deeply than it has. It needs to bring into its theory more than it has that very significant political leadership does not want conflict resolution, non-violent social change, democracy, or a stronger United Nations. Significant American political actors are` insecure, naive about international relations, naive about religion and favor the promotion of their own economic well being and that of their own oligarchic class interests. All of us who work in international relations and ethics are self-interested, somewhat provincial, sinners, and these factors of human life or nature must be accounted for in our analysis.

Secondly, many of our allies and competitor nations are governed by people no better than we are and their perspectives are limited by Communist, Hindu, Muslim, African, Latin American, and European prejudices. Nations are organized so as to be driven by many factors other than the concern for peace. National interests built into the governing structures of societies just may not be neglected when thinking about international relations. The insecurities of the elites ruling various societies are expressed not only by their personalities but by their armed forces, diplomats, corporate organization, and international relations.

Finally, even as the political scientists of the just peacemaking committee recognized, international relations is a mixture of anarchical and cooperative trends. There is not enough community in the world to build international institutions for order in the world to abolish war. The world is not a Hobbesian world of war of all against all, but neither is it a world where the people of the United States, Saudi Arabia, Rwanda, Switzerland, and China support common goals toward peace.

Gazing into the ruins of the World Trade Center confirms for me the above response to just peacemaking theory. The ruins, of course, have no single originating event but the synthesis of the humiliation of Islam, the pride of the son of the greedy family of bin Ladens, the failure of the U.S. ambassador to warn Sadam Hussein that Kuwait was a vital interest to the Bush administration, the Clinton carelessness about foreign policy, the Bush, Jr. failure to take seriously the Middle East, and the violent tendencies of some sectarian movements of Islam contributed to topple the towers of pride.

The deep-seated origins of organized violence in the human soul require more analysis of just peacemaking theory and a more profound recognition of sin. Probably, all of us have learned from Darwin's theory of evolution, Freud's theory of civilization, Marx's theory of class, Rauschenbusch's theory of human solidarity, Niebuhr's theory of sin, if not from the more recent writings of René Girard and Marjorie Suchocki of the deep connections of our human essence and violence.

Just peacemaking theory can supplement Christian or prophetic realism well. It seems unlikely to displace it. The practices of peacemaking are all useful, but they will not bring universal peace or the abolition of war. Realism needs reforming. The religious base of the realism called moral or Christian or prophetic needs to be emphasized. This prophetic realism from the Biblical base needs to be distinguished from realpolitik derived from Thucydides and Machiavelli. The realists' understandings of national interest and power need to be clarified and related to both values and ontology. The whole underlying moral perspective of prophetic realism needs to be explicated. The provisional division between international politics and international economy suggested by Hans J. Morgenthau needs to be undone and reconceptualized. The real history of prophetic moralism through its exponents from Amos, Augustine, Calvin, Wesley through Niebuhr and beyond needs a fresh narration. Finally, the deep connections between realism and peacemaking need to be explained.[9]

The containment and limitation of human violence on the international scene for as long as international politics continues will require not only the balancing of power, diplomacy, international organization, moral limitation, but also, sometimes the pursuit of peace by war. So, even as our own society drifts into greater injustice, we will work for peace by building world community, providing international human economic aid, balancing power, promoting the UNO, organizing locally for peace and justice, promoting international morality, reducing religious militancy, working for international law, struggling for ecojustice, promoting disarmament, seeking international courts, securing democratic allies, improving diplomacy, teaching our children, and saying our prayers.

NOTES

[1] *Selected Theological Statements of the Presbyterian Church (U.S.A.) General Assemblies, 1956-1998* (Louisville: Presbyterian Church U.S.A., 1998), 333.
[2] Glen Stassen, ed., *Just Peacemaking: Ten Practices for Abolishing War* (Cleveland: The Pilgrim Press, 1998), 22.
[3] Amos 5:21-24: [21]"I hate, I despise your feasts, and I take no delight in your solemn assemblies. [22]Even though you offer me your burnt offerings and cereal offerings, I will not accept them, and the peace offerings of your fatted beasts I will not look upon. [23]Take away from me the noise of your songs; to the melody of your harps I will not listen. [24]But let justice roll down like waters, and righteousness like an ever-flowing stream.
[4] Bruce Birch, *Let Justice Roll Down* (Louisville: Westminster John Knox Press, 1991), 259.
[5] Ibid., 261-69.
[6] James Muilenburg, *The Way of Israel* (New York: Harper and Brothers Publishers, 1961), 76-77.
[7] Walter Bruggemann, *Theology of the Old Testament* (Minneapolis: Fortress Press, 1997) suggests that the judgment is like a treaty of human rights or an international standard of conduct.
[8] Abraham Heschel, *The Prophets* (New York: Harper and Row, 1962).
[9] The essay is part of the work of a Lilly Faculty Fellow project of the Association of Theological Schools on prophetic realism.

A Just Peacemaking Bibliography

Theodore J. Koontz and *Michael L. Westmoreland-White*

What follows is a selective and introductory bibliography. While it is not strictly limited to American sources, its content reflects the American location of its compilers. Many have contributed to the bibliography, especially the authors of *Just Peacemaking: Ten Practices for Abolishing War*.

Late-Twentieth Century Church Peace Statements

The following church statements called for the development of a "positive theology of peacemaking," or just peacemaking theory, in addition to pacifism and just war theory. They reflected as well as fostered increased interest in active peacemaking among American Christians:

Gwyn, Douglas, et al. "For the Peace Churches." *A Declaration on Peace: In God's People, the World's Renewal Has Begun*. Scottdale, PA and Waterloo, ONT: Herald, 1991.

National Conference of Catholic Bishops. *The Challenge of Peace: God's Promise and Our Response*. Washington, DC: National Conference of Catholic Bishops, United States Catholic Conference, 1983.

Office of the General Assembly. *Christian Obedience in a Nuclear Age*. Louisville: Office of the General Assembly, Presbyterian Church, USA, 1988.

Thistlethwaite, Susan, ed. *A Just Peace Church*. New York: United Church Press, 1986.

United Methodist Council of Bishops. *In Defense of Creation: The Nuclear Crisis and a Just Peace*. Foundation Document. The United Methodist

Council of Bishops, Nashville: Graded Press, 1986.
United Presbyterian Church. *Peacemaking: The Believers' Calling.* New York: Office of the General Assembly, now part of the Presbyterian Church, USA, 1980.

Pioneers in Just Peacemaking Theory

Works by several Christian ethicists in the late twentieth century moved beyond the debate over whether (and, if so, when) Christians could participate in war making to describe moral norms for active peacemaking:

Friesen, Duane K. *Christian Peacemaking and International Conflict: A Realist Pacifist Perspective.* Scottdale, PA: Herald, 1986. Presents a biblical, theological, and social science argument that justice and peace go together and that pacifism can offer realistic possibilities for dealing with international conflict.

Geyer, Alan. *The Idea of Disarmament! Rethinking the Unthinkable.* Rev. ed. Elgin, IL: Brethren Press, 1985. A pioneering work written during the Cold War arguing for multilateral disarmament of nuclear weapons.

Geyer, Alan, and Barbara G. Green. *Lines in the Sand: Justice and the Gulf War.* Louisville: Westminster John Knox, 1992. Analyzes the Gulf War, concluding that it fell short of the standards of just war theory, pointing out the shortcomings of just war theory, and calling for a new ethic of just peace.

Herr, Robert, and Judy Zimmerman Herr, eds. *Transforming Violence: Linking Local and Global Peacemaking.* Scottdale, PA: Herald, 1998. A collection of essays stressing pro-active peacemaking, including one by Duane K. Friesen and Glen H. Stassen that gives a succinct explanation of just peacemaking.

Hollenbach, David, S.J. *Nuclear Ethics: A Christian Moral Argument.* New York: Paulist, 1983.

——. *Justice, Peace, and Human Rights: American Catholic Social Ethics in a Pluralistic World.* New York: Crossroad, 1990. Both of these books by Hollenbach reflect Catholic teaching well.

Long, Edward LeRoy. *Peace Thinking in a Warring World.* Philadelphia: Westminster Press, 1981. One of the earliest to move past the war vs. peace stalemate to work on an ethic of active peacemaking.

Stassen, Glen H. *Just Peacemaking: Transforming Initiatives for Justice and Peace.* Louisville: Westminster John Knox, 1992. The breakthrough to the new just peacemaking theory paradigm, where it is named and described convincingly, with biblical and historical grounding.

——, ed. *Just Peacemaking: Ten Practices for Abolishing War.* Cleveland, OH: Pilgrim Press, 1998. Reports the findings of twenty-three scholars who met for five years to hammer out a consensus statement on the practices of just peacemaking theory as a new paradigm for the ethics of peace and war.

Stone, Ronald. *Christian Realism and Peacemaking: Issues in U.S. Foreign Policy.* Nashville: Abingdon, 1988. Links just war theory to Reinhold Niebuhr's "Christian realism" and argues for some revision in Niebuhr in the direction of more active peacemaking because the international system has changed.

Stone, Ronald, and Dana W. Wilbanks, eds. *The Peacemaking Struggle: Militarism and Resistance.* Lanham, MD: University Press of America, 1985. Includes some articles that move toward just peacemaking theory, especially Edward LeRoy Long's "The Mandate to Seek a Just Peace."

The Practices of Just Peacemaking

Practice One: Support Nonviolent Direct Action

The place to begin in studying nonviolent direct action, both theory and practice, is with Mohandas K. Gandhi and Martin Luther King, Jr.

Bondurant, Joan. *Conquest of Violence: The Gandhian Philosophy of Nonviolence.* Rev. ed. Princeton University Press, 1988. The long-time best introduction to Gandhian nonviolence for Westerners.

Gandhi, Mohandas K. *Gandhi: An Autobiography—The Story of My Experiments with Truth.* Boston: Beacon, 1993. The personal account of Gandhi the Hindu, influenced by the Sermon on the Mount, who is the instigator of Indian independence, father of nonviolent direct action and the chief influence on King's nonviolence.

King, Martin Luther, Jr. *Stride Toward Freedom: The Montgomery Story.* New York: Harper & Row, 1958. His earliest book; the one in which he is most explicit about the theological basis of his nonviolence; also the one in which he stresses most strongly the power of love and the need to convert, not defeat, the opponent.

———. *Why We Can't Wait.* New York: Harper & Row, 1964. Describes the strategy in action in Birmingham. Includes King's famous *Letter from a Birmingham City Jail.*

———. *Where Do We Go From Here: Chaos or Community?* New York: Harper & Row, 1967. Includes King's powerful insights into "Black Power," the Vietnam War, and the need for a Poor People's Campaign.

———. *Trumpet of Conscience.* New York: Harper & Row, 1968.

———. *Strength to Love.* Minneapolis: Fortress, 1981.

Washington, James M., ed. *A Testament of Hope: The Essential Writings and Speeches of Martin Luther King, Jr.* New York: Harper Collins, 1986. A fine collection of excerpts from King's writings and speeches covering the range of racial, justice, and peace concerns that he addressed.

Religion and Nonviolence

Nonviolence often is linked to religious commitment.

Buttry, Daniel L. *Christian Peacemaking: From Heritage to Hope.* Valley Forge, PA: Judson, 1994. Provides a biblical basis and shows nonviolent direct action and conflict resolution as being effective through many examples worldwide: nicely readable for students or church groups.

Dear, John, S.J. *The God of Peace: Toward a Theology of Nonviolence.* Maryknoll, NY: Orbis, 1994. John Dear, S.J. writes with strong moral commitment. This is a good theological exposition of nonviolence from a Catholic perspective.

del Vasto, Lanza. *Warriors of Peace: Writings on the Technique of Nonviolence.* New York: Alfred A. Knopf, 1974.

Douglass, James W. *The Non-Violent Cross: A Theology of Revolution and Peace.* New York: Macmillan, 1966. A theologically incisive statement by an activist Catholic pacifist.

Dukrrani, Tehmina. *Edhi: A Mirror to the Blind.* Islamabad, Pakistan: National Bureau of Publications, 1996. A biography of Abdul-Sattar Edhi, champion of Muslim nonviolence in contemporary Pakistan.

Easwaran, Eknath. *A Man to Match His Mountains: Badshah Khan, Nonviolent Soldier of Islam.* Petaluma, CA: Nilgiri Press, 1984. The story of a Muslim from the Pathan region of Pakistan, a close associate of Gandhi, who trained his movement in remarkably disciplined, and eventually victorious, nonviolent direct action in spite of the massacre of hundreds of them by the British.

Han, Thich-Nhat. *Peace Is Every Step: The Path of Mindfulness in Everyday Life.* New York: Bantam, 1992. By a Vietnamese Buddhist monk, a nonviolent resister against the Vietnam War and part of a global movement for socially engaged Buddhism, who roots active nonviolence in a deep spiritual lifestyle of personal peacefulness.

————. *Love in Action: Writings on Nonviolent Social Change.* Berkeley, CA: Parallax, 1993. Thirty years of writings by the man nominated for the 1967 Nobel Peace Prize by Martin Luther King, Jr.

Muhaiyadeen, Bawa M.R. *Islam and World Peace: Explanations of a Sufi.* Philadelphia: Fellowship Press, 1987. Writes as a Sufi, the more mystical variety of Islam known for peacableness.

Paige, Glen D., Chaiwat Satha-Anand, and Sara Gilliat, eds. *Islam and Nonviolence.* Honolulu, HI: Center for Global Nonviolence Project. Matsunaga Institute for Peace, University of Hawaii, 1993.

Polner, Murray, and Naomi Goodman, eds. *The Challenge of Shalom: The Jewish Tradition of Peace and Justice.* Philadelphia: New Society Publishers, 1994.

Solomonow, Alan. *Roots of Nonviolence.* Nyack, NY: Jewish Peace

Fellowship, 1990. The above two entires are collections of essays by members of the Jewish Peace Fellowship.

Nonviolent National Defense

Boserup, Anders, and Andrew Mack. *War Without Weapons: Nonviolence in National Defense.* New York: Schocken, 1975.

Sharp, Gene, and Bruce Jenkins, *Civilian-Based Defense: A Post-Military Weapons System.* Princeton: Princeton University Press, 1990. An early exploration of alternative means of national defense.

Nonviolence in Latin America

Esquivel, Adolfo Perez. *Christ in a Poncho: Testimonials of the Non-violent Struggles of Latin America.* Maryknoll, NY: Orbis, 1983. The account of the Nobel Peace Prize winner who traveled throughout Latin America linking together movements for nonviolent direct action.

McManus, Philip, and Gerald Schlabach, eds. *Relentless Persistence: Nonviolent Action in Latin America.* Philadelphia: New Society Publishers, 1991. Contains numerous examples of nonviolence in the struggle for justice.

Nonviolence in Eastern Europe

Baum, Gregory, and Harold Wells, eds. *The Reconciliation of Peoples.* Maryknoll, NY: Orbis, 1997.

Burgess, John P. *The East German Church and the End of Communism: Essays on Religion, Democratization, and Christian Social Ethics.* New York: Oxford University Press, 1997.

Evangelista, Matthew. *Unarmed Forces: The Transnational Movement to End the Cold War.* Ithaca, NY: Cornell University Press, 1999.

Havel, Vaclav. *Power of the Powerless.* London: Hutchison, 1985.

Nielson, Niels. *Revolutions in Eastern Europe: The Religious Roots.* Maryknoll, NY: Orbis, 1991.

Sawatsky, Walter. "Truth Telling in Eastern Europe: The Liberation and the Burden. " *Journal of Church and State* (Autumn 1991): 701-30.

Swoboda, Jörg. *Revolution of the Candles: Christians in the Revolution of the German Democratic Republic.* Trans. Theo Lehmann and Richard Pierard. Macon, GA: Mercer University Press, 1997. The last book includes eyewitness accounts and statements by participants in the struggle that toppled the dictator, Honecker, and The Wall, with not a single death.

Nonviolence in South Africa

Wink, Walter. *Violence and Nonviolence in South Africa: Jesus' Third Way.*
Philadelphia: New Society Publishers, 1987. Argues powerfully that
nonviolence is relevant to, and can be effective, in a situation like
Apartheid South Africa.

Nonviolent Action Theory and Analysis

Lakey, George. *Strategy for a Living Revolution.* San Francisco: W. H.
Freeman, 1968.
McCarthy, Ronald M., and Gene Sharp. *Nonviolent Action: A Research
Guide.* New York: Garland, 1997. Another most useful reference book.
Powers, Roger S., and William B. Vogle, eds. *Protest, Power, and Change:
An Encyclopedia of Nonviolent Action from ACT-UP to Women's
Suffrage.* New York: Garland, 1997. A huge one volume encyclopedia of
active nonviolence, a most useful reference book.
Sharp, Gene. *The Politics of Nonviolent Action.* 3 vols. Boston: Porter
Sargent, 1973. A genuine classic that includes a fine statement of the
theory of nonviolent action, a catalogue of approximately 200 forms of
nonviolent action, and hundreds of historical examples. The most
foundational work in the field.
Taylor, Richard K. *Blockade: A Guide to Non-Violent Intervention.*
Maryknoll, NY: Orbis, 1977. A relatively early Quaker-inspired
conceptual piece.

Practice Two: Take Independent Initiatives to Reduce Threat

Osgood, Charles E. *An Alternative to War or Surrender.* Urbana, IL:
University of Illinois Press, 1962. The initial proposal of the strategy of
independent initiatives to deescalate distrust, tension, and conflict.

Additional general works include:

Lewis, Kevin, and Mark Lorell. "Confidence-Building Measures and Crisis
Resolution: Historical Perspectives." *Orbis* 28 (Summer 1984): 281-306.
Mitchell, C. R. "A Willingness to Talk: Conciliatory Gestures and
De-escalation." *Negotiation Journal* 7 (1991): 405-30.
Stassen, Glen H. *Just Peacemaking: Transforming Initiatives for Justice and
Peace.* Louisville: Westminster John Knox, 1992. Chap. 5.

On the Cold War see:

Cortright, David. *Peace Works: The Citizen's Role in Ending the Cold War.*

Boulder, CO: Westview, 1993. Esp. chap. 8.

Larson, Deborah Welch. *Anatomy of Mistrust: U.S./Soviet Relations During the Cold War.* Ithaca, NY: Cornell University Press, 1997. A carefully researched and argued assessment of missed opportunities during the Cold War, showing where independent initiatives were and were not taken.

Practice Three: Use Cooperative Conflict Resolution

For a new and comprehensive review of peacemaking, see:

Azar, Edward E., and John W. Burton. *International Conflict Resolution: Theory and Practice.* Brighton, Sussex: Wheatsheaf, 1986. A number of authors challenge the primacy of the state in favor of developing models that are not as "top-down" and models that include the important role of non-state factors such as ethnicity, religion, and class.

Burton, John W. *Resolving Deep-rooted Conflict: A Handbook.* Lanham, MD: University Press of America, 1987. A good practical guide to dealing with very complicated international conflicts.

———. *World Society.* Lanham, MD: University Press of America, 1987. Stresses the need to reperceive opponents' values in order to discover complimentary or universal needs and argues for the viability of variable-sum outcomes to conflict, especially countering the "states as billiard balls" analogy of the political realist.

Fisher, Roger, and Scott Brown. *Getting Together.* New York: Penguin, 1989.

Fisher, Roger, and William Ury. *Getting to Yes: Negotiating Agreement Without Giving In.* New York: Penguin, 1981. Perhaps the most widely read introduction to negotiation and mediation as a way of settling disputes. See also:

Gopin, Marc. *Between Eden and Armageddon: The Future of World Religions, Violence and Peacemaking.* New York: Oxford University Press, 2000. Exceptionally wise and brilliantly insightful analysis and proposals for attention to the role of religion (especially Jewish but widely applicable) and other factors in conflict resolution often systematically bypassed by rationalistic models, and many specific suggestions that apply also to other of the ten practices of just peacemaking.

Kelman, Herbert C. "Interactive Problem Solving: A Social-psychological Approach to Conflict Resolution." In *Dialogue Toward Interfaith Understanding,* ed. William Klassen. Jerusalem: Tantur Ecumenical Institute for Theological Research, 1986. Offers a fine description of a problem-solving process, based on sound social psychological research and effectively used in an interfaith setting in one of the world's flash points.

———. "Group Processes in the Resolution of International Conflicts:

Experiences From the Israeli-Palestinian Case." *American Psychologist* 52 (March 1997): 212-20. Describes how groups of highly influential Israelis and Palestinians have developed mutual understanding and paths of peacemaking in conflict resolution groups.

Laue, James H. "Ethical Considerations in Choosing Intervention Roles." *Peace and Change* 8, no. 2/3 (1982). A good delineation of distinct intervention roles: observer, go-between, and enforcer. Also deals with concepts of impartiality, power, and different kinds of advocacy.

Lederach, John Paul. *Beyond Prescription: Perspectives on Conflict, Culture, and Transformation.* Syracuse, NY: Syracuse University Press, 1995.

————. *Preparing for Peace: Conflict Transformation Across Cultures.* Syracuse, NY: Syracuse University Press, 1996. Offers an "elicitive" approach that is especially valuable because of its cultural sensitivity.

————. *Building Peace: Sustainable Reconciliation in Divided Societies.* Washington, DC: United States Institute of Peace Press, 1997.

Wallensteen, Peter. *Understanding Conflict Resolution: War, Peace, and the Global System.* London: Sage, 2002.

Practice Four: Acknowledge Responsibility for Conflict and Injustice and Seek Repentance and Forgiveness

Shriver, Jr., Donald W. *An Ethic for Enemies: Forgiveness in Politics.* New York: Oxford University Press, 1995. Elegantly written, includes biblical and historical grounding, then studies Germany's repentance after the Third Reich, U.S.-Japanese reluctance to apologize, and African-American forgiveness toward white America.

Tutu, Desmond. *No Future Without Forgiveness.* New York: Doubleday, 1999. Describes the South African experience, including the Truth and Reconciliation Commission.

Volf, Miroslav. *Exclusion and Embrace: A Theological Exploration of Identity, Otherness, and Reconciliation.* Nashville: Abingdon, 1996. Volf, who is a Croatian, is asked by his mentor, Jürgen Moltmann, whether he can embrace a Serb. Here is his theologically and ethically profound reply. Won the Grawemeyer Award.

Wink, Walter. *When the Powers Fall: Reconciliation in the Healing of Nations.* Minneapolis: Fortress, 1998. A small and accessible book briefly discussing the meaning of forgiveness, especially in dealing with dictators and human rights abusers following their fall from power.

Practice Five: Advance Democracy, Human Rights, and Religious Liberty

Democracy and Peace

Gowa, Joanne. *Ballots and Bullets: The Illusive Democratic Peace.* Princeton: Princeton University Press, 1999. Highly controversial, but the best critique of the democratic peace idea.

Owen, John. *Liberal Peace, Liberal War: American Politics and International Securit.* Ithaca, NY: Cornell University Press, 1997. Provides careful weighing of historical evidence in an array of foreign-policy crises.

Ray, James Lee. *Democracy and International Conflict: An Evaluation of the Democratic Peace Proposition.* Columbia, SC: University of South Carolina Press, 1995. An accessible review of the proposition as evaluated by a variety of social scientific methods, with historical examples.

Reiter, Dan, and Alan Stam. *Democracies at War.* Princeton: Princeton University Press, 2002. Develops an important extension of democratic peace theory to ask why democracies usually win the wars they fight.

Risse-Kappen, Thomas. *Cooperation Among Democracies: The European Influence on U.S. Foreign Policy.* Princeton: Princeton University Press, 1995. Shows how transnational actors build institutions and shared identities for joint problem solving.

Rummel, Rudolph. *Power Kills: Democracy as a Method of Nonviolence.* New Brunswick, NJ: Transaction, 1996. Empirical evidence that democracy greatly reduces violence not only between states, but also within them (as in civil wars, massacres, and terrorism).

Russett, Bruce. *Grasping the Democratic Peace: Principles for a Post-Cold War World.* Princeton: Princeton University Press, 1993. A wide-ranging review of democracy and peace in the current international system, ancient Greece, and the ethnographic record.

Weart, Spencer. *Never at War: Why Democracies Will Never Fight Each Other.* New Haven: Yale University Press, 1998. Makes a strong argument ("there never has been a war between two democracies"); a very provocative and historically rich volume.

Human Rights

Cahill, Lisa Sowle. "Toward a Christian Theory of Human Rights." *The Journal of Religious Ethics* 8 (Fall 1980): 277-301.

Donnelly, Jack. *International Human Rights.* Boulder, CO: Westview, 1993. A good general introduction.

Hennelly, Alfred, S.J., and John Langan, S.J., eds. *Human Rights in the Americas: The Struggle for Consensus.* Washington, DC: Georgetown

University Press, 1982. Combines theological ethics and political science in analyzing the struggle for human rights in Latin America, with a Catholic and Jesuit commitment to that struggle.

Hollenbach, David. *Claims in Conflict: Retrieving and Renewing the Catholic Human Rights Tradition.* New York: Paulist, 1979. Shows the historical development toward human rights in the Catholic conciliar tradition, and its flowering in Vatican II.

————. *Justice, Peace, and Human Rights.* New York: Crossroad, 1988. A very useful argument for the themes named by the book's title.

Laquer, Walter, and Barry Rubin, eds. *The Human Rights Reader.* rev. ed. New York: New American Library, 1989. Includes the seventeenth and eighteenth century classic liberal political philosophers and all the international treaties, beginning with the United Nations Universal Declaration on Human Rights (1948).

Lauren, Paul Gordon. *The Evolution of International Human Rights: Visions Seen.* Philadelphia: University of Pennsylvania Press, 1998. A broad cultural and historical survey.

Sewall, Sarah B. and Carl Kaysen, eds. *The United States and the International Criminal Court: National Security and International Law.* Lanham, MD: Rowan & Littlefield, 2000. From the American Academy of Arts and Sciences, an advocacy for the Court, but reasonably balanced with arguments against it.

Stassen, Glen H. "The Christian Origin of Human Rights." In *Just Peacemaking: Transforming Initiatives for Justice and Peace.* Louisville: Westminster John Knox, 1992. Sees human rights originating from free-church Puritan faith and the struggle for religious liberty in the 1640s in England, well before the Enlightenment, thus countering reactionary theories in pre-Hitler Germany and since that human rights arose from the Enlightenment and should be opposed by Christians.

Swidler, Arlene, ed. *Human Rights in Religious Traditions.* New York: Pilgrim Press, 1982. The chapters each develop grounding for human rights in a different religious tradition.

Tooley, J. Michelle. *Voices of the Voiceless: Women, Justice, and Human Rights in Guatemala.* Scottdale, PA: Herald, 1997. Describes and analyzes causes of systemic human rights violation and then the movement of women, including Nobel Peace Prize winner Rigoberto Menchú, with a view to inspiring women in the United States and Canada to become similarly engaged in an effective way.

Walsh, Michael, and Brian Davies, eds. *Proclaiming Justice and Peace: Papal Documents from Rerum Novarum Through Centessimus Annus.* Mystic, CT: Twenty-Third Publications, 1991. Presents the modern papal social encyclicals, undergirding the Catholic human rights tradition.

Westmoreland-White, Michael L. "Setting the Record Straight: Christian Faith, Human Rights, and the Enlightenment." *Annual of the Society of*

Christian Ethics (1995): 75-96. Argues against a view that human rights arose from the Enlightenment; they arose from the Free Church Puritan movement a century earlier. Also argues for a non-foundationalist form of universality.

Religious Liberty

Brown, Robert McAfee. *Saying Yes and Saying No: On Rendering to God and Caesar.* Philadelphia: Westminster Press, 1986.

Estep, William R. *Revolution Within the Revolution: The First Amendment in Historical Context, 1612-1789.* Grand Rapids: Eerdmans, 1990.

Hammond, Phillip E. *With Liberty for All: Freedom of Religion in the United States.* Louisville: Westminster John Knox, 1998.

Koshy, Ninan. *Religious Freedom in a Changing World.* Geneva: WCC Publications, 1992.

Levy, Leonard W. *The Establishment Clause: Religion and the First Amendment.* New York: Macmillan, 1986.

Maddox, Randy L. *Separation of Church and State.* New York: Crossroad, 1987.

Miller, Robert T., and Ronald B. Flowers. *Toward Benevolent Neutrality: Church, State, and the Supreme Court.* 4th ed. Waco, TX: Markham Press Fund, 1992.

Miller, William Lee. *The First Liberty: Religion and the American Republic.* New York: Knopf, 1986. Elegantly written and thoughtful account of the origins of the first amendment in the United States and of debate over its meaning in recent years, posing the question, "Where can we find a balanced answer?"

Murray, John Courtney, S.J. *We Hold these Truths: Catholic Reflections on the American Proposition.* London: Sheed & Ward, 1960.

————. *The Problem of Religious Freedom.* Westminster, MD: Newman Press, 1965.

————, ed. *Religious Liberty: An End and a Beginning.* New York: Macmillan, 1966. The most important influence in persuading Vatican II to give strong support to religious liberty for all, in *Dignitatus Humanae: Declaration on Religious Freedom,* which is based largely on his writing.

Second Vatican Council, The. *Dignitatus Humanae: Declaration on Religious Freedom.* In *The Documents of Vatican II.* Ed. Walter M. Abbott. Trans. Joseph Gallagher. New York: Crossroad, 1989.

Villa-Vicencio, Charles, ed. *Church and State: Classic and Contemporary Readings.* Louisville: Westminster John Knox, 1986. Begins with the early church and continues through Medieval, both Magisterial and Radical Reformation, and Confessing Church, Vatican II, Latin America, Black, African, Eastern, and South African contexts.

Wogaman, Phillip J. *Christian Perspectives on Politics.* Rev. and exp. ed.

Louisville: Westminster John Knox, 2000. A widely used text; see esp. chap. 13.

Yoder, John Howard. *For the Nations: Essays Public and Evangelical.* Grand Rapids: Eerdmans, 1997. Deals with religious liberty, but more broadly with Christian relationships to the wider society.

Periodicals

In the United States, there are five regularly published periodicals devoted to church-state concerns: *Church and State, Journal of Church and State, The Journal of Law and Religion, LIBERTY: A Magazine of Religious Freedom,* and *Report from the Capital.*

Practice Six: Foster Just and Sustainable Economic Development

The annual Worldwatch, *The State of the World* reports are essential reading.

Brundtland Commission. *Our Common Future.* World Commission on Environment and Development. Oxford/New York: Oxford University Press, 1987. Won the Grawemeyer Award and is a must read.

Cobb, Jr., John. *The Earthist Challenge to Economism: A Theological Critique of the World Bank.* New York: St. Martin's, 1999.

Daly, Herman E., and John Cobb. *For the Common Good: Redirecting the Economy Toward Community, the Environment and a Sustainable Future.* 2nd ed. Boston: Beacon Press, 1994. Won the Grawemeyer Award for ideas improving world order; it takes on economic globalization and argues for a local and communitarian alternative.

Davidson, Eric A. *You Can't Eat GNP: Economics as if Ecology Mattered.* Reading, MA: Perseus, 2001.

Deudney, Daniel H., and Richard A. Matthew. *Contested Grounds: Security and Conflict in the New Environmental Politics.* Albany: State University of New York Press, 1999.

Diehl, Paul F. and Nils Petter Gleditsch, eds. *Environmental Conflict.* Boulder, CO: Westview, 2000.

Dryzek, John S. *Rational Ecology: Environment and Political Ecology.* Oxford: Basil Blackwell, 1987.

Edwards, Michael. *Future Positive: International Co-operation in the Twenty-first Century.* London: Earthscan, 1999. A Civil Society Specialist at the World Bank and former Head of Research at Save the Children, Edwards provides extensive evidence that the key to successful sustainable growth is lasting engagement with civil society groups and communities.

Gleditsch, Nils Petter, ed. *Conflict and the Environment*. Proceedings of the NATO Advanced Research Workshop on Conflict and the Environment, Bolkesjø, Norway, 11-16 June 1996. London: Kluwer, 1997.

Homer-Dixon, Thomas. *Environment, Scarcity, and Violence*. Princeton: Princeton University Press, 1999.

Meadows, Dennis, et al. *Beyond the Limits*. Post Mills, VT: Chelsea Green, 1992. An excellent 1992 update of the influential and controversial 1972 book that deals seriously with the weaknesses of the original work: *The Limits to Growth*. New York: Universe Books, 1972.

Rasmussen, Larry L. *Earth Community Earth Ethics*. Maryknoll, NY: Orbis, 1996. Elegantly written, a strong challenge with theological depth; it won the Grawemeyer award.

Practice Seven: Work with Emerging Cooperative Forces in the International System

Adler, Emanuel, and Michael Barnett. *Security Communities*. Cambridge, UK: Cambridge University Press, 1998.

Adler, Emanuel, and Beverly Crawford, eds. *Progress in Postwar International Relations*. New York: Columbia University Press, 1991.

Cronin, Bruce. *Community Under Anarchy: Transnational Identity and the Evolution of Cooperation*. New York: Columbia University, 1999. Shows that people's sense of legitimacy and transnational identity is important for developing cooperative structural arrangements among nations. See also the footnotes on the transition within realism toward recognition of international interdependence in Glen Stassen's essay above.

Rosecrance, Richard. *The Rise of the Trading State: Commerce and Conquest in the Modern World*. New York: Basic Books, 1986.

Schroeder, Paul. "The Nineteenth Century International System: Changes in Structure." *World Politics* 39 (October 1986): 1-26.

Watson, Adam. *The Evolution of International Society*. London: Routledge, 1992.

Practice Eight: Strengthen the United Nations and International Efforts for Cooperation and Human Rights

For the finding that joint membership in international organizations is negatively correlated with conflict, see:

Russett, Bruce M., John R. Oneal, and David R. Davis. "The Third Leg of the Kantian Tripod for Peace: International Organizations and Militarized Disputes, 1950-1985." *International Organization* 52, no. 3 (Summer 1998): 441-68.

For the role of the United Nations, see:

Annan, Kofi. *We the Peoples: The Role of the United Nations in the Twenty-first Century.* New York: United Nations, 2000. An important statement by the current Secretary General, eloquent and extending the Boutros-Ghali volumes.

Art, Robert J., and Robert Jervis. *International Politics: Enduring Concepts and Contemporary Issues.* 4th ed. New York: Harper Collins, 1996. For the debate over the ethics of humanitarian intervention, see the differing articles in the final section "The Prospects for International Intervention."

Bhoutros-Ghali, Bhoutros. *An Agenda for Peace.* United Nations, 1992. Not available through the United Nations; an electronic version is at: http://www.library.yale.edu/un/un3d3.htm.

————. *An Agenda for Democratization.* New York: United Nations, 1996. These two are closely related statements by the UN Secretary General, identifying new opportunities for the United Nations to bring peace to the world.

Diehl, Paul F., ed. *The Politics of Global Governance: International Organizations in an Interdependent World.* 2nd ed. Boulder, CO: Lynne Rienner, 2001. A valuable and wide-ranging collection.

Doyle, Michael, et al. eds. *Keeping the Peace: Multidimensional UN Operations in Cambodia and El Salvador.* Cambridge, UK: Cambridge University Press, 1997. A good volume on peace-keeping.

Haas, Ernst. *The Obsolescence of Regional Integration Theory.* Berkeley, CA: Institute of International Studies, University of California, 1975. Argues from functionalist theory that governments enter into international organizations for practical reasons, and then, because of their usefulness, international organizations in turn influence the future policies of governments.

Jett, Douglas. *Why Peacekeeping Fails.* New York: St. Martin's, 2000. Presents a critical view of peacekeeping.

Russett, Bruce M., and James S. Sutterlin. "The United Nations in a New World Order." In *International Politics: Enduring Concepts and Contemporary Issues.* Ed. Robert J. Art and Robert Jervis. 4th ed. New York: HarperCollins, 1996.

Russett, Bruce M., and John R. Oneal. *Triangulating Peace: Democracy, Interdependence, and International Organizations.* New York: Norton, 2001. A major follow-on to Russett's *Grasping the Democratic Peace,* evaluating "the democratic peace" in the light of twentieth century experience.

Russett, Bruce, ed. *The Once and Future Security Council.* New York: St. Martin's, 1997. Asks whether the Security Council should be restructured, and whether it can it be.

Practice Nine: Reduce Offensive Weapons and Weapons Trade

Fortna, Page V. "A Peace That Lasts." Ph.D. dissertation. Department of Government. Harvard University, 1998. Shows that cease-fires are likely to be maintained when devices such as a buffer zones, inspections, and arms limitations are involved. See also

Geyer, Alan. *The Idea of Disarmament! Re-Thinking the Unthinkable.* Rev. ed. Elgin, IL: Brethren, 1985. Makes the case that disarmament, not arms control, should be the goal of nuclear weapons talks.

Gronlund, Lisbeth, and David Wright. *Beyond Safeguards: A Program for More Comprehensive Control of Weapons-Usable Fissile Material.* Union of Concerned Scientists, 1994.

Hartzell, Caroline A. "Explaining the Stability of Negotiated Settlements to Intrastate Wars." *Journal of Conflict Resolution* 43, no. 1 (February 1999): 3-22.

Jervis, Robert. "Cooperation Under the Security Dilemma." *World Politics* 30, no. 2 (January 1978): 167-214.

———. *The Meaning of the Nuclear Revolution.* Ithaca and London: Cornell University Press, 1989. Won the Grawemeyer Award for new ideas in improving world order; shows that deterrence does not require overkill; develops the concept of the security dilemma; gives the theoretical basis for improving security by mutual reduction of offensive weapons.

———. "Arms Control, Stability, and Causes of War." *Political Science Quarterly* 108 (Summer 1993): 239-53.

Lynn-Jones, Sean. "A Quiet Success for Arms Control: Preventing Incidents at Sea." *International Security* 9 (Spring 1985): 154-84.

Walter, Barbra F. "Designing Transitions from Civil War: Demobilization, Democratization, and Commitments to Peace." *International Security* 24, no. 1 (Summer 1999): 127-55.

Practice Ten: Encourage Grassroots Peacemaking Groups and Voluntary Associations

Boulding, Elise. *Building a Global Civic Culture: Education for an Interdependent World.* New York: Teachers College, Columbia University, 1988. Documents the growth and significance of international non-governmental organizations in building a global civic culture to contribute to a more peaceful world.

Buttry, Daniel L. *Christian Peacemaking: From Heritage to Hope.* Valley Forge, PA: Judson, 1994. Shows the effectiveness of church and citizen groups worldwide.

Cavanaugh, William T. *Torture and Eucharist: Theology, Politics, and the Body of Christ.* Oxford: Blackwell, 1998. Shows how the disciplined practice of the Eucharist in Chile during the Pinochet regime could form people into a body of resistance to state torture.

Cortright, David. *Peace Works: The Citizen's Role in Ending the Cold War.* Boulder, CO: Westview, 1993. Argues that citizen peace activists from 1980-1987 played a significant role in ending the Cold War and that grassroots social movements have the power to shape history.

Friesen, Daune K. "Religion and Nonviolent Action." In *Protest, Power and Change: An Encyclopedia of Nonviolent Act from ACT-UP to Women's Suffrage.* New York: Garland, 1997. Demonstrates how religious communities make legitimate strategies of peacemaking and support and sustain the practice of nonviolence.

Keck, Margret, and Kathryn Sikkink. *Activists Beyond Borders: Advocacy Networks in International Politics.* Ithaca, NY: Cornel University Press, 1998. Esp. chaps. 1, 3-6. A combination of theory and empirical comparison of transnational advocacy networks in such areas as human rights and environmental protection.

Putnam, Robert. "Diplomacy and Domestic Politics: The Logic of Two-Level Games." In *Double-Edged Diplomacy: International Bargaining and Domestic Politics.* Ed. Peter B. Evans, Harold K. Jacobson, and Robert D. Putnam. Berkeley, CA: University of California Press, 1993. Shows the connection between achievements in international negotiations and the pressures of groups in domestic politics.

Rasmussen, Larry L. *Moral Fragments and Moral Community: A Proposal for Church in Society.* Minneapolis: Fortress, 1993. Analyzes why and how Western society has eroded community and proposes ways in which the church can become a moral community to help improve civil society.

Sampson, Cynthia, and John Paul Lederach, eds. *From the Ground Up: Mennonite Contributions to International Peacebuilding.* New York: Oxford University Press, 2000. Chronicles, analyzes, and evaluates case studies from Ireland to Somalia to Nicaragua of the Mennonite contribution to conflict resolution and peacebuilding theory and practice.

Yoder, John H. *Body Politics: Five Practices of the Christian Community Before the Watching World.* Scottdale, PA: Herald, 1989, 2000. Shows why the recovery of practices from the Lord's Supper to binding and loosing is important for the social, economic, and political witness of the church.

Contributors

Raymond Kemp Anderson chairs philosophy and religion at Wilson College, concentrating on biblical, social, and comparative ethics. His paper draws from research undertaken with Karl Barth under title of "Love and Order: The Life-Structuring Dynamics of Grace and Virtue in Calvin's Ethical Thought." Recent projects deal with corporate personhood and ontological premises for biblical morality.

Jennifer Beste is a doctoral student in ethics at Yale University. She is currently completing her dissertation, "Trauma, Relationality, and Freedom Before God," which places trauma theory and feminist theory into conversation with Karl Rahner's theology of the fundamental option.

Lisa Sowle Cahill is the J. Donald Monan Professor of Theology at Boston College. She is the author of *Love Your Enemies: Discipleship, Pacifism and Just War Theory* (Fortress, 1994), and of "Toward Global Ethics," *Theological Studies* 63 (2002): 324-44.

Martin L. Cook is Elihu Root Professor of Military Studies and professor of ethics at the United States Army War College, Carlisle Barracks, Pennsylvania. Before joining the War College faculty in 1998, Dr. Cook was a member of the Department of Religious Studies at Santa Clara University. He has also taught at the College of William and Mary, Gustavus Adolphus College, and the United States Air Force Academy. Recent publications include "Army Professionalism: Service to What Ends?" *The Future of the Army Profession* (McGraw-Hill Primus, 2002), and "On Being a Sole Remaining Superpower: Lessons from History," *Journal of Military Ethics* (vol. 1, issue 2), 2002: 77-90.

Duane K. Friesen is professor of bible and religion at Bethel College, KS. He received his Th.D. in Christian social ethics from Harvard Divinity School. He is the author of *Artists, Citizens, Philosophers: Seeking the Peace of the City* (an Anabaptist theology of culture) (Herald Press, 2000), and

Christian Peacemaking and International Conflict: A Realist Pacifist Perspective (Herald Press, 1986).

Simeon O. Ilesanmi is Zachary T. Smith Associate Professor of Religion at Wake Forest University and an associate editor of the *Journal of Religious Ethics*. His recent publications appeared in *African Affairs: Oxford Journal of Royal African Society* and *Studies in World Christianity*.

Charles Kimball is professor and chair of the Department of Religion at Wake Forest University. He served as Middle East director for the National Council of Churches from 1983 to 1990, and is the author of *When Religion Becomes Evil*.

Theodore J. Koontz is professor of ethics and peace studies at Associated Mennonite Biblical Seminary, Elkhart, Indiana. He has taught there since 1982, except for a two-year leave/sabbatical spent teaching at Silliman University in the Philippines. He has published articles on ethics and public policy in journals such as *Mennonite Quarterly Review*, *Ethics and International Affairs*, and *Journal of Church and State*. He holds an M.A. and Ph.D. in government (international relations and modern political philosophy) and an M.Div. (ethics and church history) from Harvard.

Douglas F. Ottati teaches at Union-PSCE in Richmond, Virginia. He is the author of *Meaning and Method in H. Richard Niebuhr's Theology* (1982), *Jesus Christ and Christian Vision* (1989, 1996), *Reforming Protestantism* (1995), and *Hopeful Realism* (1999). He is also a general editor of *The Library of Theological Ethics*.

Julie Hanlon Rubio is assistant professor of moral theology at St. Louis University, where she teaches courses on marriage and social justice. She received her M.T.S. from Harvard Divinity School and her Ph.D. in Religion and Social Ethics from the University of Southern California. Her work has appeared in *Theological Studies*. Paulist Press will publish her first book, *A Christian Theology of Marriage and Family*, in 2003.

Glen H. Stassen is Lewis B. Smedes Professor of Christian Ethics at Fuller Theological Seminary in Pasadena, California. He is author of *Just Peacemaking: Transforming Initiatives of Justice and Peace* (Westminster John Knox) and coauthor and editor of *Just Peacemaking: Ten Practices for Abolishing War* (Pilgrim); *Capital Punishment* (Pilgrim); *Authentic Transformation: A New Vision of Christ and Culture* (Abingdon); and *Kingdom Ethics: Following Jesus in Contemporary Context* (InterVarsity).

Ronald H. Stone is the John Witherspoon Professor of Christian Ethics at Pittsburgh Theological Seminary. He has published *Realism and Hope* (1977) and *Christian Realism and Peacemaking* (1988) and is now writing a book, *Reforming Realism; Issues in Morality and Foreign Policy*, as Lilly Faculty Fellow of the Association of Theological Schools.

Darryl M. Trimiew is the dean of Black Church Studies at Colgate Rochester Crozer Divinity School, and the John Price Crozer Chair of Christian Social Ethics. He is a past SCE board member and the author of *God Bless the Child That's Got Its Own: The Economic Rights Debate*, and *Voices of the Silenced: The Responsible Self in a Marginalized Community.*

Andrea Vicini, S.J., is teaching fellow of moral theology and bioethics at the Faculty of Theology of Southern Italy: S. Luigi, Napoli, Italy. Current research projects include end of life issues, reproductive technologies, genetics, biotechnologies, and globalization. In Napoli, he also collaborates both with an ethics committee that overviews most of the city hospitals and with a genetic database project. He is currently writing a book on postgenomics.

Michael Westmoreland-White teaches religion and philosophy courses at several colleges and universities near Louisville, KY, and is research associate for the School of Theology of Fuller Theological Seminary. He spends much of his time implementing just peacemaking practices as a peace activist for the Louisville chapter of the Fellowship of Reconciliation and the Baptist Peace Fellowship of North America.

D. M. Yeager is an associate professor of theology at Georgetown University. Were her freedom not considerably constrained, she would content herself with making gardens. In a former life, she was an editor troubling the repose of others—who no doubt ardently wished that she would leave and go make gardens.

GEORGETOWN UNIVERSITY PRESS

INTEGRAL ETHICS

◀ Christian Love
Bernard V. Brady

"Brady introduces the reader to the major texts dealing with Christian love from the Scriptures through all the periods of church history down to the present. Students and teachers alike will learn much from the work of this very talented pedagogue."
—Charles E. Curran, author of *Catholic Social Teaching 1891-Present*

"Carefully researched and engagingly written, Brady's book will become a treasured resource for anyone wanting to explore how Christians have thought about love. Most importantly, Brady shows why the universal human vocation must be the vocation to love."
—Paul J. Wadell, St. Norbert College

0-87840-894-0, hardcover, $29.95

◀ God's Rule
The Politics of World Religions
Jacob Neusner, Editor

Resisting the tendency to separate the study of religion and politics, editor Jacob Neusner pulls together a collection of essays which explain and explore the relationship between the world's major religions and political power. From Martin Marty to John Esposito, experts explore the complex nature of how religion shapes political power, and how religion shapes itself in relation to that power.

0-87840-910-6, hardcover, $29.95

The Sacred and the Sovereign ▶
Religion and International Politics
John D. Carlson and Erik C. Owens, Editors

The first book to bring together, in dialogue, well-known figures in theology and religion with political scientists, military experts, and diplomatic leaders to consider the role religion should—and should not—play in international policy.

"A highly useful collection of thoughtful, reflective essays on the intersections, overlaps, and tensions between religion and realpolitik in humanitarian interventions, from a rich array of perspectives— theological, philosophical, diplomatic, and military.... a marvelous resource for both research and teaching."
—Albert C. Pierce, director, Center for the Study of Professional Military Ethics, U.S. Naval Academy

0-87840-908-4, paperback, $26.95

The Perversion of Autonomy ▶
Coercion and Constraints in a Liberal Society
Revised and Expanded
Willard Gaylin and Bruce Jennings

Modern psychological and political theory meet head-on in this powerful re-evaluation of America's contradictory and sometimes dangerous addiction to individualism. Best-selling author Gaylin and co-author Jennings investigate the contentious intersections of interdependence and autonomy, rights and public responsibility. They examine the painful abrasion occurring between America's tradition of personal freedom and privacy, as it rubs against the still valuable if almost vanishing ideals of sacrifice and social order.

0-87840-906-8, paperback, $21.95

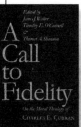

◀ A Call to Fidelity: On the Moral Theology of Charles E. Curran

James J. Walter, Timothy E. O'Connell, and Thomas A. Shannon, Editors

The contributions that Charles E. Curran has made to moral theology have reached far beyond the Catholic community and made him a touchstone figure in ethical and religious thought. *A Call to Fidelity* critically examines the impact of his scholarship.

0-87840-380-9, paperback, $27.50
Moral Traditions series
James F. Keenan, series editor

American Protestant ▶ Ethics and the Legacy of H. Richard Niebuhr

William Werpehowski

Niebuhr is one of the towering forces of Christian theology—there can be no discussion of contemporary Protestant ethics without taking his contributions into account. This book examines the moral discourse between Niebuhr and modern ethicists.

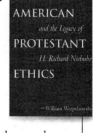

0-87840-383-3, paperback, $24.95
Moral Traditions series
James F. Keenan, series editor

Introduction to Virtue Ethics ▶
Insights of the Ancient Greeks

Raymond J. Devettere

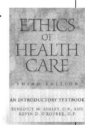

An engaging and informative introduction to the birth and development of ethics in western civilization. From Aristotle to Zeno, this volume examines the foundations on which later philosophers built their understandings of the place—and meaning—of human life.

0-87840-372-8, paperback, $21.95

◀ Josef Fuchs on Natural Law

Mark Graham

Josef Fuchs, S.J., a "theologian's theologian," is one of the Catholic Church's most distinguished moral philosophers, known for his openness to conscience and moral truth. Graham explores his contributions, suggesting developments that would make a positive contribution to rehabilitating the natural law theory dominating the landscape of moral theology today.

0-87840-382-5, hardcover, $49.95
Moral Traditions series
James F. Keenan, series editor

Ethics of Health Care ▶
An Introductory Textbook, Third Edition

Benedict M. Ashley, O.P. and Kevin D. O'Rourke, O.P.

Responds to the many developments in theology and the startlingly rapid changes in the arenas of medicine and health care over the past decade. An updated and comprehensive introduction to bioethics for physicians, bioethicists, and other health care professionals.

0-87840-375-2, paperback, $27.50

GEORGETOWN UNIVERSITY PRESS

c/o Hopkins Fulfillment Service P.O. Box 50370 Baltimore Maryland 21211-4370
1.800.537.5487 or 410.516.6956 FAX: 410.516.6998

www.press.georgetown.edu

NEW FROM OXFORD!

SACRED RIGHTS

The Case for Contraception and
Abortion in World Religions
Edited by DANIEL C. MAGUIRE

Seeking to counteract the
simplistic idea that all religions are completely antag-
onistic toward family planning, the authors—all
scholar-practitioners of the
religions about which they
write—present alternative
interpretations of religions'
views about family plan-
ning. Arguing for the existence of equally valid tradi-
tions that allow contraception and abortion, they
seek to escape the confines of oversimplified
either/or, pro-choice/pro-life arguments.

2003   paper $19.95 cloth $55.00

HEAL THYSELF

Spirituality, Medicine, and the
Distortion of Christianity
**JOEL JAMES SHUMAN and
KEITH G. MEADOR**

Keith Meador and Joel Shuman have joined
forces not only to write a book that helps us
understand the power medicine exercises in modern society and the effect that power has on our
lives as Christians, but also to make an argument
in this book with implications that reach far
beyond medical care."—From the Foreword by
Stanley Hauerwas

2002 $25.00

GETTING EVEN

Forgiveness and Its Limits
JEFFRIE G. MURPHY

"Jeffrie Murphy has writ-
ten a wonderful and sensitive book on an almost
forbidden topic, the topic
of revenge. But it is also a
book about forgiveness,
and it is striking a judi-
cious balance between
these two that makes
Murphy's book such a
challenge and a success...If
the book ends up with a
rather Christian account of forgiveness that will
please many readers, Murphy takes them through
some psychologically difficult but philosophically
clear and very readable terrain to get there."—
Robert C. Solomon, Quincy Lee Centennial
Professor and Distinguished Teaching Professor,
The University of Texas at Austin

2003 $21.00

THE ETHICS OF KILLING

Problems at the Margins of Life
JEFF MCMAHAN

"*The Ethics of Killing* is applied ethics at its best.
From now on, anyone who is serious about getting to the bottom of issues like abortion, infanti-
cide, brain death, euthanasia and the killing of
nonhuman animals will have to take account of
the novel and ingenious theory presented in Jeff
McMahan's lucidly-written, rigorously-argued
book."—Peter Singer, *Princeton University*

2002 $39.95

Prices are subject to change and apply in the US. To order, call 1-800-451-7556.
In Canada, 1-800-387-8020. Visit our web site at **www.oup-usa.org**

OXFORD
UNIVERSITY PRESS